Photoshop 5.5 for Windows

Photoshop is a registered trademark of Adobe Systems Incorporated.
Windows is a registered trademark of Microsoft Corporation.
All other trademarks quoted are the property of their respective editors.

All rights reserved. No part of this publication may be reproduced, stored in a retrieval system, or transmitted, in any form, or by any means, electronic, mechanical, photocopying, recording or otherwise, without the prior permission of the publishers.

Copyright - Editions ENI - May 2000
ISBN: 2-7460-0985-4
Original edition: ISBN: 2-7460-0258-2

ENI Publishing LDT

500 Chiswick High Road
London W4 5RG

Tel: 020 8956 2320
Fax: 020 8956 2321

e-mail: publishing@ediENI.com
http://www.publishing-eni.com

Editions ENI

BP 32125
44021 NANTES Cedex 01

Tel: 33.2.51.80.15.15
Fax: 33.22.51.80.15.16

e-mail: editions@ediENI.com
http://www.editions-eni.com

The **BY EXAMPLE** collection is directed by Corinne HERVO
Author: Cyril GUÉRIN

Overview

Introduction

This is a preliminary chapter to introduce you to the Photoshop working environment and its principal features such as menus and floating palettes. You will also learn how to use the tools that can help you work on images, such as the rulers, guides and the zoom.

pages 11 to 30

Chapter 1

This chapter is designed to show you the basic techniques for selecting items in an image so as to copy and move them. You will learn how to create a new document, to save and print it. The different colour models are described and you will see how to choose a colour and fill a selection.

pages 31 to 74

Chapter 2

Here, you will discover how to work with layers, to create them to isolate areas on the image, to retouch or distort their contents and to apply special layer effects (shadows, glows, bevelling, transparency). You will also start to use text tools.

pages 75 to 130

Chapter 3

This chapter deals with the main retouch and drawing tools, how to retouch brightness and contrast as well as colour changes and adjustments on an image.

pages 111 to 176

Chapter 4

In this chapter you will learn the blending modes you can use with drawing tools and layers. You will also explore some advanced layer functions and how to make complex retouches. This includes using the history of the work you perform. You will also discover how to create and apply patterns and textures.

pages 177 to 222

Chapter 5

This chapter gives you an idea of some more general image functions, such as converting colour models, changing an image to grayscale, changing image size and resolution and how to save an image in different formats.

pages 223 to 282

Adobe Photoshop 5.5

Chapter 6

You will discover how to create vector drawings in Photoshop and learn how to use them to draw, retouch and make complex and precise selections. You will also use Photoshop's features for importing and exporting vector graphics.

pages 283 to 320

Chapter 7

Chapter 7 deals with the channels on an image. These allow you to make special and precise selections and also to make special effects for advanced retouching or for special printing jobs.

pages 321 to 354

Chapter 8

This chapter mainly looks at how to automate work in Photoshop. Creating automated tasks allows you to carry out fastidious and repetitive work in a single action.

pages 355 to 390

Extra information

You will find in this chapter more advanced Photoshop features not dealt with previously, such as image digitisation, creating brush types, using specific filters and other tools, setting preferences and linking with other applications.

pages 391 to 418

Appendices

A list of the various shortcut keys and mouse shortcuts is included to help you work more quickly in Photoshop.

pages 419 to 424

Glossary

Definitions of various technical terms used in this book

pages 425 to 429

Index

pages 430 to 439

Adobe Photoshop 5.5

Foreword

Designed by a team of professionals specialised in training, this course has been created for anyone who works on a PC and wants to develop a good understanding of the Adobe Photoshop 5.5 application.

HOW THE BOOK IS SET OUT

*The learning process used is based on concrete exercises. In order for the exercise in progress to make perfect sense, it is important to adopt a **step-by-step** method for all the modifications described, from the first to the last line. The practice exercises provided at the end of each chapter will allow you to revise the techniques you have just learnt.*

The different stages you must follow to complete the exercise are numbered and begin with a title:

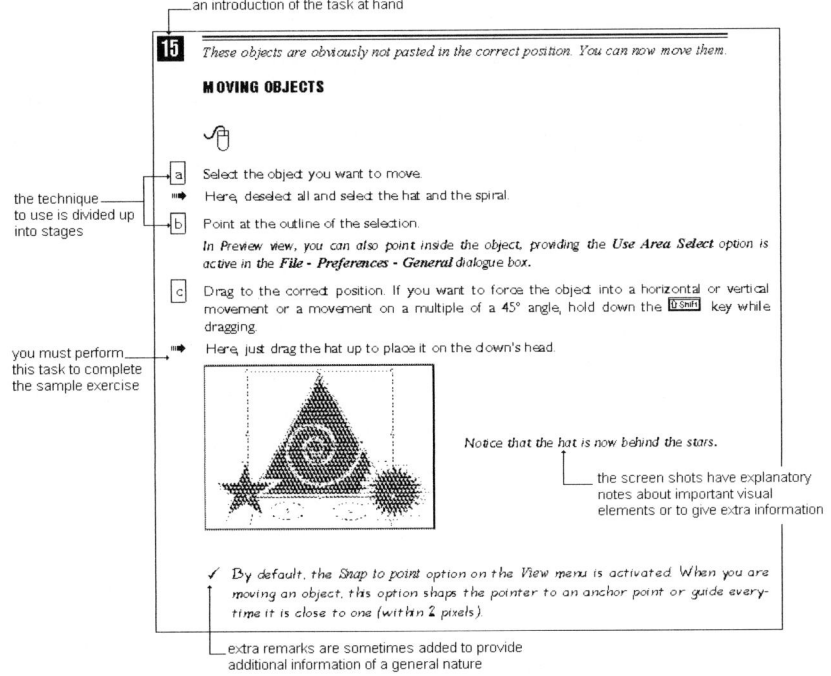

Also, keep in mind that there are different ways to perform tasks: using menus, the mouse or the keyboard. In order for this book to be as comprehensive as possible, all possible solutions are demonstrated: they are identified by these icons:

Foreword

INSTALLING THE CD-ROM

▶ Insert the CD-ROM into the CD-ROM drive of your computer.

▶ From the Windows desktop, click the **Start** menu then activate the **Run** option.

▶ Type **"D:\ENI PHOTOSHOP 5.5.exe"** and enter.

If your CD-ROM drive is not called drive D, replace D with the appropriate drive letter.

*A dialog box called **Training in Photoshop 5.5** appears.*

▶ Click **Next**.

*The installation application offers to create a folder called **ENI Photoshop 5.5**.*

▶ If required, change the proposed folder name then click **Next**. If several people will be using the course on the same computer, it may be wise to change the name so that each person works in their own separate folder.

▶ Confirm the creation of the **ENI Photoshop 5.5** folder by clicking **Yes**.

The installation application decompresses the files then copies the sample documents into the created folder. The ENI Photoshop 5.5.exe file contains the sample documents in a compressed format. The same documents appear in an uncompressed form in the Examples folder on the CD-ROM.

▶ Click **Finish** to end the installation process.

INTRODUCTION

1 - STARTING PHOTOSHOP 5.5 12
2 - A DESCRIPTION OF THE SCREEN 13
3 - LOOKING AT THE TOOLBOX 14
4 - WORKING WITH PALETTES 16
5 - DEFINING THE POINTER'S PRESENTATION 19
6 - WORKING WITH RULERS 20
7 - USING GUIDES 21
8 - USING THE GRID 23
9 - USING THE NAVIGATOR PALETTE 24
10 - CHANGING THE ZOOM 25
11 - DISPLAYING A FULL SCREEN IMAGE 27
12 - LOOKING AT THE INFO PALETTE 27

CHAPTER 1

1 - SELECTING ALL OF AN IMAGE 33
2 - DEACTIVATING A SELECTION 34
3 - SELECTING A REGULAR ZONE ON AN IMAGE 34
4 - MOVING PART OF AN IMAGE 37
5 - POSITIONING PART OF AN IMAGE WITH PRECISION 38
6 - COPYING PART OF AN IMAGE 39
7 - CREATING A NEW DOCUMENT 41
8 - COPYING AN IMAGE INTO ANOTHER DOCUMENT 43
9 - SELECTING AN IRREGULAR PART OF AN IMAGE 45
10 - SAVING A SELECTION 49
11 - LOADING A SELECTION 50
12 - MOVING OR COPYING ONTO A NEW LAYER 51
13 - UNDERSTANDING COLOUR MODELS 52
14 - SELECTING A COLOUR 54
15 - USING THE SWATCHES PALETTE 59
16 - COLOURING A SELECTION 61
17 - ADDING STROKE TO A SELECTION 64
18 - FEATHERING A SELECTION 65
19 - SELECTING AN AREA OF THE IMAGE BY ITS COLOUR 66
20 - EXPANDING OR CONTRACTING SELECTIONS 67

21 - INVERSING A SELECTION 69
22 - DEFINING PRINT OPTIONS 70
23 - PRINTING AN IMAGE 72
      PRACTICE EXERCISE 1 74

CHAPTER 2

1 - ACCESSING LAYERS 76
2 - CHANGING THE LAYER STACKING ORDER 78
3 - CHANGING A LAYER'S ATTRIBUTES 79
4 - CREATING A NEW LAYER 82
5 - SELECTING NON-TRANSPARENT PARTS OF A LAYER 83
6 - DELETING A LAYER 85
7 - APPLYING FILTERS 86
8 - IMPROVING A LAYER'S OUTLINE 88
9 - APPLYING A TRANSFORMATION TO A SELECTION OR A LAYER 90
10 - DUPLICATING A LAYER 97
11 - LINKING LAYERS 99
12 - ALIGNING THE CONTENTS OF LINKED LAYERS 100
13 - SPACING THE CONTENTS OF LINKED LAYERS 100
14 - MERGING LAYERS 101
15 - INSERTING TEXT INTO AN IMAGE 102
16 - MODIFYING TEXT ON A TYPE LAYER 107
17 - CONVERTING TEXT INTO IMAGE 108
18 - APPLYING EFFECTS TO LAYERS 108
19 - MODIFYING OR DELETING EFFECTS APPLIED TO LAYERS 114
20 - COPYING LAYER EFFECTS 115
21 - DELETING PART OF AN IMAGE 117
22 - FILLING A SELECTION OR A LAYER WITH A GRADIENT 121
23 - APPLYING LAYER MASKS 126
24 - APPLYING A LAYER MASK'S EFFECTS OR DELETING IT 129
      PRACTICE EXERCISE 2 130

CHAPTER 3

1 - DRAWING WITH THE PENCIL, PAINTBRUSH OR AIRBRUSH 132
2 - DRAWING STRAIGHT LINES OR ARROWS 136
3 - USING THE PAINT BUCKET TO CHANGE THE COLOUR OF PIXELS 138
4 - EXTRACTING THE FOREGROUND OF AN IMAGE 140
5 - USING THE SMUDGE TOOL 142
6 - BLURRING OR SHARPENING PART OF AN IMAGE 144
7 - DARKENING OR LIGHTENING PART OF AN IMAGE 146
8 - CHECKING THE TONAL RANGE OF A PICTURE 148
9 - ADJUSTING CONTRAST AND/OR BRIGHTNESS ON AN IMAGE 150
10 - ADJUSTING THE PROPORTIONS OF COLOUR IN AN IMAGE 159
11 - MODIFYING COLOUR SATURATION ON AN AREA OF AN IMAGE 162
12 - ADJUSTING INDIVIDUAL COLOUR COMPONENTS 163
13 - REPLACING CERTAIN COLOURS ON AN IMAGE 167
14 - CREATING A NEGATIVE 169
15 - TRANSFORMING AN IMAGE AREA INTO A BITMAP 170
16 - CREATING FLAT AREAS OF COLOUR 172
17 - DUPLICATING PART OF AN IMAGE WITH THE RUBBER STAMP 173
   PRACTICE EXERCISE 3 176

CHAPTER 4

1 - APPLYING A TEXTURE TO AN IMAGE 179
2 - ASSOCIATING A BLENDING MODE WITH A LAYER 181
3 - DESCRIBING BLENDING MODES 181
4 - CONVERTING A BACKGROUND INTO A LAYER 188
5 - SOFTENING THE EFFECT OF A FILTER, ADJUSTMENT OR TOOL 189
6 - COPYING OR MOVING ONE SELECTION INTO ANOTHER 190
7 - CREATING A CLIPPING GROUP 192
8 - REMOVING A LAYER FROM A CLIPPING GROUP 193
9 - COPYING IMAGES LOCATED ON SEVERAL LAYERS 194
10 - CREATING AN ADJUSTMENT LAYER 195
11 - MODIFYING AN ADJUSTMENT LAYER 198
12 - CREATING A PATTERN 199
13 - APPLYING A PATTERN 200
14 - WRAPPING AROUND THE EDGES OF A PATTERN OR TEXTURE 202

15 - SELECTING A RANGE OF COLOURS 205
16 - MANAGING THE HISTORY PALETTE 208
17 - CREATING SNAPSHOTS OF IMAGES 213
18 - REPRODUCING A PREVIOUS STATE OR SNAPSHOT 217
19 - CREATING AN ART REPRODUCTION OF AN EARLIER STATE OF THE IMAGE 220
    PRACTICE EXERCISE 4 222

CHAPTER 5

1 - CHANGING THE DEPTH OF COLOURS 224
2 - CONVERTING A COLOUR IMAGE FROM ONE COLOUR MODEL TO ANOTHER 225
3 - CONVERTING AN IMAGE INTO GRAYSCALE 230
4 - CONVERTING A GRAYSCALE IMAGE TO BITMAP 231
5 - CONVERTING AN IMAGE TO DUOTONE 234
6 - CONVERTING AN RGB IMAGE INTO INDEXED COLORS 238
7 - MANAGING AN IMAGE'S COLOR TABLE 242
8 - COLORIZING A GRAYSCALE IMAGE 245
9 - MODIFYING THE SIZE OF THE CANVAS 249
10 - APPLYING A TRANSFORMATION TO A SELECTION BORDER 251
11 - CHANGING THE SIZE AND/OR RESOLUTION OF AN IMAGE 252
12 - CROPPING AN IMAGE 257
13 - SAVING A DOCUMENT IN A SPECIFIC FORMAT 259
14 - SAVING AN IMAGE FOR USE ON THE WEB 274
    PRACTICE EXERCISE 5 282

CHAPTER 6

1 - USING THE FREEFORM PEN 284
2 - SAVING A WORK PATH 286
3 - DELETING A PATH 286
4 - CREATING A PATH 287
5 - RENAMING A PATH 287
6 - USING THE MAGNETIC PEN TOOL 288
7 - USING THE PEN TOOL 290
8 - EDITING A PATH 296
9 - SHOWING /HIDING PATHS 301
10 - CONVERTING A SELECTION BORDER INTO A PATH 302
11 - CONVERTING A PATH INTO A SELECTION BORDER 303

12 - APPLYING COLOUR TO A PATH OUTLINE 306
13 - APPLYING FILL COLOUR INSIDE A PATH AREA 307
14 - DUPLICATING A PATH 309
15 - CLIPPING AN IMAGE 312
16 - EXPORTING PATHS TO ILLUSTRATOR 314
17 - IMPORTING AN ILLUSTRATOR IMAGE 315
     PRACTICE EXERCISE 6 319

CHAPTER 7

1 - ACCESSING CHANNELS 322
2 - USING ALPHA CHANNELS 324
3 - MODIFYING ALPHA CHANNEL OPTIONS 326
4 - MODIFYING A CHANNEL 327
5 - DUPLICATING A CHANNEL 330
6 - DELETING A CHANNEL 331
7 - COMBINING TWO CHANNELS 332
8 - COMBINING CHANNELS FROM TWO IMAGES 335
9 - SELECTING WITH QUICK MASK MODE 337
10 - MIXING COLOUR CHANNELS 339
11 - USING SPOT CHANNELS 342
12 - CONVERTING AN IMAGE INTO MULTICHANNEL MODE 349
13 - SPLITTING CHANNELS INTO SEVERAL DOCUMENTS 351
14 - MERGING CHANNELS INTO A SINGLE DOCUMENT 351
     PRACTICE EXERCISE 7 354

CHAPTER 8

1 - CREATING A CONTACT SHEET 356
2 - CREATING A WEB PHOTO GALLERY 359
3 - CREATING A PICTURE PACKAGE 363
4 - CONVERTING AN IMAGE WITH CONDITIONAL MODE CHANGE 365
5 - WORKING WITH THE ACTIONS PALETTE 366
6 - USING RECORDED ACTIONS 367
7 - CREATING AN ACTION SET 369
8 - CREATING AN ACTION 370
9 - INSERTING A STOP 372
10 - INCLUDING A PATH IN AN ACTION 374

11 -	INSERTING A MENU ITEM INTO AN ACTION	375
12 -	DUPLICATING AN ACTION OR A SET	377
13 -	DELETING AN ACTION/AN ACTION ITEM/A SET	378
14 -	MODIFYING AN ACTION'S OPTIONS	378
15 -	MODIFYING AN ACTION	380
16 -	MODIFYING THE PLAYBACK OPTIONS ON AN ACTION	384
17 -	SAVING A SET OF ACTIONS	385
18 -	PLAYING AN ACTION ON A GROUP OF IMAGES	386
	PRACTICE EXERCISE 8	389

EXTRA INFORMATION

1 -	SELECTING A DIGITISATION SOURCE	392
2 -	SCANNING AN IMAGE	392
3 -	MANAGING THE BRUSHES PALETTE	395
4 -	SMOOTHING A SELECTION	400
5 -	USING SEVERAL VIEWS ON AN IMAGE	401
6 -	CONVERTING AN ACROBAT DOCUMENT INTO A PHOTOSHOP IMAGE	402
7 -	DEFINING DOCUMENT INFORMATION	403
8 -	DELETING DISSIMILAR PIXELS	404
9 -	INCREASING IMAGE SHARPNESS	405
10 -	APPLYING A 3D EFFECT TO AN IMAGE	405
11 -	DEFINING THE RESOLUTION AUTOMATICALLY	407
12 -	AUTOMATICALLY MODIFYING AN IMAGE'S BRIGHTNESS AND CONTRAST	408
13 -	THROWING LIGHT ONTO PART OF AN IMAGE	409
14 -	USING THE TOOL	412
15 -	USING THE TOOL	413
16 -	AUTOMATICALLY SELECTING A LAYER WITH THE TOOL	414
17 -	SETTING THE GENERAL PHOTOSHOP PREFERENCES	414
18 -	SETTING PREFERENCES FOR SAVING FILES	415
19 -	SETTING PREFERENCES FOR THE WORK DRIVES	416
20 -	SETTING MEMORY PREFERENCES	416
21 -	CONFIGURING COLOUR MANAGEMENT	417

APPENDICES

SHORTCUT KEYS 419
GLOSSARY 425

INDEX 430

INTRODUCTION

1 - STARTING PHOTOSHOP 5.5 12
2 - A DESCRIPTION OF THE SCREEN 13
3 - LOOKING AT THE TOOLBOX 14
4 - WORKING WITH PALETTES 16
5 - DEFINING THE POINTER'S PRESENTATION 19
6 - WORKING WITH RULERS 20
7 - USING GUIDES 21
        ADDING A GUIDE 21
        MOVING A GUIDE 21
        DEFINING THE GUIDES' APPEARANCE 22
        DELETING GUIDES 22
8 - USING THE GRID 23
9 - USING THE NAVIGATOR PALETTE 24
10 - CHANGING THE ZOOM 25
11 - DISPLAYING A FULL SCREEN IMAGE 27
12 - LOOKING AT THE INFO PALETTE 27

Introduction

This introduction has been designed as a guided tour of the Photoshop working environment and its principal components (menus, palettes...).

1 Firstly, start up the Photoshop application.

STARTING PHOTOSHOP 5.5

[a] Click the **Start** button.

[b] Point to the **Programs** menu, then the **Adobe** menu and finally the **Photoshop 5.5** menu.

[c] Click the **Adobe Photoshop 5.5** option.

The Photoshop application is loaded into the computer's memory and the application window appears; in the window you can see that some palettes appear by default.

The first time you start Photoshop, the application prompts you to calibrate your monitor and define your colour settings. For now, skip this step. If you find that you need to adjust your configuration, you can start the **Adobe Colour Management Wizard** some other time (cf. Extra Information).

➤ Here click the **Next** button twice, then click **Finish**.

✓ *If there is a Photoshop shortcut on the Desktop, you can double-click it to start Photoshop.*

Introduction

2 *You are probably impatient to start work, but first take the time to look at the application window.*

A DESCRIPTION OF THE SCREEN

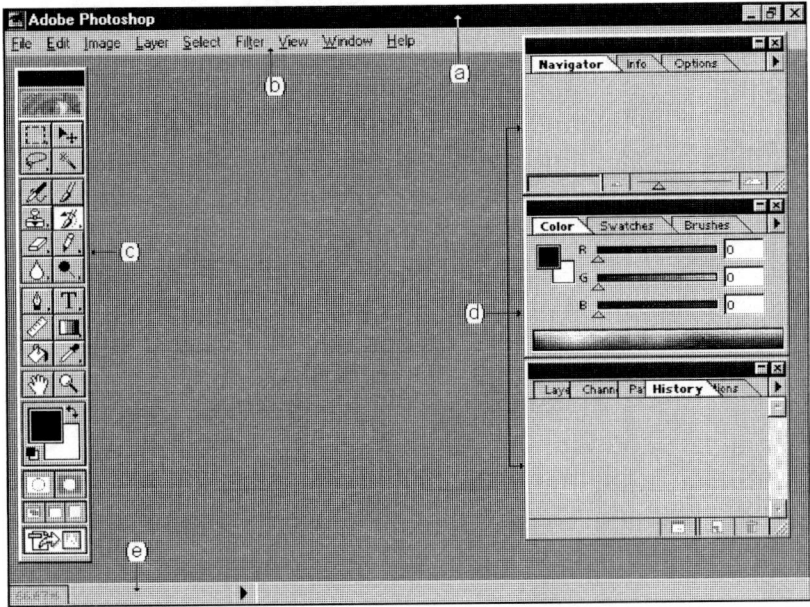

The **title bar (a)** contains the **Control** menu ( ) button, the application name and the **Minimize** ( ), **Restore** ( ) (or **Maximize**) and **Close** ( ) buttons.

The **menu bar (b)** contains nine menus (which for now are closed). They allow you to access the different Photoshop commands.

The **toolbox (c)** contains your working tools as well as buttons used to control colour choice and different screen viewing modes. Some tools have hidden tools attached to them (these are indicated by a small black triangle on the tool button). The toolbox can be moved by dragging its title bar.

The **palettes (d)** let you access different options. By default, all eleven palettes are visible on the screen and are collected into groups from three to five palettes.

The **status bar (e)** displays information concerning the magnification (or zoom) level, the size of the active document, the current work status and other information. It can be hidden by using the **Hide Status Bar** command in the **Window** menu.

✓ *The Windows taskbar may be seen below the status bar.*

Adobe Photoshop 5.5

Introduction

3

The toolbox contains lots of different buttons. It would be a good idea to get to know them.

LOOKING AT THE TOOLBOX

[a] If necessary, show the toolbox by activating the **Show Tools** option in the **Window** menu. The toolbox can be hidden by choosing **Hide Tools** in the **Window** menu.

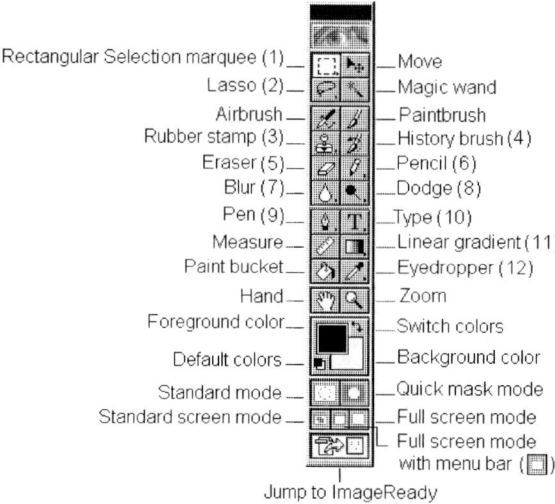

Some tools, for example the Pencil, display a tiny black triangle, which indicates that there are tools hidden underneath. Hold down the tool button to access the hidden tools. When you point to a tool, its name appears after a second as a ScreenTip.

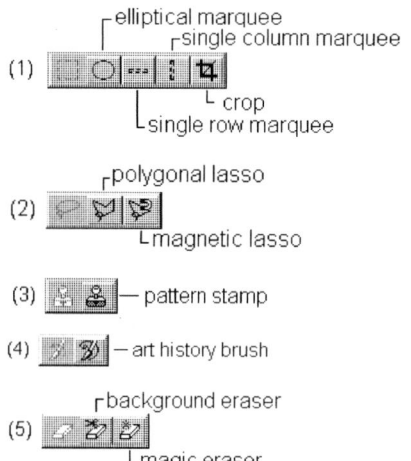

Adobe Photoshop 5.5

Introduction

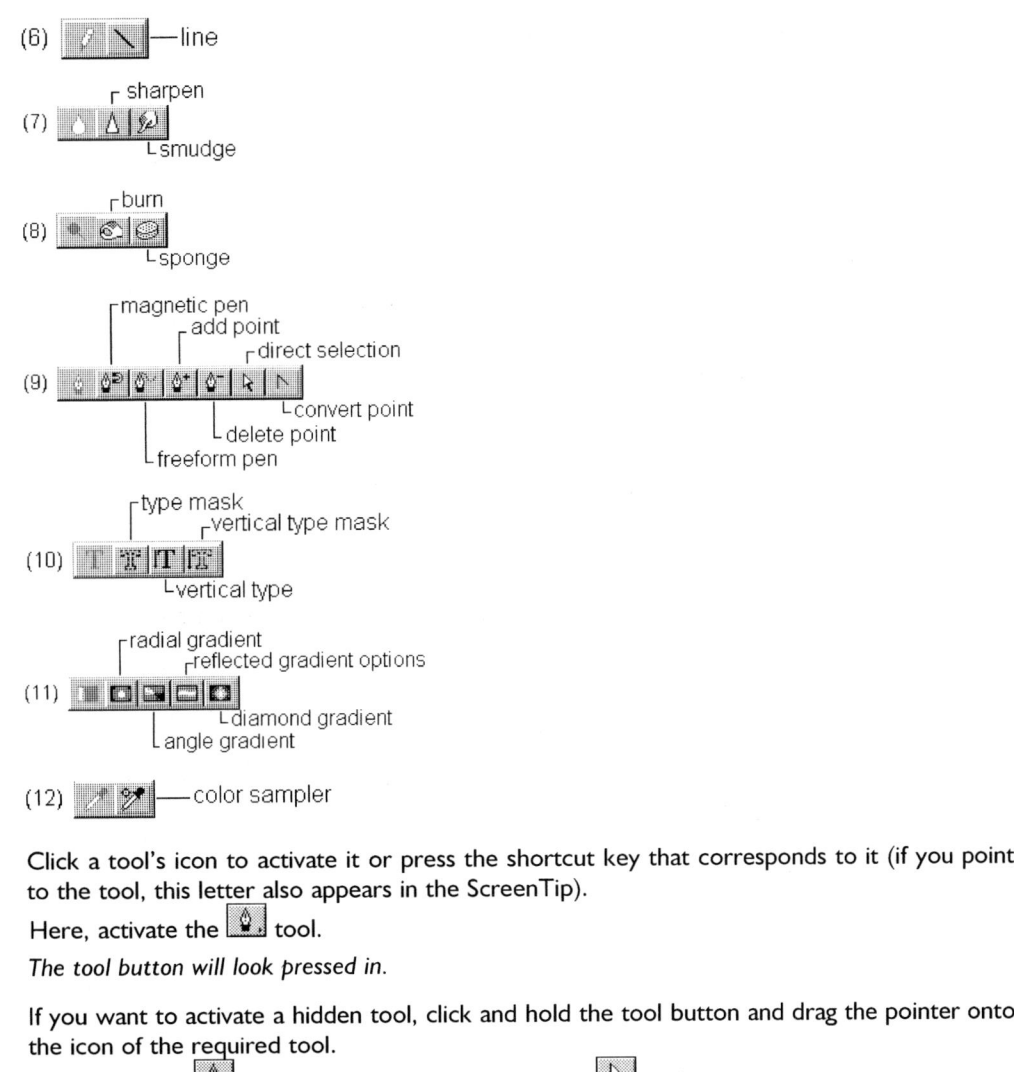

- **b** Click a tool's icon to activate it or press the shortcut key that corresponds to it (if you point to the tool, this letter also appears in the ScreenTip).
- ➣ Here, activate the tool.

   The tool button will look pressed in.

- **c** If you want to activate a hidden tool, click and hold the tool button and drag the pointer onto the icon of the required tool.
- ➣ Here, click the tool and drag until you reach the tool.

   The button will now replace that of the tool on the toolbox.

- ➣ For this example, activate the tool.

   You can see that, although you are no longer using the tool, its icon stays on the toolbox (the tool is now the hidden one). You can also see the importance of mastering the names and locations of the different tools so as not to be confused.

- ➣ For this example, click the tool then drag to to reactivate the Pen tool.

Adobe Photoshop 5.5   15

Introduction

☑ *When a tool is active you can adjust its parameters using the* Options *palette. You can access this palette more easily by simply double-clicking the tool in question.*

4 *Photoshop has eleven palettes full of information and options. Spend some time now making sure you know how to use them.*

WORKING WITH PALETTES

Each palette within a palette group is identified by a tab (on the example below, you can see three tabs on the palette group. Navigator *is the name of the first palette).*

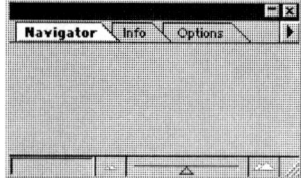

[a] To activate a palette, click the corresponding tab. If the palette you want to use is hidden, you can show it by activating the **Show [Palette Name]** option in the **Window** menu.

➤ Here, click the **Info** tab.

The palette tab becomes white and its contents are visible in the foreground of the group.

[b] It is possible to separate the palettes by dragging one of the tabs onto the work area. You can regroup them in the same way, by dragging one palette tab onto another.

➤ Here, drag the **Info** palette onto the work area.

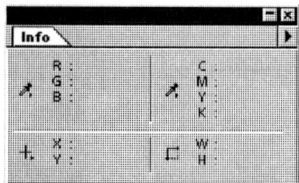

The palette now exists in its own separate window.

[c] Like the toolbox, these palettes have a title bar, which you can use to move them around. To reduce the height of a palette, click the 🔲 button.

➤ Here, click the 🔲 button on the **Info** palette.

Only the title bar and the tab are now visible. The 🔲 button has replaced the 🔲 button: it is used to expand the palette.

16   **Adobe Photoshop 5.5**

Introduction

- [d] To hide a palette, activate the **Hide [Palette Name]** option in the **Window** menu or click the ⊠ button.
- ➤ Here, hide the **Info** palette.

  The palette disappears from the screen.

- [e] To open the palette menu, click the ▶ button situated opposite the tab.
- ➤ Here, open the palette menu on the **Color** palette.

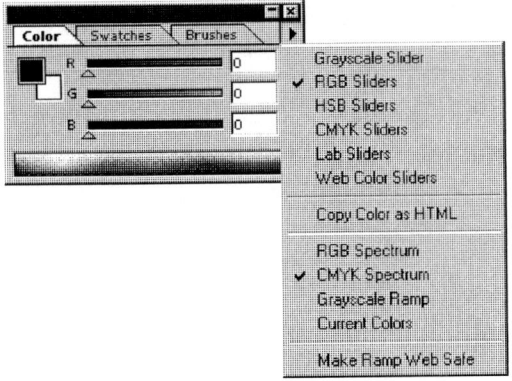

The menu options naturally depend on the active palette.

- ➤ For this example, click outside this menu to close it.

  ✓ *Some palettes can be resized by dragging their bottom right corner.*

  ✓ *To put the palettes back into their original location, go into the Preferences dialog box (File - Preferences - General) and click Reset Palette Locations to Default.*

  ✓ *While you work, it is possible that the palettes might be getting in your way; you can hide all of them by pressing the ⇥ key. Press it again to bring them back.*

  After all those tools and commands, you may be glad actually to open a Photoshop document. You are going to start with one which already exists on your disk.

- ➤ **File - Open** or Ctrl O
- ➤ Use the **Look In** list to access the folder containing the document you want to open. To open a folder which is visible in the list, double-click the folder's icon.

  The 📁 button will send you to the folder above.

  The 📑 and 📋 buttons allow you to display a simple list (limited to the document names) or a detailed list (also containing the document size, type, and last modification date).

- ➤ Open the **Look in** list so as to select the **C:** drive. Double-click the **ENI Photoshop 5.5** folder to open it.

Adobe Photoshop 5.5 17

Introduction

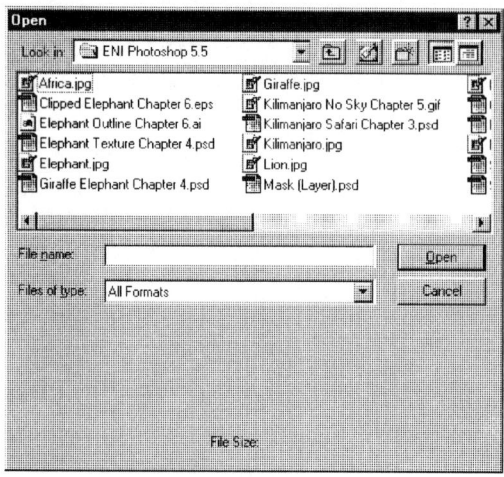

You can see the list of documents contained in the ENI Photoshop 5.5 folder. These documents were copied onto your disk when you installed the CD ROM accompanying the book.

➠ Double-click the **Giraffe** document.

The document window appears on the screen: like any other window, it has a title bar, ▭, ▭ and ▨ buttons. The document name appears on the title bar as well as the active zoom level (100%) and the image's colour mode (here, RGB is not visible because the document window is not wide enough).

☑ *The Open As option in the File menu will let you open images for which the file type is unknown (a wrong extension for example). All the files can be seen in the Open As dialog box. The document is opened in the usual way, but the file type will also be displayed in the Open As box.*

➠ For this example, click the 🖉 tool to select it then move the pointer onto the document window.

Depending on the option set, the pointer might take the same form as the chosen tool's icon on the toolbox, or it might appear as a circle or target.

Introduction

5 You will be pleased to learn that Photoshop includes a whole series of features that make your work easier. Here is the first: you can decide how to represent the pointer for each tool.

DEFINING THE POINTER'S PRESENTATION

a **File**
Preferences
Display & Cursors

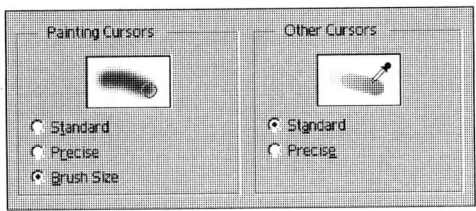

Two different groups exist so that you can define the painting cursors (pointers) independently of the other cursors.

b Define the pointer for the painting tools and/or for other tools:

Standard   The pointer takes the shape of the active tool's icon.

Precise   The pointer takes the form of a cross or a target.

Brush Size   The pointer takes the shape defined in the **Brushes** palette. It also indicates the size and shape of the selected tool.

➤ Here, leave **Brush Size** for painting tools and activate **Precise** for the others.

The pointer form is visible in the dialog box.

c Click **OK**.

➤ Here, confirm then move the pointer onto a light-coloured part of the image.

The pointer associated with the ▱ *tool is represented by a circle that corresponds to the brush shape selected in the* ***Brushes*** *palette.*

> ✓ *If the pointer form is* Standard *or* Brush Size, *press the* ⬚ *(caps-lock) key so that the pointer takes a* Precise *form. If* Precise *has been chosen for painting tools, pressing* ⬚ *will change it to* Brush Size *form. To go back to the form chosen in the* Preferences *dialog box, just undo the uppercase lock by pressing* ⬚.

Adobe Photoshop 5.5

Introduction

6 *Now look at how working with the rulers can help you create your image.*

WORKING WITH RULERS

[a] To show (or hide) the rulers, use the command:
View   [Ctrl] **R**
Show Rulers
or
Hide Rulers

➔ Here, activate the **View - Show Rulers** option.

[b] If the 0 point, located by default in the top left corner of the image, does not suit your needs, point to the ruler origin and drag it on to the required place on the image.

➔ Here, drag the 0 point onto the giraffe's nose.

While you drag, two dotted lines can be seen. The meeting point of the two determines the new 0 point. The horizontal and vertical rulers now show the 0 point as being on the giraffe's nose.

[c] To take the 0 point back to its default position, double-click the ruler origin square.

➔ Here, double-click the square.

The 0 point returns to its original location.

✓ *The default unit used on the ruler is either the centimetre or the inch, depending on your configuration. If that does not suit, use the* File - Preferences - Units & Rulers *to select a new unit of measurement in the* Units *text box.*

Introduction

 Now that you have displayed the rulers, you can set guides to help you position the items in your composition.

USING GUIDES

ADDING A GUIDE

[a] Point to either the vertical or horizontal ruler depending on what sort of guide you want to create.

➜ Here, point to the vertical ruler.

[b] Drag the dotted line onto the image until you have placed the guide in the required position.

➜ Here, drag from the vertical ruler to the 2 cm position (or to 1 inch).

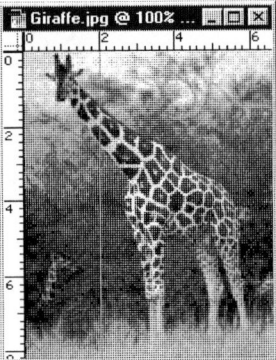

A guide is now visible in that position.

✓ While you drag, you can press [Alt] to change the vertical guide into a horizontal guide and vice versa.

✓ By default, the guides are "magnetic", that is, when you move elements close to them, the elements are "snapped" or attracted by the guides. If you do not wish to use this option, cancel it by deactivating Snap to Guides in the View menu (or [Ctrl][⇧ Shift] ;).

MOVING A GUIDE

[a] Select the tool.

[b] Point to the guide you want to move (the pointer takes the shape of a double-arrow).

➜ Here, point to the one existing guide.

[c] Drag the guide into its new position.

➜ Here, drag the guide until it reaches the giraffe's front legs.

Adobe Photoshop 5.5

Introduction

- ✓ You can temporarily activate the ▸₊ tool by pressing Ctrl, no matter what the active tool.

- ✓ To lock the guides into position, activate the View - Lock Guides option (or Ctrl Alt ;).

DEFINING THE GUIDES' APPEARANCE

[a] **File** Double-click a guide with the ▸₊ tool
Preferences
Guides & Grid

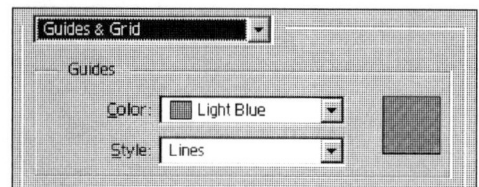

[b] Select the desired colour in the **Color** list and the style of the guides in the **Style** list.

▸ Here, select **Magenta** as the **Color**.

[c] Click **OK**.

The guide stands out much more now!

DELETING GUIDES

[a] Select the ▸₊ tool.

▸ Here, the tool is already selected.

[b] Point to the guide you want to delete (the pointer takes the form of a double arrow).

▸ Here, point to the one guide on the image.

[c] Drag the guide outside of the image or drag it back onto the ruler.

▸ Here, delete the guide you created.

- ✓ You can also delete all the existing guides by choosing *Clear Guides* in the *View* menu.

Introduction

8 Guides are not the only way in which Photoshop helps you position items in a picture: you should try out the grid as well.

USING THE GRID

a To show or hide the grid, use:
View
Show Grid or **Hide Grid**

⟹ Here, show the grid.

`Ctrl` "

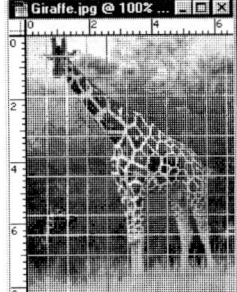

The major grid appears in grey. By default, the spacing between each major line is 2.54 cm (1 inch). The minor grid appears in light grey: by default, four minor grid lines appear between each major line.

b To define the grid parameters, use the command:
File
Preferences
Guides & Grid

c In the **Grid** section, define the **Color** and **Style** for the major grid.

⟹ Here, choose the **Medium Blue** colour.

d Indicate in the **Gridline every** box how far apart to space the major lines.

⟹ Here, enter **1**

e Specify the number of **Subdivisions**, that is the number of minor grid lines between each major one.

⟹ Here, enter **2**

f Click **OK**.

The major grid now appears in a blue colour. The interval between each minor grid line is now equal to 5 mm (if you are working in inches, half an inch).

✓ *By default, items snap to the grid. To deactivate snapping, use the command View - Snap to Grid (or* `Ctrl` `⇧ Shift` *").*

Adobe Photoshop 5.5

Introduction

9 The last in the series of helpful features, at least for now, is the zoom control. But before you get to grips with that, take a look at the **Navigator** palette.

USING THE NAVIGATOR PALETTE

[a] If necessary, show the palette by clicking its tab or by activating the **Show Navigator** option in the **Window** menu.

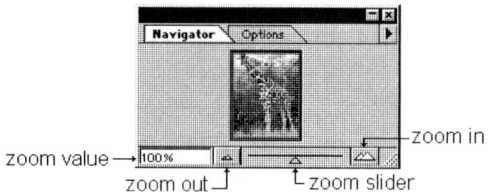

[b] To change the zoom level, click the ▲ or ▲ button or enter a percentage into the zoom value box or drag the zoom slider.

➤ Here, click ▲.

The image has been enlarged and the zoom value has changed. The view box represents the part of the image that can be seen in the document window.

[c] Click the thumbnail (the miniature picture) in the palette to see another part of the image.

➤ Here, click the giraffe's head.

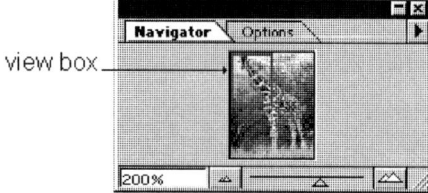

You can now see the giraffe's head and the view box has moved to the place you clicked.

➤ For this example, click ▲.

The image returns to the previous zoom level.

☑ You can also zoom in on a part of the picture by dragging around a section of the thumbnail while holding down [Ctrl].

☑ The colour of the view box can also be changed. To do this, open the palette menu (▶), activate *Palette Options* then select the colour you wish.

Introduction

10 But the **Navigation** palette is not the only way of changing the magnification of your picture.

CHANGING THE ZOOM

a. Click the tool.

When the pointer moves onto the image, it takes the shape of a magnifying glass with a plus sign (+) in it.

b. Click the part of the image you wish to zoom in on or drag a selection marquee (a dotted rectangle) around this part to limit what is seen in the document window to just that part.

➤ Here, click the giraffe's head three times.

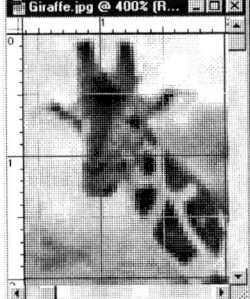

The giraffe's head is enlarged in the window and the zoom value is indicated on the window's title bar.

c. To reduce the zoom, make sure the 🔍 tool is active, hold down [Alt] and click.

➤ Here, hold down [Alt] and click the centre of the image.

The zoom is now equal to 300%. When you press [Alt], a minus sign (-) appears in the magnifying glass.

d. To take the image back to a 100% zoom level, double-click the 🔍 tool.

✓ No matter what tool is active, you can temporarily activate the zoom-in by pressing [Ctrl][space] or the zoom-out by pressing [Alt][space].

✓ When the image is larger than the window, you can use the scroll cursors or the 🖐 tool to scroll the window's contents. Using this tool, drag the image so as to show the parts which are hidden. Even when another tool is active, you can also hold down the [space] bar to temporarily activate the 🖐 tool.

Adobe Photoshop 5.5

Introduction

☑ *If you wish the document window to resize itself automatically depending on the zoom, click Resize Windows to Fit on the Options palette (when the tool is active).*

[a] Use one of these shortcuts:
`Ctrl` +	Increases the zoom.
`Ctrl` `Alt` +	Increases the zoom while enlarging the window accordingly.
`Ctrl` -	Reduces the zoom.
`Ctrl` `Alt` -	Reduces the zoom while reducing the window accordingly.
`Ctrl` `Alt` 0	Resets the zoom at 100%.
`Ctrl` 0	Enlarges the window and adjusts the zoom to the window size.

[a] Open the **View** menu.

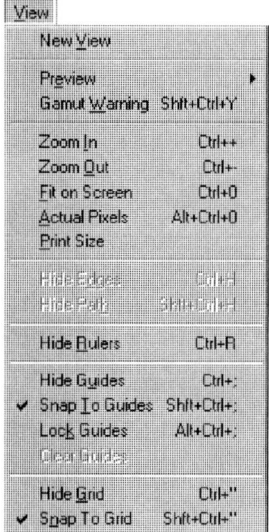

[b] Activate one of these options:
Zoom In   Increases the zoom level.
Zoom Out   Reduces the zoom level.

Adobe Photoshop 5.5

Introduction

    Fit on Screen   Enlarges the document window and adjusts the zoom to the size of the screen.

    Actual Pixels   Fixes the zoom at 100%.

    Print Size   Displays the image at the size it will be printed. This display depends on the image resolution. If the resolution is 72 ppi, the zoom will be set at 100%, if it is 144 ppi, the zoom will equal 50%...

11

In some cases, you can get the best overall view of a picture by displaying it full screen.

DISPLAYING A FULL SCREEN IMAGE

a To display the image window over the entire work area, while keeping the menu bar, click the ▢ button near the bottom of the toolbox.

There are no scroll bars when in this mode. You must use the ✋ tool if you want to move your picture.

b To obtain a larger displaying surface, click the ▢ button.

The menu bar is no longer visible, but can be accessed from the title bar of the toolbox by pressing ▶. Again there are no scroll bars in this mode, so you should use the ✋ tool to move the image.

c To return to a standard screen mode, click the ▣ button.

    ✓ *When working on an image, remember to use the different zoom possibilities open to you. They will allow you select, create and retouch with much more precision.*

12

*A little while ago, you were introduced to the **Navigation** palette. Now here is another palette which can be useful when you are using any of a whole set of tools and commands: the **Info** palette lets you see exactly what the command is doing to your picture.*

LOOKING AT THE INFO PALETTE

a Show the **Info** palette by clicking its tab or using the **Window - Show Info** command.

➤ Here, select **Window - Show Info**, as the palette was previously hidden. Drag the tab onto that of the **Navigator** palette, where it was originally. Next, position the pointer on the image without clicking.

Introduction

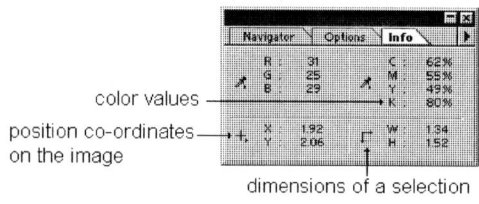

color values
position co-ordinates on the image
dimensions of a selection

Various pieces of useful information are shown on the palette.

[b] The colour values for the pixels under the pointer are displayed using two colour modes. The first set of information refers to the real colors on the image, the second to the printing colours. For the second set of information, the values are indicated by default as percentages; if the % symbol is replaced by a !, this means that the pixel to which you are pointing cannot be printed exactly as it is.

It is possible to adjust the colour modes displayed by clicking the ✎ icon in the palette. You will learn more specific information later concerning colour modes.

[c] The co-ordinates of the pointer on the image are also shown. These co-ordinates are displayed in the unit of measure selected in the **Units** option in the **File - Preferences - General** dialog box.

It is possible to change this unit by clicking the ✚ icon (but this will change the unit used in the whole of Photoshop).

[d] The **Info** palette also provides information when selecting and modifying objects (but you will see more on this in later chapters).

The information in the ⌐⌐ frame shows you the dimensions of what is currently selected. These are described in the same unit of measure used for the pointer co-ordinates.

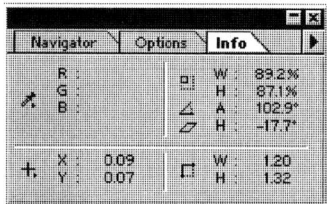

When you make a transformation on a selection or layer, the information concerning the colour components is replaced by the transformation parameters: changes in scale are indicated by the ▫ icon, and the letters W (width) and H (height). The △ icon indicates the rotation angle and the ⟋ icon indicate the skew (slanting) angle.

For now, leave the explanations about selections and modifications, you will look at those at a later time. For now, deactivate the grid before closing the Giraffe document.

➤ For this example, use the command **View - Hide Grid**.

You are coming to the end of this tour of the Photoshop environment. It is time to close the picture document, although you will not be leaving Photoshop just yet.

➤ Click the ⊠ button on the document window.

Introduction

➤ Photoshop will offer to save, but click **No**.
The picture of the giraffe is no longer on the screen.

> ☑ *If several images are open simultaneously, you can close all the documents by using the Close All option in the Window menu.*

You have now reached the end of this introduction. All that is left to do in this chapter is to close the Photoshop application.

➤ Click the ☒ button on the Photoshop window.
The Photoshop window disappears from the screen. If no other application is open, you will find yourself back on the Windows Desktop.

Introduction

CHAPTER 1

1 - SELECTING ALL OF AN IMAGE 33
2 - DEACTIVATING A SELECTION 34
3 - SELECTING A REGULAR ZONE ON AN IMAGE 34
4 - MOVING PART OF AN IMAGE 37
5 - POSITIONING PART OF AN IMAGE WITH PRECISION 38
6 - COPYING PART OF AN IMAGE 39
7 - CREATING A NEW DOCUMENT 41
8 - COPYING AN IMAGE INTO ANOTHER DOCUMENT 43
9 - SELECTING AN IRREGULAR PART OF AN IMAGE 45
      USING THE [ ] TOOL 45
      USING THE [ ] TOOL 46
      USING THE [ ] TOOL 47
10 - SAVING A SELECTION 49
11 - LOADING A SELECTION 50
12 - MOVING OR COPYING ONTO A NEW LAYER 51
13 - UNDERSTANDING COLOUR MODELS 52
      THE COLOUR WHEEL 52
      THE RGB MODEL 52
      THE CMYK MODEL 53
      THE LAB MODEL 53
      THE HSB MODEL 54
      THE GRAYSCALE MODEL 54
14 - SELECTING A COLOUR 54
      USING THE COLOR PALETTE 54
      USING THE COLOR PICKER 56
      USING THE SWATCHES PALETTE 57
      USING THE [ ] TOOL 57
      USING A CUSTOM COLOR PICKER 58
15 - USING THE SWATCHES PALETTE 59
      ADDING COLOURS TO THE SWATCHES PALETTE 59
      DELETING COLOURS FROM THE SWATCHES PALETTE 59
      SAVING OR OPENING A SWATCH LIBRARY 60
16 - COLOURING A SELECTION 61
17 - ADDING STROKE TO A SELECTION 64
18 - FEATHERING A SELECTION 65
19 - SELECTING AN AREA OF THE IMAGE BY ITS COLOUR 66

20 - EXPANDING OR CONTRACTING SELECTIONS	67
USING THE MOUSE	67
EXPANDING A SELECTION USING ITS COLOURS	68
EXPANDING A SELECTION ACCORDING TO ITS OUTLINE	68
CONTRACTING A SELECTION ACCORDING TO ITS OUTLINE	69
21 - INVERSING A SELECTION	69
22 - DEFINING PRINT OPTIONS	70
23 - PRINTING AN IMAGE	72
PRACTICE EXERCISE 1	74

Chapter 1

Throughout this course, imagine that you are working on a project, with an African theme. This project consists of several different documents (flyers, leaflets etc), each containing various illustrations obtained from photographs. Photoshop will help you to create these illustrations.

During this first chapter, you will learn mainly how to select items. This is very important, as knowing the various selection techniques will let you create, edit and retouch with precision, considering the selection acts like a stencil when you are retouching. You will also learn the basic principals of saving and printing your work.
By the end of this chapter, you will have produced an illustration which looks like this:

➠ If you have previously quit Photoshop, restart it now.

You will be working on the document called Mask.jpg.

➠ Open the **Mask.jpg** document in the **ENI Photoshop 5.5** folder.

1 *Start with a simple selection.*

SELECTING ALL OF AN IMAGE

[a] Select   [Ctrl] **A**
All
A selection marquee appears around the image in the form of a black-and-white dotted line which flashes.

Adobe Photoshop 5.5

Chapter 1

☑ If this selection marquee bothers you, you can hide it by activating the *Hide Edges* option in the *View* menu or by pressing [Ctrl] H. To show the marquee again, activate *Show Edges* in the *View* menu or press [Ctrl] H. Be careful, hiding the marquee does not mean that the object is no longer selected.

2

If the selection does not suit you or is no longer needed, you can cancel it.

DEACTIVATING A SELECTION

[a] **Select**   [Ctrl] **D**
Deselect
The dotted rectangle representing the selection disappears and no part of the image is currently selected.

☑ By using this command, you deselect everything. You will see later on how to cancel only part of a selection.

3

Continue working on the basic selections.

SELECTING A REGULAR ZONE ON AN IMAGE

[a] Select the ▢ tool or the ○ tool (which is one of the tools hidden by ▢).
➤ Here, activate the ▢ tool.

[b] If the **Options** palette is not visible, show it to check the tool preferences (click the **Options** tab or use the **Window - Show Options** command).

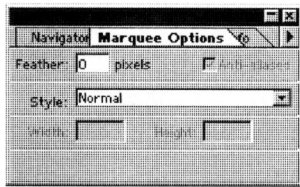

[c] Use the **Feather** option to create a transition boundary between the selected object and the pixels surrounding it. If the value is 0, the selection marquee will be hard-edged. The higher the feathering value, the more the selection marquee will be blurred and will integrate the neighbouring pixels with varying degrees of transparency.

Adobe Photoshop 5.5

Chapter 1

The mask on the left has been selected without feathering while the one on the right was selected with a feathering value of 5.

To demonstrate more clearly the impact of feathering on the selection, the marquees have been overdrawn identically in black on both of these selections. Notice that on the right mask, even if it is essentially the outside pixels which are blurred, the pixels inside the selection are also a little blurred at the edges. Furthermore, the selection marquee has rounded corners: feathering changes the appearance of the selection marquee. For this reason, it is recommended at this stage to leave the feathering value at 0 in the **Options** palette so as not to be confused by the visual appearance of the selection marquee. You will see that it is possible to produce a feathering effect after having completed the selection.

▫▶ Here, leave the value at **0** to obtain a hard-edged marquee.

[d] If the selection was made with the ⬚ tool, activate the **Anti-aliased** option to obtain a regular border without a "staircase effect" (where the edge pixels are showing) on the selected item's border.

 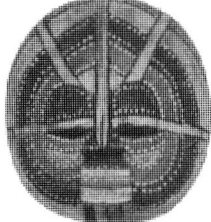

*The mask on the left was selected normally, while the one on the right was selected with the **Anti-aliased** option active. You can see clearly the edge pixels on the left mask, while the mask on the right has a smoother outline.*

▫▶ Here, the **Anti-aliased** option is not available.

[e] Define the **Style** for the selection:

    Normal   To define the rectangular or elliptical selection with no constraints.

    Constrained Aspect Ratio   To define the rectangular or elliptical selection with width and height constraints. Select the ratio between width and height by entering values in the **Width** and **Height** text boxes. By default, the values are equal to 1, which forces you to create a square or a circular marquee (with equivalent width and height).

    Fixed Size   To define a rectangular or elliptical selection marquee of a specific size. Indicate the size in pixels in the **Width** and **Height** text boxes. The selection marquee will be drawn just by clicking the image.

Adobe Photoshop 5.5

Chapter 1

▸ Here, leave the **Normal** style active.

For this example, use the options proposed by default.

[f] Drag to draw a selection rectangle or ellipse. If you have chosen the **Fixed Size** option, just click the image.

▸ Here, select the mask by dragging a rectangle around it (starting at one corner).

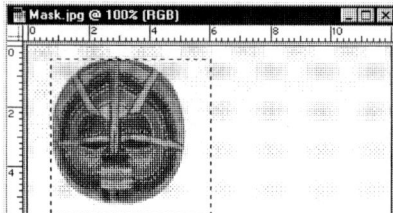

The selection marquee appears around the mask.

[g] If the marquee is incorrectly placed, point inside the selection and hold down the mouse button. You can now drag the selection marquee around to fit it over the image.

The pointer takes this form: .

▸ Here, centre the marquee around the mask.

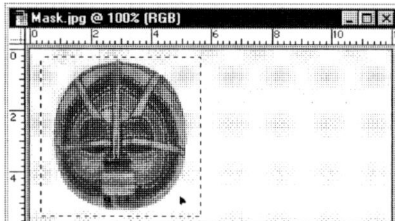

The selection marquee is now correctly placed around the mask.

Now try using the ⬚ tool to select the mask, as its shape is rounded.

▸ Cancel the first selection using **Select - Deselect**.

▸ Click the ⬚ tool to see the hidden ⬚ tool, activate it, then drag the marquee around the mask, as close to its edges as possible. If necessary, adjust the marquee's position.

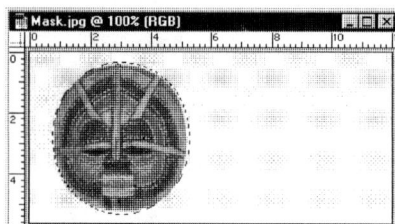

The mask is not entirely circular, but the ⬚ tool lets you make a fairly good selection.

Chapter 1

- ✓ When creating a rectangular or elliptical marquee, you can make a perfectly proportioned circle or square by holding down [⇧ Shift] while you drag.
- ✓ When creating a selection marquee, you can also use the [Alt] key to draw the marquee (rectangle or ellipse) from the object's centre. Point to the centre of the object when you start dragging.
- ✓ You can reposition the marquee while dragging by pressing [space]. Release the [space] bar but not the mouse button to continue selecting.
- ✓ For very specific tasks, you can use the [⋯] and [⋮] tools which allow you to only select a row or column of pixels.

4 Using this first selection, you are going to see how to move an object.

MOVING PART OF AN IMAGE

[a] Select the part of the image or activate the layer containing the image you wish to move.
You may not yet be familiar with the idea of layers. It will be discussed in Chapter 2.

➤ Here, keep the mask selected.

[b] Activate the [▶+] tool or press [Ctrl] to use the tool temporarily.

➤ Here, click [▶+].

[c] Point inside the selection and drag to the desired location.
The pointer takes this form: ▶✂.

➤ Here, move the mask to the right of the image.

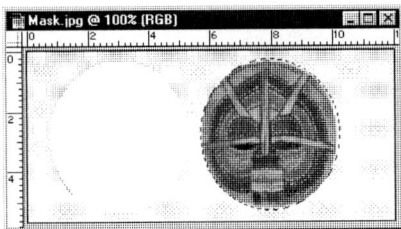

The mask is correctly placed. Notice the appearance of a "hole" in the place where the object used to be. The space is filled with the active background colour.

- ✓ Hold down [⇧ Shift] while dragging to obtain a horizontal, vertical or 45° movement.
- ✓ Use the arrow keys to move the image pixel by pixel. An arrow key plus [⇧ Shift] will move the image 10 pixels.

Adobe Photoshop 5.5

Chapter 1

☑ Use snapping to guides or to the grid if you want the object to be attracted to them while being moved.

As you work on an image, it is easy to make a false manoeuvre, and you should learn how to correct this.

➤ **Edit - Undo...** or Ctrl Z

The **Undo** option is followed by the name of the last action performed.

The mask returns to its original position.

☑ To undo several actions, you can use the History palette (which will be described in detail in Chapter 5).

☑ If you cannot undo (if the history has been erased for example), you can activate the *Revert* option in the *File* menu, which will replace the current version of the open document with that existing on the hard disk.

---

5 You can also move an object by indicating the co-ordinates of its new position or by providing move values.

POSITIONING PART OF AN IMAGE WITH PRECISION

|a| Select the part of the image or activate the layer to be moved.

➤ Here, keep the mask selected.

|b| **Edit**
Transform
Numeric

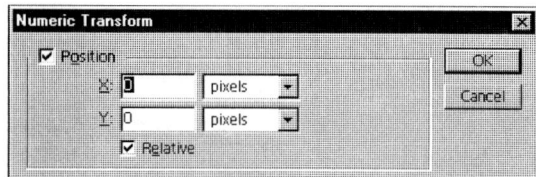

|c| Deactivate the **Scale**, **Skew** and **Rotate** options.

|d| Activate the **Relative** option to give a movement value in relation to the current position of the selection. Deactivate this option if you want to define the new location relative to the upper left corner of the image.

➤ Here, activate the option if it is not already active.

Chapter 1

[e] If the **Relative** option is active, enter the horizontal movement value in the **X** text box and the vertical movement in the **Y** text box. If the **Relative** option is deactivated, enter the horizontal and vertical position of the selection's new location. Also, select which unit to apply to **X** and **Y** from the drop-down list box.

⟹ Here, enter **4** in box **X** and select **cm** as the unit and leave **0** as the **Y** value (if you prefer to work in inches, enter **1.5** and select **inches**).

[f] Click **OK**.

The mask moved four centimetres to the right.

As you do not really want to move the mask, cancel the move.

⟹ **Edit - Undo Numeric Transform**

Perhaps you would prefer to copy the mask. To help you position the copy correctly, set some guides.

⟹ If necessary, show the rulers (**View - Show Rulers**).

⟹ Click the **Info** palette tab to show it.

⟹ Point to the vertical ruler then drag to create a guide as close to position **X = 11.3** (centimetres) as possible (use the **Info** palette to find this location). If you are working in inches, set the guide at **X = 4.5**.

⟹ From the horizontal ruler, create a guide, using the **Info** palette to help you, at position **Y = 0.35** (in inches, this is a mere **0.1**).

6 *Make a copy of the mask.*

COPYING PART OF AN IMAGE

[a] Select the part of the image or activate the layer to be copied.

⟹ Here, keep the mask selected.

[b] Activate the ![tool] tool or hold down [Ctrl] to use the tool temporarily.

⟹ Here, activate the ![tool] tool.

[c] Point inside the selection and hold down [Alt].

The pointer will take this form: ![pointer].

[d] Drag to the desired location.

⟹ Here, drag the copy to the right of the original until it touches the guides you created.

Adobe Photoshop 5.5   **39**

Chapter 1

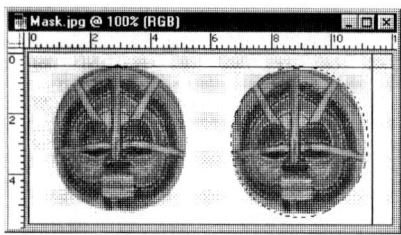

A second mask now appears to the right of the first one. It is the second mask that is selected and not the original.

- ✓ Copying is still a type of moving, so you can use the arrow keys as well as ⇧Shift to place the copy precisely. You can also constrain it to a horizontal, vertical or 45° movement by holding down the ⇧Shift key as you drag.

- ✓ As long as the copy is selected, you can move it with the ⊕ tool without a "hole" appearing in the background.

The guides are no longer useful, so you can remove them.

➠ Drag the guides out of the window.
➠ **View - Hide Rulers**

You can also use the Windows clipboard to move or copy part of an image. Try this out by copying the mask from the document Mask.jpg into a new document.

➠ Leave the mask selected.
➠ **Edit - Copy**

- ✓ If you move or copy a large area of the image into the clipboard, the memory may be overloaded and will slow down your computer. Even after you paste data in, the item you transferred into the clipboard will still be there. If you do not need the information anymore, it may be a good idea to empty the clipboard (and the part of the memory reserved for it) by using *Edit - Purge - Clipboard*.

Chapter 1

 If you want to copy the content of the clipboard into a new document, you will first have to learn how to create the document.

CREATING A NEW DOCUMENT

[a] File **N**
     New

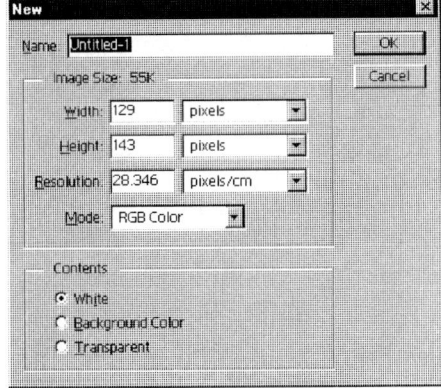

[b] If you wish, enter the name of the new document in the **Name** text box.

This can also be done when you are saving the new document.

▸ Here, type in **My mask**

[c] Enter the document size into the **Width** and **Height** text boxes, selecting the correct unit of measurement.

The default size listed corresponds to the dimensions of the selection inside the clipboard.

▸ Here, leave the default values, as you wish to obtain an image the size of the previously-copied mask.

[d] Define the image resolution in the **Resolution** box. It is best to use **pixels per inch** (or **ppi**) as the measurement unit as this is the most commonly used unit when dealing with graphics. The 72 ppi resolution corresponds to the resolution of the monitor and is suitable for images destined to stay on screens (photos used for CD ROMs, Web pages etc). For images made for printing, you should choose a resolution between 150 and 600 ppi depending on the quality required (150 ppi is the minimum resolution possible for satisfactory printing results).
Be careful, the higher the resolution chosen, the more resources it will use on your computer. It is also worth noting that to the average person's eye, there is really very little difference between 300 ppi and 600 ppi resolution. Keep these high resolutions for "deluxe" professional printing tasks or for when making enlargements.

▸ Here, leave the proposed resolution which corresponds to that of the mask.

Adobe Photoshop 5.5

Chapter 1

|e| Select the image's colour mode in the **Mode** list.
For images to be displayed on a screen, opt for **RGB Color** or **Grayscale**. For images which will be printed, **CMYK Color** or **Grayscale** are preferable.

⟹ Here, leave **RGB Color**.

|f| Define the background using the **Contents** options, choosing between:

White to make the background white.

Background Color to use the active background colour.

Transparent to create a transparent layer. This transparent "colour" is shown on the screen as a grey and white chessboard.

⟹ Here, activate **Transparent** to create a new image on a transparent layer.

|g| Click the **OK** button.

A new window appears on the screen. The background of this window, represented by a grey and white chessboard, is transparent.

- ✓ *Image resolution is a complex problem, so an entire chapter is devoted to it later in this volume.*

- ✓ *It is possible to define the parameters of the transparent colour. To do this, choose File - Preferences - Transparent & Gamut.*

You can now paste in the mask that you have copied.

⟹ **Edit - Paste**

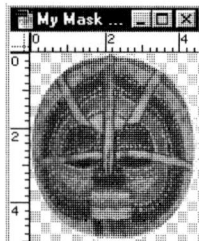

The mask just fits into the created document and is not selected. It appears in the centre of the image.

Chapter 1

At this point, it would be a good idea to save the document you have just created.

⟹ **File - Save As** or **Save** or Ctrl ⇧Shift **S** or Ctrl **S**

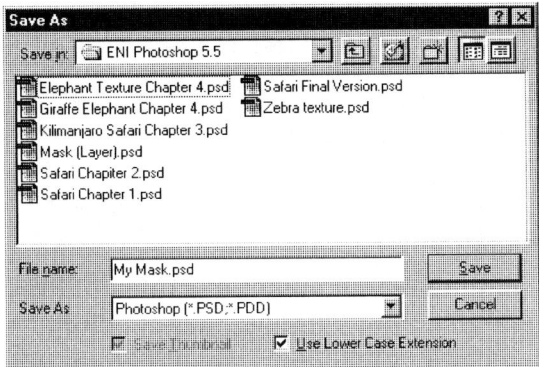

The Save As dialog box appears.

⟹ Open the **ENI Photoshop 5.5** folder located in C: drive.

⟹ The name **My mask** is already displayed. Do not change it.

If the document contains one or more layers, it is impossible to save it in any other format than Photoshop. Generally speaking, it is a good idea to keep one version of the document in Photoshop format as it is the only format capable of memorising every element of work in an image.

⟹ Click the **Save** button.

*The image is saved on the hard disk and is called **My Mask.psd** (PSD for PhotoShop Document).*

You do not need to use this image for the moment, so you can close it.

⟹ **File - Close** (do not close **Mask.jpg**).

---

8 *You now know how to copy part of a selected image onto the same document, or even onto another using the clipboard. There is another technique you can use to copy images from one document to another.*

COPYING AN IMAGE INTO ANOTHER DOCUMENT

[a] If necessary, open the two documents to be used.

⟹ Here, open the document **Africa.jpg**. If the **Africa.jpg** and **Mask.jpg** documents overlap too much, use the title bars to move the windows so you can see each window clearly.

[b] Go into the document which contains the image you wish to copy.

⟹ Here, activate the **Mask.jpg** window by clicking the title bar.

Chapter 1

[c] Select the part of the image to copy or activate the layer containing the image.

➠ Here, select the mask again, if it is not still selected.

[d] Activate the ![tool] tool or press [Ctrl] to use the tool temporarily.

➠ Here, activate the ![tool] tool.

[e] Point inside the selected item.

The pointer takes this form: ▶⛯.

[f] Drag the selected item onto the destination document window.

➠ Here, drag the mask onto the **Africa.jpg** document window, as shown in the following illustration:

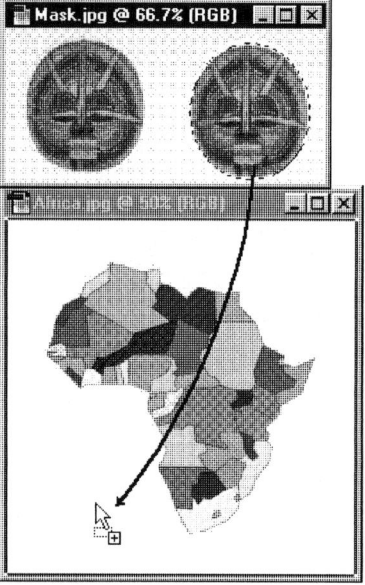

While you drag, the pointer is accompanied by a small cross which symbolises a copy. When you release the mouse, the mask is correctly copied into the Africa.jpg document, at the point where you stop dragging.

- ✓ If the image that you want to copy is in the clipboard, you can also use the *Paste* option in the *Edit* menu.

- ✓ Whatever method you use to copy onto another document, the copied image will be placed on a layer.

Chapter 1

You can test this for yourself:

▸ Show the **Layers** palette by using **Window - Show Layers** if necessary.

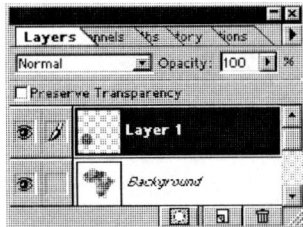

*The created layer is called **Layer x** (x may vary depending on the number of existing layers already in the document).*

*The **Mask.jpg** document is not useful for you at the moment, so you can close it.*

▸ Click the ⊠ button on the **Mask.jpg** window.

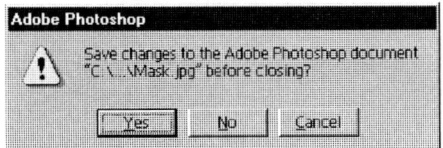

This dialog box appears because you did not save your document before closing it.

▸ Click the **No** button, because you do not need to save the changes made.

Now you just need to place the mask in the correct position.

▸ Activate the ⊕ tool then point to the mask and drag it so as to place it at the bottom left beside Africa.

---

9 *You now know how to select regular-shaped items. Here, you will see how to select irregular-shaped ones.*

SELECTING AN IRREGULAR PART OF AN IMAGE

USING THE ⌒ TOOL

[a] Activate the ⌒ tool.

[b] If the **Options** palette is hidden, show it to check the tool preferences. Define these options in the same way as for a regular-shaped item.

Adobe Photoshop 5.5   45

Chapter 1

➔ Here, enter **0** as a feathering value and ensure that the **Anti-aliased** option is active to smooth any jagged edges around the selection border.

[c] Activate the layer in which you want to make the selection.

➔ Here, click the **Background** layer on the **Layers** palette to continue this exercise on the map of Africa.

You will learn more about layers in the following chapter.

[d] Drag along the outline of the required section. To finish selecting, release the mouse button.

➔ Here, drag along the outline of the map.

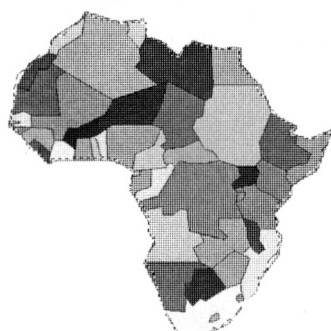

The map is selected, but the marquee is not very precise.

The [🔲] tool is interesting when selecting small sections, but on such a large item, it is difficult to obtain a satisfactory result first time.

As the selection is really not very good, cancel it.

➔ **Select - Deselect**

USING THE [🔲] TOOL

[a] Activate the [🔲] tool (it is one of the tools hidden by [🔲]).

[b] Define the **Options** as you did with the [🔲] tool.

➔ Here, leave the default options.

[c] Activate the layer containing the item you are working on.

➔ Here, you are still working on the map.

[d] Proceed with a series of subsequent clicks to draw around the outline of the object. To finish off the selection, double-click or click the starting point (when you reach this point, the pointer takes this form: [🔲]).

➔ Here, select the map.

Chapter 1

This selection should be much more precise than the previous one. The map lends itself particularly well to this type of selection, as its outline is composed of lots of straight lines.

As you are going to make a final selection of the map with another tool, deselect this one.

■➤ **Select - Deselect**

USING THE ![] TOOL

[a] Activate the ![] tool (which is one of the tools hidden by ![]).

[b] If the **Options** palette is hidden, show it to check the tool preferences.

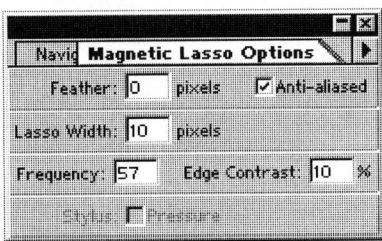

[c] Use the **Lasso Width** option to determine the automatic detection width for the edges. This value can vary from 1 to 40. Use a lower value if there is little contrast between the object you are selecting and its surroundings and a higher value if the contrast between object and background is very marked.

You can change the Lasso width while you are selecting, using the ![←] and ![→] keys to respectively decrease or increase it by a pixel.

■➤ Here, enter **20** as the **Lasso Width**.

[d] Use the **Frequency** option to set the rate at which fastening points will be created. You can use a value between 0 and 100. For an image with low contrast, use a high value. On the example below, the image on the left was selected with a **Frequency** rate equal to 10 and you can see on its border six fastening points (represented by tiny squares). The image on the right was selected with a **Frequency** of 50 and you can see nine fastening points.

■➤ Here, choose a **Frequency** of **10**.

Adobe Photoshop 5.5

Chapter 1

[e] Use the **Edge Contrast** option to define the lasso's sensitivity towards the image's edges. If the edges are soft, use a higher value. If the edges change direction abruptly, enter a lower value. On the following figure, the image on the left is selected with an **Edge Contrast** equal to 10% while that on the right is selected with a value of 100%. Notice that the pointed corner on the right-hand image has not been included in the selection.

➡ Here, leave the **10%** value proposed by default.

[f] Activate the layer on which the selection will be made.

➡ Here, you are still working on the same layer.

[g] Click to start outlining then drag the pointer over the object's edges. As you select, if you are unsatisfied with the selection, drag the pointer backwards. Press the [Del] key to remove the last fastening point. You can also click to manually create a fastening point. To finish off the selection, double-click or click the starting point (when this point is reached, the pointer takes this form :).

➡ Here, select the map: click the edge then drag the pointer around the whole outline.

The selection is perhaps not as perfect as the one created with the tool but it can be done much more quickly and is a little less angular.

✓ You can temporarily deactivate the snapping properties of the tool. To do this, hold down the [Alt] key and drag over a portion of the border as with the tool or make a series of clicks as with the tool. Release the key to bring back snapping.

Chapter 1

10 *In order to use the map selection on other occasions, you can save the selection.*

SAVING A SELECTION

a Select
Save Selection

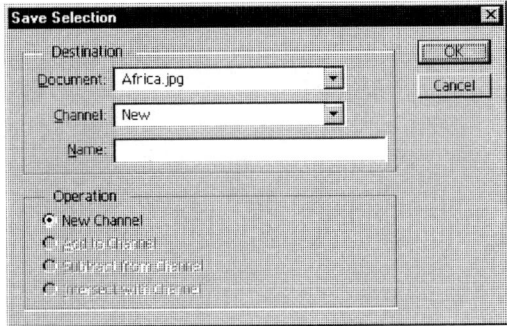

b Use the **Document** option to indicate in which document the selection should be saved. If several images of the same dimensions are open in Photoshop, you can save the selection in one of these documents. Generally, you would save it in the same document or in a new one.

▸ Here, leave the **Africa.jpg** option selected.

c If a selection has already been saved, you can replace it with a new selection by choosing the corresponding option in the **Channel** drop-down list. To create a new channel, leave the New option active.

▸ Here, only the New option is available because no other selection has yet been saved.

d Use the **Name** option to give a title to the selection you want to save. If you leave this box blank, Photoshop will attribute a default name **Alpha x**, x being a number between 1 and 23 (which is the maximum number of selections you can save).

▸ Here, enter **Map** in the **Name** box.

e If you have chosen an existing selection in the **Channel** box, use the **Operation** option to define how the two selections are to be combined.

Replace Channel	This option replaces New Channel in the dialog box. It will erase the previous selection and replace it with the new one.
Add to Channel	Combines the previously saved selection with the new one.
Subtract from Channel	Deletes the area corresponding to the selection you are saving from the selection already saved in the channel.
Intersect with Channel	Saves the parts of the new selection that intersect with the previously saved selection.

Adobe Photoshop 5.5

Chapter 1

➡ Here, these options are not available.

[f] Click **OK**.

The selection is saved.

Before going any further, you should deselect the map.

➡ **Select - Deselect**

✓ *This technique creates an alpha channel, a sort of additional level to the document. You will see more about channels in chapter 7.*

---

11 *You can now retrieve the selection you have saved by loading it into an image.*

LOADING A SELECTION

[a] **Select**
Load Selection

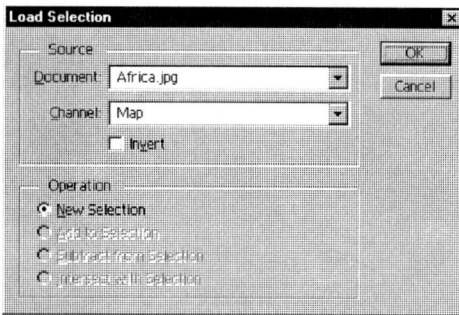

[b] Use the **Document** option to indicate which document Photoshop should look in to retrieve the selection. If several images of the same size are open in Photoshop, you can retrieve a saved selection in one of these documents from the document you are currently using.

➡ Here, you want to pick it out of the **Africa.jpg** document.

[c] Choose the selection's name from the **Channel** drop-down list.

➡ Here, the only channel listed is **Map**.

[d] Activate the **Invert** option to select the entire image except the part which corresponds to the saved selection.

➡ Here, do not activate this option.

Chapter 1

|e| If the destination image already contains a selected item, specify how to combine it with the one you are about to load.

New Selection — to replace the existing selection with the one you are loading.

Add to Selection — to combine the existing selection with the new one.

Subtract from Selection — to remove from the existing selection the part of it that corresponds to what you are loading.

Intersect with Selection — to keep the intersecting areas of the existing and new selection.

➡ Here, these options are not available because nothing is currently selected.

|f| Click **OK**.

The selection is loaded and the map is automatically selected.

✓ *When a selection is cancelled, you can retrieve it by using the Reselect command in the Select menu, or by pressing* [Ctrl][⇧ Shift] *D. However, this only reselects the last item selected, whereas the Load Selection command will let you apply any saved selection. Also, the selection you can retrieve using Reselect is not saved anywhere in the document and cannot be recovered if you quit Photoshop.*

---

12 *You have already seen some basic techniques for moving and copying selected areas of an image. Here is a special type of move/copy operation, which you will find useful. You are going to move the selected map onto a new layer.*

MOVING OR COPYING ONTO A NEW LAYER

|a| If it is not already selected, select the part of the image as required.

➡ Here, the map is already selected.

|b| To move a selection, use: [Ctrl][⇧ Shift] **J**
Layer
New
Layer Via Cut

|c| To copy a selection, use: [Ctrl] **J**
Layer
New
Layer Via Copy

➡ Here, move the selection onto a new layer using **Layer - New - Layer Via Cut** then if the **Layers** palette is hidden, choose **Window - Show Layers**.

Adobe Photoshop 5.5

Chapter 1

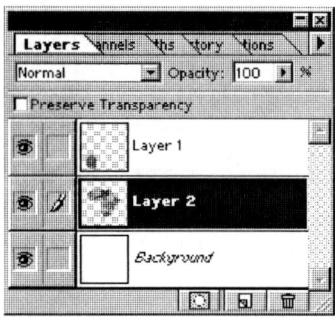

The map appears on a layer called **Layer 2** and the preview picture of the **Background** layer seems empty.

Layers and the **Layers** palette will be discussed in detail in the next chapter.

---

13 To make your various retouches and creations, you will need to use colours and shades of grey. In order to do this, you will need to have a good understanding of colour models. This information may seem a little theoretical, but it is necessary to use Photoshop correctly.

UNDERSTANDING COLOUR MODELS

THE COLOUR WHEEL

Before looking at the main colour models available, you should get to know the colour wheel which indicates the various colour separations and will give you a better understanding of colour mixing.

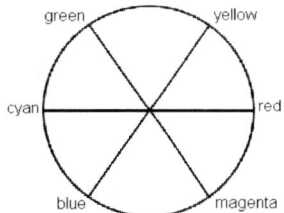

THE RGB MODEL

The primary colours on this model are red, green and blue. Colours are obtained by mixing these three components. This is an additive system: the three components combined at their maximum level give white. Black is obtained when none of these components is present, that when all their values are at 0. The value of each component can range from 0 to 255.

Chapter 1

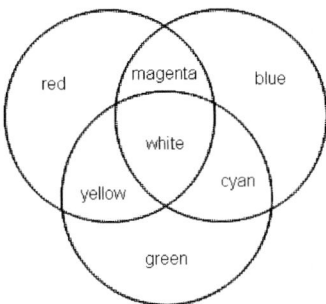

This is the model used by all electronic equipment (televisions, monitors etc). Some colours obtained by using this model are very bright and cannot be printed correctly. You should therefore use this model when producing images that will only be shown on screen.

THE CMYK MODEL

The primary colours in this model are cyan, magenta and yellow. As for the RGB model, colours are obtained by mixing the three components. A fourth colour is added to this model: black. It is essentially used to produce colour depth and contrast and also replaces a mix of the three primary colours when colouring black or grey. The CMY model is a subtractive system: each colour "absorbs" elements of the other colours, so all colours mixed at maximum values gives black. White is obtained when none of these components is present, when they all have 0 values. Each component can have a value from 0 to 100%.

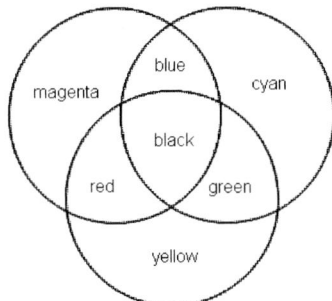

This model is used in printing. The colours obtained are duller than those made with the RGB model. You should use this model for all images that are to be printed.

THE LAB MODEL

You cannot really speak of primary colours when describing this model. Colours are created from lightness (L) and the chromatic components a and b. a spreads from green to magenta and b from blue to yellow. Lightness has a value from 0 to 100 (0 for black and 100 for white) and a and b stretch from -128 to +127. For example, values of +127 for a and +127 for b will give you a red which will be either light or dark depending on the lightness value.

Adobe Photoshop 5.5

Chapter 1

This model is specific to Photoshop and is independent of the reproduction system used. Its colour gamut encompasses both the RGB and CMYK models. This model is usually used internally by Photoshop to convert colours. Its main advantage is that it dissociates lightness from colour. This makes it possible to correct an image without affecting the shades of colour used. It is also useful for certain effects.

THE HSB MODEL

Three characteristics make up this model: hue (colour), saturation (colour purity), and brightness (colour lightness factor). Hue corresponds to a point on the colour wheel, that is an angle varying from 0 to 360. Saturation varies from 0 (totally impure colour = grey, either light or dark depending on the brightness) to 255 (perfectly pure). Brightness ranges from 0 (zero brightness = black) to 255 (maximum brightness = an extremely light colour, white if saturation is nil).

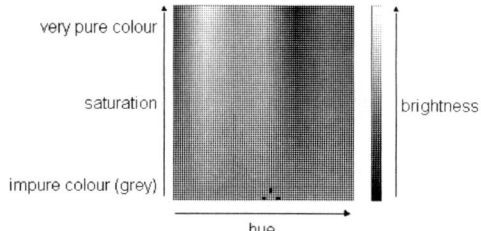

This model is based on the human eye's perception of colour. It is usually easier to choose colours in it, as they are defined in a way which corresponds to our natural appreciation of colours. This model is used in Photoshop only for choosing colours and for some retouches but not as a colour model.

THE GRAYSCALE MODEL

There is only one primary colour in this model and that is black. Grey varies according to the percentage of black ink used: 0% for white up to 100% for black. This model is used for black and white digital images and for preparing duotone and tritone images. It can be used both for images viewed on-screen and for images made to be printed.

Now that you have some basic information concerning colours, you can choose a colour using the various possibilities offered by Photoshop.

SELECTING A COLOUR

USING THE COLOR PALETTE

[a] If the palette is not visible, click the **Color** tab or click the **Window** menu and choose **Show Color**.

Chapter 1

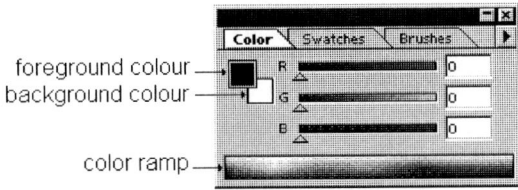

foreground colour
background colour
color ramp

[b] If the colour model does not suit your needs, open the palette menu (▶) and choose the option you prefer.

➤ Here, keep the **RGB** model.

[c] To choose a foreground colour, make sure that the colour selection box has a double frame around it (and is thus active). If this is not the case, click it once.
You would proceed in the same way when choosing the background colour.

[d] Drag the different sliders △ to define each colour component or enter a colour value in the corresponding text box.

➤ Here, drag the slider corresponding to red to its maximum value and the green and blue to minimum.

The foreground colour selection box becomes red and the symbol △▨ appears in the palette.

[e] If the △▨ symbol appears in the palette, you have defined a non-printable colour, that is a colour outside the CMYK colour gamut. If the image you are working on is to be printed, correct the colour by clicking the symbol which will select the printable colour closest to the original (the visual difference may be quite noticeable).

➤ Here, click the symbol.

The foreground colour has been corrected and now contains more orange.

☑ *The default colour model proposed corresponds to the image's colour model.*

☑ *To select a colour quickly, you could also click in the Color Ramp. By default, this bar uses the CMYK model. To use another model, open the palette menu (▶), and activate an option: RGB Spectrum, CMYK Spectrum, Grayscale Ramp and Current Colors. This last option creates a gradient from the foreground colour to the background colour. The make Ramp Web Safe option ensures that the colour bar only contains colours supported by Web browsers with a 256 colour display.*

☑ *You can copy the selected colour as a hexadecimal value which can be used in a Web page. Open the palette menu (▶) and take the Copy Color as HTML option. To make the colour available for use in your HTML editor, simply paste in the corresponding clipboard object.*

☑ *If you click the box displaying the selected colour, the Color Picker opens.*

Adobe Photoshop 5.5

Chapter 1

USING THE COLOR PICKER

[a] Click the foreground or background colour selection box on the toolbox or on the **Color** palette to open the **Color Picker**.

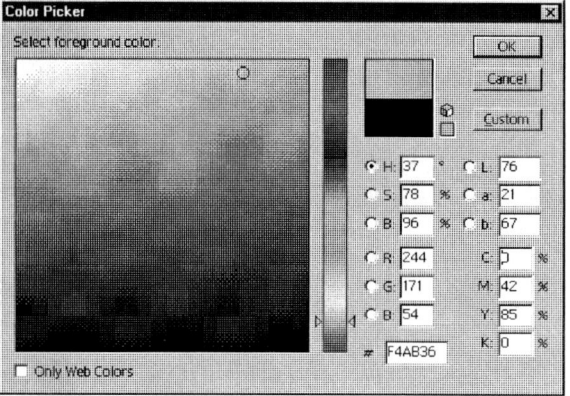

The active colour is shown by a circle. The components of this colour appear in the dialog box, as defined in each of the four colour models.

[b] If the dialog box shown is the **Custom Colors** dialog box, click the **Picker** box to reach the **Color Picker**.

[c] If appropriate, activate the **Only Web Colors** check box to limit your choice to colours supported by Web browsers with a 256 colour display.

➤ Here, leave do not activate this option.

[d] Drag the slider (▶ ◀) to select the hue then click the colour field to select the desired colour. You can also directly enter the chromatic components in the model of your choice into the text boxes on the right of the dialog box. The # text box gives the colour as a hexadecimal value, like the colour codes used in HTML: the first two digits (from 00 to FF) represent the red component, the next two represent green and the last two, blue.

➤ Here, drag the slider to the blue section and click a very bright blue in the color field.

The colour indicated in the rectangle to the right of the slider is now blue, underneath it is the former colour (here, red).

[e] If the selected colour is not printable, the ⚠️ symbol appears. Click the symbol to convert to the closest available printable colour.

➤ Here, click the symbol if it happens to appear.

[f] If Web browsers displaying 256 colours do not support the colour you select, the symbol appears. Click the symbol to convert to the closest available colour.

➤ Even if this symbol appears, do not click it.

[g] Click **OK**.

Chapter 1

- ✓ The *Custom* button allows you to access books of predefined colours, like the *Pantone* books.

- ✓ Although it is not as effective, it is possible to use the Windows Color Picker instead of the Photoshop picker. Activate *File - Preferences - General.* Choose *Windows* in the *Color Picker* list and click OK.

USING THE SWATCHES PALETTE

[a] If the palette is not visible, click the **Swatches** tab or click the **Window** menu and choose **Show Swatches.**

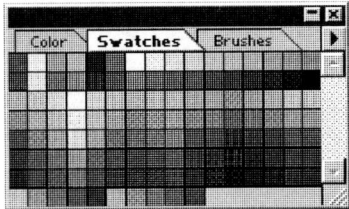

[b] Click one of the colours to select the foreground colour.
Hold down Alt and click a colour to select the background colour.

▶ Here, select a fairly dark green as a foreground colour.

The colour selection box on the toolbox should now display that green.

- ✓ You can also modify the swatches (see further on).

USING THE 🖉 TOOL

[a] Click the 🖉 tool.

[b] If the **Options** palette is not visible, click the **Options** tab or click the **Window** menu and choose **Show Options.**

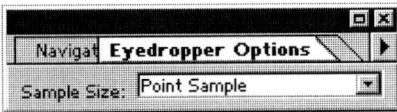

[c] Select the size of the sample used for the eyedropper:

Point Sample   Picks up the colour of the pixel that you click. Point samples are more useful for drawing than when retouching.

3x3 Average   Takes a colour based on the average of the nine pixels surrounding the one you click. This sample size is well-suited for subtle retouches.

Chapter 1

|5x5 Average| Takes a colour based on the average of the twenty-five pixels surrounded the one you click. You may often find that this sample is a bit too large.

➡ Here, keep **Point Sample**.

[d] Click the part of the image whose colour you want to pick up to select the foreground colour.
Hold down [Alt] and click to choose a background colour.
Be careful, the choice of foreground/background colours may be inverted if the **Color** palette is shown and if the background colour selection box has been activated.

➡ Here, click one of the colours on the map.

✓ The *Info* palette will show you the different colour components of the image as you move the pointer over it.

✓ You can temporarily activate the [🖉] tool by holding down [Alt] when the Airbrush, Paintbrush, Pencil, Line, Type, Linear Gradient or Paint Bucket tools are active.

USING A CUSTOM COLOR PICKER

[a] Open the **Color Picker**.

➡ Here, click the foreground colour selection box on the toolbox.

[b] If necessary, click the **Custom** button.

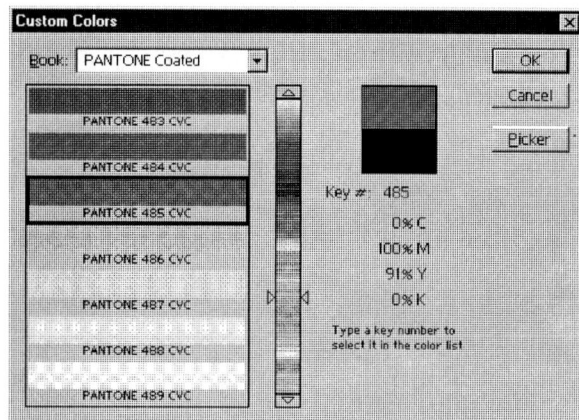

[c] Select a colour system in the **Book** list.

➡ Here, select, if not already selected, **PANTONE Coated**.

[d] Drag the slider (▷ ◁) to select a colour then click a specific shade. You can also type in the colour reference.

➡ Here, type **485** which is the reference of a red colour (type this in quickly on the keyboard).

Chapter 1

➤ Click **OK**.

✓ *These custom colours, also called spot colours, are generally used to create or redraw logos or to create duotones based on a logo's colours. Using spot colours ensures visual consistency. The best-known custom colours are the Pantone colours used by printers.*

---

15 *Now that you have seen the basics of using the* **Swatches** *palette, you can learn to customise this palette.*

USING THE SWATCHES PALETTE

[a] If the palette is hidden, click the **Swatches** tab or click the **Window** menu and choose **Show Swatches**.

ADDING COLOURS TO THE SWATCHES PALETTE

[a] Select the foreground colour you want to add to the swatches.

➤ Here, keep the colour called 485.

[b] Click after the final colour on the palette to add the active foreground colour.

➤ Here, add the 485 colour.

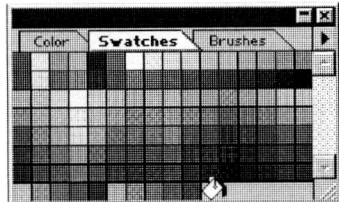

The pointer must first turn into a paint bucket for the operation to be successful. If you point to the new swatch, its name should appear on the tab.

[c] Hold down [Alt] and [⇧ Shift] and click a swatch to insert the new colour in front of it.

[d] Hold down [⇧ Shift] and click a swatch to replace it with a new colour.

DELETING COLOURS FROM THE SWATCHES PALETTE

[a] Hold down [Ctrl] and click a swatch to delete it from the palette.

The pointer must first turn into a pair of scissors for the operation to be successful.

➤ Here, delete the colour that you have just added.

Adobe Photoshop 5.5

Chapter 1

SAVING OR OPENING A SWATCH LIBRARY

[a] Open the palette menu (▶) and activate the **Load Swatches** or the **Save Swatches** option.

⟶ Here, activate **Load Swatches**.

*The folder selected is **ENI Photoshop 5.5**. The dialog box is empty because this folder does not contain any Swatches files (extension ACO).*

[b] Access the folder containing the swatches. By default, the swatches are contained in **\Program Files\Adobe\Photoshop 5.5\Goodies\Adobe Photoshop Only\Color Swatches**.

⟶ Here, open the **Look in** list to look for **C:** drive. Double-click **Program Files**, then **Adobe**, then **Photoshop 5.5**, then **Goodies**, then **Adobe Photoshop Only** and finally **Color Swatches**.

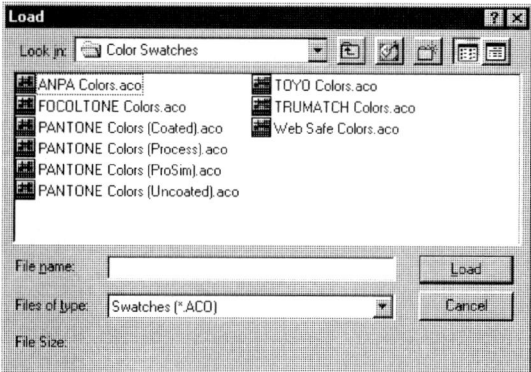

You do not have to save swatch libraries in this folder, it is simply a good way of keeping them grouped together on the hard disk.

[c] Click the name of the swatch library you want to load or give a name to your library if you are saving it.

⟶ Here, select the **PANTONE Colors (Coated)** library.

[d] Click **Load** (or **Save** if you are saving something).

⟶ Here, click the **Load** button.

The new colours will appear in the palette.

⟶ Here, use the palette's scroll cursors to view the new swatches then point to one of the colours.

Chapter 1

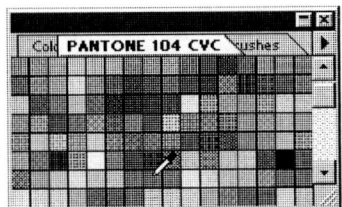

You see that the tab will briefly indicate the name of the colour when you point to it.

[e] To return to the default palette, open the palette menu (▶) and activate the **Reset Swatches** option. Confirm in the dialog box with **OK**.

➤ Here, reset the swatches and then confirm when asked to do so.

> ✓ *In the palette menu, there is yet another option, which is Replace Swatches. Unlike the Load Swatches option, which adds a new library to the existing one, Replace Swatches will erase the current library and replace it with the new one.*
>
> ✓ *The last swatch palette used is saved when you quit Photoshop.*

---

16 *You have had a lot of information to digest about working with colours. Turn your attention back to the map now and put some of it into practice. You are going to apply a single colour to the whole continent.*

COLOURING A SELECTION

[a] If necessary, select the colour that will be used for the fill.

➤ Here, using the **Color** palette (foreground colour), select a green where $R = 60$, $G = 160$ and $B = 40$.

[b] Select the part of the image you want to paint.

➤ Here, retrieve the **Map** selection:
Select - Load Selection
Select the **Channel** called **Map**.
Click **OK**.
This step is optional when painting a whole layer.

[c] **Edit**
Fill

Adobe Photoshop 5.5   61

Chapter 1

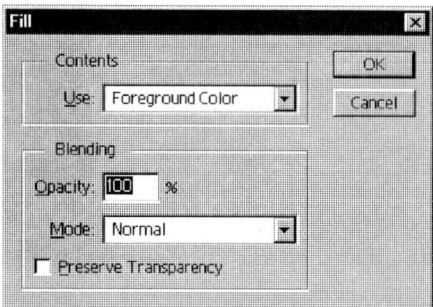

|d| Open the **Use** list to select the fill colour to use: active **Foreground Color**, active **Background Color, Black, 50% Gray, White.**
You will see how to use the **Pattern** and **History** options at a later time.

➡ Here, leave the **Foreground Color**.

|e| Use the **Opacity** option to define the degree of transparency of the fill colour. The lower the value entered, the more the fill colour will be transparent.

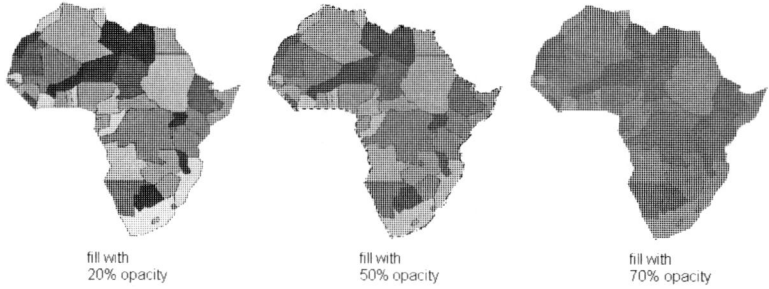

fill with 20% opacity   fill with 50% opacity   fill with 70% opacity

➡ Here, enter **50**

|f| Use the **Mode** option to apply special fill effects.

➡ Here, you do not need to use these effects for now.

|g| Activate the **Preserve Transparency** option if you do not want to fill in the transparent areas on a layer.

➡ Here, leave this option deactivated as you are colouring a specific selection.

|h| Click **OK**.

The map appears to be covered in a translucent wash of green. On the illustration below, several opacity levels have been used.

Chapter 1

*Try making a few other changes using the **Fill** command.*

➧ **Edit - Fill**

➧ Indicate 100% in **Opacity** and click **OK**.

The map should be coloured in green, with the individual countries no longer visible.

To see the result more clearly, hide the selection border.

➧ **View - Hide Edges**

The outline still shows a few coloured slivers, as the ⟨tool icon⟩ tool did not provide a perfect selection.

Continue by showing the edges again and then undoing the last action performed.

➧ **View - Show Edges**
Edit - Undo Fill
Select - Deselect
Edit - Fill

➧ Leave the **Opacity** at 100%, activate the **Preserve Transparency** option and click **OK**.

This produces a result identical to the previous fill. Even though there was no active selection, only the non-transparent zones of the layer were filled (the mask was not affected as it is not contained within the same layer as the map).

Now, continue by filling in the background of this image.

➧ On the **Layers** palette, click the **Background** layer.

➧ Select a brown colour (using components **R = 186**, **G = 127** and **B = 52** should give a satisfactory colour).

➧ **Edit - Fill**

➧ Leave the values as set and click **OK**.

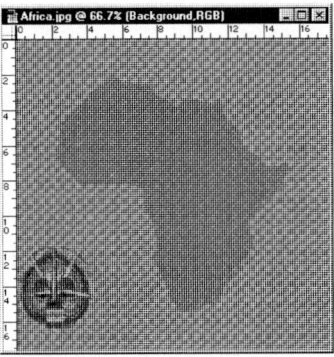

*The **Background** of the image has been filled, the map and the mask are not affected as they are on different layers. They are still visible as the layers containing them are situated above the Background layer.*

✓ *If you wish to make a fill using the foreground colour at 100% Opacity, and in Normal mode, you can use the shortcut ⟨Alt⟩⟨←⟩.*

Adobe Photoshop 5.5

Chapter 1

17 *In addition to the fill colour, you can now apply a colour to the selection's border.*

ADDING STROKE TO A SELECTION

[a] If necessary, select the colour you want to use for the border.

➠ Here, select a yellow, you could use the components R = **250**, G = **240** and B = **44** for example.

[b] Select the part of the image that needs to have a stroked outline.

This is optional if you are going to apply stroke to all the images contained within one layer.

➠ Here, simply activate the layer **Layer 2** by clicking it on the **Layers** palette.

[c] **Edit**
Stroke

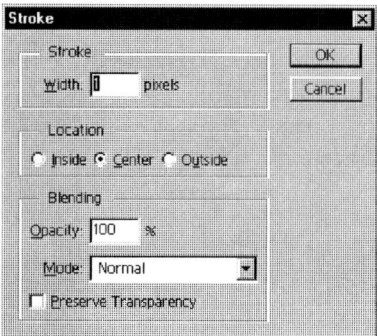

[d] Use the **Width** option to define the stroke (or outline) width which can attain a maximum of 16 pixels.

➠ Here, type in **1**

[e] Use the **Location** option to determine where the stroke should be placed in relation to the selection's outline.

➠ Here, click **Outside**.

[f] Use the **Opacity** option to define the degree of transparency of the colour.

➠ Here, leave **100%**. You do not need to use the effects associated with the **Mode** option for now.

[g] Activate the **Preserve Transparency** option if the stroke is not to be applied to the transparent areas of a layer. On a layer, do not use this option when choosing an **Outside Location**.

[h] Click **OK**.

A highly-contrasted outline appears around the map.

Chapter 1

In fact, it is too contrasted, so undo the stroke.

⟩⟩▸ **Edit - Undo Stroke**

Retrieve the selection of the Map again.

⟩⟩▸ **Select - Load Selection**
⟩⟩▸ Select the **Channel** called **Map**.
Click **OK**.

---

18 *You saw previously some basic details about using feathering when selecting. Now you are going to see how to apply a feathered outline to a selection that does not already have one.*

FEATHERING A SELECTION

[a] **Select**
Feather   Ctrl Alt **D**

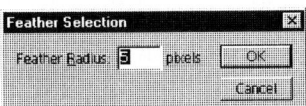

[b] Specify the feathering width up to a maximum of 250.

⟩⟩▸ Here, enter a **Feather Radius** of **10**

[c] Click **OK**.

The selection border is a little out of shape.

✓ *If the selection border was already feathered when first selected, the new feathering value will be added to the existing one.*

Use this selection to add stroke to the object.

⟩⟩▸ **Edit - Stroke**
⟩⟩▸ Leave the default values as set and click **OK**.

The stroked outline is much softer than before.

The result is interesting, but later you will be able to make an outline that is much more precise and easier to obtain.

⟩⟩▸ **Edit - Undo**
⟩⟩▸ **Select - Deselect**
⟩⟩▸ **File - Save**

Adobe Photoshop 5.5

Chapter 1

*The Africa document has already been created; however, Photoshop opens the **Save As** dialog box. As you have created layers, Photoshop can only save the document under its own Photoshop format. Rename this document.*

➠ Call the document **Safari** and click **Save**.

The document carries the PSD extension characteristic of Photoshop documents.

*Add to this image the picture of a lion contained in the **Lion.jpg** document.*

➠ Open the **Lion.jpg** document located in the **ENI Photoshop 5.5** folder.

19

You know now how to select an image using the traditional selection tools in different ways: there is another method which is selecting by colours.

SELECTING AN AREA OF THE IMAGE BY ITS COLOUR

[a] Activate the tool.

[b] If the **Options** palette is hidden, show it now.

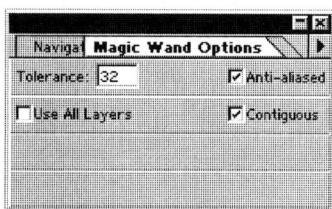

[c] Use the **Tolerance** option to specify the colour detection range. The lower the tolerance rate, the more similar the colours have to be in order for the pixels to be selected. This rate varies from 0 to 255. The tolerance chosen depends largely on the image contrast present. If the object you are selecting is highly-contrasted with its surrounds, you can use a higher value.

You can see below the selected areas (in white) created with different degrees of tolerance.

Tolerance=30   Tolerance=60   Tolerance=130

➠ Here, set the **Tolerance** at **60**.

Chapter 1

- [d] Leave the **Anti-aliased** option active to avoid a "staircase effect".
- [e] Activate the **Use All Layers** option to select zones that may not be on the active layer.
- ➤ Here, leave this option deactivated.
- [f] Leave **Contiguous** option active if you only want Photoshop to select pixels which are adjacent to one another. If you deactivate this option, any pixel which satisfies the **Tolerance** criterion is selected.
- [g] Click the required colour to select it.
- ➤ Here, click the bottom left corner of the image.

  A part of the sky appears as selected.

  This is not suitable as you need to select the whole of the sky.

- ➤ **Select - Deselect**
- ➤ Set the **Tolerance** at **130** and click the same place on the image.

  A much larger selection is made which encompasses the whole of the sky, except for the bottom right corner where the corner of sky is cut off from the rest by the lion's legs and tail.

20

To make complete selections, you may often have to enlarge or reduce the selection made, as it is rare to be able to correctly select a part of an image on the first try.

EXPANDING OR CONTRACTING SELECTIONS

USING THE MOUSE

- [a] Hold down [⇧ Shift] while using the selection tool to spread the selection out. The pointer should have a small + sign attached.
- ➤ Here, hold down [⇧ Shift] and click the sky between the lion's legs and tail.

  This portion of sky has now been selected.

- [b] Hold down [Alt] while using the selection tool of your choice to reduce a selection The mouse pointer has a small - sign attached.
- ➤ Here, hold down [Alt] and click the bottom left corner of the image.

  Only the part of the sky between the lion's legs and tail is now selected (and possibly some stray pixels near the outline of the lion).

- ➤ For this example, press [Ctrl] **Z** to undo this last action.

  You have returned to the selection made previously.

Adobe Photoshop 5.5

Chapter 1

EXPANDING A SELECTION USING ITS COLOURS

a Set the **Tolerance** for the tool in the **Options** palette.

▸ Here, use **40** as the **Tolerance** level.

b Open the **Select** menu and activate the option:

Grow   To spread out the selection to neighbouring pixels, depending on the tolerance used.

Similar   To spread the selection to all the pixels on the layer or the image which are similar in colour to those present in the selection.

▸ Here, activate the **Select - Similar** option, because the part of sky still unselected is not attached to the currently selected zone.

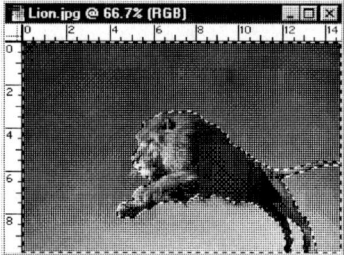

The sky is now entirely selected.

EXPANDING A SELECTION ACCORDING TO ITS OUTLINE

a **Select**
Modify
Expand

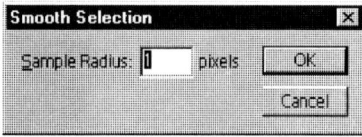

b Choose an expansion value for the selection.

▸ Here, enter **2** for a highly visible result.

c Click **OK**.

The selection has now spread to a part of the lion.

As you do not want the lion affected, undo this last action.

▸ **Edit - Undo**

Chapter 1

CONTRACTING A SELECTION ACCORDING TO ITS OUTLINE

[a] **Select**
Modify
Contract

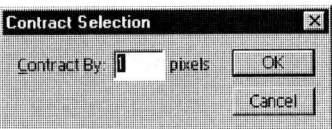

[b] Choose a contraction value for the selection.

▸ Here, leave it as **1**.

[c] Click **OK**.

The selection border has shrunk away from the lion, notably on its mane, stomach and tail.

> ✓ To make perfect selections, take full advantage of the various tools by combining their different uses. You can for example, create a selection with the ▨ tool and expand or contract that selection using the ▨ tool. Or you could create a selection with the ▨ tool set at a certain *Tolerance* and expand or contract the selection with the same tool but another *Tolerance*. Any combination is possible!

---

21 On some images, it is easier to select the exterior surroundings of an object, than the object itself, which is the case in this example. You now merely have to inverse the selection, or turn it inside out, to select the lion.

INVERSING A SELECTION

[a] **Select**   `Ctrl` `⇧ Shift` **I**
Inverse

The lion is now selected instead of the sky.

*Copy the lion into the **Safari** document then close the **Lion.jpg** document.*

▸ **Edit - Copy**
▸ Activate the **Safari** document by clicking its window or by using the **Window** menu.
▸ **Edit - Paste**

Adobe Photoshop 5.5

Chapter 1

The lion appears in the middle of the image. It is possible that there are still a few blue pixels attached to the lion.

➡ Close the **Lion.jpg** document without saving it.
➡ Save the changes made to the **Safari.psd** document.

---

22 *Even though your document is still only a rough draft, you can print it. But first, you need to prepare your print setup.*

DEFINING PRINT OPTIONS

[a] File 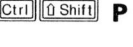 **P**
Page Setup

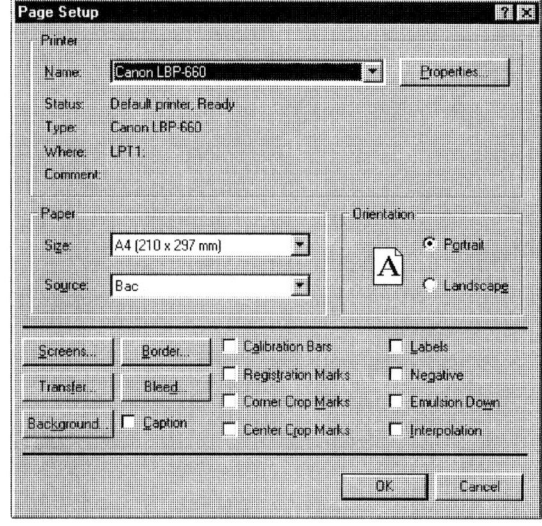

[b] Specify the paper **Size** that you wish to use for printing.
[c] Select the appropriate page **Orientation** for the item you are printing.
➡ Here, leave the **Portrait** option active.
[d] Using the various check boxes, specify the elements that are to be printed with the image:

Caption   Prints the caption defined in the **File Info** option, found in the File menu (cf. Advanced Options).

Calibration Bars   Prints the CMYK and RGB colours as well as a CMYK colour bar. This option requires a Postscript printer.

Chapter 1

Registration Marks	Prints registration marks for aligning colour films. This option is only useful if printing with colour separation (primarily used by professional printers).
Corner Crop Marks	Prints guides on corners where the page will be trimmed. Use the **Bleed** button to print crop marks within the image.
Center Crop Marks	Performs the same task as the previous option, but prints crop marks in the centre of the image.
Labels	Prints the document's name. If a single layer is active, its name will also be printed.
Negative	Prints a negative of the image.
Emulsion Down	Specifies when the light-sensitive side of a film is face down. This is frequent when printing on photographic film. This option requires a Postscript printer.
Interpolation	Resamples a low-resolution image to reduce the jagged appearance which often occurs. This option requires a Postscript printer.

|e| The **Screens** button regulates the attributes of halftone screens. These are relatively complicated and really require specialised printing knowledge to use. Leave the default values for personal or office printing.

|f| The **Transfer** button is used to correct a poor printer calibration.

You will be better-equipped to understand how this option works as time goes on. For now, do not use it.

|g| The **Background** button allows you to print the page background using a particular colour. When you click it, Photoshop displays the **Color Picker**.

➤ Here, do not use this option.

|h| The **Border** button allows you to print a black border around your image. Click the button to define the border's thickness.

➤ Here, you do not need to print a border.

|i| Click **OK**.

|j| To check that the image will be contained within the page, click the status bar where Photoshop shows the document size.

Adobe Photoshop 5.5 71

Chapter 1

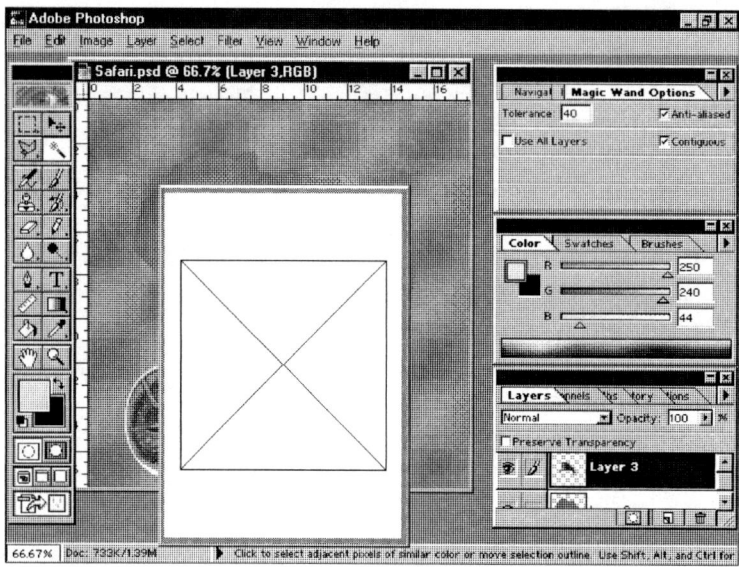

The page appears with a rectangle inside, which represents the place taken up by the image on the hypothetical printed page. The image is always centred on the page. If crop marks or other options have been activated, they too will appear.

23 Now that your page has been correctly configured, you may print.

PRINTING AN IMAGE

[a] **File** Ctrl **P**
Print

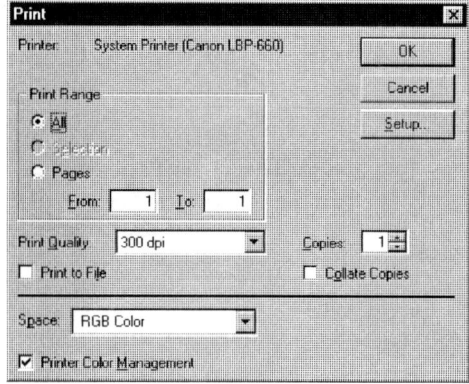

72   Adobe Photoshop 5.5

Chapter 1

|b| If a rectangular selection has been made on the screen, you can limit printing to just this selection by activating the **Selection** option.

➤ Here, this option is not available as nothing has been selected.

|c| If your image takes up several pages, specify the pages to print by activating the **Pages** option and entering the number of the first page in the **From** box and the last page in the **To** box.

➤ Here, you will be printing a single page.

|d| Specify the **Print Quality** in dpi (dots per inch). The higher the value, the better the result, although this does depend on the image resolution too. The quality available depends on the printer you are using.

➤ Here, leave the quality proposed by default.

|e| If necessary, indicate the number of copies you want to print in the **Copies** box. The **Collate Copies** option allows you to sort the various copies printed. For example, the image to be printed takes up two pages and you want to print three copies. If the option is active, the copies will print as 1-2-1-2-1-2, whereas if it is not active they will print 1-1-1-2-2-2.

➤ Here, a single copy is sufficient.

|f| The **Print to File** option will print onto a file on the hard disk and not directly to the printer. This file can be transferred to the printer at a later time.

|g| The **Space** option determines the printing type. You generally select **Grayscale** for a black and white printer and **Adobe RGB (1998)** or **ColorMatch RGB** for colour printers. With this option, you can also request colour separation, which is useful for professional printers.

➤ Here, leave the colour **Space** as it is proposed.

|h| The **Printer Color Management** lets you ask for a colour conversion if the colour **Space** used is **RGB Color**. This option is replaced by **Postscript Color Management** if using a Postscript printer.

➤ Here, if necessary, activate the **Printer Color Management**.

|i| Click **OK**.

After a few seconds' waiting time, the image is printed.

✓ The *Setup* button lets you modify the print setup you saw before.

Chapter 1

PRACTICE EXERCISE 1

- Open the **Giraffe.jpg** document.
- Select the giraffe as precisely as possible, using the selection tools of your choice.
- On your **Safari.psd** document, create a horizontal guide at 7 cm and a vertical one at 11 cm.
- Copy the giraffe onto the **Safari.psd** document, placing it in the bottom right corner bordered off by the guides.
- Close the **Giraffe.jpg** document without saving.
- Save **Safari.psd** and close.

You will find a corrected version of the exercise in the document **Safari Chapter 1.psd**.

CHAPTER 2

1 - ACCESSING LAYERS	76
2 - CHANGING THE LAYER STACKING ORDER	78
3 - CHANGING A LAYER'S ATTRIBUTES	79
4 - CREATING A NEW LAYER	82
5 - SELECTING NON-TRANSPARENT PARTS OF A LAYER	83
6 - DELETING A LAYER	85
7 - APPLYING FILTERS	86
8 - IMPROVING A LAYER'S OUTLINE	88
REMOVING FRINGE PIXELS	88
REMOVING JAGGED EDGES	89
9 - APPLYING A TRANSFORMATION TO A SELECTION OR A LAYER	90
FLIPPING/ROTATING	90
APPLYING A PRECISE TRANSFORMATION	91
APPLYING OTHER TRANSFORMATIONS	93
10 - DUPLICATING A LAYER	97
11 - LINKING LAYERS	99
12 - ALIGNING THE CONTENTS OF LINKED LAYERS	100
13 - SPACING THE CONTENTS OF LINKED LAYERS	100
14 - MERGING LAYERS	101
15 - INSERTING TEXT INTO AN IMAGE	102
16 - MODIFYING TEXT ON A TYPE LAYER	107
17 - CONVERTING TEXT INTO IMAGE	108
18 - APPLYING EFFECTS TO LAYERS	108
DEFINING A GLOBAL ANGLE FOR EFFECTS	108
APPLYING A DROP SHADOW EFFECT	109
APPLYING A GLOW EFFECT	111
APPLYING A BEVEL AND EMBOSS EFFECT	112
APPLYING A COLOUR FILL EFFECT	113
19 - MODIFYING OR DELETING EFFECTS APPLIED TO LAYERS	114
20 - COPYING LAYER EFFECTS	115
21 - DELETING PART OF AN IMAGE	117
USING A SELECTION	117
USING THE [tool icon] TOOL	118
22 - FILLING A SELECTION OR A LAYER WITH A GRADIENT	121
USING A PRESET GRADIENT	121
CREATING A CUSTOMIZED GRADIENT	123
23 - APPLYING LAYER MASKS	126
24 - APPLYING A LAYER MASK'S EFFECTS OR DELETING IT	129
PRACTICE EXERCISE 2	130

Chapter 2

During this chapter, you are going to look at layers and basic techniques for using them. You are going to modify your Safari document so it looks like this:

▸ If you have quit Photoshop, start it again.

▸ Open the document called **Safari Chapter 1** (it was the correction you looked at for the first practice exercise).

1 *Start by looking at the **Layers** palette.*

ACCESSING LAYERS

|a| **Window**   Click the **Layers** tab
    Show Layers

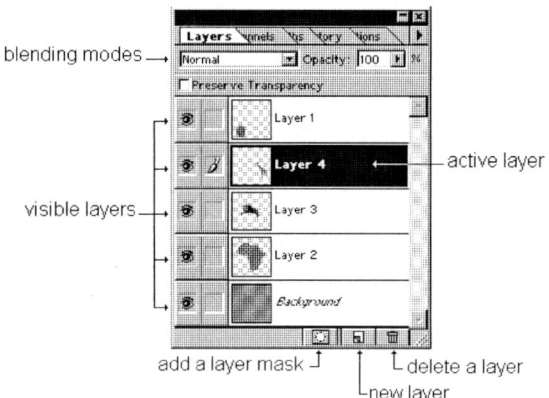

76   Adobe Photoshop 5.5

Chapter 2

[b] To view all the existing layers, maximize the palette by clicking the ▫ button on the palette's title bar.

*The layer situated at the top of the list is the foremost layer on the screen, while the one at the bottom of the list in the one furthest in the background. The **Background** layer is the only one not to have transparent zones.*

[c] To activate a layer, click its thumbnail (the small "preview" picture) or its name.

Any selections, alterations, retouches or moves made will only occur on this layer and will not affect any other one. Visible layers are represented by this icon 👁.

[d] To hide a layer, click the 👁 icon that corresponds to it. To hide all layers except one, hold down [Alt] and click the eye icon of the one that interests you.

➠ Here, click the eye icon corresponding to **Layer 2**.

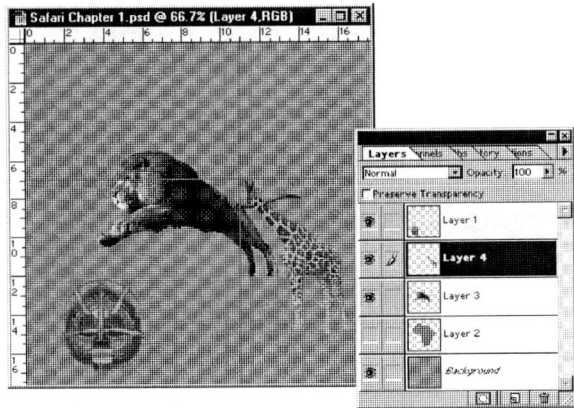

The map of Africa is no longer visible and the layer does not have a 👁 icon on the palette.

[e] To display the layer again, click the small square to bring back the 👁 icon.

➠ Here, click again in the small square which contained the eye icon for **Layer 2**.

The map reappears on the screen and the icon reappears on the palette.

✓ To hide or show several layers, you can drag the pointer over the 👁 icon squares.

✓ You can modify the size of the thumbnails in the palette by activating the *Palette Options* in the palette menu (click ▶).

Before continuing, erase the guides currently visible on the screen.

➠ **View - Clear Guides**

Adobe Photoshop 5.5 77

Chapter 2

As layers are stacked one on top of the other, it is possible to change this stacking order to hide or show certain parts of the image.

CHANGING THE LAYER STACKING ORDER

[a] Select the layer concerned.

➡ Here, click **Layer 2**.

[b] **Layer**
Arrange

[c] Choose one of these options:

Bring to Front	`Ctrl` `⇧ Shift`]	Places the active layer on top of all the others.
Bring Forward	`Ctrl`]	Shifts the active layer one level towards the front.
Send Backward	`Ctrl` [	Shifts the active layer one level towards the back.
Send to Back	`Ctrl` `⇧ Shift` [	Places the active layer underneath all the others, but not under the **Background** layer (if there is one).

➡ Here, use the **Bring to Front** option.

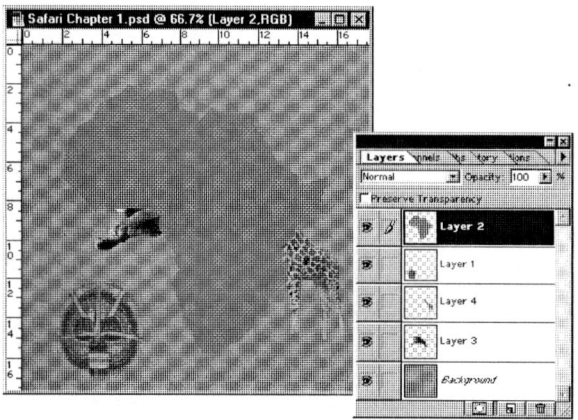

The map covers the lion and the giraffe.

➡ **Layer - Arrange - Send to Back**

The map returns under the lion and the giraffe.

Chapter 2

» **Layer - Arrange - Bring Forward**
 The map hides the lion, but not the giraffe.

» **Layer - Arrange - Send Backward**
 The map returns to its original position.

[a] Point to the layer you want to move and drag it up in the list to bring it closer to the front and down in the list to send it further to the back.

» Here, activate **Layer 3** and drag it between **Layer 1** and **Layer 4**.

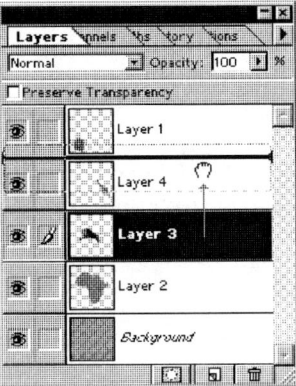

When a thick black line appears between the layers, you can release the mouse. The layer stacking order has been modified; the lion moves in front of the giraffe.

Move the lion so that he is not obstructing the giraffe.

» Activate the tool and drag the lion up and to the right until his back legs are touching the eastern point of Africa.
 As the layer containing the lion is active, only the lion is moved.

3

The layers all have fairly generic names (Layer 1 etc), but you can rename them.

CHANGING A LAYER'S ATTRIBUTES

[a] Select the layer.

[b] **Layer**   Double-click the layer's thumbnail
 Layer Options

» Here, double-click **Layer 4**.

Adobe Photoshop 5.5

Chapter 2

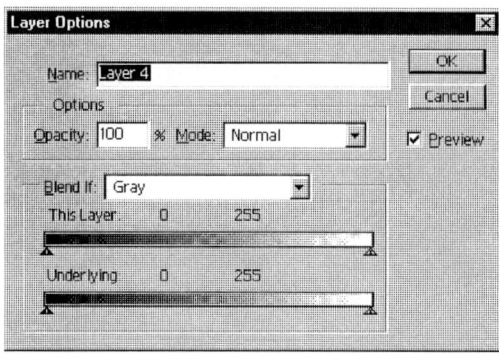

*You can also open the **Layers** palette menu and click **Layer Options**. The **Preview** option will let you see the result of your work on the image before confirming the changes.*

c Enter the layer **Name** in the corresponding text box.

➤ Here, type **Giraffe** in the **Name** text box.

d Define the layer's transparency with the **Opacity** option.

*This can also be defined directly on the **Layers** palette using the **Layer Blending Modes** list.*

➤ Here, do not change the level of transparency: you can use this option at a later time.

e Set the blending mode from the **Mode** list.

*You can also define this directly in the **Layers** palette.*

➤ Here, do not change anything. You will have a chance to use these effects later on in this book.

*In the **Blend If** box, you can make some parts of the layer transparent according to the brightness of the pixels present on **This Layer** or an **Underlying** layer. Select **Gray** to create a global transparency or opt for a colour to create blending according to the brightness of that colour (you will look at blending in more detail at a later time).*

f Drag the black *This Layer* slider to make the dark pixels on the layer transparent. Use the white slider to make the light pixels on the layer transparent.

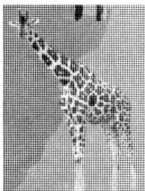
normal giraffe

with dark pixels transparent

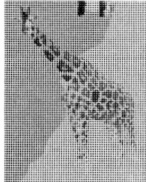
with light pixels transparent

➤ Here, leave the default values as set for now: you can test the option a bit later.

Chapter 2

> [g] Drag the black **Underlying** slider to make the dark pixels of the underlying layers show through. Use the white slider to make the light pixels of the underlying layers show through.
>
> *On this example, the option would not produce a very startling effect as the background pixels are all the same colour.*

> [h] Click **OK**.
>
> *The layer appears in the palette with its new name.*

> ✓ The *This Layer* and *Underlying* sliders are made up of two halves. To separate them, press [Alt] before dragging. Separating the sliders allows you to create transparency gradients on given areas instead of creating a more violent overall transparency. To group the sliders together again, drag one of the halves onto the other.

*Do a test to see what happens if you change the **Blend If** options in the **Layer Options** dialog box.*

➤ Double-click the **Giraffe** layer thumbnail.
➤ Set the **This Layer** black slider at **90** then click **OK**.

The giraffe's spots have become transparent as their brightness is less than 90.

➤ Double-click the **Giraffe** layer thumbnail.
➤ Set the **This Layer** black slider back at **0** and the white slider at **160** then click **OK**.

Now it is only the spots that are visible as the whiteness factor of the giraffe itself is greater than 160.

Show the giraffe normally again and rename the other layers.

➤ Double-click the **Giraffe** layer thumbnail.
➤ Set the **This Layer** white slider at **255** then click **OK**.
➤ Double-click the thumbnail of **Layer 1**.
➤ Enter **Mask** as the layer **Name** and click **OK**.
➤ Rename **Layer 2** as **Map**
➤ Rename **Layer 3** as **Lion**

Adobe Photoshop 5.5

Chapter 2

4

You saw in the previous chapter how to add an outline to the map but the result was not really perfect. Try to improve on that by creating a layer for the outline.

CREATING A NEW LAYER

[a] Activate the layer below the place you want to insert the new layer.

➠ Here, activate the **Giraffe** layer.

[b] Click the button in the **Layers** palette.

*A new layer called **Layer 1** appears in the palette above the **Giraffe** layer.*

[a] Activate the layer below the place where you want to insert the new layer.

➠ Here, drag the corner of the palette to lengthen it and scroll its contents until you can activate the **Background** layer.

[b] **Layer**   Alt -click the button   Ctrl û Shift **N**
   New   on the **Layers** palette
   Layer

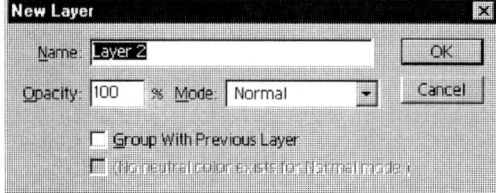

Using this method lets you define some of the new layer's characteristics as you create it.

82   **Adobe Photoshop 5.5**

Chapter 2

|c| Enter the **Name** of the new layer.

⟶ Here, type in **Outline** in the **Name** text box.

|d| If needed, define the other layer characteristics (you will see this function in more detail later on).

|e| Click **OK**.

The **Outline** layer appears in the palette between the **Background** and **Map** layers (click to see all the layers).

☑ If the document does not have a background, you can create one using *Layer - New - Background*. The new background will be placed at the back, behind all existing layers and will be filled with the background colour.

---

5 To create a correct outline, you have to select the map. The objects placed in layers being independent, Photoshop is able to retrieve selections according to the elements of a layer. Here is how to achieve this.

SELECTING NON-TRANSPARENT PARTS OF A LAYER

|a| Hold down `Ctrl` and, on the **Layers** palette, click the layer thumbnail whose selection you want to retrieve.

⟶ Here, hold down `Ctrl` and click the **Map** layer thumbnail.

The map selection appears.

|b| If a selection already exists, you can enlarge or reduce it by clicking a layer while holding down one of these:

`Ctrl` `⇧ Shift`   to add the existing selection to the new one.

`Ctrl` `Alt`   to remove from the existing selection the pixels corresponding to the new one.

`Ctrl` `⇧ Shift` `Alt` to obtain a selection corresponding to the intersection between the existing selection and the new one.

⟶ Here, hold down `Ctrl` `⇧ Shift` then click the **Giraffe** layer.

The giraffe is now included in the selection.

⟶ For this example, hold down `Ctrl` `Alt` then click the **Lion** layer.

The lion has now been excluded from the selection.

Adobe Photoshop 5.5

Chapter 2

Before trying the second solution, deselect.

⟹ **Select - Deselect**

[a] Activate the layer where you want to load the selection.

⟹ Here, activate the **Map** layer.

[b] **Select**
Load Selection

[c] In the **Channel** list, select **[Layer Name] Transparency**.

⟹ Here, the **Map Transparency** option is already highlighted in the **Channel** list.

[d] If the selection has previously existed, you can use a particular **Operation** option (cf. Chapter 1 - Loading a selection).

⟹ Here, keep the **New Selection** choice active.

[e] Click **OK**.

Whatever the method used, you will still end up with the map selected.

Complete the selection then draw your outline.

⟹ Hold down [Ctrl][⇧ Shift] then click the **Giraffe** and **Lion** layers.
The selection will now take in the map, lion and giraffe.

⟹ Activate the **Outline** layer.

⟹ **Select - Feather** (to create a blurred outline).
Set the feather radius as **7** and click **OK**.

⟹ Activate the **Color** palette.
Select for example a yellow using the components **R**= 250, **G**= 250 and **B**= 190.

⟹ **Edit - Stroke**
Set the stroke **Width** as **1** and **Center** as the **Location** then click **OK**.

⟹ **Select - Deselect**

Chapter 2

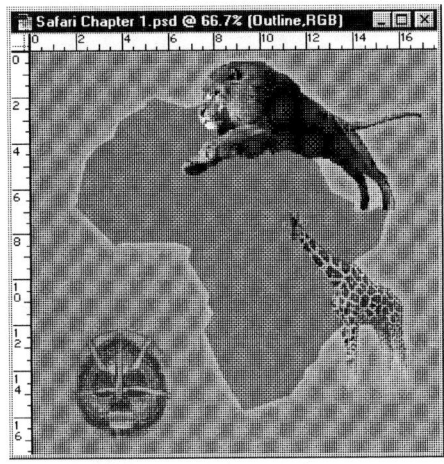

A luminous outline, of better quality than the one made in Chapter 1, appears in the image.

---

6 *You created **Layer 1** which you do not need to use, so now you can delete it.*

DELETING A LAYER

|a| Activate the layer to be deleted.

➠ Here, activate **Layer 1**.

|b| **Layer** Click the 🗑 button in the **Layers** palette
Delete Layer

If you use the 🗑 button on the Layers palette, you will be asked for confirmation:

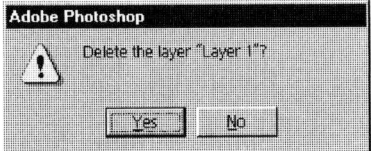

|c| In this case, click **Yes** to delete the layer.

The layer no longer exists in the palette.

✓ *You can also drag the thumbnail of the layer you want to delete onto the 🗑 button. Using this method, you will not be asked to confirm.*

Adobe Photoshop 5.5

Chapter 2

*Before going on, you should add to your document an extra element which you will find in the **Tusk.jpg** document.*

▸ Open the **Tusk.jpg** document.

▸ Activate the ▭ tool, show the **Options** palette if you need to then set the **Tolerance** at **80**. Click the red zone.

*The red background should be entirely selected. If this is not the case, spread out the selection using **Select - Modify - Expand**.*

▸ **Select - Inverse**

The tusk should be selected.

▸ **Edit - Copy**

▸ **File - Close**
Reply **No** when asked to save.

▸ **Edit - Paste**

*The tusk appears in the middle of the **Safari Chapter 1** document on a new layer called **Layer 1**.*

Rename this layer.

▸ Double-click the **Layer 1** thumbnail.

▸ Enter **Tusk** in the **Name** box and click **OK**.

7

Before continuing work on the layers, you should learn how to apply Photoshop filters.

APPLYING FILTERS

[a] Activate the layer on which you wish to apply a filter and, if necessary, select part of that layer if you need to limit its application.

▸ Here, activate the **Mask** layer.

[b] Open the **Filter** menu and select a category then the filter you wish to use.

There are numerous filters available in Photoshop; you may not use all of them here, but you will be able to experiment with them by yourself, to see the results produced.

▸ Here, for example, activate **Filter - Distort - Glass**.

Chapter 2

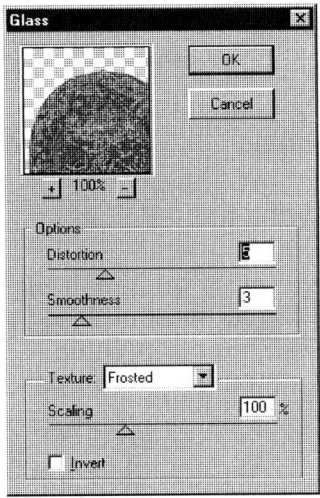

Most of the filters contain various settings that you can adjust.

|c| Adjust the settings as required using the sliders or entering values.

Some filters have a preview screen in the dialog box.

|d| To change the part of the image visible in this preview, point at the preview and drag. You can also adjust its zoom by clicking the ⊞ and ⊟ buttons.

➧ Here, move the various sliders to see the results on the preview screen.

|e| Click **OK**.

➧ Here, click the **Cancel** button because you do not want to keep the result.

✓ You can interrupt the application of a filter by pressing [Esc].

✓ You can reapply a filter using the same parameters by choosing the first command in the *Filter* menu (the name of this command corresponds with the filter used) or by pressing [Ctrl] F.

✓ You will see later how to modify a filter's effect.

Adobe Photoshop 5.5

Chapter 2

8 *When some items are selected and copied, some pixels from the original image outline may stay on the copy, or the outline may have a jagged edge. Look now at how to improve the outline of the Mask layer.*

IMPROVING A LAYER'S OUTLINE

REMOVING FRINGE PIXELS

a Activate the layer whose outline is too contrasted with the rest of the layer.

➠ Here, leave the **Mask** layer, whose outline is too light, active. Zoom in on the mask to make the effect more noticeable.

b **Layer**
   Matting

c Select one of the proposed methods:

Defringe	Replaces the outline pixels over a certain width with the colour of the pixels found inside the object.
Remove Black Matte	Lightens the layer outline, you can use this option on layers coming from a black or very dark background.
Remove White Matte	Darkens the layer outline, use this option for layers coming from white or light coloured backgrounds.

➠ Here, use **Remove White Matte**.

The mask was taken from a fairly light background, but not enough for the result to be really satisfactory. In this case, the top of the mask stays too light while the bottom has become too dark.

d If you use the **Defringe** option, a dialog box opens: set the outline **Width** to be modified in the corresponding text box and click **OK**.

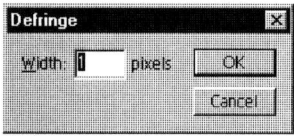

Avoid using too large a width. If the object was badly selected, reselect it, or erase the surplus parts of its outline.

Undo your last action and try the defringing method.

➠ **Edit - Undo**

➠ **Layer - Matting - Defringe**
   Leave the default value which should be **1** and click **OK**.

The result is more interesting, the lightest parts have been replaced and no part of the outline is too dark.

➠ Reduce the zoom so you can see the whole image again.

Chapter 2

*The tusk that you copied probably has some elements of red still attached to it. You can defringe it, but don't forget to activate the **Tusk** layer before doing so.*

REMOVING JAGGED EDGES

|a| Activate the layer with the jagged edge.

➠ Here, activate the **Lion** layer.

|b| Select the layer's contents by pressing [Ctrl] and clicking the layer thumbnail.

➠ Here, [Ctrl]-click the **Lion** layer thumbnail.

|c| Select
Modify
Border

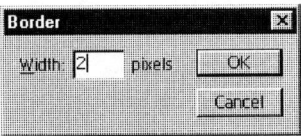

This command allows you to select just an object's outline by doubling the selection border, changing it to a width between 1 and 64 pixels

|d| Set the **Width** at 1 or 2 depending on how jagged the edge is.

➠ Here, set the **Width** at **2**.

|e| Click **OK**.

The selection's black and white border seems thicker: it has been doubled. Only the pixels of the layer's outline are currently selected.

|f| Filter
Blur

|g| Activate one of the following filters:

    Blur   To blur lightly. Use this filter for a slightly jagged edge.

    Gaussian Blur   To create a highly blurred effect. Use this filter for an extremely jagged edge. As the effect produced is quite extreme, avoid entering too high a **Radius** value.

    Blur More   To create a medium blur. Use this filter for a very jagged edge.

➠ Here, activate **Filter - Blur - Blur**.

|h| Deselect using **Select - Deselect** to see the result clearly.

The outline should be mostly, or even completely, smooth.

Adobe Photoshop 5.5

Chapter 2

Repeat these actions to remove the jagged edge on the tusk and on the map.

➠ Hold down [Ctrl] and click the **Tusk** layer.
Select - Modify - Border
Click **OK**.

➠ **Filter - Blur - Blur**
Press [Ctrl] **D** to deselect.

➠ Do the same set of actions on the **Map** layer.

➠ Press [Ctrl] **S** to save the document.

---

9 *Some items in the image are not very suitably placed. You can transform them.*

APPLYING A TRANSFORMATION TO A SELECTION OR A LAYER

FLIPPING/ROTATING

[a] Activate the layer or select the part of the image.

➠ Here, activate the **Tusk** layer.

[b] **Edit**
Transform

[c] Choose between these options:

Rotate 180°	Turns the element completely around. It performs simultaneously a horizontal and vertical flip.
Rotate 90° CW	Rotates the element 90° towards the right (clockwise).
Rotate 90°CCW	Rotates the element 90° towards the left (counter-clockwise).
Flip Horizontal	Turns the element upside down, over the horizontal axis.
Flip Vertical	Flips the element over the vertical axis.

➠ Here, apply a **Rotate 90°CW** rotation.

The tusk is now vertical.

✓ *You can apply the same operation to the entire image (all layers included) by using the options found in Image - Rotate Canvas.*

Chapter 2

Position the tusk correctly.

▶ Activate the [move] tool and move the tusk in this way:

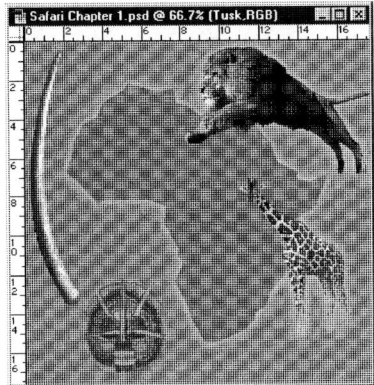

APPLYING A PRECISE TRANSFORMATION

[a] Activate the layer or select the part of the image.

▶ Here, activate the **Lion** layer.

[b] **Edit**
Transform
Numeric

[c] Deactivate the **Position** option, unless, in addition to the transformation, you wish to move the item.

▶ Here, deactivate this option.

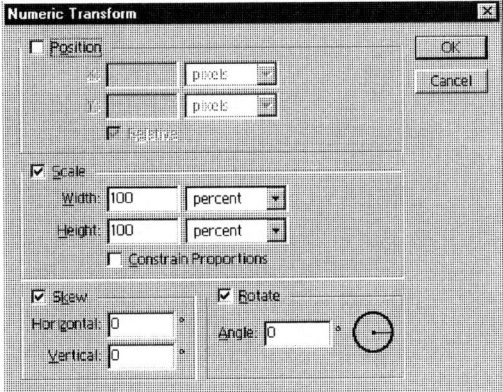

Adobe Photoshop 5.5   91

Chapter 2

[d] To change the size of an object, use the **Scale** option. Activate the **Constrain Proportions** option if you wish to keep the same ratio between **Width** and **Height**. Then enter the desired size, selecting an adequate measurement unit.

➤ Here, activate the **Constrain Proportions** option then enter **87** in the **Width** text box.
An identical Height value will be entered automatically.

[e] To skew an object, or make it lean over, activate the **Skew** option. Indicate the skew value in the **Horizontal** or **Vertical** text boxes. The permitted values range from -89.99 to 89.99.

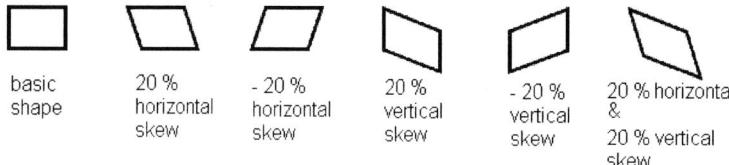

basic shape | 20 % horizontal skew | - 20 % horizontal skew | 20 % vertical skew | - 20 % vertical skew | 20 % horizontal & 20 % vertical skew

➤ Here, you do not need to skew this object.

[f] Activate the **Rotate** option to rotate the object through a certain angle. The permitted values are between -360 and 360.

➤ Enter **23** in the **Angle** text box.
You can also drag the Radius visible on the dial next to the Angle text box.

[g] Click **OK**.

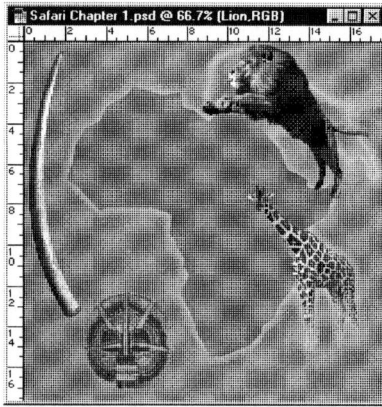

The lion is a little smaller and seems to be jumping higher. However the outline you drew before is no longer appropriate!

✓ You can also make a precise rotation for the whole image (all layers included) by choosing **Image - Rotate Canvas - Arbitrary**.

Undo the outline and move the lion.

➤ Drag the **Outline** layer thumbnail onto the 🗑 button on the **Layers** palette.

Chapter 2

➟ Activate the tool and move the lion so that its back legs press onto the eastern point of the map, it almost touches the edge of the image.

*Before continuing, save the image under the name **Safari**.*

➟ **File - Save As**

➟ Access the **ENI Photoshop 5.5** folder click **Safari** then click **Save**.
Confirm replacing the **Safari** document by clicking **OK**.

APPLYING OTHER TRANSFORMATIONS

Free transformation allows you to apply five different transform options and to combine them: scale, rotate, skew, distort and perspective.

[a] Activate the layer or select part of the image.

➟ Here, activate the **Giraffe** layer.

[b] **Edit**   Ctrl T
Free Transform

A bounding border (the rectangle with handles) appears around the giraffe. When the pointer is inside the bounding border, it takes this form ▶ : you can then move the bordered object.

[c] To rescale the object, point to one of the handles and drag.

When the pointer is on one of the side handles, it takes one of these forms: ↔ or ↕ and will let you "stretch" the object horizontally or vertically. When the pointer is on a corner handle, it takes one of these forms: ↖ or ↗ and lets you scale in both directions at once.

To keep the object's original proportions, hold down ⇧ Shift while dragging.

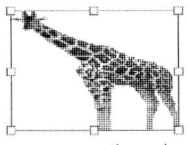
unproportioned

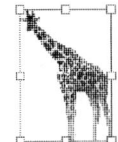
kept in proportion

Chapter 2

▸ Here, rescale the giraffe without its proportions then with the proportions then press `Esc` to cancel the scale.
Then press `Ctrl` **T** to try the next transform option.

[d] To rotate the object, point outside the bounding border and drag.

The pointer must have one of these forms: ↙, ↘, ↗, ↖, ↶, ↷. To force a 15 angle rotation, hold down `⇧ Shift` as you drag. To move the rotation centre represented by this symbol ✥ (by default, it is placed in the centre of the bounding border), point to it (the pointer will take this form ▸✥) and drag it.

▸ Here, point above the top left corner handle and drag to the left to obtain this result:

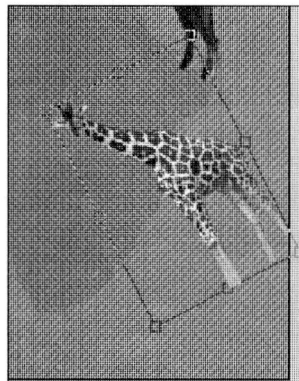

▸ Next move the rotation centre before applying a new rotation.
Press `Esc` to cancel the rotation, then press `Ctrl` **T** to try the next transform option.

[e] To skew an object, hold down `Ctrl` `⇧ Shift` and drag one of the side handles. The pointer should take one of these forms ▸↔ or ▸↕ to make respectively a horizontal or vertical skew. To make a symmetrical skew in relation to the centre of the bounding border, hold down `Alt` while you drag.

▸ Here, hold down `Ctrl` `⇧ Shift` and drag the middle handle on the top side towards the left.

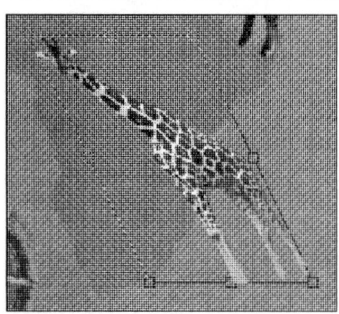

The giraffe is leaning towards the left.

Chapter 2

- For this example, point to the middle handle on the left side, hold down [Ctrl] [⇧ Shift] and drag upwards to skew the giraffe vertically.
- Press [Esc] then [Ctrl] **T**.

[f] To distort an object, which is a complete deformation in fact, hold down [Ctrl] and drag one of the handles. The pointer should have this form: ▶. To make a symmetrical distortion in relation to the centre, hold down [Alt] while you drag.

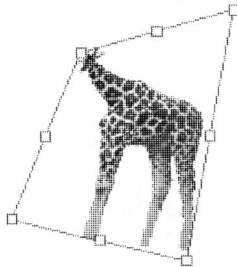

- Here, point to the upper right corner handle, hold down [Ctrl] and [Alt] then drag upwards. Hold down [Ctrl] and drag the upper left corner handle downwards.

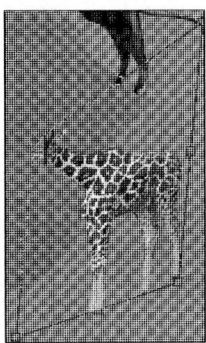

Our giraffe is starting to look a little strange!

- Press [Esc] then press [Ctrl] **T**.

[g] To finish, you can try the perspective effect. To do this, press [Ctrl] [Alt] [⇧ Shift] and drag a corner handle. The pointer should take this form: ▶.

Chapter 2

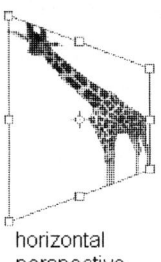
horizontal perspective

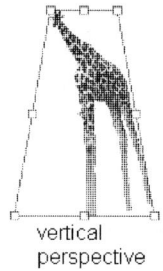
vertical perspective

⟹ Here, point to the handle on the upper left corner, hold down `Ctrl` `Alt` `⇧ Shift` and drag upwards to obtain a horizontal perspective.

[h] When the transformation(s) applied seem suitable, press `Enter`. If not, press `Esc`.

⟹ Here, press `Esc`, you will have another chance to scale later on.

> ✓ *The whole point of the free transform options is that you can combine the various effects: if only one effect interests you, you could very well do it using one of the Edit - Transform options. These function in exactly the same way as the free transform options:*
>
> | | |
> |---|---|
> | *Scale* | *To change an object's size.* |
> | *Rotate* | *To rotate an object.* |
> | *Skew* | *To skew, or lean an object over.* |
> | *Distort* | *To deform an object* |
> | *Perspective* | *To apply a "perspective" effect, or an illusion of depth, to the object.* |
>
> ✓ *You can reproduce the last transformation using the Edit - Transform - Again command or by pressing* `Ctrl` `⇧ Shift` *T.*

You can now scale the giraffe.

⟹ If you made an error while testing the transform tools that you cannot manage to remove, you can close the document without saving and open it again to find the original giraffe shape.

⟹ Activate the **Info** palette by clicking its tab or using **Window - Show Info**.

⟹ **Edit - Transform - Scale**

⟹ Hold down `⇧ Shift` to keep the same proportions and drag the top left handle to reduce the giraffe to about 27 percent of its size (use the **Info** palette to help you to see the scale percentage being applied).

⟹ Press `Enter` to confirm your transformation.

The giraffe should now appear much smaller than the other items.

Chapter 2

 *Now you can add a second tusk to your image. To do this, you can duplicate the **Tusk** layer.*

DUPLICATING A LAYER

|a| Point to the layer thumbnail and drag it onto the ⬜ button on the **Layers** palette.

➟ Here, point to the **Tusk** layer and drag it onto the ⬜ button.

*A new layer called **Tusk copy** is created above the **Tusk** layer. The second tusk created does not seem to appear on the image. This is because the two tusks are stacked one on top of the other.*

*To check this, move the **Tusk copy** layer.*

➟ Activate the ⬜ tool, point to the tusk and drag towards the right.

You can now see two tusks.

|a| Activate the layer you want to duplicate.

➟ Here, activate the **Giraffe** layer.

|b| **Layer**
Duplicate Layer

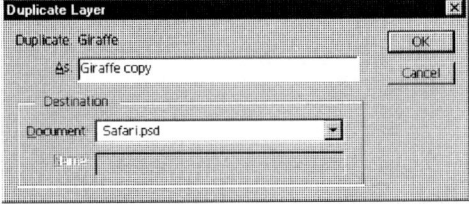

Using this method allows you to duplicate the layer onto the document of your choice.

|c| Enter the name of the new layer in the **As** text box.

➟ Here, enter **Giraffe Shadow** in the **As** box.

|d| Use the **Document** option to indicate where you want to duplicate the layer: on an open document or on a **New** document (at which point, the **Name** option will let you name the new document).

➟ Here, leave the **Safari.psd** document which is offered by default because you are going to duplicate the layer into the active document.

Chapter 2

[e] Click **OK**.

The *Giraffe Shadow* layer appears above the *Giraffe* layer.

✓ *Whatever the duplication method used, the copied layer is always placed above the original.*

*Leave this layer where it is for now, you will have a chance to add a shadow to your giraffe later on. Now, rename the **Tusk** and **Tusk copy** layers.*

➟ Double-click the **Tusk** layer thumbnail.
➟ Enter **Left Tusk** in the Name text box and click **OK**.
➟ Double-click the **Tusk copy** layer thumbnail.
➟ Enter **Right Tusk** in the Name text box and click **OK**.

You need to turn the right tusk around and position it correctly.

➟ **Edit - Transform - Flip Horizontal**
➟ Activate the tool and move the tusk over to the right hand edge of the page, so it is facing the left tusk (but not at the same height; the giraffe's head will be covered a little).

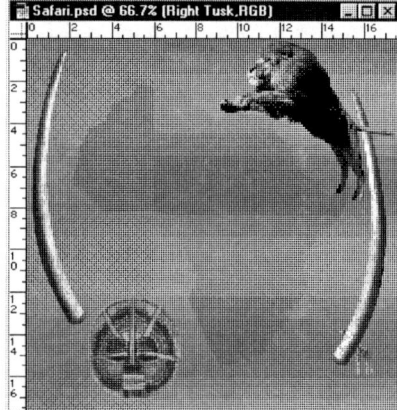

98　　　　　　　　　　　　　　　　　　　　Adobe Photoshop 5.5

Chapter 2

11 As you now need to work on both tusks at the same time, you will have to link the layers.

LINKING LAYERS

a Activate, if necessary one of the layers that need linking.

▸ Here, leave the **Right Tusk** layer active.

b In the row representing the other layer that you want to link, point to the small square situated between the thumbnail and the 👁 icon.

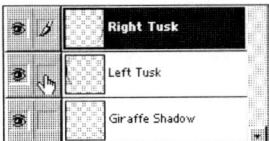

▸ Here, place the pointer as shown above.

c Click.

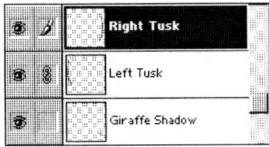

The 🔗 icon appears on the **Left Tusk** layer. This is the symbol that the layer is linked with the active layer.

You can link as many layers as you want. When layers are linked, your actions affect them in an identical way: moves and free or numeric transformations are simultaneously applied to all the linked layers. On the other hand, only the active layer will be affected by any filters or adjustments made.

d To delete a link, click the 🔗 icon again.

Be careful, simply activating another layer does not delete a link.

Activate another layer.

▸ Activate the **Giraffe** layer.

The 🔗 icon disappears from the **Left Tusk** layer because the **Giraffe** layer is not linked to it.

▸ Activate the **Right Tusk** layer.

The 🔗 icon reappears in the **Left Tusk** layer.

▸ Activate the **Left Tusk** layer.

The 🔗 icon is now visible on the **Right Tusk** layer.

Adobe Photoshop 5.5

Chapter 2

12 *Now that your layers are linked, line up the two tusks so that they sit at the same height.*

ALIGNING THE CONTENTS OF LINKED LAYERS

a Activate the layer which will be the point of reference for the alignment.

➜ Here, leave the **Left Tusk** layer active.

b **Layer**
Align Linked

c Choose one of the alignments on offer:

	Top	To align the top of the linked layers with the highest point of the active layer.
	Vertical Center	To align the vertical centre of the linked layers with the vertical center of the active layer.
	Bottom	To align the bottom of the linked layers with the lowest point of the active layer.
	Left	To align the left side of the linked layers with the left-most point of the active layer.
	Horizontal Center	To align the horizontal centre of the linked layers with the horizontal centre of the active layer.
	Right	To align the right side of the linked layers with the right-most point of the active layer.

➜ Here, activate the **Top** option.

The right tusk has moved upwards so that its highest pixel is lined up with the highest pixel on the Left Tusk layer.

Try another alignment then cancel it to come back to the current state.

➜ **Layer - Align Linked - Left**

The tusk of the Right Tusk layer is lined up on the left of the Left Tusk active layer.

➜ **Edit - Undo**

13 *As well as aligning, you can also distribute the contents of several layers to space them out evenly; use this function to centre the map between the two tusks.*

SPACING THE CONTENTS OF LINKED LAYERS

a If necessary, link the layers you wish to line up. At least three layers must be linked to perform this operation.

➜ Here, link the **Map** layer to the **Left Tusk** and **Right Tusk** layers.

100   Adobe Photoshop 5.5

| b | **Layer**
Distribute Linked

| c | Specify how to distribute the contents of the various layers:

    ⧉ **Top**   To space the uppermost point of each layer evenly.

    ⧉ **Vertical Center**   To space the vertical centre of each layer evenly.

    ⧉ **Bottom**   To space the lowest point of each layer evenly.

    ⧉ **Left**   To space the left-most pixels on each layer evenly.

    ⧉ **Horizontal Center**   To space the horizontal centres of each layer evenly.

    ⧉ **Right**   To space the right-most pixels of each layer evenly.

Vertical distribution is applied in relation to the layer whose contents are highest and the layer whose contents are lowest. Horizontal distribution is applied relative to the layer whose contents are the furthest left and the layer whose contents are the furthest right.

▸ Here, activate the **Horizontal Center** option.

The map is now perfectly centred between the two tusks because the central points of these three elements are equidistant.

Try another distribution then cancel it to return to the current state.

▸ **Layer - Distribute Linked - Right**

*The pixel situated on the far right of the **Map** is now at equal distance to the far right edge of the **Left Tusk** and the far right edge of the **Right Tusk**.*

▸ **Edit - Undo**

---

14 *When certain layers have been correctly placed in relation to each other, you can group them on a single layer, which will use less memory.*

MERGING LAYERS

| a | Link the layers that you want to merge or mask the layers that are not to be grouped.

▸ Here, remove the link with the **Map** layer (click the 🔗 icon) so that only the **Left Tusk** and **Right Tusk** layers are linked. Make sure the **Left Tusk** layer is active.

Chapter 2

b. Use one of the following commands:

Layer Merge Down	Ctrl E	To merge two adjacent layers on the **Layers** palette. This command is only accessible when there is no other layer linked with the active layer.
Layer Merge Linked	Ctrl E	To merge all layers linked with the active layer. If the **Background** layer is linked, the merge will systematically occur on this layer.
Layer Merge Visible	Ctrl ⇧ Shift E	To merge all the visible layers with the active layer. If the **Background** layer is visible, the merge will occur on it.
Layer Flatten Image		To merge all the layers visible onto the **Background** layer. If the image does not have a **Background** layer, one will be created. If certain layers are masked, Photoshop will ask for confirmation before deleting them.

➣ Here, use **Layer - Merge Linked**.

The **Left Tusk** and **Right Tusk** are merged onto the **Left Tusk** layer because it is the active layer.

Now that the two layers are merged, rename this layer.

➣ Double-click the **Left Tusk** layer thumbnail.

➣ Enter **Tusks** in the **Name** text box and click **OK**.

Save the changes made.

➣ **File - Save**

---

15 *Your image is starting to resemble the one illustrated at the beginning of the chapter. The item which is missing is the text.*

INSERTING TEXT INTO AN IMAGE

a. Activate one of the following tools:

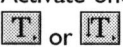 To create a layer onto which the text will be placed. It will be a layer specifically for text, which offers the advantage of letting you modify the text at any time. On the other hand, most of the retouch options and filters are not available for this layer. These layers are called **type layers** and are represented by a **type** icon on the **Layers** palette:

Chapter 2

 To create a selection whose outlines make a text. You can fill this selection with colour. But these tools are primarily used to erase or copy part of the layer, depending on the form of the text. This allows you to create text that has a photographic background rather than a text filled with a block of colour. You can also use them to apply certain retouch effects or distortions.

▶ Here, activate the T tool.

[b] Click the place on the image where you wish to insert the text.

▶ Here, click the left of the image.

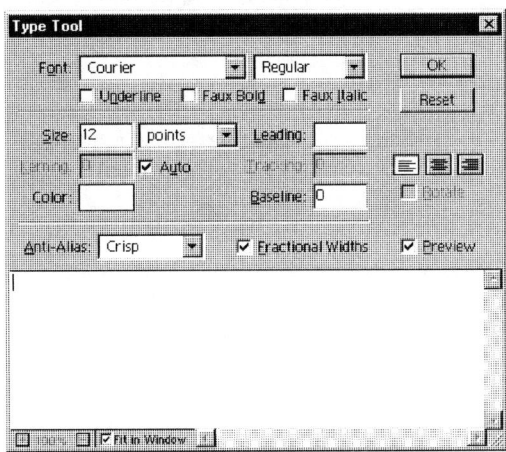

A dialog box opens: the top half allows you to set the parameters for the text. An insertion point blinks in the lower part of the box which is designed for entering your text.

[c] Select the **Font**. Define its style in the list box to the right of the **Font** list. You are probably already familiar with these styles:

Bold   To produce characters in dark, bold type.

Bold Italic   To produce characters in bold type and also in a sloping italic style.

Italic   To produce a sloping italic type.

Regular   To produce standard characters with no special style.

If the police you have selected is not compatible with certain font styles, such as bold, activate one of the following simulation styles:

Underline   To underline the selected characters. This tool cannot be used with vertical text or text which has been rotated using the **Rotate** option in the dialog box.

Faux Bold   To apply a simulated bold effect to the selected characters.

Faux Italic   To apply a simulated italic effect.

Chapter 2

▸ Here, select an attractive font (for example **Comic Sans MS**) and **Bold** style.

[d] Select the character size in the **Size** text box. It is possible to enter a value between 0.10 and 1296 points.

▸ Here, enter **60** points.

[e] Use the **Leading** option to set the spacing between two lines. If your text runs over several lines, make sure you use a leading value that is at least equal to the largest font size used to prevent the lines from overlapping. You can use a value between 0.10 and 1296.

Text in 18 pt and 18 pt leading   Text in 18 pt and 24 pt leading

▸ Here, you do not need to enter any value as your text will only be on one line.

[f] Deactivate the **Auto** option if you want to manually define the **Kerning** value, that is the spacing between two characters. Any value between -1000 and 1000 is permissible. A negative value brings the two characters closer together and a positive value separates them. Kerning can be used to create diphthongs.

The **Tracking** option is similar to the **Kerning** option but is used to provide uniform spacing over a block of text. Before setting the **Tracking**, select the characters where you wish to apply this new spacing. You can use a **Kerning** value for a specific pair of characters and tracking for the larger block text:

SAFARI
auto kern and 0 tracking on the whole text

S A F A R I
auto kern and 300 tracking on the whole text

SAFARI
-150 kerning between F and A and 0 tracking on the whole text

S A F A R I
-150 kerning between F and A and 300 tracking on the whole text

▸ Here, you do not need to modify these options.

[g] Click the **Color** box to choose a colour for the text.

This option is not available when using the [icon] *and* [icon] *tools.*

▸ Here, click this box, specify these colour components: C= **0**, M= **0**, Y= **0**, K= **90** then click **OK**.

[h] Use the **Baseline** option to shift some characters vertically (sub- or super-script). You can use any value between -1296 and 1296. With a negative value, you will move the character down (sub-script) and with a positive value, the character will move up (super-script).

Chapter 2

SAFARI   SAFARI

baseline=0   baseline=12
for all characters   for the AFAR characters

⟩⟩▶ Here, you do not need to apply a baseline shift.

[i] Use the ▤, ▤ or ▤ buttons to align the text respectively on the left, in the centre and on the right of the part of the image where you clicked. These options are generally only useful if you are entering several lines of text.

⟩⟩▶ Here, activate the ▤ option.

[j] If using the 🆃 or 🆃 tools; activate the **Rotate** option to turn the vertical letters towards the right.

```
S                    ┌─┐
A                    │S│
F                    │A│
A                    │F│
R                    │A│
I                    │R│
                     │I│
                     └─┘
without rotation    with rotation
```

⟩⟩▶ Here, you are not using these tools.

[k] Select an **Anti-Alias** option to define how the outline of the letters will look.

None	Individual pixels are visible at the edges of the letters (staircase effect).
Crisp	The outline of the letters is smoothed as much as possible without affecting the quality of the text.
Strong	The text is bolder. The edges of the letters are a little blurred.
Smooth	The outline of the letters is smooth. Smoothing takes priority over the quality of the text.

⟩⟩▶ Here, leave the **Crisp** option.

[l] Deactivate the **Fractional Widths** option if you do not want Photoshop to optimise the spacing between letters (wich involves leaving fractions of pixels between letters). Deactivating this option makes text more readable when the font size is less than 20 points.

⟩⟩▶ Here, leave the option active, because the font size is well above 20 points.

[m] Enter your text in the large text box. Press ⏎ to change lines.

⟩⟩▶ Here, type in **SAFARI PHOTO**

Adobe Photoshop 5.5

Chapter 2

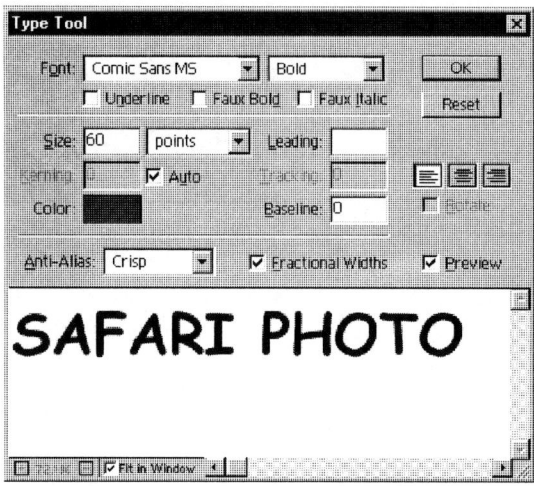

|n| To change the parameters of existing text, drag to select the characters you wish to modify then change the options.

|o| Click **OK**.

The text appears in the place you clicked and a new type layer called SAFARI PHOTO is now present on the Layers palette.

> ✓ To change the orientation of a text after having typed it, activate the corresponding type layer and use the commands *Layer - Type - Horizontal* or *Layer - Type - Vertical* depending on which way you want to orient your text. This is only possible for a type layer and not for texts created using the ▦ and ▦ tools.

> ✓ You can modify the zoom in the *Type Tool* dialog box using the ⊞ and ⊟ buttons underneath the large text box (in the left corner). The *Fit in Window* option lets you automatically change the zoom so that the whole text is visible in the text box as you write. This zoom does not change the font size being used, but just the way the text box is displayed.

Chapter 2

16 *The text you have entered is not satisfactory, so you will need to change it.*

MODIFYING TEXT ON A TYPE LAYER

a Double-click the name of the layer which corresponds to the text. Be careful to click the name and not the thumbnail or you will obtain the **Layer Options** dialog box and not the **Type Tool** box.

➡ Here, double-click the SAFARI PHOTO layer name.

*The **Type Tool** dialog box opens.*

b To change the parameters of the text, drag to select the text concerned then make your changes.

➡ Here, select the word PHOTO by double-clicking it then enter **10** as the font **Size**.

*The word PHOTO is now dramatically smaller. If the **Preview** option is active, the changes made can be seen in the document window, unless the whole word is now hidden by the lion.*

c To modify the text, click in the text box (if you are not already there) then make your changes.

➡ Here, click in the text box and delete the word **PHOTO**.

d Click **OK**.

*The word **PHOTO** has disappeared and in the **Layers** palette the layer should be renamed automatically as **SAFARI**.*

✓ *If the layer is not renamed, you can do it by double-clicking its thumbnail and renaming it.*

Return to the text and position it correctly.

➡ **Edit - Transform - Rotate 90° CCW**

➡ Activate the [tool icon] tool and move the text into the top left corner of the image:

Adobe Photoshop 5.5

Chapter 2

17

When the text requires no further modification, you can transform it into an image. This will enable you to apply different filters or retouches to it.

CONVERTING TEXT INTO IMAGE

[a] Activate the type layer containing the text you wish to convert.

➜ Here, leave the **SAFARI** layer active.

[b] **Layer**
Type
Render Layer

The **T** icon which was visible on the **Layers** palette disappears.

☑ *The converted text can no longer be modified as text after its conversion. To avoid any difficulties, you should only convert text into an image if you need to apply a filter or retouch it.*

➜ At this point, if you want to modify your text at a later date, undo this conversion.

18

You have seen how to create an outline around a selection. Photoshop offers other solutions for applying different effects to a layer, in simple ways. You can now look at these techniques.

APPLYING EFFECTS TO LAYERS

DEFINING A GLOBAL ANGLE FOR EFFECTS

*The **Global Angle** lets you apply different effects using one single angle. This is useful when you combine several different effects or when applying effects to several layers.*

[a] **Layer**
Effects
Global Angle

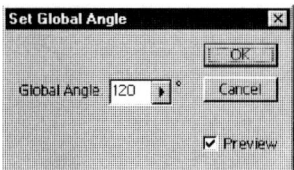

[b] Set the angle between -180° and 180°.

Depending on the angle given, the results can be very different.

Chapter 2

drop shadow effect
made with a 120° angle

drop shadow effect
made with a -40° angle

|c| Click **OK**.

⟩⟩ Here, you can click **Cancel** because you can use the default angle set.

APPLYING A DROP SHADOW EFFECT

|a| Activate the layer to which you are applying the effect. You cannot apply any effect to the **Background** layer.

⟩⟩ Here, activate the **Mask** layer.

|b| **Layer**
Effects

|c| Select one of the following options:
Drop Shadow   To apply a shadow to the outside of the layer.
Inner Shadow   To apply a shadow inside the layer.

⟩⟩ Here, activate **Drop Shadow**.

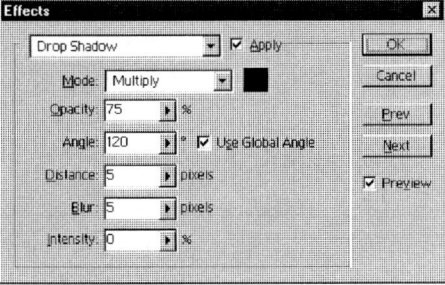

This dialog box allows you to set the various parameters of the effect. If the Preview option is active, the effect can be seen in the document window.

|d| Check that the **Apply** option is activated to be able to adjust and apply the effect.

|e| Select the blending **Mode** for the effect.

*The most frequently used modes for these effects are **Normal**, **Multiply**, **Soft Light**, **Hard Light** or **Color Dodge**.*

You will see the characteristics of these modes later in the book.

|f| Click the **Color Box** situated next to the **Mode** list to choose the colour of the shadow.

⟩⟩ Here, leave the default colour.

Adobe Photoshop 5.5

Chapter 2

[g] Use the **Opacity** option to set the opacity for the shadow's starting point. The higher the opacity of this starting point, the more pronounced the shadow will be.

» Here, leave the **75%** value proposed by default.

[h] If necessary, change the effect's **Angle**. If you change this value while the **Use Global Angle** option is active, you will also change the global angle. If this is the case, all the layers which have effects using the global angle will be modified. To use an angle different from the global angle, simply check that the **Use Global Angle** option is deactivated before setting a new **Angle**.

» Here, leave the **Angle** at **120**.

[i] If necessary, modify the **Distance** option. This option depends on the type of shadow selected:

Drop Shadow   Lets you adjust the offset between the layer and the shadow.
Inner Shadow   Lets you adjust the area covered by the shadow on the layer.

drop shadow distance=10   drop shadow distance=30   inner shadow distance=10   inner shadow distance=30

» Here, set the **Distance** at **7**.

[j] Use the **Blur** option to set the distance at which **Opacity** will equal 0. The higher this value is, the greater the area covered by the shadow.

blur=5   blur=20

» Here, leave the value at **5**.

[k] Use the **Intensity** value to counteract the softening of the shadow produced by the **Blur** option. The higher the intensity, the denser the shadow produced.

intensity=0   intensity=90

» Here, leave the **Intensity** as nil.

*The **Prev** (previous) and **Next** buttons allow you to access the parameters of the other effects available, so you can apply several effects if you wish.*

Chapter 2

☐ Click **OK**.

A shadow appears under the mask and a specific icon can be seen on the Layers palette.

APPLYING A GLOW EFFECT

☐ Activate the layer to which you will apply the effect. The **Background** layer cannot take on any effect.

➔ Here, activate the **Map** layer on the **Layers** palette.

☐ **Layer**
Effects

☐ Select one of the following options:
Outer Glow   to apply a soft edge, or halo effect on the outside of the layer.
Inner Glow   to apply a soft edge, or halo effect inside the layer.

➔ Here, activate **Outer Glow**.

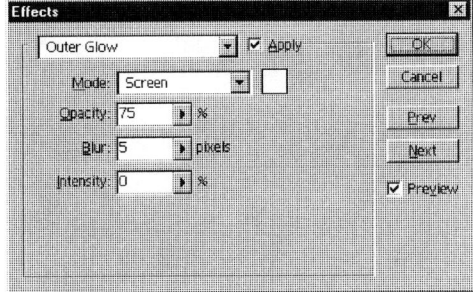

☐ Check that the **Apply** option is activated to be able to adjust and apply the effect.

☐ Choose the blending **Mode** for the effect.

*The most frequently used modes for these effects are **Normal, Screen, Soft Light, Hard Light** and **Color Dodge**.*

You will see more on these modes in later chapters.

☐ Click the **Color Box** situated next to the **Mode** list to choose the colour used on the glow.

➔ Here, click the box and check that the colour shown is made up of C= **2**, M= **0**, Y= **35** and K= **0**.

☐ Define the **Opacity, Blur** and **Intensity** as you saw for the shadow effects.

➔ Here, set the **Blur** at **15**.

Adobe Photoshop 5.5

Chapter 2

[h] If using the **Inner Glow** effect, you could choose one of these options:

Center   To create a luminous halo effect in the centre of the layer. To avoid masking the whole layer with this halo, use a high **Blur** setting.

Edge   To create a luminous glow on the inside edge of the outline.

original image   center   edge

➽ Here, these options are not accessible.

[i] Click **OK**.

A glow appears around the map.

APPLYING A BEVEL AND EMBOSS EFFECT

[a] Activate the layer to which you will apply the effect. The **Background** layer cannot take on any effect.

➽ Here, activate the **SAFARI** layer on the **Layers** palette.

[b] **Layer**
Effects
Bevel and Emboss

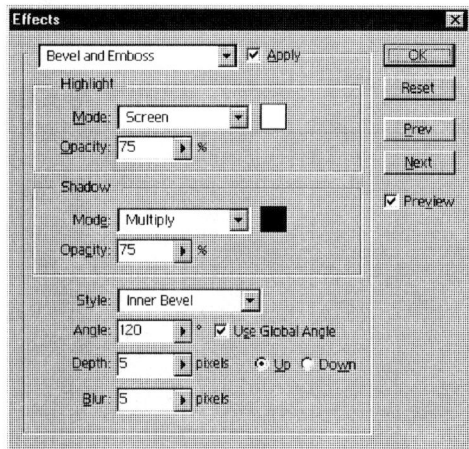

[c] Define the **Highlight** options as for those seen on the glow effects.
Define the **Shadow** options as for those seen on the shadow effects.

➽ Here, leave the default values as set.

Chapter 2

[d] Select the desired effect **Style**.

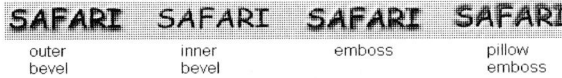

outer bevel   inner bevel   emboss   pillow emboss

The *Emboss* effect is the equivalent of the *Outer Bevel* and the *Inner Bevel* effects combined.

➡ Here, activate **Outer Bevel**.

[e] Define the **Depth** which will determine the thickness of the bevelling or embossing.

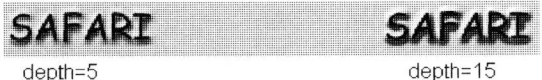

depth=5   depth=15

➡ Here, set the **Depth** at **10**.

[f] Activate the **Up** or **Down** option to determine the "source" of the illumination, or what will be the lightest part.

➡ Here, leave the **Up** option active.

[g] Click **OK**.
The layer's letters are bevelled.

APPLYING A COLOUR FILL EFFECT

[a] Activate the layer to which the effect will apply. You cannot apply an effect to the **Background** layer.

➡ Here, activate the **Map** layer.

[b] **Layer**
Effects
Color Fill

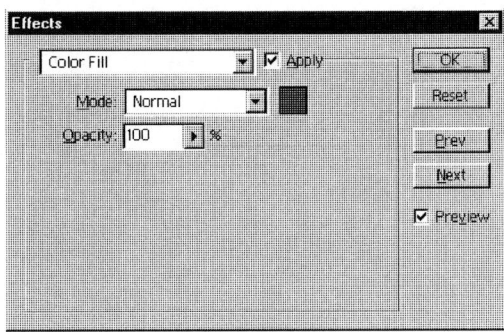

[c] Check that the **Apply** button is active so that you can adjust and apply the effect.

Adobe Photoshop 5.5   **113**

Chapter 2

[d] Choose the blending **Mode** for the effect.
The different modes will be discussed later on.

➟ Here, leave the **Normal** mode.

[e] Click the **Color Box** located next to the **Mode** list to choose the colour for the fill.

➟ Here, keep the red which is selected by default.

[f] Use the **Opacity** option to specify how opaque the fill will be.

➟ Here, set the opacity to **50%**.

[g] Click **OK**.

The red fill applied to the map is only semi-opaque, so that the green shows through. The result is that the map is coloured brown.

> ✓ You can achieve the same result if you use the *Edit - Fill* command and set the *Preserve Transparency* option, but you not be able to modify the fill as easily as you can with a layer effect.
>
> ✓ You can transform the effect or effects applied to layers by using the *Layer - Effects - Create Layer (or Layers* as the case may be*)*. The effects can no longer be modified by the *Effects* commands in the *Layer* menu but you can retouch them using other methods.
>
> ✓ You can temporarily mask the applied effects by activating *Layer - Effects - Hide All Effects*. To show them again, use the *Layer - Effects - Show All Effects* command.

---

19 *If any effect does not satisfy you, you can change it*

MODIFYING OR DELETING EFFECTS APPLIED TO LAYERS

[a] Activate the layer whose effect must be modified.

➟ Here, activate the **SAFARI** layer.

[b] Double-click the 🅕 icon corresponding to the layer or select the effect to modify using the **Layer - Effects** command.

➟ Here, double-click the 🅕 icon on the **SAFARI** layer.

[c] If several effects have been applied, use the list of effects at the top of the **Effects** dialog box to choose which effect to modify.

➟ Here, select the **Bevel and Emboss** effect if it is not already active.

Chapter 2

[d] Adjust the parameters which are not suitable in order to modify the effect or deactivate the **Apply** option to delete it.

▸ Here, set the **Depth** at **5**.

[e] Click **OK**.

The effect has been modified and the bevelling effect is not so pronounced.

> ✓ You can also delete an effect by holding down [Alt] and activating the option which corresponds to the effect in the *Layer - Effects* menu.
>
> ✓ To delete all the effects applied on a layer, you can also use the *Layer - Effects - Clear Effects* command.

On second thoughts, it would be better to go back and remove the red fill from the map.

▸ Activate the **Map** layer.

▸ **Layer - Effects - Color fill**

▸ Deactivate the **Apply** option.

▸ Click **OK**.

The map goes back to its previous green colour.

---

20 When one or more effects have been created, you can duplicate them to apply them to other layers.

COPYING LAYER EFFECTS

[a] Activate the layer whose effects you want to copy.

▸ Here, activate the **Map** layer.

[b] **Layer**
Effects
Copy Effects

[c] Activate the layer onto which you want to apply the copied effects.

▸ Here, activate the **Lion** layer.

[d] **Layer**
Effects

Adobe Photoshop 5.5

Chapter 2

➤ <u>e</u> Select one of the following options:
   Paste Effects   To apply the effects only to this layer.
   Paste Effects to Linked To apply effects to all linked layers.

➤ Here, select **Paste Effects**.
   The outer glow effect has been applied to the lion.

   The results are disappointing. Cancel the effect and instead create a shadow behind the giraffe using a different method.

➤ **Edit - Undo**
➤ Activate the **Giraffe Shadow** layer.
➤ **Edit - Fill**
➤ In the **Use** list, choose **Black**, activate the **Preserve Transparency** option and click **OK**.
   As the Giraffe Shadow layer is above the Giraffe layer, the giraffe has turned black.
➤ **Filter - Blur - Gaussian Blur**
➤ Using the hand, push around the contents of the **Preview** box until you can see the giraffe.
➤ Set the **Radius** at **3** and click **OK**.
   The giraffe shadow now has a blurred outline.

   Reshape this shadow to produce a more realistic shadow than that produced by the Drop Shadow effect.

➤ If the **Info** palette is hidden, show it.
➤ **Edit - Free Transform**
➤ Point to the top centre handle, hold down <u>Ctrl</u> and drag down and to the right. Use the **Info** palette to help you see the transformation values. The vertical scale should be around 20% and the skew to the right at -70%.
➤ Press <u>Enter</u>.
   The shadow has been slightly flattened, like the shadow produced when the sun is very high.

Chapter 2

Position the shadow correctly.

▶ If necessary, activate the [move] tool and move the shadow so that it is placed at the giraffe's feet (do not use the layer alignment options, the shadow would be placed too low):

Place the shadow underneath the giraffe.

▶ In the **Layers** palette, drag the **Giraffe Shadow** layer underneath the **Giraffe** layer.

You can make the shadow look even more realistic.

▶ In the **Layers** palette, double-click the **Giraffe Shadow** thumbnail and set the **Opacity** at 60%.

The shadow becomes translucent and the background colour shows through it.

You can now save this image.

▶ **File - Save**

---

21 *The rounded bases of the tusks do not look quite right in this image. Perhaps you should delete them.*

DELETING PART OF AN IMAGE

USING A SELECTION

[a] If necessary, activate the layer on which you want to delete something.

▶ Here, activate the **Tusks** layer.

[b] Select the part to be deleted.

▶ Here, activate the [marquee] tool and select the lower extremity of the tusks.

[c] **Edit**   [Del]
Clear

Adobe Photoshop 5.5   117

Chapter 2

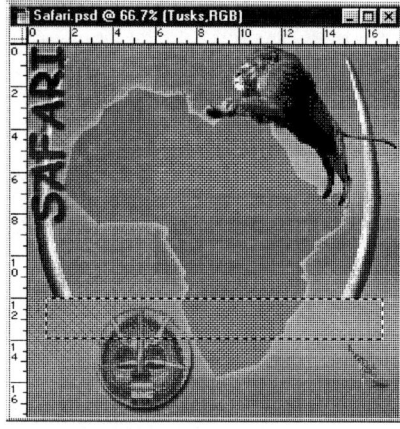

The selected portion is deleted, without any alteration to the background, as you are on a layer.

You probably do not think that this looks any better.

⟹ **Edit - Undo**
⟹ **Deselect** using **Select - Deselect**

USING THE ⌫ TOOL

[a] If necessary, activate the layer in which you want to delete something.

⟹ Here, leave the **Tusks** layer active.

[b] Activate the ⌫ tool.

[c] If the **Options** palette is hidden, show it by clicking its tab or by using **Window - Show Options**.

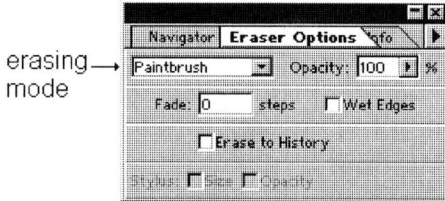

erasing mode

[d] Use the **Erasing Mode** list to select one of these four tools:

Paintbrush allows you to rub out using the characteristics of the 🖌 tool, which means that the eraser's outlines will be blurry to avoid jagged edges after rubbing out.

Airbrush allows you to rub out using the characteristics of the 🖌 tool, which means that the eraser's outlines stay blurry and the erasing effect is softer than with the 🖌 tool.

Chapter 2

    Pencil   allows you to rub out using the characteristics of the  tool, which means that eraser's outlines will be hard, producing a jagged edge after rubbing out.

    Block   allows you to rub out with a fixed size eraser, producing a jagged edge after rubbing out.

➧ Here, you should use the **Paintbrush** type.

☐e Use the **Opacity** option to rub out more or less superficially, in order to keep a certain amount of the rubbed-out pixels visible.

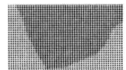
original image

erasing with 100 % opacity

erasing with 50 % opacity

*If you select the **Airbrush** eraser tool, the **Opacity** option is replaced by **Pressure**. This acts similarly to **Opacity** but the effect is cumulative: the longer you stay in the same spot, the more the eraser will rub out. To create a homogenous erasure you must drag as evenly as possible.*

➧ Here, leave a value of **100%**.

☐f Use the **Fade** option to make a graded effect. The value specified lets you set the distance at which the eraser no longer makes any effect. This value can vary between 1 and 9999. To remove any graded effect, delete the value.

original image

erasing with 100 % opacity

erasing with 100 % opacity plus fade

➧ Here, you do not need to apply a fade effect.

☐g If you have chosen the paintbrush eraser, activate the **Wet Edges** option to give a water-colour effect when using the brush, which corresponds to an erasure using 50% less opacity.

➧ Here, leave this option deactivated.

☐h If necessary, activate the **Erase to History** option in order to rub out in relation to the previous states of the image. You can temporarily activate this tool by holding down [Alt] while you drag.

➧ Here, leave this option deactivated as you will see how to use **History** later on.

Adobe Photoshop 5.5

Chapter 2

[i] If you have chosen any other eraser than the **Block** type, show the **Brushes** palette by clicking its tab or using **Window - Show Brushes**.

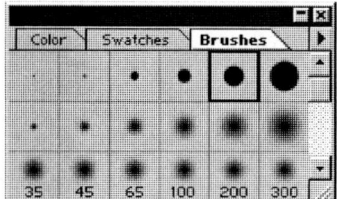

The active brush is surrounded by a black square. The brushes that cannot be shown actual size are shown in miniature with their diameter in pixels underneath.

[j] Select an eraser brush type.

➠ Here, activate the brush with a diameter of **65**

[k] Point to the item you want to erase and drag to rub out.

➠ Here, point to the bottom part of one of the tusks and drag.

The end of the tusk has been rubbed out.

✓ If you apply the tool to the *Background* layer, the rubbed-out area will be filled with the active background colour.

✓ You can also use one of two special erasers:

  The background eraser erases an area of the image and makes it transparent. It works like a mixture of the [ ] and [ ] tools. You drag to erase, but the areas which are actually rubbed out depend on the *Tolerance* and *Sampling* settings you have chosen. In the *Sampling* list, you choose the colour to erase (Photoshop interprets this option according to the tolerance you define): if *Continuous* is active, the reference colour changes as you drag; if *Once* is active, only the colour you first click is erased; if *Background Swatch* is active, only the current background colour is erased.

The magic eraser erases an area of the image and makes it transparent. It works rather like the [ ] tool.

You can erase more accurately if you select and then clear the selected area rather than using the [ ] and [ ] tools. If you use one of these tools on the *Background*, it will automatically be converted into a layer.

Chapter 2

Go back to the previously-saved version of the document and try rubbing out again, this time with a fade effect.

➤ **File - Revert**
➤ Make sure that the **Tusks** layer is active and that the ✐ tool is selected.
➤ In the tool **Options** set the **Fade** option to **10**.
➤ Point to the base of one of the tusks and drag over it.

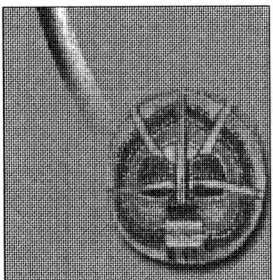

After a certain distance, the eraser loses its effectiveness. The tusk is almost completely rubbed out at the tip but remains untouched further up.

As you will create a more regular effect later on, revert to the previous version again.

➤ **File - Revert**

---

22 *You now know how to rub out part of an image using a fade effect to produce progressive erasing of an image. You can also use a different technique that will produce a more even result. To do that you need to first see how the gradient tools work.*

FILLING A SELECTION OR A LAYER WITH A GRADIENT

USING A PRESET GRADIENT

[a] If necessary, activate the layer to which you want to apply the gradient or make a selection to limit the gradient.

➤ Here, activate the **Map** layer.

[b] When working on a layer, activate the **Preserve Transparency** option on the **Layers** palette if you want to limit applying the gradient just to the items on the layer. If the option is not active, the whole layer will be filled by the gradient.

➤ Here, activate the option.

[c] Activate one of the following tools: ▨, ▨, ▨, ▨ or ▨, depending on which type of gradient you want to use.

➤ Here, activate the ▨ tool.

Adobe Photoshop 5.5

Chapter 2

[d] If the **Options** palette is hidden, show it by clicking its tab or by choosing **Window - Show Options**.

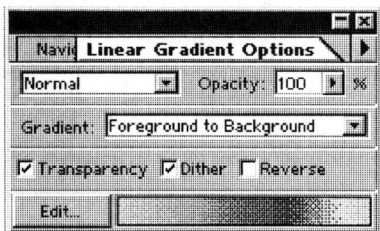

[e] If necessary, reset the **Painting Mode** for the gradient and the opacity value.
The various modes are described in detail in chapter 4.

▸ Here, leave the options that are set by default.

[f] Select an existing gradient fill using the **Gradient** list.

▸ Here, select the **Gradient** that is called **Copper**.

[g] Activate the **Transparency** option for those gradients using a transparent colour. If this option is not active, there will be no transparency in the gradient apart from that applied by the **Opacity** option.

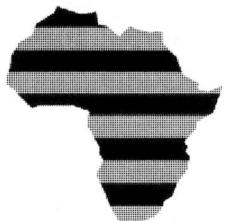 

preset transparency stripes gradient with transparency option active

preset transparency stripes gradient with no transparency

▸ Here, leave this option active.

[h] Activate the **Dither** option to create gradients with smoother, more diffuse transitions from shade to shade. This option is especially useful when working with high-resolution images or for very long gradients.

[i] Activate the **Reverse** option to make the same gradient, but with its colours reversed.

▸ Here, the **Foreground to Background** gradient would become a **Background to Foreground** type, but do not activate this option.

Chapter 2

[j] Drag over the item to define the length of the gradient. You can use the ⇧Shift key if you want to make a horizontal or vertical gradient, or one that slopes at 45°.

▶ Here, press down ⇧Shift and drag over the map from top to bottom.

The map is filled by the gradient.

Undo this gradient.

▶ **Edit - Undo**

CREATING A CUSTOMIZED GRADIENT

[a] Activate one of the following tools: ▨, ▨, ▨, ▨ or ▨ depending on the gradient you wish to use.

▶ Here, leave the ▨ tool active.

[b] If the **Options** palette is hidden, show it by clicking its tab or using **Window - Show Options**.

[c] Click the **Edit** button on the **Options** palette.

[d] Click the **New** button to create a gradient or the **Duplicate** button to create a gradient based on one selected from the list of existing gradients.

If you do not create a new gradient, you will modify the gradient selected in the list.

▶ Here, click the **New** button.

[e] Enter the **Name** of the new gradient in the corresponding text box.

▶ Here, enter **Test Gradient**

[f] Click **OK** if you have created or duplicated a gradient.

Adobe Photoshop 5.5

Chapter 2

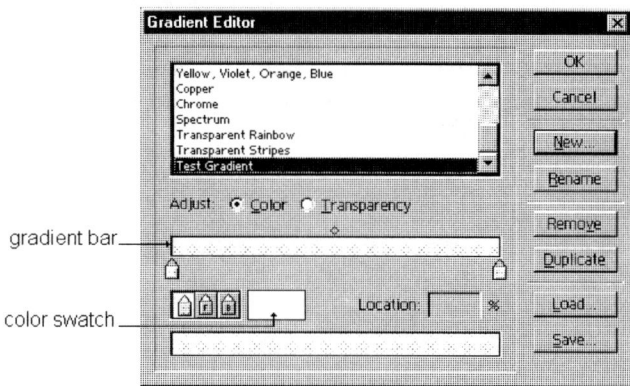

gradient bar

color swatch

|g| To change the colour of a gradient, click the ⌂ color stop that corresponds to it.

➟ Here, click the color stop located on the left.

The tip of the color stop turns black.

|h| Click:

The color swatch   To select any colour.

The [ ] button   To use the foreground colour in the gradient.

The [ ] button   To use the background colour.

➟ Here, click the color swatch in order to select the colour by its components: **R= 85**, **G= 200** and **B= 75**.

➟ Click **OK**.

The gradient now spans from green to yellow.

|i| To set the transition distance between the two colours of the gradient, drag the color stop ⌂ or enter a value in the **Location** text box. Between each color stop ⌂, you have a mid-point (◆) which allows you to regulate at what point in the gradient the start and end colours will be evenly mixed. You can drag this mid-point to adjust it or enter a value in the **Location** text box.

mid-point at 25 %   mid-point at 50 %   mid-point at 75 %

➟ Here, drag the mid-point to **85 %** to see the result, then return it to the **50 %** position.

Chapter 2

[j] To add a colour to the gradient, click under the **Gradient Bar** where the other ⌂ color stops are located to add a new one then define the colour by clicking the color swatch. To remove a colour, drag the ⌂ downwards.

➤ Here, add an intermediate colour at the **50% Location** using the components **R= 45, G= 100** and **B= 40** then click the color stop at Location **100%**, click the color swatch and define the components as **R= 230, G= 230** and **B= 30**.

[k] To create or modify a gradient with transparency, activate the **Transparency** option once you have defined the colours (if you wish). In the same way as for the colours you can change, add or remove transparencies using the color stops ⌂. To define the transparency rate, click the corresponding color stop ⌂ and enter an **Opacity** value.

➤ Here, the gradient does not contain any transparencies.

[l] Click **OK**.

The set gradient now appears in the Options palette.

> ✓ You can *Rename* or *Remove* a gradient by selecting it in the list of existing gradients and clicking the corresponding button.
>
> ✓ You can *Save* or *Load* gradients by clicking the appropriate button. By default, the \Program Files\Adobe\Photoshop 5.5\Goodies\Photoshop Only\Gradients folder is intended for saving gradients, but you can choose another folder if you wish.

Try out the new gradient.

➤ Drag from the top to the bottom of the map.

The gradient appears.

Undo the gradient.

➤ **Edit - Undo**

*Before continuing, you should temporarily separate the two tusks on the **Tusks** layer. You can regroup them at a later time.*

➤ Activate the **Tusks** layer.
➤ Activate the ⬚ tool and select the right tusk by dragging a marquee around it.
➤ **Layer - New - Layer Via Cut**

*The right tusk is now situated on a new layer called **Layer 1**, situated just above the **Tusks** layer.*

➤ Activate the default colours by clicking the ⬛ icon on the toolbox.

Adobe Photoshop 5.5

Chapter 2

23 You can now create an even and progressive rubbing-out of the base of the tusks using a layer functionality: layer masks. These allow you to mask certain sections of a layer without modifying the contents. Look now at how to apply them.

APPLYING LAYER MASKS

a Activate the layer that will be masked.

➧ Here, leave **Layer 1** active.

b **Layer**
Add Layer Mask

c Use one of the following options to create the layer mask:

Reveal All	Click the ▣ button on the **Layers** palette	To leave the whole layer visible by default. The layer mask will be white.
Hide All	[Alt]-click the ▣ button	To mask the whole layer. The layer mask will be black.
Reveal Selection	[Ctrl]- or [Shift]-click the ▣ button with a selection made	To reveal only the items on the layer which are included in the selection. The layer mask will be white on the selected zone and black on the rest.
Hide Selection	[Alt]-click the ▣ button	To hide the items on the layer that have been selected. The layer mask will be black in the selected part and white on the rest.

➧ Here, activate **Reveal All**.

A layer mask thumbnail appears next to the layer thumbnail.

The 🔗 icon located between the two thumbnails indicates that the layer mask is linked to the layer. If you move the layer, the mask moves with it. You can unlink them by clicking the 🔗 icon and relink them by clicking the empty space between the two thumbnails.

d Before modifying the layer mask, make sure that the ▣ icon is displayed next to the 🖌 icon. If you see the ✏ icon in this place, it means that you are working on the layer itself.

To modify the layer mask, click its thumbnail to make the ▣ icon appear (click the layer thumbnail when you wish to work on the layer itself again).

Chapter 2

[e] Change the layer mask using the drawing or retouching tools or by using certain filters. The drawing on the layer mask is in grayscale; you need to apply:

  black To mask completely the corresponding pixels on the layer.

  grey To give a certain level of transparency to the pixels on the layer. For example, black at 40% is equivalent to having 40% less opacity. In this case, if the layer is applied with 100% opacity, the pixels on the layer affected by the layer mask grey will have a real opacity value of 60% (100%-40%).

  white To not affect the layer pixels at all.

» Here, select the tool then click the double arrow you can see near the color boxes on the toolbox to switch the foreground and background colours: the foreground colour will then be black.
Access the **Brushes** palette and select a wide brush. Draw a line through the bottom part of the right tusk.

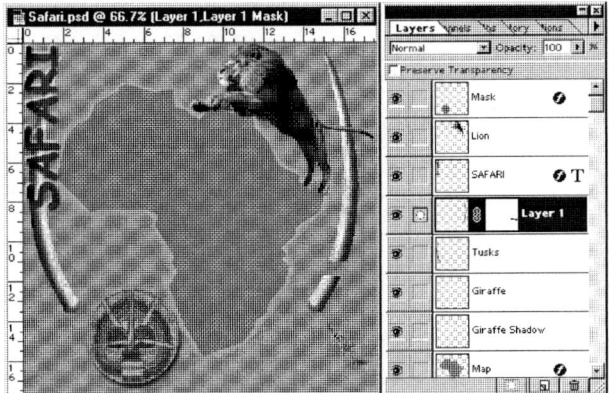

On the layer mask thumbnail, you can see the black line. The corresponding pixels on the **Layer 1** *layer are no longer visible: a part of the tusk seems to have been erased. In fact, the pixels have just been masked.*

» For this example, select white as the foreground colour, then a narrower brush. Click the part of the tusk that you have already masked.
The corresponding pixels become visible again.

[f] To make certain changes on the layer mask easier, you can show only the layer mask by [Alt]-clicking its thumbnail. To show both again, perform the same task or click the layer thumbnail.

» Here, [Alt]-click the layer mask thumbnail.

  The layer mask now only contains a black line with a white spot.

» For this example, drag the tool over the black line to make it disappear. Then click the layer thumbnail.

Adobe Photoshop 5.5

Chapter 2

- ✓ You can also create a layer mask by dragging the layer thumbnail onto the ▢ button on the *Layers* palette. This lets you create a layer mask, which has as its masked areas the transparent areas of the layer used.

- ✓ You can temporarily mask the effect produced by a layer mask by pressing ⇧Shift and clicking its thumbnail or using the command *Layer - Disable Layer Mask*. This will be displayed in the *Layers* palette in this way:

- ✓ To show the layer mask effect again, click its thumbnail or use the *Layers - Enable Layer Mask* command.

Apply a gradient to the layer mask.

➤ Activate the ▢ tool and select the **Foreground to Transparent** gradient in the **Options** palette.
Make sure that the foreground colour is black.
Click the layer mask thumbnail.
Drag from the bottom of the tusk on the right upwards over the tusk for about a centimetre.

The base of the tusk disappears, progressively becoming more and more transparent.

*Apply the same effect as on the layer mask to the **Tusks** layer.*

➤ Hold down Alt and click the layer mask thumbnail on **Layer 1**.

Only the layer mask should be visible.

➤ **Select - All**

➤ **Edit - Copy**

➤ **Select - Deselect**

➤ Activate the **Tusks** layer and create a layer mask by clicking the ▢ button on the **Layers** palette.

*A layer mask thumbnail appears on the **Tusks** layer.*

➤ Hold down Alt and click the layer mask thumbnail on the **Tusks** layer.

Only the layer mask should be visible (it is completely white).

➤ **Edit - Paste**

➤ **Select - Deselect**

➤ Click the 8 icon between the layer thumbnail and the layer mask thumbnail to remove the link between the layer and the layer mask.

➤ **Select - All**

Chapter 2

➠ **Edit - Transform - Flip Horizontal**
 The layer mask is turned upside down, but not the tusk as the two are no longer linked.
➠ Click the layer thumbnail to display the photo again.
 The two tusks are progressively erased, in a symmetrical way.

---

24 *When you are satisfied with the effects produced using a layer mask, you can apply its effects to the layer then remove it.*

APPLYING A LAYER MASK'S EFFECTS OR DELETING IT

|a| Activate the layer whose layer mask needs to be applied or deleted by clicking the layer mask thumbnail (the 🖼 icon should be visible next to the 👁 icon).

➠ Here, activate the **Layer 1** mask.

|b| **Layer**   Click the 🗑 button on the **Layers** palette
 Remove Layer Mask

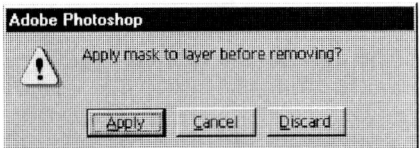

|c| Click the **Apply** button to remove the layer mask after applying it or the **Discard** button to remove the mask without applying it.

➠ Here, click the **Apply** button.
 The layer mask thumbnail for Layer 1 disappears from the Layers palette but the mask's effect can still be seen on the layer itself.

 ✓ *If you apply a layer mask to a Type layer, the layer will be converted to an ordinary layer and the text could no longer be modified.*

 ✓ *If you merge layers containing layer masks, the layer mask(s) are automatically applied and deleted.*

 You can test this.

➠ Activate the **Tusks** layer.
 Merge this layer with **Layer 1** by clicking the square next to the **Layer 1** 👁 icon.
➠ **Layer - Merged Linked**
➠ Save the document.

Adobe Photoshop 5.5

Chapter 2

PRACTICE EXERCISE 2

- Open the **Kilimanjaro.jpg** document.
- Copy this image onto the **Safari.psd** document and close **Kilimanjaro.jpg**.
- Name the layer containing this picture **Kilimanjaro**.
- Place this layer under the **Giraffe Shadow** layer.
- Scale the **Kilimanjaro** layer to 50% of its original size, keeping its proportions.
- Place the **Kilimanjaro** layer to the extreme right of the photo and line it up with the bottom of the **Map** layer (the map should not move).
- Place the **Tusks** layer under the **Kilimanjaro** layer.
- Move the **Giraffe** and **Giraffe Shadow** layers simultaneously to the bottom right corner of the **Kilimanjaro** image.
- Copy the left tusk from the **Tusks** layer onto a new layer called **Crossed Tusks**.
- Apply to the **Crossed Tusks** layer a transformation, consisting of a 30 rotation and a proportional scale of about 40%.
- Duplicate the **Crossed Tusks** layer and apply a horizontal flip to that duplicate. Bring the tusk on the **Crossed Tusks** layer a little closer to the one on the **Crossed Tusks Copy** layer.
- Merge the **Crossed Tusks** and the **Crossed Tusks Copy** layers into one **Crossed Tusks** layer.
- Place this layer above the **Mask** layer and move the tusks to sit above the mask image.
- Create a horizontal type layer whose text will read **ENI TRAVEL**. The attributes for this text are: **Bookman Old Style** or **Times New Roman** font, in bold type, with a font size of 44 for Bookman and 46 for Times, and a font colour consisting of **C**=0, **M**=25, **Y**=56 and **K**=0.
- Apply a **Drop Shadow** and an **Inner Shadow** effect to the **ENI TRAVEL** layer, using a 5 pixel **Distance** and **Blur** for each effect.
- Place the **ENI TRAVEL** layer in the bottom right corner of the image.
- Add a layer mask to the **Kilimanjaro** layer.
- Use the tool with a **Foreground to Transparent** gradient to modify the layer mask. Create a first gradient to mask the sky a second to mask the left side of the picture (up to the tree) and a third small gradient on the bottom of the image.
- Save the **Safari.psd** document and leave Photoshop.

The correct version of this photo is saved as **Safari Chapter 2.psd**.

CHAPTER 3

1 - DRAWING WITH THE PENCIL, PAINTBRUSH OR AIRBRUSH	132
2 - DRAWING STRAIGHT LINES OR ARROWS	136
3 - USING THE PAINT BUCKET TO CHANGE THE COLOUR OF PIXELS	138
4 - EXTRACTING THE FOREGROUND OF AN IMAGE	140
5 - USING THE SMUDGE TOOL	142
6 - BLURRING OR SHARPENING PART OF AN IMAGE	144
7 - DARKENING OR LIGHTENING PART OF AN IMAGE	146
8 - CHECKING THE TONAL RANGE OF A PICTURE	148
9 - ADJUSTING CONTRAST AND/OR BRIGHTNESS ON AN IMAGE	150
THE SIMPLIFIED METHOD	150
BY MODIFYING THE HISTOGRAM	151
USING AUTOMATIC LEVELS	153
USING AUTOMATIC CONTRAST	154
BY ADJUSTING THE CURVES	154
USING THE BLACK POINT AND WHITE POINT OF AN IMAGE	157
10 - ADJUSTING THE PROPORTIONS OF COLOUR IN AN IMAGE	159
USING THE SIMPLIFIED METHOD	159
BY ADJUSTING THE COLOR BALANCE	160
BY CHANGING THE HISTOGRAM OR THE CURVES	161
11 - MODIFYING COLOUR SATURATION ON AN AREA OF AN IMAGE	162
12 - ADJUSTING INDIVIDUAL COLOUR COMPONENTS	163
BY MODIFYING THE HUE OR SATURATION	163
USING SELECTIVE COLOR	166
13 - REPLACING CERTAIN COLOURS ON AN IMAGE	167
14 - CREATING A NEGATIVE	169
15 - TRANSFORMING AN IMAGE AREA INTO A BITMAP	170
16 - CREATING FLAT AREAS OF COLOUR	172
17 - DUPLICATING PART OF AN IMAGE WITH THE RUBBER STAMP	173
PRACTICE EXERCISE 3	176

Chapter 3

Throughout this chapter, you are going to discover the main drawing and retouching tools, the commands for changing image contrast and luminosity as well as different ways in which colours can be changed. You will be working on the documents used in the previous chapters in order to improve their quality.

➟ If you left Photoshop at the end of the last chapter, restart it.

➟ **File - New**
Select **pixels** as the **Width** and **Height** unit then enter **400** in these two text boxes.
Check that the colour mode is **RGB** then click **OK**.

Use a filter to apply a background to the image.

➟ Select a neutral foreground colour, neither too light nor too dark (a blue for example).

➟ **Filter - Render - Clouds**
The image is filled with the foreground colour, which has a cottonwool effect added to it.

---

1 *The drawing tools are used naturally for drawing but also for retouching. Start now to master these tools.*

DRAWING WITH THE PENCIL, PAINTBRUSH OR AIRBRUSH

[a] If necessary, activate the layer on which you want to draw or select a part of the image to delineate the drawing area.

[b] Activate one of these tools: ✏️, 🖌️ or 🖍️.

You looked briefly at the characteristics of these tools when the 🧽 tool was described in chapter 2.

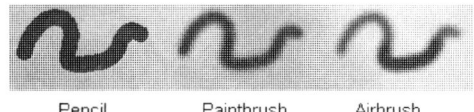

Pencil   Paintbrush   Airbrush

Notice the slightly rough, highly contrasted outline produced by the ✏️ tool compared with that produced by the 🖌️ tool. The 🖍️ tool gives a result similar to that of the paintbrush. Note however the difference in line thickness produced by this tool. This is due to the Airbrush's pressure setting: the longer you hold the tool on one area, the thicker the line produced, as there will be a build-up of colour.

➟ Here, activate the 🖌️ tool.

Chapter 3

[c] If the **Options** palette is hidden, show it by clicking its tab on the palette group or double-click the [/] tool.

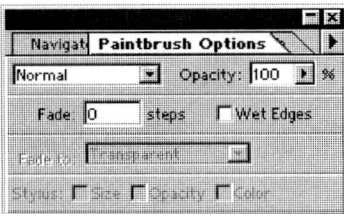

[d] Select a **Painting Mode** if necessary.

The various modes let you obtain special effects (cf. Chapter 4).

➤ Here, you do not need to use another mode than **Normal** for now.

[e] Change the path's **Opacity** if necessary: the lower the opacity value, the more transparent the path.

*The **Opacity** option is replaced by a **Pressure** option when using the [/] tool. This allows you to adjust how fast colour builds up when using the airbrush.*

➤ Here, leave the **Opacity** at **100%**.

[f] Use the **Fade** option to draw a path that fades to transparency or to the background colour.

As with the [/] tool, the number of fade steps varies between 1 and 9999. A value of 0 ensures no fade is added.

Fade to transparent   Fade to background

➤ Here, leave the fade value at **0**.

[g] Activate the **Wet Edges** option if required (this is specific to the [/] tool). This produces a watercolour effect by leaving extra pigment on the brush outline:

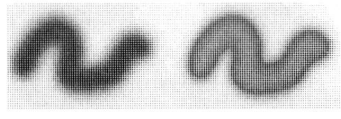

Without wet edges   With wet edges

Adobe Photoshop 5.5

Chapter 3

An *Auto Erase* option replaces the *Wet Edges* option for the ▭ tool. *This option lets you paint using the foreground colour, providing the pixels where you start painting are not the same as the foreground colour. If these pixels are already in the foreground colour, you will paint with the background colour. This technique is especially helpful when used in conjunction with masks, as you will see later on.*

➠ Here, you do not need to activate the **Wet Edges** option.

☐h Select a foreground colour for your drawing. If you are using a fade to background, select a background colour too.

➠ Here, select a colour of your choice that is sufficiently contrasted with the image's background colour (red, for example).

☐i If the **Brushes** palette is hidden, display it by clicking its tab or using **Window - Show Brushes** then select a brush type.

➠ Here, select a medium-sized brush, avoiding the very large types at the bottom of the palette.

☐j Point to the place where you wish to start drawing and drag the pointer to draw. You can hold down ⇧Shift as you drag to make a horizontal or vertical line. To draw lines at different angles (creating zigzags, polygons...), hold down ⇧Shift and start to draw then click another point on the canvas: the line will be drawn to that point.

➠ Here, draw anything you like.

Your drawing appears in the document.

Try out some of the various tools and options to see the different effects produced.

➠ Reduce the **Opacity** value to **40%** and drag to draw a line on the image.

The drawing is transparent and the background shows through it.

➠ **Edit - Undo**

➠ Return the **Opacity** to **100%**, activate the **Wet Edges** option and draw a line.

The outline of the path is opaque and the central part of it is slightly transparent.

➠ **Edit - Undo**

➠ Deactivate the **Wet Edges** option, set the **Fade** to **50** steps towards **Transparent** and draw a line.

The path becomes more and more transparent as you draw.

➠ **Edit - Undo**

➠ Set the **Fade** option towards **Background** and draw a line.

The path is a gradient, running from the foreground colour into the background colour.

➠ **Edit - Undo**

➠ Set the **Fade** at **0** steps to deactivate the fade option.

» Now, activate the [✎] tool, select a medium-sized brush type from the **Brushes** palette and draw a line.

The path drawn has stark, slightly rough edges.

» Activate the **Auto Erase** option and drag firstly over your previous path then draw a new line near it.

The first path drawn appears in the background colour and the second in the foreground colour.

» **Edit - Undo**
» Deactivate the **Auto Erase** function.
» Activate the [✎] tool and draw a line, holding the tool over some areas (that is, drag very slowly from time to time).

On these areas, the path appears thicker.

*Try using the Airbrush tool to draw in the lion's whiskers on the **Safari Chapter 2** drawing. You may remember that the whiskers were not correctly selected when the lion was inserted into the document.*

» Open the **Safari Chapter 2.psd** document (you could also use the **Safari.psd** document if you completed the whole of the second chapter).
» Zoom in on the lion's face to see it more clearly.
» Activate the **Lion** layer.
» Activate the [✎] tool and select a colour by clicking one of the white hairs on the lion's face.
» Activate the [✎] tool, set the **Fade** option at 8 steps towards **Transparent**. Select the smallest brush type possible in the **Brushes** palette and drag to draw four or five small lines from the lion's cheek outwards. If you are not satisfied with the result, cancel and try again.

This shows how the [✎] tool can be used for retouching.

» Close the **Safari Chapter 2.psd** document without saving it.

Chapter 3

2

You have just seen how to use the drawing tools to make lines, but there is also a tool specifically designed to draw straight lines or arrows.

DRAWING STRAIGHT LINES OR ARROWS

[a] If necessary, activate the layer on which you wish to draw your line or arrow.

➺ Here, the document only contains one layer.

[b] Select a foreground colour for the line.

➺ Here, select the colour of your choice.

[c] Activate the ◩ tool (it can be found in the same tool group as the ◲ tool).

[d] If the Options palette is hidden, show it by clicking its tab or double-clicking the ◩ tool.

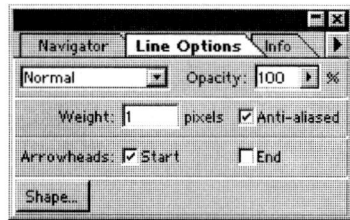

[e] If necessary, adjust the **Painting Mode** (cf. Chapter 4) as well as the **Opacity** value for the drawing.

➺ Here, keep the **Normal** mode and **100% Opacity**.

[f] Define the stroke's **Weight** (width) in pixels in the corresponding text box.

➺ Here, enter **2** pixels.

[g] Activate the **Anti-aliased** option to draw arrows or diagonals without a jagged edge.

➺ Here, leave this option active.

[h] Activate the **Start** and/or **End** options to draw a line with an arrowhead at the beginning or the end of the line.

➺ Here, activate the **End** option.

[i] If drawing an arrowhead, click the **Shape** button to define the arrowhead shape.

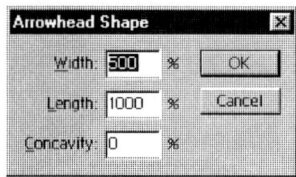

You will not be able to draw an arrow with different arrowheads at the beginning and at the end.

Chapter 3

Define the shape:

Width determines the width of the arrowhead relative to the line. If the width of the line is 2 pixels and the arrow width is set at 500%, the arrow width will be 10 pixels (or five times greater than the line width). This width can vary from 10 to 1000%.

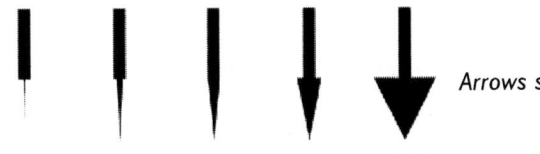

Arrows showing various arrowhead widths.

10% 50% 100% 200% 500%

Length determines the length of the arrowhead relative to the width of the line. This length can vary from 10 to 5000%.

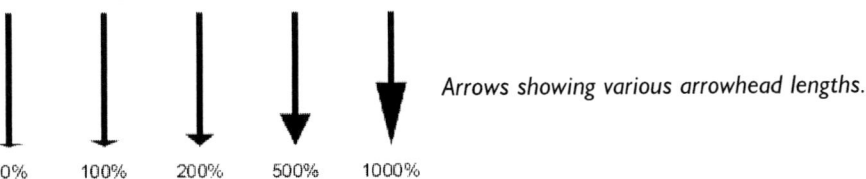

Arrows showing various arrowhead lengths.

50% 100% 200% 500% 1000%

Concavity modifies the part of the arrowhead that joins the line, to make it concave or convex. This value can vary between -50% and 50%.

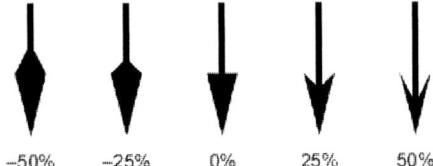

−50% −25% 0% 25% 50%

➤ Here, leave the default values as entered.

[j] Drag to draw the line. You can use the [⇧ Shift] key to draw the line vertically or horizontally or along a 45° angle.

➤ Here, draw the line of your choice.

A line complete with an arrowhead is drawn.

If you wish you can change the various option values to draw lines with different arrowheads before closing the document.

➤ Close the document and open the one called **Lion.jpg**.

Adobe Photoshop 5.5

Chapter 3

There is one last drawing tool, which has some special qualities: this is the paint bucket tool.

USING THE PAINT BUCKET TO CHANGE THE COLOUR OF PIXELS

[a] If necessary, activate the layer on which you wish to colour an area.

➡ Here, the document only contains a **Background** layer.

[b] Select a foreground colour as a fill colour or define a pattern (you will look at this possibility later on).

➡ Here, select red as the foreground colour.

[c] Activate the ⬚ tool.

[d] If the **Options** palette is hidden, show it by clicking its tab or double-clicking the ⬚ tool.

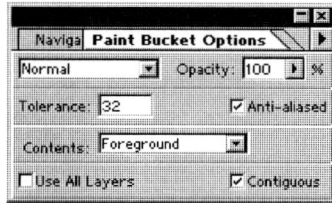

[e] If necessary, adjust the **Painting Mode** (cf. Chapter 4) as well as the **Opacity** value for the drawing.

➡ Here, keep a **Normal** mode and **50% Opacity**.

[f] Set a tolerance level between 0 and 255. If the **Tolerance** is very low, only similarly coloured pixels to the one you click will be filled.

The ⬚ tool has a similar function to that of the ⬚ tool. In the first case, you fill in pixels of a certain colour, whereas for the second you select them. In both cases, the tools identify and use similar colours.

➡ Here, set the **Tolerance** at **120**.

[g] Activate the **Anti-aliased** option to avoid jagged edges on the outline of the filled area.

➡ Here, this option should be active.

[h] Choose what you wish to fill with from the **Contents** list, either the **Foreground** colour or a **Pattern** if one has been defined.

➡ Here, leave the **Foreground** option active.

[i] Activate **Use All Layers** to fill in the active layer with sampled colour taken from all layers present.

➡ Here, leave this option deactivated.

Chapter 3

- [j] Activate the **Contiguous** option to fill adjacent pixels only. If the option is not active, all the pixels which meet the tolerance criterion are filled.
- ➤ Here, leave this option active.
- [k] Click one of the pixels whose colour you want to modify.
- ➤ Here, click in the bottom left corner of the image.
  The sky becomes purple, as you are using 50% Opacity and red plus blue produces purple.

> ✓ The [🪣] tool depends greatly on the use of *Tolerance* and tends to produce an unpredictable result. It can be quicker to fill pixels by selecting an area and using *Edit - Fill* or by creating a specific layer for the fill and using the *Use All Layers* option with the [🪣] tool to fill the layer.

Try this method.

- ➤ **Edit - Undo**
- ➤ Create a new layer: type `Ctrl` `⇧ Shift` **N** then click **OK**.
- ➤ Activate the **Use All Layers** option in the paint bucket **Options** palette and set the **Opacity** at **100%**.
- ➤ Check that the new layer is active then click the bottom left corner of the image then under the lion's tail and between his back legs.
  The sky becomes red.
- ➤ On the **Layers** palette, set the **Opacity** to **50%**.
  The sky has the same purple colour you created before. This colour does however seep onto the lion: this is due to an overly high Tolerance level.

Since the results are not satisfactory, you had better return to the last saved version of this document. You are going to try out another tool but, before you do, you will need to make a copy of the background.

- ➤ **File - Revert**
- ➤ **Layer - Duplicate Layer**
- ➤ Enter **Leap** in the As text box and click **OK**.
  A layer called Leap is created automatically.
- ➤ Hide the **Background** layer.

Chapter 3

4 *Some images do not have a clear outline, which makes them difficult to select. The lion is a good example of this. Its fur and whiskers do not stand out sharply from the background, making it difficult to separate the animal from its background without cropping it. Photoshop provides an effective solution to this problem.*

EXTRACTING THE FOREGROUND OF AN IMAGE

[a] If you are working on an image made up of several layers, activate the layer containing the detail to extract.

⟹ Here, the **Leap** layer should be active.

[b] **Image**
     Extract   Ctrl Alt **X**

A dialog box appears.

[c] Define the **Brush Size** for the **Edge Highlighter** (the tool which selects the area to extract). To make the best selection possible, use a fine brush where the outline is sharp and a thicker brush in places where it is less clear, like the lion's belly or whiskers.

⟹ Here the default value of **10** will work very well for the lion.

[d] If the default colours are too close to the colours of the image, change the **Highlight** and **Fill** colours, so that you can see what you are selecting.

⟹ Here, leave the default colours.

[e] Set a value for the **Smooth** option, which removes stray background pixels from the selection.

⟹ Here, enter a value of **50**

Chapter 3

[f] Activate the **Force Foreground** option if the background does not contrast well with the object which you are extracting (and especially if the background is solid colour). Click the **Color** box and choose the colour to use for highlighting the selection or activate the ![] tool and click the colour in the preview area.

▶ Here, the lion stands out well and there is no need to set these options.

[g] If you have already selected an object to extract and saved the selection, you can restore it via the **Load Highlight** list.

▶ Here, the option is greyed out because there is no selection saved.

[h] Activate the ![] tool to outline your selection.

[i] Point to the edge of the object and drag to outline it. Make sure your outline overlaps both the object you are selecting and (importantly) the background. If you have activated the **Force Foreground** option, you should also fill in the outline with the ![] tool.

▶ Here, outline the lion as shown:

[j] If you go wrong with your outline, activate the ![] tool and drag over the part you need to correct. Then reactivate ![] and continue outlining.

▶ Here, make corrections if you need to.

[k] Activate the ![] tool to fill in your outline, defining the area of the foreground to extract. If you are working with the **Force Foreground** option, your outline is already filled in: miss out this step and the next one.

▶ Here, you are not working with **Force Foreground**. Activate the tool.

[l] Click inside the outline.

▶ Here, click the lion.

The lion is coloured with the blue from the Fill list.

[m] Click the **Preview** button.

You can see the results of the extraction in the preview area of the dialog box. The parts of the image which you are discarding appear transparent.

Adobe Photoshop 5.5

Chapter 3

[n] Use the **Show** list to check the quality of the extraction. You can choose to see the extracted object on a background of a specific colour or presented as a **Mask** (similar to a stencil).

➠ Here, select **White Matte** from the **Show** list.

You can see exactly what you have extracted. If you have been successful, the lion's whiskers should be present, without any blue sky between them.

[o] If necessary, go back and modify your outline until you obtain a perfect result. Use the following options to help you:

View	To switch between the **Extracted** and **Original** views, so that you can see what effect your corrections are having.
Show Highlight	To show the selection outline.
Show Fill	To show the filled area of the foreground.

➠ Here, if you are not satisfied with your extraction, correct the outline.

[p] Click **OK**.

*The sky disappears from the **Leap** layer and only the lion remains.*

➠ Here, make the **Background** layer visible again. The sky is still there.

- ✓ *If the edges still need sharpening a little, you can use one of the following tools:* ▢ ▢ *or* ▢

- ✓ *The Extract dialog box includes a* ▢ *tool, which you can use to zoom in or out on the preview.*

- ✓ *If you have chosen a large zoom, use the dialog box's* ▢ *tool to see different parts of the image.*

5

You can apply a movement effect to the lion by using a rather interesting retouch tool called the Smudge tool. Imagine that your photo has been painted and the paint is still wet. The smudge tool produces an effect similar to spreading wet paint with your finger.

USING THE SMUDGE TOOL

[a] If necessary, activate the layer on which you want to work.

➠ Here, you are working on the **Leap** layer.

[b] Activate the ▢ tool (in the same tool group as the ▢ tool).

Chapter 3

|c| If the **Options** palette is hidden, show it by clicking its tab or double-clicking the ![tool] tool.

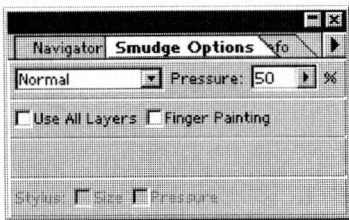

|d| Adjust the **Effect Mode** to the one you want to use (cf. Chapter 4).
➤ Here, once again, use **Normal** mode.

|e| Define the tool's **Pressure**. The higher it is, the more the colours you touch will be spread out.
➤ Here, leave **Pressure** at **50%**.

|f| Activate the **Use All Layers** option to spread a colour featured on another layer than the active one.
➤ Here, you can leave this option deactivated.

|g| Activate the **Finger Painting** option if you wish to spread the foreground colour as opposed to the colours on the image (as if you had dipped your fingers in paint beforehand).
➤ Here, leave this option deactivated.

|h| If the **Brushes** palette is hidden, display it by clicking its tab or using **Window - Show Brushes** then select a brush type.
➤ Here, select the brush with a diameter of **65**.

|i| Drag the zone you wish to smudge.
➤ Here, point to the lion's face and drag towards the left.
The lion's nose becomes "stretched out" and blurred.
This produces quite a humorous effect but it is not really the result you are looking for!
➤ **Edit - Undo**

You are aiming to give the impression that the lion is in motion.

➤ Select the brush type located above the active brush (or at least a smaller brush).

Adobe Photoshop 5.5   143

Chapter 3

Try to obtain a similar result to this one by using the technique described below.

Before using the tool   After using the tool

▶ Make a series of small "drags" with the mouse from the edge of the lion outwards. If any of these appear incorrect do not hesitate to cancel them and try again. You should choose different tools for different areas: when retouching under the lion's tail or around his back legs, you may need a smaller brush.

Close the picture of the lion, saving it under another name then open a different picture.

▶ **File - Save As**
▶ Enter **Leaping Lion** as the File Name, click the Save button then OK.
▶ **File - Close**
▶ Open the **Tusk.jpg** document.

---

6 You have already seen how to blur a layer or selection using filters. To retouch smaller areas, there are other retouching tools that you can use.

BLURRING OR SHARPENING PART OF AN IMAGE

[a] If necessary, activate the layer you want to work on.

▶ Here, the document only has a **Background** layer.

[b] Activate one of the following tools:

     To blur the chosen area.
     To obtain a greater contrast over the chosen area.

 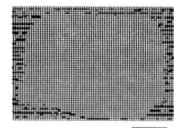 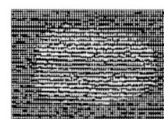

Original image   After using the tool   After using the tool

Chapter 3

Be careful, these tools may produce opposite effects but you should not use one to correct unsatisfactory work made with the other one, as you will probably not obtain the image you started out with. If the image turns out too blurry or too sharp, it would be best to cancel and start again.

➠ Here, activate the ⬙ tool.

c If the **Options** palette is hidden, show it by clicking its tab or double-clicking the ⬙ tool or the ⬙ tool.

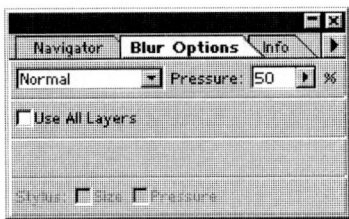

d Select the **Effect Mode** for the tool (cf. Chapter 4).

➠ Here, you will be using **Normal** mode.

e Adjust the **Pressure** you want to exert on the image. The higher the pressure, the more quickly the effect is produced. As an image is generally quite focussed, the ⬙ tool produces its effect more slowly. It is preferable to use a low level of pressure to avoid jagged edges.

➠ Here, adjust the **Pressure** to **70%**.

f Activate the **Use All Layers** option if you want the tools to blur or sharpen using data from all visible layers.

➠ Here, this option can be left inactive.

g If the **Brushes** palette is hidden, display it by clicking its tab or using **Window - Show Brushes** then select a brush type.

➠ Here, select a medium-sized brush.

h Drag over the area that should be more blurred or sharper. You can press ⌥Alt to switch to the ⬙ tool momentarily while you are using the ⬙ tool, and vice versa.

➠ Here, drag over part of the red area of the image.

The area where you used the ⬙ tool has become blurred.

✓ *To blur or sharpen large areas of a picture, it would be better to work with selections and/or layers and apply a Blur filter (Blur, Blur More and Gaussian Blur) or a Sharpen filter (Sharpen, Sharpen Edges, Sharpen More and Unsharp Mask).*

Adobe Photoshop 5.5

Chapter 3

Now try the ▲ tool.

- Activate the ▲ tool.
- Drag over the part of the image where you just used the ▲ tool, then drag over another area.

  Both areas are now more highly contrasted. The second area has pink, and maybe even white pixels within it.

You can use a sharpen filter on another picture.

- **File - Close** and click **No** when prompted to save.
- Open the **Giraffe.jpg** document.
- **Filter - Sharpen - Unsharp Mask**, which hardens the outlines and produces a more highly focussed image.
- Adjust the **Amount** of contrast to **50%** if necessary.
- Adjust the **Radius** surrounding the edge pixels that will be affected by the filter. Set it to **0.7**.
- The **Threshold** can be left at **0**.
- Click **OK**.

  The giraffe is noticeably sharper.

- If at first you do not really see any difference, watch the picture carefully then cancel the effect by pressing Ctrl **Z** and immediately redo the effect by pressing Ctrl **Z** again.

  *As a general rule, unless that is what you specifically require, avoid sharpening images too much as this tends to produce over-contrasted images. You will see in the last chapter entitled Extra Information more detailed explanations on how to use the **Sharpen** filters.*

  Save your picture.

- Close it then open the **Kilimanjaro.jpg** document.

---

7 *Some of the retouching tools allow you to modify the luminosity of an image.*

DARKENING OR LIGHTENING PART OF AN IMAGE

[a] If necessary, activate the layer on which you want to work.
- Here, there is only a **Background** layer.

[b] Activate one of the following tools:
- ● to lighten an area of the image.
- ● to darken an area of the image.

146 Adobe Photoshop 5.5

Chapter 3

Be careful, these tools may produce opposite effects but you should not use one to correct unsatisfactory work made with the other one, as you will probably not obtain the image you started out with.

▸ Here, activate the ▨ tool.

[c] If the **Options** palette is hidden, show it by clicking its tab or double-clicking the ▨ tool.

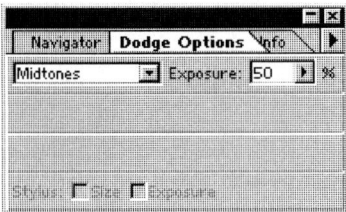

[d] Define which tones within the image you want to retouch:

Shadows	To work on dark parts of the image. This option adds white when you are working with the ▨ tool. If you are using this option, avoid using the ▨ tool on light or medium-coloured areas as they will fade to white.
Midtones	To change the luminosity over most areas of the image.
Highlights	To work on light tones. This option adds black when you use it with the ▨ tool. When choosing this option, avoid using the ▨ tool on midtones as they will fade towards black.

▸ Here, leave the **Midtones** option active.

[e] Modify the **Exposure** option to adjust how fast the image will be lightened or darkened.

▸ Here, leave a value of **50%**.

[f] If the **Brushes** palette is hidden, display it by clicking its tab or using **Window - Show Brushes** then select a brush type.

▸ Here, select a fairly large brush type.

[g] Drag over the area that should be lightened or darkened. You can press [Alt] if you wish to switch briefly from the ▨ tool to the ▨ tool and vice versa.

▸ Here, drag over the leaves on the tree to the left of the picture.

The tree loses some black colour and becomes yellow-green.

Adobe Photoshop 5.5

Chapter 3

Now use the ▨ tool.

▸ Activate the ▨ tool.

▸ Drag over the path seen at the bottom of the picture.
   The path was a beige colour but now is more brown.

This result is not really satisfactory, revert to the last saved version of the photo.

▸ **File - Revert**

---

8 *You have seen how to adjust the luminosity and contrast on small areas of a picture, now you can learn how to do this over an entire image or layer. First, you must analyse your photo.*

CHECKING THE TONAL RANGE OF A PICTURE

[a] For a document made of several layers, hide all the layers except the one that you wish to check. If you leave several layers visible you will obtain an overall information about all these layers.

[b] **Image**
Histogram

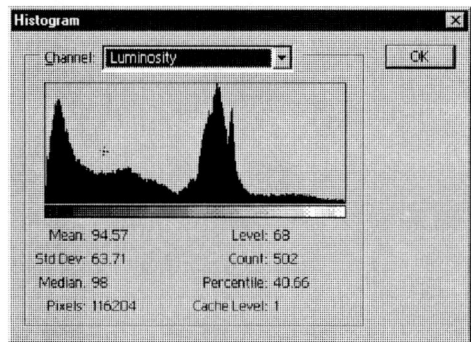

*You can make an overall analysis of the picture using the **Luminosity** option or by each layer of colour to trace any colour dominants.*

Various information is provided:

Mean Indicates the average luminosity (or brightness).

Std Dev Indicates how far values differ from the average.
(standard deviation)

Median Indicates the luminosity threshold between 50% of light pixels and 50% of dark pixels. This information can be helpful if you wish to obtain a better balance in the image's brightness.

Chapter 3

Pixels	Indicates the number of pixels used in calculating the histogram. This number can vary, depending on the **Cache Level** value shown opposite. Generally **Cache Level 1** is shown, which means all the pixels on the image.
Level	When you move the pointer over the histogram, Photoshop indicates for which brightness level it is showing the other values, **Count** and **Percentile**.
Count	Indicates the number of pixels at this **Level** of brightness.
Percentile	Indicate the percentage of pixels located at or below the **Level** shown.

With a poor quality image you will obtain a histogram with large gaps and a low number of pixels, like this:

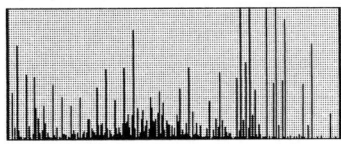

In this case, retouching is useless because there are not enough details on the picture. You should digitize your picture again if you wish to print a correct result.

[c] To be sure that the quality of your image is good, check its **black point** by pointing to the left edge of the histogram.

*If the value which appears in **Level** is greater than 10, the image lacks detail in its dark areas.*

[d] Next check its **white point** by positioning the pointer at the right edge of the histogram. If the **Level** value is less than 240, detail is poor in the light areas of the image.

If the dark areas of your image are more detailed than the light ones, the histogram will look like this one:

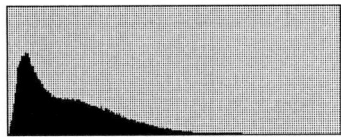

If the light areas of your image are more detailed, the histogram will look like this one:

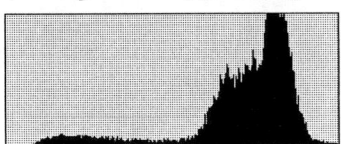

Adobe Photoshop 5.5

Chapter 3

If your image is more homogenous, with an average tonal range, the histogram will appear more like this:

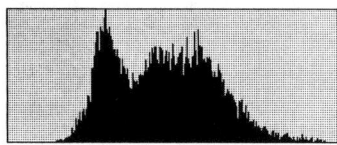

▶ Here, note the **Median** value (98), you will use it a little later on.

[e] Click **OK**.

- ✓ *If the image has Alpha channels or spot colour channels, you can make them available in the Channel list in the Histogram dialog box by holding down the Alt key while you run the Image - Histogram command.*

- ✓ *The histogram is not always absolutely accurate. To confirm the black point and white point readings, use the Image - Adjust - Levels command.*

9 *Now, modify the image contrast and brightness.*

ADJUSTING CONTRAST AND/OR BRIGHTNESS ON AN IMAGE

THE SIMPLIFIED METHOD

[a] If necessary, activate the layer on which you want to work. You can also make a selection to limit your retouching to that selection.

[b] **Image**
Adjust
Brightness/Contrast

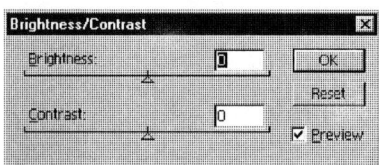

[c] Drag the sliders to adjust the **Brightness** and/or **Contrast** levels or enter a value between -100 and 100 in the corresponding text boxes.

A negative value darkens the picture or dims the contrast and a positive values lightens or increases contrast.

▶ Here, drag the sliders in different ways to view the effects produced.

Chapter 3

|d| Click **OK**.

➠ Here, click the **Reset** button because you are going to try another method.

✓ This method is easy to use but has the disadvantage of being imprecise and can quickly distort the picture quality, especially in relation to brightness:

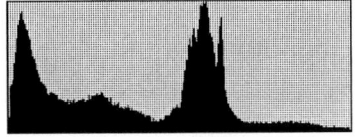
Before lightening with
Brightness/Contrast

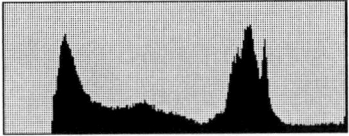
After lightening with
Brightness/Contrast

You can see a noticeable shift in the histogram, with a loss of data in the dark areas of the image.

Before continuing, open another image without closing the one of Kilimanjaro.

➠ Open the **Mask (Layer)** document.

BY MODIFYING THE HISTOGRAM

|a| If necessary, activate the layer on which you need to work.

➠ Here, there is only one layer.

|b| **Image**
Adjust
Levels

Ctrl L

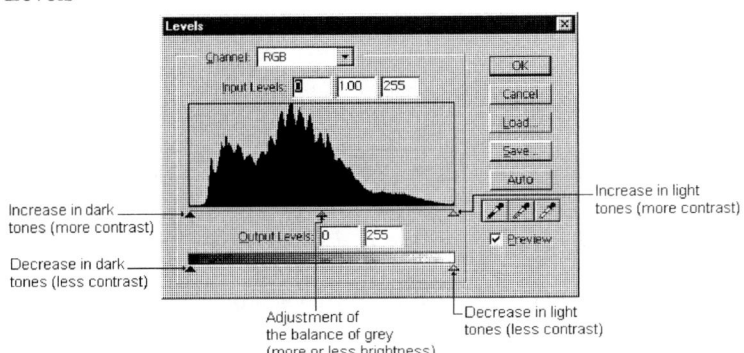

Adobe Photoshop 5.5   151

Chapter 3

[c] Adjust the various sliders depending on whether you wish to increase or decrease the contrast. To increase brightness, move the slider for the balance of grey towards the left; to decrease it, move the slider to the right. You can also enter values straight into the text boxes. For the grey balance, a value greater than 1 lightens the image whereas a value less than 1 darkens it. For a quick, but generally good retouch, adjust the contrast sliders to meet each edge of the histogram, as shown here:

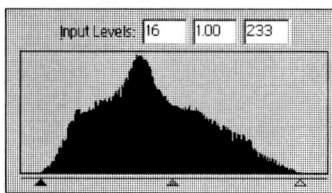

For a more precise retouch, use the **Channel** option and work in the same way on each colour channel on the picture instead of just treating the **RGB** composite. However, avoid using this method unless you are correcting a colour dominant.

➠ Here, the mask contains a rather marked yellow dominant. Since there is only a negligible amount of pixels at each extreme of the histogram, you can bring the sliders a little closer to the centre in order to see a noticeable difference in the contrast (leave the **Channel** choice as **RGB**):

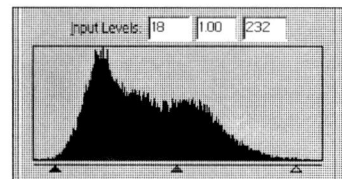

[d] Click **OK**.

The mask has a clearer contrast but retains its yellow dominant.

✓ *This retouch command is better adapted to the RGB, Lab or grayscale modes. You should avoid using it on images in CMYK mode as the histogram produced for these types of images is very different and you will doubtless end up with an imprecise result. When working with Lab mode, only work on the L channel so as not to alter the colour dominants.*

✓ *It is possible to Save the adjustments made and to Load them into another picture, using the corresponding buttons.*

✓ *The Auto button produces the equivalent effect to the Image - Adjust - Auto Levels command.*

Chapter 3

Cancel this retouch.

▸ **Edit - Undo**

USING AUTOMATIC LEVELS

|a| If necessary, activate the layer you wish to retouch.

▸ Here, that is not necessary.

|b| Define the options for automatic levels and contrasts if necessary: use the command **Image - Adjust - Levels** or **Image - Adjust - Curves**. Hold down the [Alt] key and the **Auto** button changes into an **Options** button.

|c| Click this **Options** button.

▸ Here, use **Image - Adjust - Levels**, hold down [Alt] and click **Options**.

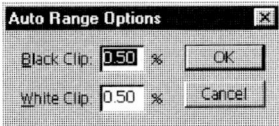

|d| Set the **Black Clip** and **White Clip** values between 0 and 9.99%. The higher the clip, the higher (or even more excessive) the contrast produced. However you should always specify a value of at least 0.01 (or a value higher than zero) so that small defects in the picture do not interfere with the automatic contrast.

▸ Here, specify a value of **0.10** for both options.

|e| Click **OK** on the **Auto Range Options** dialog box then the **Cancel** button on the **Levels** or **Curves** dialog box.

▸ Here, click **OK** then **Cancel**.

|f| **Image**   [Ctrl] [⇧ Shift] **L**
Adjust
Auto Levels

The contrast is automatically adjusted and the yellow dominant is removed.

> ✓ *With an image in RGB mode, any colour dominant will be removed, if it is not too exaggerated.*

> ✓ *As this method changes the histogram, avoid using it on images in CMYK.*

> ✓ *To make an automatic adjustment on the brightness as well as the contrast, you can also use the Image - Adjust - Equalize command (cf. Extra Information).*

Adobe Photoshop 5.5

Chapter 3

The contrast is now too high on this picture. Cancel your last action.

➡ **Edit - Undo**

USING AUTOMATIC CONTRAST

[a] If necessary, activate the layer on which you will be working.

➡ This is not necessary here.

[b] Change the **Auto Range** settings, as described in the previous section on automatic levels.

➡ Here, leave the options as you set them.

[c] **Image**   `Ctrl` `Alt` `⇧ Shift` **L**
Adjust
Auto Contrast
The contrast is adjusted, but the yellow dominant remains.

☑ *On an RGB image, the Auto Contrast command increases the contrast without affecting the image's dominant colours. This is the difference between this command and Image - Adjust - Auto Levels.*

☑ *Because this method changes the histogram, you should not use it on CMYK images.*

The contrast produced by this command is still too marked for your picture. Cancel again.

➡ **Edit - Undo**

*Go back to the image of Kilimanjaro, without closing the **Mask (Layer).psd** document.*

➡ **Window - Kilimanjaro.jpg**

BY ADJUSTING THE CURVES

[a] If it is not already active, activate the layer on which you want to work.

➡ Here, you are working on the **Background** layer.

[b] **Image**   `Ctrl` **M**
Adjust
Curves

Chapter 3

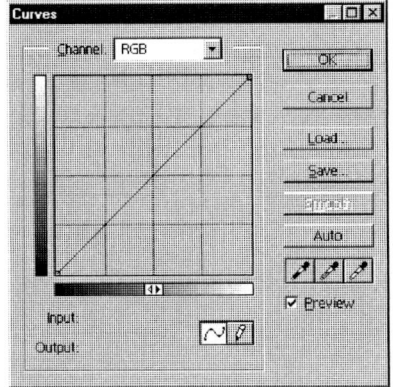

*The horizontal axis represents the original pixel values (or **Input** values), and the vertical axis represents the new values (or **Output** values). At the outset, the diagonal line is straight.*

|c| Before making any corrections, check the luminosity bar situated below the curve. If you are working with an image in RGB, this bar should be like this by default: . With an image in CMYK, Lab or grayscale, the bar will run in the other direction: . This is very important, because, when the orientation of this bar changes, the brightness curve will be inverted to achieve the same result. You can click the double arrow in the middle of this bar to switch over its orientation.

|d| To define a curve, use the buttons:

To define an even curve from selected points along it. To add a point, click along the curve or point to the area on the image you wish to correct and Ctrl-click: the output point corresponding to the pixel you have clicked will be created on the curve. You can adjust the points created by dragging them. Up to 14 points can be added in this way.

To draw a curve manually by dragging it or by using ⇧Shift-clicks to draw straight lines. You can click the **Smooth** button to smooth out the new curve.

With an RGB image whose luminosity bar looks like this: , depending on the result required, define your curves in the following ways:

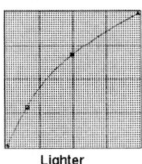
Lighter

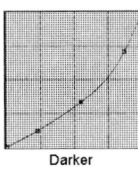
Darker

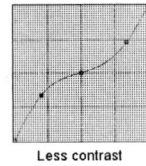
Less contrast

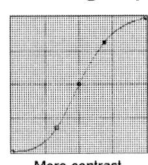
More contrast

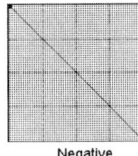
Negative

Adobe Photoshop 5.5

Chapter 3

To change an image's contrast you can add a point in the middle of the curve to lock the midpoint. This allows you to work exclusively on the dark and/or light tones.

With an image in CMYK, Lab or grayscale mode, whose luminosity bar is like this: ▬▬▬▬, use curves similar to these:

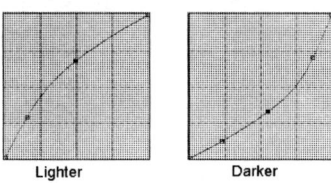

Lighter   Darker

The same types of contrast and negative curves are used for both RGB, CMYK and grayscale images. For those in Lab mode, you need to work on the **L**, **a** and **b** **Channels** separately to achieve an equivalent contrast or negative effect.

Unless you wish to make a particular effect (the result of which may be difficult to predict), avoid curves that could be cut in several places by an imaginary horizontal line:

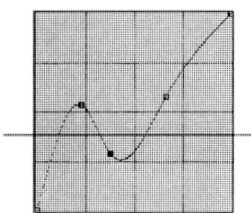

In this example, the curve can be cut in three places by the black line shown.

[e] When you add a point, the **Input** and **Output** values are indicated. Instead of changing the curve by dragging you can add specific values in these text boxes.

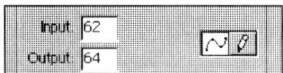

These values range between 0 and 255 for an RGB image and between 0 and 100% for images in CMYK, Lab or grayscale. If the luminosity bar faces this way: ▬▬▬▬ *(RGB images) an output value higher than the input value produces a lightening (more light) effect, and vice versa. If the luminosity bar faces the other way:* ▬▬▬▬ *(CMYK, Lab or grayscale images), an output value higher than the input value produces a darkening (more dark tones) effect and vice versa.*

In the same way as for the levels, you can work on the individual **Channels** *in an image by using the corresponding option. For images in Lab mode, this is compulsory as you cannot work on a composite channel as you can with RGB or CMYK images.*

➤ Here, define an input point at level 98 with an output point of 128. Click next to the curve, select the number in the **Input** text box and enter **98**, then select what is in the **Output** box and enter **128**.

Chapter 3

The input level of 98 was chosen according to the *Median* level shown earlier using **Image - Histogram**. The output level of 128 corresponds to the average brightness value. This allows you to achieve a better brightness balance in the picture.

[f] To delete a fixed point, drag it out of the curve area, or click it and press [Del].

[g] Click **OK**.

The image has been significantly brightened.

- ✓ This method is less easy to use when you are starting out, but gives a more precise result than the *Image - Adjust - Levels* command, because it does not only adjust according to the dark or light tones but in relation to all the tones in the image. Furthermore, it is suitable for all types of images.

- ✓ You can also hold down the [Ctrl] [⇧ Shift] keys and click the image to fix a point, not on its composite channel but on the curves of all the colour component channels. This can produce a more precise correction in relation to a given hue.

- ✓ It is possible to *Save* the adjustments made and to *Load* them into another picture, using the corresponding buttons.

- ✓ The *Auto* button produces the equivalent effect to the *Image - Adjust - Auto Levels* command.

Check how the image's brightness has been redistributed.

➤ **Image - Histogram**

The *Median* is now 126, which means an almost equal distribution of dark and light tones. Note that this may be useful for this particular image but this may not be the case for every photo you work on.

Go back now to the image of the mask, without closing the picture of Kilimanjaro.

➤ **Window - Mask (Layer).psd**

USING THE BLACK POINT AND WHITE POINT OF AN IMAGE

[a] If necessary, activate the layer on which you will be working.

➤ Here, this is not necessary.

[b] If the **Info** palette is hidden, click its tab or display it with the **Window - Show Info** command.

Adobe Photoshop 5.5

Chapter 3

[c] **Image**
Adjust
Levels or Curves

[Ctrl] **L** or [Ctrl] **M**

➡ Here, select the **Levels** command in order to see the modifications made to the histogram.

[d] Select the ![] tool in the dialog box and click an area on the image or layer that corresponds to the darkest tones. Use the information supplied by the **Info** palette to select a pixel whose RGB components are the lowest.

➡ Here, select the tool then click the black vertical bar located at the bottom of the mask.

The mask has more contrast in the dark areas and the histogram builds up towards the left.

[e] Select the ![] tool in the dialog box then click on the lightest part of the image. Use the **Info** palette to help you find the pixel whose RGB components are the highest (the first piece of data shows the initial value and the second shows the value as corrected with the ![] tool).

➡ Here, select the tool then click the golden triangle located over the left eye.

The mask is now highly contrasted and the histogram becomes more balanced.

[f] Click **OK**.

➡ Here, click the **Cancel** button as the contrast is too great.

✓ *This method can be useful when the images already have fairly good brightness and contrast.*

✓ *You can modify the preferences of the ![] tool to define the black and white points from the average values and not from the values of the most extreme pixels (Point Sample option). To do this, show the Options palette and adjust the tool before proceeding.*

✓ *You can define the white and black points at a certain value by double-clicking the ![] tool to display the Color Picker. Set the components for the black point then click OK. Proceed in the same way for the ![] tool.*

✓ *The ![] tool is used when you want to change the balance of greys in the image. Be careful: only use this tool on a very neutral area (a grey) or on a very dominant colour in order to correct it. If you click another area in an image, a very random correction is made, resulting in a marked distortion of colours.*

A correct contrast of the mask can be achieved without losing the yellow dominant.

➡ **Image - Adjust - Levels**

➡ Move the output level slider to **18** for the dark tones and **232** for light tones then click **OK**.

Chapter 3

10 You can now remove the yellow dominant from the mask by adjusting the image's colour proportion.

ADJUSTING THE PROPORTIONS OF COLOUR IN AN IMAGE

USING THE SIMPLIFIED METHOD

[a] If necessary, activate the layer on which you wish to work or select an area of the image to limit your retouching.

[b] **Image**
Adjust
Variations

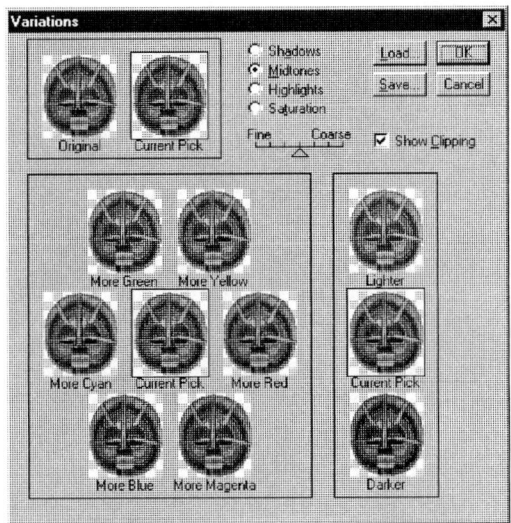

[c] Select the tones with which you want to work: **Shadows**, **Midtones** or **Highlights**. To change the intensity of the colours, use the **Saturation** option.

➤ Here, check that you are working on the **Midtones**.

[d] Change the speed of the adjustment by moving the **Fine/Coarse** slider. Each marker on this scale indicates that this speed is doubled (or halved).

➤ Here, leave the speed as set.

[e] Leave the **Show Clipping** option active to display the pixels in a bright colour that will become black or white (depending on whether the active option is **Shadows** or **Highlights**). If the **Saturation** option is being used, the **Show Clipping** option allows you to see if any pixels exceed the maximum saturation.

Adobe Photoshop 5.5

Chapter 3

[f] To adjust the colour proportions, click one of the **More [Colour]** variations (**More Green**, **More Yellow**...). You can also click the **Lighter** or **Darker** choices to modify the image brightness.

➤ Here, click once on the **More Blue** variation, as blue is opposite to yellow and this should correct the yellow dominant.

Each time you click a variation, all the variations consequently change: the Original preview allows you to compare the picture before and after retouching.

➤ Click **OK**.

The mask no longer has its yellowish tint.

- ✓ *This method, which is very easy to use, can be used on images that do not require a very precise adjustment.*

- ✓ *The Image - Adjust - Variations command requires considerable memory, so do not use it on large documents or if you do not have a lot of available memory.*

- ✓ *It is possible to Save the adjustments made and to Load them into another picture, using the corresponding buttons.*

Cancel this to look at another method.

➤ **Edit - Undo**

BY ADJUSTING THE COLOR BALANCE

[a] If necessary, activate the layer on which you wish to work or select an area of the image to limit the adjustment to that area.

[b] **Image**
Adjust
Color Balance

[Ctrl] **B**

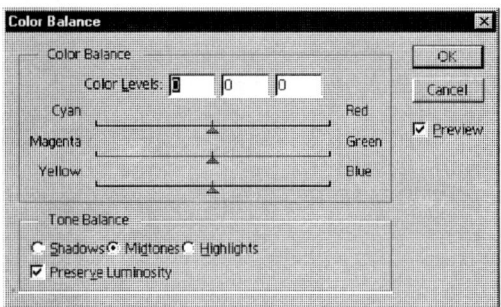

[c] Select the tones with which you want to work: **Shadows**, **Midtones** or **Highlights**.

▸ Here, leave **Midtones** active.

[d] With an image in RGB, leave the **Preserve Luminosity** option active to preserve the harmony between dark, light and midtones, without changing the image brightness.

[e] Drag a slider to increase the proportion of a specific colour in the chosen image or layer. You can also enter a value of between -100 and +100 in the **Color Levels** text boxes (the first box corresponds to the first slider, and so on).

▸ Here, remove the yellow dominant by dragging the **Yellow/Blue** slider towards blue to a value of **+34**.

[f] Click **OK**.

The yellow tint is removed but in a more subtle way than before.

> ✓ *This method is more precise than the variations method but tends to alter the image. This is especially the case for images not in RGB mode, where the brightness may be affected.*

Cancel this effect to see the last method.

▸ **Edit - Undo**

BY CHANGING THE HISTOGRAM OR THE CURVES

[a] If necessary, activate the layer on which you wish to work or select an area of the image to limit the adjustment to that area.

[b] To adjust the histogram, use:

Image   [Ctrl] **L**
Adjust
Levels

To adjust using the curves, use:

Image   [Ctrl] **M**
Adjust
Curves

▸ Here, use the **Image - Adjust - Levels** command.

Adobe Photoshop 5.5

Chapter 3

[c] To modify an image's colours, use the **Channel** option on the various dialog boxes (**Levels** or **Curves**) and adjust each channel on the image or layer.
To make the adjustment, look back at the section on Adjusting contrast and/or brightness on an image.

➠ Here, select the **Red** channel and set the output slider that increases the dark tones (the slider on the left) to **10**.
Select the **Green** channel and set the output slider for dark tones to **11**.
Select the **Blue** channel and set the output slider for light tones (the slider on the right) to **213**.
This last adjustment should eliminate the yellow dominant.

[d] Click **OK**.
The yellow dominant has been removed.

✓ *These last two methods are the more precise. Avoid other methods when you require a high quality result.*

11 *To improve an image you can work on the colour saturation in addition to adjusting the brightness and contrast. The mask could use some localized retouching.*

MODIFYING COLOUR SATURATION ON AN AREA OF AN IMAGE

[a] Activate if necessary the layer where the retouch is to be made.
[b] Activate the 🖫 tool situated in the same tool group as the ● and 🖫 tools.
[c] If the **Options** palette is hidden, show it by clicking its tab or double-clicking the 🖫 tool.

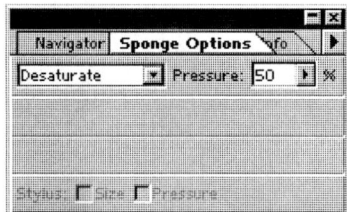

[d] Select the **Tool operations** mode:

Desaturate To dull the colour. The excessive use of this mode on an area will turn that section grey.

Saturate To give brilliance to a colour. If you accentuate a colour too much, it may become unprintable. In this case the printed image will no longer conform to the one viewed on the screen.

Chapter 3

- ⏵ Here, select the **Saturate** mode.
- ⓔ Adjust the **Pressure** to determine how quickly the image area will be saturated or unsaturated.
- ⏵ Here, set the **Pressure** to **60%**.
- ⓕ If the **Brushes** palette is not visible, display it with **Window- Show Brushes** then select a brush type.
- ⏵ Here, select the brush type that lies above the 65 diameter type.
- ⓖ Drag over the part of the image you want to modify.
- ⏵ Here, drag over the red part of the mask.

    The more you hold the 🖼 *tool on the image, the redder these areas become.*

    Try to desaturate the colour now.

- ⏵ Select the **Desaturate** mode in the **Options** palette then drag firstly over the red areas then over the yellow areas.

    The red zones become rapidly duller because they were quite intense. The yellow areas become practically grey.

    Close the **Mask (Layer).psd** *document without saving it then go back to the picture of Kilimanjaro.*

- ⏵ **File - Close** then click **No** to close without saving.

12
You can now see how to modify the hue and saturation for the various colour components of an image.

ADJUSTING INDIVIDUAL COLOUR COMPONENTS

BY MODIFYING THE HUE OR SATURATION

- ⓐ **Image**
  Adjust
  Hue/Saturation   　　　　　　　　　　　　　　　　　　Ctrl U

- ⓑ From the list, select the hue that you want to correct. The **Master** choice lets you work on all the image's colours at the same time. You can also work separately on the **Reds**, **Yellows**, **Greens**, **Blues**, **Cyans** or **Magentas**.

- ⏵ Here, select **Blues**.

Adobe Photoshop 5.5

Chapter 3

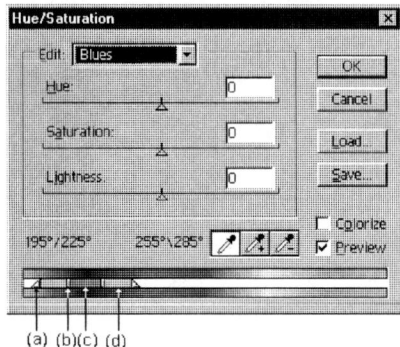
(a) (b)(c) (d)

Sliders appear in the color bar at the bottom of the dialog box. These sliders are placed along this bar according to the colour chosen. The triangular sliders (a) cordon off the total correction range, which by default takes in a 90° zone on the colour wheel. The rectangular sliders (b) show the main correction range corresponding to the selected colour; this covers a 30° zone on the colour wheel.

c You can drag these sliders to extend or compress the correction range. The values (in degrees) on the colour wheel that correspond to the range represented by the four sliders are seen above the color bar on the left.
Moving the dark grey area (c) moves the entire correction range, while dragging the light grey areas (d) changes the main correction range without affecting the "fall-off" ranges on either side (which show where the selected colour fades off into the next colour).

d When you select a colour other than **Master**, the [🖉] tool on the dialog box is activated. Click on the part of the image that contains the colour you want to modify.

➤ Here, click the section of sky that lies above Mount Kilimanjaro.

The total correction range is automatically adjusted to correspond to this colour (some of the cyan range is now included). You can increase the main correction range by activating the [🖉] tool then clicking part of the image. In the same way, you can reduce it with the [🖉] tool. You can also hold down [⇧ Shift] *with the* [🖉] *tool to activate the* [🖉] *tool momentarily or* [Alt] *to use the* [🖉] *tool momentarily.*

One of the sliders has moved down to the other end of the spectrum bar. If you find this difficult to work with, hold down [Ctrl] *then slide the spectrum bar along until the sliders are correctly placed again. Before moving the bar, make sure the mouse pointer has taken this form:* [✋].

e Make your corrections by dragging the sliders (located higher up in the dialog box):

Hue   To modify the colours. If you wish, the colour used can be completely changed. You can also define the **Hue** in the corresponding text box by setting a value between -180 and +180.

Saturation   To modify the brilliance of colours, much as with the [⊙] tool, but in an overall way on the image, layer, selection or to the chosen colour. You can also enter a value between -100 and +100 into the corresponding text box. The -100 value corresponds to a complete desaturation of the image and changes all the colours to grey.

Chapter 3

|Lightness|To modify the brightness with the same method as used by the **Image - Adjust - Brightness/Contrast** command. This method, as you have already seen, is not precise when working on a combination of all colours. Set a value here only for selected colours and not on the **Master** to avoid a loss of picture quality. For this option too you can enter a value of between -100 and +100 in the corresponding text box.|

⇒ Here, set the **Hue** at **+9** and the **Saturation** at **+7** to make the sky and the volcano a more vibrant blue.

[f] Click **OK**.

The sky and the whole top half of the image are a more significant blue colour. The bottom of the image, showing the earth and grass should not be modified.

- ✓ The *Colorize* option in the *Hue/Saturation* dialog box can modify all the colours on an image to give them the same hue and saturation. The brightness is not affected by this option. This can be used to colour an image that is in grayscale or even, when used with a layer or a selection, to simulate a two-tone picture from a colour picture. You will see more on that later on.

- ✓ You can also use this command to remove a colour dominant by selecting the corresponding colour and adjusting it, particularly by reducing the saturation.

- ✓ It is possible to *Save* the settings applied and to *Load* them into another picture, using the corresponding buttons.

- ✓ To unsaturate a picture rapidly, you can use the *Image - Adjust - Desaturate* or press [Ctrl][⇧ Shift] U. This will fade all the colours to grey. You can use this function to make one element of a picture stand out: part of the image would be in grayscale and the item you wish to highlight could be coloured.

Test this now by making a desaturation.

⇒ Open the **Giraffe.jpg** document.

⇒ Select the giraffe. Make a precise selection to obtain a high quality result. To do this, use several selection tools.

⇒ **Select - Inverse**

The whole image is selected apart from the giraffe.

⇒ **Image - Adjust - Desaturate**

The picture is now in grayscale except the giraffe which is no longer selected.

⇒ **Select - Deselect**

The selection border disappears and you can see that the giraffe clearly stands out from the background.

Adobe Photoshop 5.5

Chapter 3

Save this image under another name then close it.

▸ **File - Save As**
Enter **Highlighted Giraffe** as the **File name**, click the **Save** button then **OK**.

▸ **File - Close**

There is another method which allows you to adjust each colour component.

You are going to make the ground at the bottom of the picture less red and make the dark areas in the trees and bushes greener.

USING SELECTIVE COLOR

[a] If necessary, activate the layer you wish to retouch or select an area to limit the retouch effects.

[b] **Image**
Adjust
Selective Color

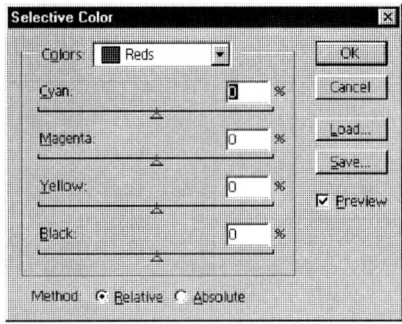

[c] In the **Colors** list, select the colour you wish to correct. You can work independently on the **Reds, Yellows, Greens, Cyans, Blues, Magentas, Whites, Neutrals** or **Blacks**.

▸ Here, you should select **Reds**.

[d] Under **Method**, activate:

Relative   If you want to keep the current colour proportions for each different hue.

Absolute   If you want to change the hues without taking the colour proportions into account. This can be used when changing one colour into another.

▸ Here, leave the **Relative** option active.

Chapter 3

[e] Drag the various sliders or enter a value of between -100 and +100 in the corresponding text boxes.

*The colours are modified according to their CMYK components, which necessitates a good understanding of this colour model. For example, red is mainly composed of **Magenta** and **Yellow**. This does not mean that you cannot add **Cyan** or **Black** to a red to dull or darken it. Whatever the hue, you can use all four sliders to correct it so as to tone it down, to accentuate it or even transform it into another colour.*

➤ Here, move the **Magenta** slider to **-20%**.
Select **Blacks** in the **Colors** list and set the **Cyan** slider at **+11%**, the **Yellow** slider at **+25%** and the **Black** slider at **-9%**.

[f] Click **OK**.

The trees are lighter and greener; the ground is now more orange than red.

✓ *Black is used in an image to supply contrast. Avoid excessively reducing or increasing the Whites, Neutrals or Blacks sliders, which may result in a marked deterioration in contrast.*

✓ *This technique can also be used to remove a colour dominant. To do this, select the colour with the corresponding option and adjust the components. If, for example, the dominant colour is blue, select Blues and reduce the Cyan and Magenta components.*

✓ *It is possible to Save the adjustments made and to Load them into another picture, using the corresponding buttons.*

13 *Change the colour of the sky by using a different technique from the Hue/Saturation command.*

REPLACING CERTAIN COLOURS ON AN IMAGE

[a] If necessary, select the layer that you want to retouch. Making a selection will help you achieve a better colour result unless you specifically want to work on an entire layer.

➤ Here, you are working on the whole image.

[b] **Image**
Adjust
Replace Color

Adobe Photoshop 5.5   167

Chapter 3

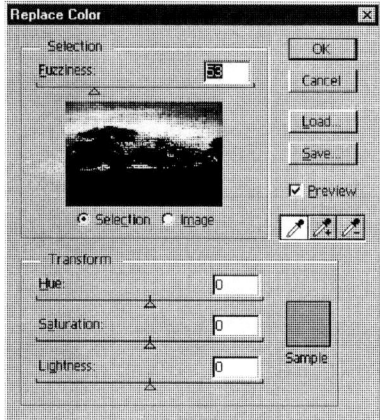

|c| To make your selection, use the following options:

Selection Lets you view the parts of the image that will be modified in the form of a mask. The white pixels will be changed, but not the black ones. The grey pixels will be partially modified.

Image Lets you view a thumbnail of the entire picture in the dialog box. This can be interesting when the document is viewed with a high zoom level. If you are using this option, remember to check the **Selection** result with the corresponding option.

➤ Here, leave the **Selection** option active.

|d| Select the colour you want to modify by using the 🖉 tool in the dialog box. Click the area on the image that corresponds to the chosen colour or on the preview screen in the dialog box. You can enlarge the selection by activating the 🖉 tool then clicking a place on the image. You can reduce the selection in the same way with the 🖉 tool. You can also hold down [Shift] with the 🖉 tool to activate the 🖉 tool momentarily or [Alt] to use the 🖉 tool momentarily.

➤ Here, click the sky.

|e| Vary the **Fuzziness** option so it takes into account more or less similar shades. If the selection was made before the command was activated, and you want to work on the entire image, set the **Fuzziness** to maximum level (200).

➤ Here, set the **Fuzziness** level to adjust the selection in the best way (you will have to select the volcano as well).

Chapter 3

[f] Select the new colour with the **Hue**, **Saturation** and **Lightness** sliders. The definition of this colour is identical to the method used with the **Image - Adjust - Hue/Saturation** command you saw previously. You can also enter values in the text boxes corresponding to the various sliders.

➤ Here, set the **Hue** slider to **+146** to give a setting sun effect.

[g] Click **OK**.

The sky becomes orange. Of course, to achieve a very realistic effect, the brightness and colours of the whole picture would need changing, which is a time-consuming process.

- ✓ As this method does not allow you to make very precise selections, you should restrict it to images with high colour contrast.

- ✓ For the best quality results, you should make a selection using the traditional selection tools. In this case, using this command becomes redundant as you need to make another selection. Use instead the *Image - Adjust - Hue/Saturation* command which allows you to make more delicate colour changes.

- ✓ It is possible to *Save* the adjustments made and to *Load* them into another picture, using the corresponding buttons.

This sky effect is not really suitable, so you can cancel it.

➤ **Edit - Undo**

---

14 *You are now going to look at the other possibilities offered by Photoshop to change the colours on an image. Start with a simple command: the **Invert** command, which creates a negative.*

CREATING A NEGATIVE

[a] If necessary, activate a layer or make a selection.

➤ Here, that is not necessary.

[b] **Image**
Adjust
Invert

[Ctrl] I

The image appears with its colours inverted.

Adobe Photoshop 5.5

Chapter 3

✓ The quality of the negative depends on the colours present in the image:

 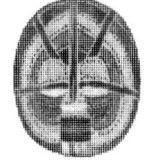 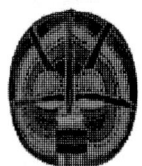

Inverted RGB image   Inverted Lab image   Inverted CMYK image

The negative produced with RGB and Lab images are similar except that the Lab image has more contrast and saturation. The negative produced from a CMYK image is however very different. On the example above, the negatives from the RGB and Lab images are blue, while the CMYK one is brown. If you wish to obtain a photographic-type negative, use this command on an image in RGB (or at a stretch Lab) or grayscale format.

✓ If you apply this command again, you will obtain a positive image, that is, the original. However if you try to recover a positive from a scanned photographic negative, this method will probably not suffice to produce a high quality image. The reason for this is that photographic colour negatives contain a coloured filter, generally orange which varies in intensity from film to film. Certain top-of-the-range scanners can offer to create a positive image directly from a negative.

Reapply a negative to return to the positive image and save the picture under another name.

➟ **Image - Adjust - Invert**

➟ **File - Save As**
Enter **Retouched Kilimanjaro** in the **File name** box, click **Save** then **OK**.

---

15 *Now you can create a very marked contrast effect on the bottom of the picture.*

TRANSFORMING AN IMAGE AREA INTO A BITMAP

a   Activate a layer or make a selection to constrain the effect to a part of the image.

➟ Here, activate the [ ] tool and select the bottom half of the image (the area containing the bushes and dirt path).

To ensure a softer transition between the highly contrasted area and the rest of the picture, use a higher feathering value.

➟ **Select - Feather**
Set the value as **10** and click **OK**.

Chapter 3

b **Image**
   Adjust
   Threshold

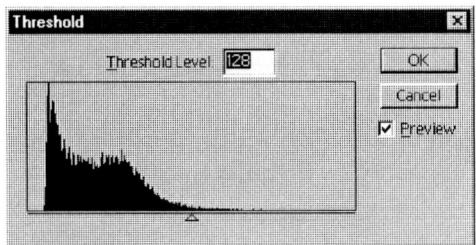

c Drag the cursor to define the threshold or enter a value between 1 and 255: the pixels to the left of the slider in the histogram will be black and the ones to its right will be white.

⟹ Here, position the slider at **56**

d Click **OK**.

⟹ Here, cancel you selection with **Select - Deselect**.

The bottom part of the image appears snow-covered!

✓ *There is little real interest in using this command on an entire image because it would be preferable to convert the image into a specific colour mode: Bitmap.*

You do not wish to keep this result, so revert to the previous version of the document.

⟹ **File - Revert**

Chapter 3

16 *To finish this overview of the image-retouching commands, you can modify the histogram by deliberately limiting the number of tonal levels.*

CREATING FLAT AREAS OF COLOUR

[a] If necessary, activate a layer or make a selection.

▸ Here, that is not necessary.

[b] **Image**
Adjust
Posterize

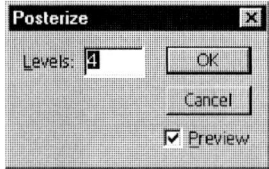

[c] Define the number of brightness **Levels** for each colour channel in the corresponding text box. You can enter a value between 2 and 255.
On grayscale images, the effect is very noticeable as they only contain one colour channel. For these images, you will obtain a bitmap image if you only use two **Levels**. For colour RGB or CMYK images, there will be the same number of levels for each channel. For example, if you set 2 **Levels** for a RGB image, you will obtain six colours (two for red, two for green and two for blue).

▸ Here, adjust the **Levels** to **4**

[d] Click **OK**.

The image now looks more like a drawing than a photo.

✓ *On an image in Lab mode, the result is usually disappointing. The reason for this is that Lab images contain three channels but only one of these concerns contrast and brightness, the other two channels being colour channels with no contrast or brightness. As the* Posterize *command acts on all channels, you will obtain considerable colour modification.*

Undo the **Posterize** *command.*

▸ **Edit - Undo**

Chapter 3

17 You are now going to see how to remove or modify unwanted items in an image, without creating holes as you do with the **Eraser** tool.

DUPLICATING PART OF AN IMAGE WITH THE RUBBER STAMP

The rubber stamp paints with a sampled area of an image rather than with any individual colour.

a If your image contains several layers, activate the layer which will act as the reference for this duplication. You can also open another image if you want to reproduce an area from that image.

b Activate the ![tool] tool.

c If the **Options** palette is not visible, click its tab or double-click the ![tool] tool.

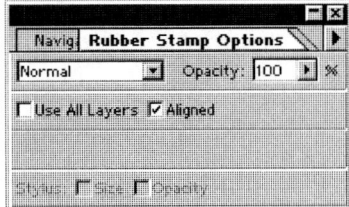

d Choose an **Effect Mode** for the tool (cf. Chapter 4) and an **Opacity** level.

➔ Here, leave the tool in **Normal** mode and the **Opacity** at **100%**.

e Use the **Use All Layers** option to reproduce an area of the image without taking into account which layer is active. In this case, the duplication will be made from the whole image, including all layers together.

➔ Here, this option is not applicable as there is only one layer.

f Leave the **Aligned** option active to apply the sampled area once, as a whole, whether or not you stop and start your painting. If the option is deactivated, the duplication will begin again from the initial sampling point each time you stop dragging then start again.

➔ Here, deactivate the **Aligned** option.

g If the **Brushes** palette is not visible, click its tab or show it using **Window - Show Brushes** then select a brush type.

➔ Here, select for now the brush type seen above the 65 diameter type.

Adobe Photoshop 5.5   173

Chapter 3

|h| Indicate the initial sampling point by pointing to the area you want to reproduce. Hold down [Alt] and click.

➤ Here, point to the grassy area at the bottom of the picture (as shown on the illustration below) and [Alt]-click:

The initial sampling point has been determined.

|i| Point to the area you want to retouch and drag to start painting.

➤ Here, click the bush and drag the pointer towards the right.

*Two pointers appear on the screen: the cross hair indicates the part of the image that is being reproduced and the second pointer shows the tool as it is being used. If the **Aligned** option is active in the **Options** palette, the gap between the two pointers will not alter until a new sampling point is defined.*

Chapter 3

You are going to paint over the large bush at the bottom of the image. Reproduce the result below using the following tips to help you:

- Use **Edit - Undo** to cancel your first attempt.
  Redefine the sampling point for the duplication.
- Start dragging from the left side of the bush.

  After a while, the bush is no longer rubbed out because the image was memorised when you started dragging. The sampling point has moved, and is now at the place where the bush initially started.

- Start dragging again from the path to rub out the bush. Be careful to use a fairly straight line when painting in the lighter coloured path between the grass and the earth.
- To erase the top part of the bush, redefine a sampling point (Alt-click) from the ground under the tallest tree (above the very first sampling point).
- Use small drags (at least seven) to erase this area.
- When painting the earthy patches, to avoid a texture that is too repetitive, redefine the sampling point at various places on the picture to achieve an uneven, and more realistic, texture. Each time you redefine the sampling point, make a click or small drag over the area where the top half of the bush was.
- Define a sampling point on the path again and widen the path.
- Select smaller brush types to ensure a perspective effect on the path.

  The bush should be well-erased, although it is possible that some areas of the path may be a little blurred.

- Save the picture.

Adobe Photoshop 5.5

Chapter 3

PRACTICE EXERCISE 3

- Leave the **Retouched Kilimanjaro.jpg** document open.
- Refocus the areas on the image where you used the Rubber Stamp tool, especially the path (use the Sharpen tool).
- Using the Paintbrush tool, erase Mount Kilimanjaro without removing the clouds or their outlines. Use a sky blue colour.
- Hide the outline of your painting to blend in with the rest of the sky using an appropriate retouching tool.
- Open the **Giraffe.jpg** document.
- Select the giraffe with precision, "inventing" its hooves where they are hidden in the grass.
- Copy the giraffe into the **Retouched Kilimanjaro** document then close the giraffe photo.
- Reduce the size of the giraffe so it is in proportion with the rest of the picture.
- Adjust the hue and saturation of the giraffe so that it fits in better with its surroundings.
- Remove the grass from the giraffe's hooves so you can restore the patches on its fur as you can see further up.
- Blend its hooves into the picture so the giraffe does not look as if it is levitating!
- Create a new layer under the giraffe layer.
- Use the Airbrush tool to make a freeform shadow for the giraffe. Use black.
- Set the opacity at 50% for the layer containing the shadow.
- Save the image as **Kilimanjaro Safari** and close it.
- Open the **Elephant.jpg** document in the **ENI Photoshop 5.5** folder.
- Fill in the hole located near the base of its left ear.
- Lighten the image using the **Levels** and **Curves** commands.
- Adjust the elephant's colour so it contains more brown and is a little duller.
- Save that picture as **Retouched Elephant** and leave Photoshop.

The corrected versions of these documents are called **Kilimanjaro Safari Chapter 3.psd** and **Retouched Elephant Chapter 3.jpg**.

CHAPTER 4

1 - APPLYING A TEXTURE TO AN IMAGE 179
2 - ASSOCIATING A BLENDING MODE WITH A LAYER 181
3 - DESCRIBING BLENDING MODES 181
        NORMAL 181
        DISSOLVE 182
        BEHIND 182
        CLEAR 183
        MULTIPLY 183
        SCREEN 183
        OVERLAY 184
        SOFT LIGHT 184
        HARD LIGHT 184
        COLOR DODGE 185
        COLOR BURN 185
        DARKEN 185
        LIGHTEN 185
        DIFFERENCE 186
        EXCLUSION 186
        HUE 186
        SATURATION 186
        COLOR 187
        LUMINOSITY 187
4 - CONVERTING A BACKGROUND INTO A LAYER 188
5 - SOFTENING THE EFFECT OF A FILTER, ADJUSTMENT OR TOOL 189
6 - COPYING OR MOVING ONE SELECTION INTO ANOTHER 190
7 - CREATING A CLIPPING GROUP 192
8 - REMOVING A LAYER FROM A CLIPPING GROUP 193
9 - COPYING IMAGES LOCATED ON SEVERAL LAYERS 194
10 - CREATING AN ADJUSTMENT LAYER 195
11 - MODIFYING AN ADJUSTMENT LAYER 198
12 - CREATING A PATTERN 199
13 - APPLYING A PATTERN 200
        USING THE PATTERN STAMP TOOL 200
        USING THE FILL COMMAND 201
14 - WRAPPING AROUND THE EDGES OF A PATTERN OR TEXTURE 202
15 - SELECTING A RANGE OF COLOURS 205
16 - MANAGING THE HISTORY PALETTE 208
        ACCESSING THE HISTORY PALETTE 208
        UNDOING SEVERAL ACTIONS 210
        DELETING HISTORY STATES 211

	EMPTYING THE HISTORY PALETTE 211
	MODIFYING THE HISTORY PREFERENCES 212
17 -	CREATING SNAPSHOTS OF IMAGES 213
	DEFINING A SIMPLE SNAPSHOT 213
	DEFINING A SPECIFIC SNAPSHOT 215
	CREATING A DOCUMENT FROM A STATE OR A SNAPSHOT 215
18 -	REPRODUCING A PREVIOUS STATE OR SNAPSHOT 217
	USING THE HISTORY BRUSH 217
	USING THE FILL COMMAND 219
19 -	CREATING AN ART REPRODUCTION OF AN EARLIER STATE OF THE IMAGE 220
	PRACTICE EXERCISE 4 222

Chapter 4

In this chapter you will be looking at more specialised retouching techniques as well as advanced functions of layers. Before starting, you need to create a new document.

➠ If you left Photoshop, restart it.

➠ **File - New**

➠ Set the **Width** at **180** pixels, the **Height** at **85** pixels and the **Resolution** at **72** ppi. Select the **RGB Color Mode** with a **White** background then click **OK**.

➠ Click the fill color box on the toolbox then in the **Color Picker** select a colour whose components are **R= 186**, **G= 127** and **B= 52** then click **OK**.

➠ **Filter - Render - Clouds**

---

1 *Apply a texture to the background of this document.*

APPLYING A TEXTURE TO AN IMAGE

[a] If necessary, activate the layer to which the texture will be applied or select something.

➠ Here, you are working on the **Background**.

[b] **Filter**
Texture
Texturizer

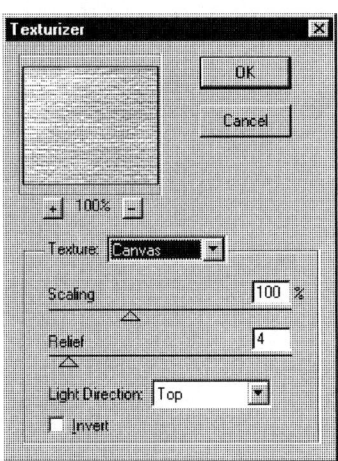

[c] Determine which **Texture** you wish to apply by choosing in the corresponding list. By default you have the choice of **Brick**, **Burlap**, **Canvas** or **Sandstone**. You can also use **Load Texture**. If you choose this option, an **Open** dialog box appears so you can select a texture from another file.

Adobe Photoshop 5.5

Chapter 4

You can use any file with a Photoshop format. However, if you want to create high-quality textures, make sure that the pixels at the top of the image in the file match the ones at the bottom and that those on the right (imagine wrapping the image round so that the opposite edges meet: the pattern should be continuous over the join). This will allow you to fill areas larger than the image in your texture file, without creating a tile effect (for more details cf. *Wrapping around the edges of a pattern or texture*).

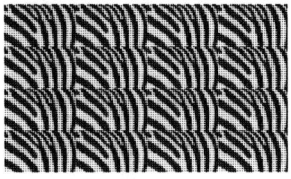 

texture which does not wrap correctly   texture of the same size which wraps correctly

Some extra textures are supplied with Photoshop. They are in the **Program Files\Adobe\Photoshop 5.5\Goodies\Textures** folder.

⇒ Here, select the **Load Texture** option. Access the folder described above then open the **Hard Linear Grain.psd** texture.

[d] Define the other texturizer options:

Scaling To change the size of the texture. This can vary between 50 and 200% of the original size.

Relief This determines the depth of the texture "engraved" on the image. This value can be between 0 and 50.

Light Direction This determines how the texture is lit. You have the choice between several lighting options. The **Invert** option reverses the lighting direction. For example, if the **Light Direction** is set at **Top**, clicking **Invert** will change it to **Bottom**.

⇒ Here, leave the default parameters: **Scaling** at **100%**, **Relief** of **4** and **Top Light Direction**.

[e] Click **OK**.

The result resembles a plank of light-coloured wood with a deep grain.

Create a text over this wood effect and save the document.

⇒ Activate the [T] tool and click in the centre of the image.

⇒ Select a calligraphy font like **Comic Sans MS** with a size and leading of **36**.
Click the **Color** box to select a colour consisting of **R= 68, G= 186** and **B= 52**.

⇒ Make sure the type is centre-aligned then type **Nature** [Enter] **reserve** in the text box.
Click **OK**.

⇒ Move the layer contents so they are correctly centred on the "wood".

⇒ Save this image under the name **Reserve signpost**

Chapter 4

2 *You have seen several references to painting/effect modes, especially when using the drawing tools. These various modes (known collectively as blending modes) also intervene when working with layers. Look at how to associate a mode with a particular layer.*

ASSOCIATING A BLENDING MODE WITH A LAYER

☐ a   Select the layer concerned in the **Layers** palette.

▶ Here, you are working on a type layer called **Nature reserve**.

☐ b   Select the blending mode from the drop-down list at the top of the **Layers** palette.

▶ Here, for example, choose **Color Burn**.

The layer contents turn out differently.

3 *Now look in detail at the different blending modes available.*

DESCRIBING BLENDING MODES

Blending modes determine how a drawing tool behaves when used. For layers, they determine how the elements on the active layer will be applied in relation to elements on underlying layers. You will also see that these modes can be used when applying filters, when adjusting images or for channels (this will be looked at in Chapter 7).

These modes act mainly on colours but can also affect the luminosity of an image. The result produced by these modes depends on two factors:

The base colour   This corresponds to the image's original colour.

The blend colour This refers to the foreground colour, in the case of drawing tools. For layers, each pixel on the layer is considered as a specific blend colour.

*The blending mode applied with a **blend colour** over a **base colour** gives a **result colour**.*

NORMAL

The blend colour totally covers the base colour if opacity equals 100%. The result colour is therefore the same as the blend colour.

▶ Here, select **Normal** again: on the signpost the green text colour hides the wood background of the image.

> ✓ *This mode is called Threshold when you work on Bitmap images or images in Indexed Color mode.*

Adobe Photoshop 5.5   **181**

Chapter 4

DISSOLVE

This replaces the base colour by the blend colour in a random manner. This replacement depends on the opacity used. This mode causes pixelation (jagged edges of rough-looking pixels) in areas whose opacity is less than 100%. The opacity effect is replaced by a higher or lower density of pixels of the blend colour.

▸ Here, apply the **Dissolve** mode to the **Nature reserve** layer.

The effect is not so marked here as there are few areas whose opacity is less than 100%. You can however see that the letters now have a jagged outline.

Apply this mode to another image to see the effect in a more dramatic way.

▸ Open the **Kilimanjaro.jpg** document.

▸ **Select - All**

▸ **Layer - New - Layer Via Cut**

The image is on a new layer and the **Background** layer is white.

▸ **Select - All**

▸ **Select - Modify - Border**
Set the border width at **20** pixels and click **OK**.

▸ **Edit - Clear**

The border is erased and the white background shows through, gradually fading back to the picture.

▸ **Select - Deselect**

▸ Apply the **Dissolve** mode to **Layer 1**.

The effect can be very clearly seen here. The areas that were almost transparent are replaced by opaque pixels, widely spaced and the areas that were almost opaque are now completely opaque with some white pixels.

Close this image without saving it and return to the signpost.

▸ **File - Close** then click **No** to close without saving.

BEHIND

This mode only works for drawing tools or for the commands **Edit - Fill** or **Edit - Stroke**.

It is identical to **Normal** mode for the transparent areas of a layer. On opaque areas, this mode has no effect and the base colour remains unaltered. On partially transparent areas, the blend colour is applied with a reduced opacity, proportional to the transparency of the base colour.

✓ On a layer which has a layer mask, the *Behind* mode considers black areas on the mask as being opaque, even if the corresponding areas on the layer are transparent.

CLEAR

This can only be used with the ▨ and ▨ tools as well as with the **Edit - Fill** or **Edit - Stroke** commands.

It makes the layer areas you are working on transparent. It is the equivalent of the ▨ tool on a large scale. It is more like a blend "colour" than a blending mode.

✓ This mode can only be applied to a layer and not to an image background.

MULTIPLY

As its name implies, this multiplies the blend colour by the base colour to obtain the result colour. From a photographic point of view, it is as if you were showing two superimposed slides simultaneously. The result colour is always darker. To attenuate this darkening, you can adjust the opacity on the drawing tool or on the layer.
If one of the colours is black (the base colour or the blend colour), the result will be black. On the other hand, white is a neutral colour. If the blend colour is white, the base colour will remain the same. If the base colour is white, the blend colour will be applied as with **Normal** mode.

➢ Here, apply the **Multiply** mode to the **Nature Reserve** layer.

The wood texture can be seen through the green colour. This colour is darker because green has been multiplied with brown. The result is not too dark as the colours used are relatively light.

SCREEN

This mode is exactly the opposite of the **Multiply** mode. It multiplies the negative of the base colour with the negative of the blend colour to achieve its result colour. In photographic terms, it is as if you superimpose two negatives simultaneously then inverse their combined colours to create a positive image. The result colour is always lighter.
If one of the colours (base or blend) is white, the result colour will be white.
Black is a neutral colour. If the blend colour is black, the base colour will not be changed. If the base colour is black, the blend colour will be applied as with **Normal** mode.

➢ Here, apply the **Screen** mode to the **Nature reserve** layer.

The wood texture is not so visible as the green is very light. The result is very light here as the colours used were originally very light.

Chapter 4

OVERLAY

This mode applies **Multiply** or **Screen** mode depending on the base colour. If that colour is lighter than the blend colour, **Multiply** mode will be used. If the base colour is darker than the blend colour, **Screen** mode will be applied.
However, contrary to the **Multiply** and **Screen** modes, this mode preserves the base colour's luminosity.
A 50% grey is a neutral colour. If the blend colour is this grey, the base colour remains unchanged. If the base colour is this grey, the blend colour will be applied as with **Normal** mode.

➡ Here, apply the **Overlay** mode to the **Nature reserve** layer.

The result is an average of the results obtained with ***Multiply*** *and* ***Screen*** *modes.*

SOFT LIGHT

This mode lightens or darkens the base colour, depending on the blend colour. If the blend colour has a luminosity greater than 50%, the base colour will be lightened, taking into account the blend colour. If the luminosity is less than 50%, the base colour will be darkened.
The effect of this mode is the equivalent of shining a diffused (coloured) light on the image. If you are using grey as the blend colour, you will obtain a result similar to that achieved with the ▣ and ▣ tools. A white blend colour will considerably lighten the colour and a black will strongly darken it, without the image becoming completely black or white.
A 50% grey is again the neutral blend colour. When this is used, the base colour will remain unchanged.

➡ Here, apply the **Soft Light** mode to the **Nature reserve** layer.

The text is now almost completely illegible but the wood gives the impression of being lit by a diffuse green light.

HARD LIGHT

This mode lightens or darkens the base colour depending on the blend colour. If the blend colour has more than 50% luminosity, a process similar to **Screen** mode will lighten the base colour. If the luminosity is less than 50%, a darkening will occur, much in the same way as with the **Multiply** mode.
The effect of this mode is similar to shining a direct light on the image. White will give white and black will give black. 50% grey is the neutral blend colour. When this is used, the base colour will remain unchanged. If the base colour is this grey, the blend colour will be applied as with **Normal** mode.

➡ Here, apply the **Hard Light** mode to the **Nature reserve** layer.

The text gives the effect of a harsh light shining on the wood. The wood grain in those areas becomes indistinct.

Chapter 4

COLOR DODGE

This mode lightens the base colour, taking into account the blend colour. This lightening effect occurs in relation to each colour channel.

Black is a neutral blend colour. If the blend colour is black, the base colour will remain unaltered.

⟫ Here, apply the **Color Dodge** mode to the **Nature reserve** layer.

The text becomes very light and takes on a colour that is a mixture of the green in the text and the brown of the wood. The wood grain under the text becomes almost invisible.

COLOR BURN

This mode is the opposite of **Color Dodge**. It darkens the base colour, relative to the blend colour. This darkening occurs for each colour channel.

White is neutral as a blend colour. If the blend colour is white, the base colour stays the same.

⟫ Here, apply the **Color Burn** mode to the **Nature reserve** layer.

The text is darker and the wood grain stands out more through it.

DARKEN

This mode uses the blend colour to darken the base colour. Contrary to the **Color Burn** mode, the two colours are not mixed. For each colour channel, the darkest colour is preserved: if the blend colour is darker than the base colour, the blend colour is used, and vice versa.

If one of the colours (blend or base colours) is black, the resulting colour will be black. White is a neutral colour. If the blend colour is white, the base colour will stay the same. If the base colour is white, the blend colour will be applied as with **Normal** mode.

⟫ Here, apply the **Darken** mode to the **Nature reserve** layer.

The text appears almost as it did with Normal mode because the green used is darker than the brown. However the wood grain is visible through the text.

☑ *On some images, using this mode can produce flat areas of colour.*

LIGHTEN

This is the opposite mode to **Darken**. It lightens the base colour using the blend colour. Contrary to the **Color Dodge** mode, the colours are not mixed. For each colour channel, the lightest colour is kept: if the blend colour is darker than the base colour, the base colour is used and vice versa.

If one of the colours (base or blend) is white, the result colour will be white.

Black is the neutral colour. If the blend colour is black, the base colour will stay the same. If the base colour is black, the blend colour will be applied as with **Normal** mode.

⟫ Here, apply the **Lighten** mode to the **Nature reserve** layer.

Adobe Photoshop 5.5

Chapter 4

The text is all but invisible, because its green is darker than the brown of the wood. The parts of the wood grain that have become green have lost their relief.

☑ On some images, using this mode can produce flat areas of colour.

DIFFERENCE

For each colour channel, this mode performs a subtraction between the base and blend colours. If the blend colour has a higher brightness value than the base colour, the base colour will be subtracted from the blend colour and vice versa.
If one of the colours (blend or base) is white, the result colour will be the negative of the non-white colour. Black is the neutral colour. If the blend colour is black, the base colour stays the same. If the base colour is black, the blend colour will be applied as with **Normal** mode.

➤ Here, apply the **Difference** mode to the **Nature reserve** layer.

The text becomes magenta, while still letting the wood grain show through.

EXCLUSION

This mode is identical to the **Difference** mode but is more subtle. It does have two special qualities:
— the brightness is reduced which can smooth a relief.
— if one of the colours (blend or base) is a 50% grey, the result colour will be 50% grey.

➤ Here, apply the **Exclusion** mode to the **Nature reserve** layer.

The text stays magenta but the wood grain cannot really be seen on the text.

HUE

This mode replaces the base colour by the blend colour. The brightness and saturation of the base colour are preserved.
This mode works in the same way as modifications to the **Hue** option in the **Image - Adjust - Hue/Saturation** command. It is very useful when replacing a colour on an area of an image with a drawing tool.

➤ Here, apply the **Hue** mode to the **Nature reserve** layer.

The wood becomes green where the text is written.

SATURATION

This mode replaces the saturation of the base colour with that of the blend colour. The hue and luminosity of the base colour remain unchanged.
This mode works in the same way as modifications to the **Saturation** option in the **Image - Adjust - Hue/Saturation** command.

➤ Here, apply the **Saturation** mode to the **Nature reserve** layer.

The wood where the text is written becomes bright orange rather than brown.
The green colour is no longer visible, because the base colour takes priority. The colours are bright because the green was highly saturated.

COLOR

This mode replaces the hue and saturation of the base colour with those of the blend colour. The base colour's luminosity stays the same.

This mode works in an identical way to when the **Hue** and **Saturation** options are activated in the **Image - Adjust - Hue/Saturation** command. It can be useful to colour with a drawing tool an image in grayscale that has been converted to colour.

➽ Here, apply the **Color** mode to the **Nature reserve** layer.

The wood becomes bright green in the areas where the text is written, which corresponds to the **Hue** *and* **Saturation** *modes combined.*

LUMINOSITY

This mode replaces the luminosity of the base colour by that of the blend colour. The hue and saturation of the base colour are preserved.

➽ Here, apply the **Luminosity** mode to the **Nature reserve** layer.

The text becomes brown. The green cannot be seen because the base colour is used. The wood grain does not show through the text at all.

> ☑ If you use this mode with a flat area of colour, you will lose all signs of relief on the image areas concerned. This is especially the case with the drawing tools, the Edit - Fill command (except when filling with a snapshot or pattern) and the Edit - Stroke command, or on certain type layers. For layers containing photographic elements, the result could be more interesting.

Apply now a more appropriate mode to the text and change its colour.

➽ Apply the **Multiply** mode to the **Nature reserve** layer.
➽ Modify the type layer by double-clicking its name.
➽ Select the text in the text box and change its colour, with new components of **R= 186**, **G= 52** and **B= 127**.

Chapter 4

4 *You want to apply a bevelled edge to the wood. For the moment this is not possible because the wood is on the image background. Convert this background into a layer.*

CONVERTING A BACKGROUND INTO A LAYER

a Double-click the **Background** layer thumbnail.

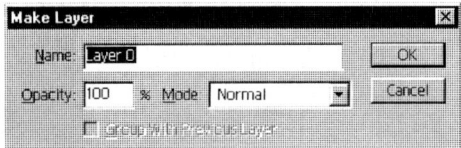

b Enter the **Name** of the layer in the appropriate text box.

▬▶ Here, enter **Signpost** in the **Name** box.

c Set the **Opacity** and blending **Mode** for the layer.

*These options are offered in case you are not leaving this layer in the background of your image. If this layer is staying in the background and you are not creating a new **Background** layer, you can use the **Opacity** option, which will function normally. On the other hand, the blending **Modes** will not produce any result with the exception of **Dissolve** if the layer has less than 100% **Opacity**, **Soft Light** which will make a grey result, **Color Dodge** which will turn the layer black and **Color Burn** which will make it white.*

▬▶ Here, leave the options as set by default.

d Click **OK**.

The background is now a layer like any other and can contain transparent zones.

*Apply a bevel effect to the **Signpost** layer.*

▬▶ **Layer - Effects - Bevel and Emboss**

▬▶ Set the **Opacity** under **Highlight** at **90%**, select an **Inner Bevel** type of **Style** then click **OK**.

There is now an impression of depth on the edges and the signpost looks a little more like a real piece of wood.

Apply a filter to tone down the wood grain.

▬▶ **Filter - Brush Strokes - Accented Edges**
Set the **Edge Width** at **1**, the **Edge Brightness** at **25** so that the result is not lightened or darkened and the **Smoothness** at **15** then click **OK**.

The wood grain practically disappears, giving a polished appearance to the wood.

Chapter 4

5 *To retrieve a correct wood grain, you can tone down the effect of the last filter applied.*

SOFTENING THE EFFECT OF A FILTER, ADJUSTMENT OR TOOL

[a] After having applied a **Filter**, or made an adjustment with one of the **Image - Adjust** commands or used one of the drawing or retouching tools, use the command:

Filter [Ctrl] [⇧ Shift] **F**
Fade [Name] (of filter, or adjustment name, or tool name)

▸ Here, the option is called **Fade Accented Edges**.

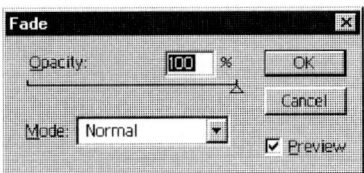

[b] Define the **Opacity** to soften the effect's intensity.

▸ Here, set the **Opacity** between **50** and **60%**.

[c] Select, if necessary, a blending mode to create an extra effect.

▸ Here, leave the **Mode** as **Normal**.

[d] Click **OK**.

The wood grain stands out again but is less pronounced than on the original version.

✓ *Softening changes made with drawing or retouching tools can let you avoid cancelling your work, when you have forgotten to make suitable settings on the tool Options.*

✓ *As long as you have not used another command, you can modify your work further by using the Filter - Fade command again.*

▸ Save the signpost then close that image and open two other documents: **Safari Chapter 2.psd** and **Elephant.jpg**.

Adobe Photoshop 5.5 189

Chapter 4

*You are going to modify the **Safari Chapter 2.psd** document in order to obtain this result.*

6 *Start by copying the elephant so that it is contained within the map of Africa.*

COPYING OR MOVING ONE SELECTION INTO ANOTHER

[a] Select the area of the image you want to copy.

▸ Here, activate the ![ ] tool and set the **Tolerance** to **30** in the **Options** palette.
Click the white area that surrounds the elephant.
Select - Inverse

[b] Activate the **Edit - Copy** command (or `Ctrl` **C**) to copy the selection or **Edit - Cut** (`Ctrl` **X**) to move it.

▸ Here, select the **Copy** command then close the **Elephant.jpg** document without saving.

[c] Select the area in the image into which you want to paste the item you have just cut or copied.

▸ Here activate the **Map** layer then `Ctrl`-click the **Map** layer thumbnail to load the map selection.

[d] **Edit**   `Ctrl` `⇧ Shift` **V**
Paste Into

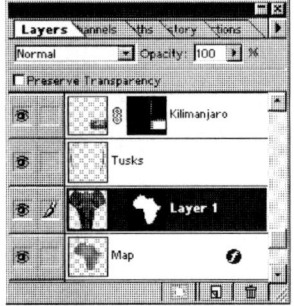

The elephant is pasted onto a new layer, which is associated with a layer mask corresponding to the second selection (in this case, the map). Only the part of the elephant that matches up with the map can be seen. You can also see that by default there is no link between the layer and its mask. The ![ ] *icon is not there, contrary to what you can see on the Kilimanjaro layer. This means you can move the layer without changing the transparent areas of the mask.*

- ✓ The layer mask that has been created has no special qualities. You can work on it as with any layer mask.

- ✓ This command is especially useful if you wish to create specific effects on the layer mask or more particularly when working with images that do not accept layers, like Indexed colour or Bitmap mode images. In this case there will be no layer mask but the result will be the same as long as you do not deselect.

- ✓ Depending on the elements you may have to move the pasted object to achieve an optimum result.

Move the elephant so it entirely fills the map then rename the layer.

➔ Activate the tool.

➔ Drag the elephant until the map is covered by the elephant (no more green should be visible).

➔ Double-click the layer thumbnail, enter **Elephant** in the **Name** box and click **OK**.

You are now going to use another technique to achieve the same result. Delete the layer mask.

➔ **Layer - Remove Layer Mask**
Click the **Discard** button to avoid applying the mask.
The elephant is now completely visible.

➔ Save this image under the name **Safari**, replacing the existing document.

Chapter 4

7 *For images that can support layers, it may be more interesting to create a clipping group (where the contents of the lowest layer act as a mask over the other layers) than use the **Paste Into** command.*

CREATING A CLIPPING GROUP

[a] If the **Layers** palette is hidden, click its tab or activate the **Window - Show Layers** command.

[b] If necessary, place the layer that will act as the mask under the layer(s) that are to be clipped. If several layers are to be in the group, they must be stacked one on top of the other. They must not be separated by any layer not contained in the group.

➡ Here, the **Map** layer will be the mask for the **Elephant** layer.

[c] Activate the layer you want to clip and which is located above the masking layer. If several layers are to be clipped, you can link them to the masking layer so the clipping group can be created in one operation.

➡ Here, leave the **Elephant** layer active.

[d] Use one of the following commands (which one is available depends on whether or not the active layer is linked):

Layer **Group with Previous**	Ctrl **G**	To group the active layer with the layer underneath it.
Layer **Group with Linked**	Ctrl **G**	To group all the linked layers with the layer directly beneath them.

➡ Here, activate **Layer - Group with Previous**.

The elephant has been clipped to the shape of the **Map** *without any layer mask being created.*

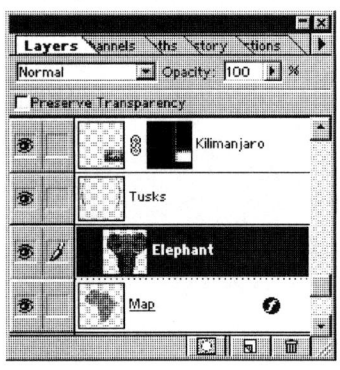

*The layer that acts as a mask is called the **base layer**. The name of this layer is underlined in the **Layers** palette. The layers contained in the clipping group are separated by a dotted line and the thumbnail of the clipped layer is slightly indented from the others.*

✓ *When a new layer is created with* Layer - New - Layer, *a clipping group can be created by activating the* Group with Previous Layer *option in the* New Layer *dialog box.*

Chapter 4

- ✓ You can add a layer to an existing clipping group by stacking this layer over the group and using [Ctrl] G again.

- ✓ You can also create a group directly in the *Layers* palette: point to the line that separates the two layers. Hold down [Alt] (the pointer should take this form: ◄🖐) and click: the two layers will be grouped.

Cancel your group and try this method.

➤ **Edit - Undo**

➤ Point to the line between the **Map** and **Elephant** layers.

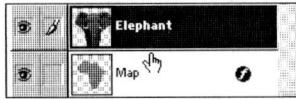

➤ [Alt]-click this line.

The clipping group has been created once more.

---

8 *When the clipping group is no longer required it can be undone without affecting the various layers.*

REMOVING A LAYER FROM A CLIPPING GROUP

[a] If the **Layers** palette is hidden, click its tab or activate the **Window - Show Layers** command.

[b] Activate the layer that you wish to remove from the clipping group. If the layer selected is not the layer in the group foreground, all the layers in the group placed above it will be removed too. If you want to undo the whole group, activate the base layer.

➤ Here, activate the **Map** layer.

[c] **Layer**   [Ctrl] [⇧ Shift] **G**
Ungroup

The elephant is now longer cut out in the shape of the map.

- ✓ You can ungroup two layers directly in the *Layers* palette by using the line separating them. Hold down [Alt] (the pointer will take this form: ◄🖐) and click to ungroup the two layers.

Adobe Photoshop 5.5

Chapter 4

You wish to keep this clipping group, so cancel your last action.

➠ **Edit - Undo**

9

You now know how to copy selected elements. These copies were made on the active layer as the selection only took into account the pixels on that layer. You can also copy part of an image without worrying about which layer is active.

COPYING IMAGES LOCATED ON SEVERAL LAYERS

[a] If necessary, hide all the layers whose contents are not to be copied.

➠ Here, hide all the layers except for **Elephant**, **Map** and **Background**: drag the pointer over the 👁 icons from the **ENI TRAVEL** layer to the **Tusks** layer on the **Layers** palette.

[b] Select the area of the image that you want to copy.

➠ Here, activate the 🔲 tool and select the map, including its glowing edges.

[c] **Edit**   Ctrl ⇧Shift **C**
Copy Merged

[d] Position the pointer or activate the layer where you wish to paste the copy.

➠ Here, create a new document using **File - New** and click **OK**.

[e] **Edit**   Ctrl **V**
Paste

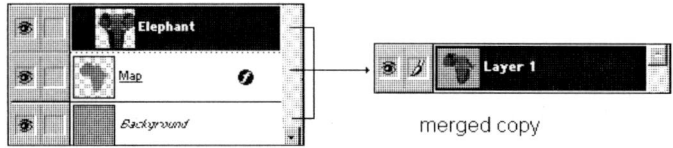

merged copy

The images selected on all the visible layers appear on a single merged layer.

➠ Save this new image under the name **Elephant Map** and close it.

*You are back in the **Safari.psd** document. Remove the selection and show all the layers before continuing.*

➠ **Select - Deselect**

➠ Show all the layers by dragging the pointer upwards over each square where the 👁 icon should appear.

Chapter 4

In the previous chapter you saw the adjustment commands. Another adjustment possibility becomes available when you are working with layers.

CREATING AN ADJUSTMENT LAYER

[a] Activate the layer that will act as the reference for the adjustment layer. The adjustments made will apply to this layer and by default to all its underlying layers.

▶ Here, activate the **Kilimanjaro** layer.

[b] If necessary, make a selection to limit the adjustment to one part of the image.

▶ Here, that is not necessary.

[c] **Layer**
New
Adjustment Layer

or [Ctrl]-click the ![button] button on the **Layers** palette

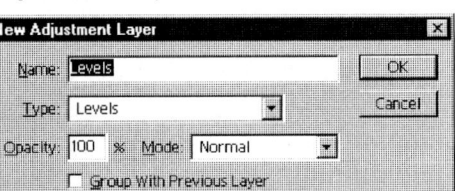

[d] Select an adjustment **Type**. You can choose between all the adjustments available in **Image - Adjust** except the auto-adjustments such as **Auto Levels**, **Desaturate**, **Equalize** as well as **Replace Color** and **Variations**.

▶ Here, select **Curves** as the **Type**.

When a Type of adjustment is chosen the layer Name is automatically changed, unless you have already renamed it. It is a good idea to keep the adjustment type as part of the layer name, especially if you superimpose several adjustment layers.

[e] Modify if necessary the layer **Name**.

▶ Here, change the **Name** to **Kilimanjaro Curves**

[f] Reset the **Opacity** and blending **Mode** on the layer to tone down the adjustment effect.

▶ Here, leave the default options as set.

[g] Activate the **Group With Previous Layer** option if you wish to limit the retouch to the previously selected layer. This would create a clipping group between the adjustment layer and the active layer. If this option is not activated, all underlying layers will be affected by the correction made.

▶ Here, leave this option inactive.

[h] Click **OK**.

Adobe Photoshop 5.5

Chapter 4

*The dialog box corresponding to the chosen adjustment appears on the screen. In this example, the **Curves** dialog box appears.*

[i] Make your adjustment according to the type chosen and click **OK**.

➤ Here, add a point on the curve whose input value is **128** and whose output value is **148** and click **OK**.

All the layers situated under the adjustment layer have been lightened.

The adjustment layer appears in the palette above the previously active layer. Note that a ⬤ icon is present on the layer which indicates that it is an adjustment layer.

*What if you wanted only the **Kilimanjaro** layer to be lightened? In that case the **Group with Previous** option should have been activated when the adjustment layer was created. This can be corrected by creating a clipping group.*

➤ Point to the line between the **Kilimanjaro** and the **Kilimanjaro Curves** layers and [Alt]-click.

*The rest of the image returns to its original brightness level but the **Kilimanjaro** layer remains lightened.*

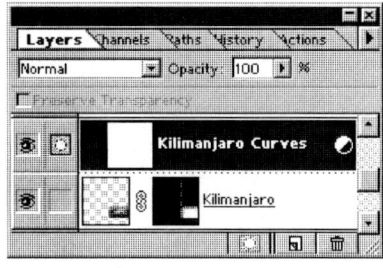

When an adjustment layer is active, you can see that a ▧ icon appears next to the 👁 icon as is the case for layer masks. An adjustment layer does indeed have similar properties to a layer mask. Layer masks affect opacity and adjustment layers make corrections but each one is able to make changes to specific areas of an image. You can also, in the same way as for a layer mask, draw on adjustment layers in grayscale in order to modify the correction zone.

✓ *If the adjustment is suitable, you can merge the adjustment layer with the layer underneath it. However in doing that you will render the adjustment permanent and you will not be able to modify it further.*

Chapter 4

✓ *If a selection were made before the adjustment layer was created, the layer thumbnail would show the selected area in white and the rest of the image in black.*

Create a new adjustment layer to see how the correction zone can be modified.

- Activate the **Elephant** layer.
- Activate the ▢ tool and select the bottom half of the map.
- **Layer - New - Adjustment Layer**
- Select the **Hue/Saturation** adjustment **Type**, activate the **Group with Previous Layer** option and click **OK**.
- Leave the **Edit** option as **Master** and set the **Hue** slider at **+90**. Click **OK**.

The bottom half of the elephant becomes green and the adjustment layer thumbnail is black with a white rectangle that corresponds to the selected area.

Modify the adjustment layer as you would do for a layer mask.

- If the adjustment layer that you have just created is not active, activate it.
- Restore the default colours by clicking the ▢ icon in the toolbox.
- Activate the ▢ tool and select a **Foreground to Background Gradient** in the **Options** palette.
- Drag from the top of the map to the bottom.

The elephant retains a normal colour at the top and becomes progressively green. The adjustment layer thumbnail displays the gradient made. An identical layer mask would have produced a gradient with varying degrees of transparency: on an adjustment layer, the gradient is made from the specified correction (for example using changes in hue, in saturation, in luminosity...).

You do not need to keep this adjustment layer.

- Click the 🗑 button on the **Layers** palette then the **Yes** button to delete the layer.

Apply an adjustment layer to the giraffe to harmonise it a little more with the picture of Mount Kilimanjaro.

- Activate the **Giraffe** layer.
- **Layer - New - Adjustment Layer**
- Select the **Hue/Saturation** adjustment **Type** and name the layer **Giraffe Hue/Saturation**. Activate the **Group with Previous Layer** option and click **OK**.
- Leave the **Edit** option as **Master**, set the **Hue** slider at **+45** and the **Lightness** slider at **-25** then click **OK**.

The giraffe takes on similar colour tones to the Kilimanjaro picture.

Adobe Photoshop 5.5

Chapter 4

Create two new adjustment layers for the mask.

➟ Activate the **Mask** layer.

➟ **Layer - New - Adjustment Layer**

➟ Select the **Levels Type** and name this layer **Mask Levels**.
Activate the **Group with Previous Layer** option and click **OK**.

➟ Set the output levels for the dark tones at **16** and then set the light tone output to **232** and click **OK**.

The mask has more contrast.

➟ **Layer - New - Adjustment Layer**

➟ Select the **Hue/Saturation** adjustment **Type** and name the layer **Mask Hue/Saturation**.
Activate the **Group with Previous Layer** option and click **OK**.

➟ Activate the **Colorize** option, set the **Hue** slider at **200**, leave the **Saturation** at **25** then click **OK**.

A two-tone effect is obtained with a cyan blue mask with black details.

---

11 *The adjustment made to the **Kilimanjaro Curves** layer is not entirely suitable, so you should modify it.*

MODIFYING AN ADJUSTMENT LAYER

[a] If the **Layers** palette is hidden, click its tab or activate the **Window - Show Layers** command.

[b] Activate the adjustment layer you wish to modify.

➟ Here, activate the **Kilimanjaro Curves** layer.

[c] **Layer**   Double-click the layer name
Adjustment Options

*A dialog box that corresponds to the chosen type of adjustment is displayed. In this example, the **Curves** dialog box appears.*

[d] Make the necessary modifications.

➟ Here, modify the central point of the curve so that the input value is **98** and the output value is **128**.

[e] Click **OK**.

The image of Kilimanjaro is a little lighter still.

Chapter 4

✓ If you double-click the Layers palette, do not double-click the adjustment layer thumbnail because you will open the Layer Options dialog box and not the adjustment options. Make sure you double-click the layer name only.

Before continuing, save your document.

➟ **File - Save**

---

12 *You are going to create a pattern to apply to the edges of your picture.*

CREATING A PATTERN

[a] Select the area of the image that is going to be used to make the pattern. You can only select it with the ▯ tool or by using **Select - All**.

➟ Here, open the **Giraffe.jpg** document.
Activate the ▯ tool and select an area on the giraffe's back. Try to select as large an area as possible without selecting any of the surrounding foliage.

[b] **Edit
Define Pattern**

*The pattern is defined (if you experience difficulties with this command check in the tool options that a **Feather** value of **0** is specified).*

[c] In order to improve or reuse the pattern for other things, copy it into a new document (which will only contain one layer) then save that document (use **Photoshop *.PSD** or ***.PDD** format if you want to load the pattern from the **Texturizer** at a later time).

➟ Here, use **Edit - Copy**
File - New and click **OK** straight away.
Edit - Paste
Merge the created layer with the **Background** using **Layer - Flatten Image**.
Save the pattern under the name **Giraffe Texture**

✓ *You cannot use several patterns at the same time. If a pattern has already been defined, any new pattern will replace it.*

✓ *If you have created a very large pattern and you no longer wish to use it, you can free some memory by using Edit - Purge - Pattern.*

Adobe Photoshop 5.5

Chapter 4

☑ You can create a texture in the same way without worrying about the **Edit - Define Pattern** command.

Before moving on, close the giraffe document.

➟ Show the **Giraffe.jpg** document by clicking its window or using **Window - Giraffe.jpg**.
➟ **File - Close**

---

13 *Try this pattern out on a new layer.*

APPLYING A PATTERN

USING THE PATTERN STAMP TOOL

[a] Activate the layer on which you wish to use the pattern.
➟ Here, show the **Safari.psd** document by clicking its window or using **Window - Safari.psd**. Activate the **Background** layer then click the [⬚] button on the **Layers** palette.
[b] Activate the [🖰] tool (it is in the same tool group as the [🖰] tool).
[c] If the **Options** palette is hidden, click its tab or double-click the [🖰] tool.

The options on offer are the same as for the [🖰] tool.

[d] Set the **Opacity** and **Effect Mode**.
➟ Here, leave the default options.
[e] If you leave the **Aligned** option active, the **Pattern Stamp** tool will apply the "tiles" of pattern regularly, positioning each one next to an existing one, even if you drag rather haphazardly. If you deactivate the option then drag the Pattern Stamp over an area where the pattern is already applied, you can overlap the tiles of pattern.
➟ Here, leave the **Aligned** option active.
[f] If the **Brushes** palette is not displayed, click its tab or use **Window - Show Brushes**.
[g] Select a brush type.
➟ Here, select the type with a **100** diameter.
[h] Drag over the area that you wish to fill with the pattern.
➟ Here, drag over the bottom left quarter of the image to paint it with the pattern.

Chapter 4

The giraffe pattern fills the area of the image concerned. However you can notice a slight "checkerboard" effect. This is caused by a lack of continuity in the edge pixels as you saw when you looked at applying textures earlier in the chapter.

USING THE FILL COMMAND

[a] Activate the layer on which you wish to use the pattern.

➠ Here, leave **Layer 1** active.

[b] If necessary, make a selection if you wish to limit the fill to a particular area.

➠ Here, this is not necessary.

[c] **Edit**
Fill

⇧ Shift ⌫

[d] Select **Pattern** in the **Use** list.

[e] If required, reset the **Opacity** and blending **Mode**.

➠ Here, leave the options set by default.

[f] Activate the **Preserve Transparency** to limit the fill to the visible pixels on the layer.

➠ Here, if the **Preserve Transparency** option is available, deactivate it.

[g] Click **OK**.

The whole background layer is filled with the pattern. Some areas are masked by other items in the picture as the background layer lies underneath all the rest.

The checkerboard effect due to the lack of pixel continuity is still visible. Erase the contents of this layer.

➠ **Edit - Fill**

➠ Select **Clear** as the blending **Mode** and click **OK**.

Adobe Photoshop 5.5

Chapter 4

14
You may have to improve the pattern quality to avoid the checkerboard effect.

WRAPPING AROUND THE EDGES OF A PATTERN OR TEXTURE

[a] Create your pattern or texture in a new document as previously explained.

➡ Here, show the **Giraffe Texture.psd** document by clicking its window or using **Window - Giraffe Texture.psd**.

[b] **Filter**
Other
Offset

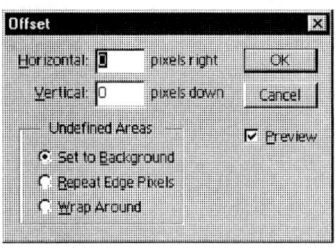

This filter will show you how the edges of the pattern are joining up by moving the image so that some of the pixels are pushed off the canvas, then putting these pixels back on the other side.

[c] Set the **Horizontal** and **Vertical** move distances in the corresponding text boxes. You can enter a value between -30 000 and +30 000. To wrap around a texture or pattern, use both the horizontal and vertical movement, not just in one direction.

➡ Here, set the **Horizontal** and **Vertical** offsets at **15**

[d] Determine how to fill the emptied spaces on the image:

Set to Background   Fills the undefined areas with the background colour. If the offset is being made on a layer, the **Set to Transparent** option replaces this.

Repeat Edge Pixels   The empty areas are filled by the remaining edge pixels. This method produces a flattening effect by repeating the same pixels.

Wrap Around   The areas of the image that were hidden by the moved portion now reappear on the opposite side of the picture. This lets you see the pattern's various edges stacked against each other so you can spot possible continuity problems when the pattern is tiled.

  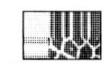

original image   offset with blank areas set to background   offset with blank areas set to repeat edge pixel   offset with blank areas set to wrap around

➡ Here, activate **Wrap Around**.

|e| Click **OK**.

The image is moved and the edges shifted around, which imitates the repetition of the image over a large area. If there is a continuity problem, a distinct cross can be perceived on the image. The cross effect should be corrected if you want to achieve a smooth tiling effect for the pattern or texture.

|f| Correct the image so the cross effect is no longer visible. To do this, use mainly the [icon], [icon] and [icon] tools. For very specific needs, you can also use other tools.

▸ Here, activate the [icon] tool and mask the cross by reproducing other areas of the image over it.

|g| Check that the result is correct by making an offset in the opposite direction. If you used positive values in the first offset, use negative values and double them in relation to the first ones used (or vice versa). If the result is not correct, use the retouching tools again.

▸ Here, use **Filter - Other - Offset**, set the **Horizontal** and **Vertical** offsets at **-30**, activate the **Wrap Around** option and click **OK**. If the cross effect can still be seen, correct it.

|h| If you wish, you can return the pattern or texture to its original position by making an offset identical to the very first one you did.

▸ Here, use **Filter - Other - Offset**, set the **Horizontal** and **Vertical** offset at **15**, activate the **Wrap Around** option then click **OK**.

|i| Save the final result to keep your corrected texture or pattern.

▸ Here, use **File - Save**.

> ✓ *On a layer containing transparent areas, the Offset filter will often produce a move similar to what you would obtain using the* [icon] *tool.*

Try out your improved pattern.

▸ **Select - All**
▸ **Edit - Define Pattern**
▸ **File - Close** (you do not need to use this document again for now).

*You should now be in the **Safari.psd** document once again; if this is not the case, display it now.*

▸ If the **Layer 1** layer is not active, click to activate it.
▸ **Edit - Fill**
▸ Leave the **Use** option as **Pattern** and select **Normal** as the blending **Mode**. Click **OK**.

Chapter 4

The pattern is now tiled smoothly with no chequered effect. There may still be a slight undulating look to the pattern. This is due to the variations in the patches on the giraffe's fur. To correct this, you can modify the pattern by making the size of these patches more uniform.

Turn your attention back to the Safari.psd document.

➠ Open the **Zebra Texture.psd** document.
➠ **Select - All**
➠ **Edit - Define Pattern**
➠ **File - Close**
➠ **Edit - Fill**
➠ Select **Clear** as the blending **Mode** and click **OK**.

The layer containing the giraffe pattern has been cleared.

Before you apply the pattern, it would be a good idea to rename the layer.

➠ Double-click the **Layer 1** layer thumbnail.
➠ Enter **Zebra Border** in the **Name** text box and click **OK**.
➠ **Select - All**
➠ **Select - Modify - Border**; set the **Width** at **30** and click **OK**.
➠ **Edit - Fill** and select **Normal Mode**, check that **Pattern** is selected in the **Use** list. Click **OK**.

The image now has a zebra stripe border.

There is still more work to do on this document.

➠ **Select - Deselect**
➠ Activate the **SAFARI** type layer and apply a **Soft Light** or **Color Dodge** blending mode to it to lighten it.
➠ Activate the **Crossed Tusks** layer and apply a **Difference** blending mode to it.
➠ Activate the **Background** layer.
➠ **Filter - Textures - Texturizer**
➠ Use the **Texture** list to select **Load Texture**. Open the **\Program Files\Adobe\Photoshop 5.5\Goodies\Textures** folder, choose the **Bumpy Leather** document and click the **Open** button.
➠ Set the **Scaling** to **100%**, the **Relief** to **4** and the **Light Direction** to **Top Right** then click **OK**.

The texture appears in the background of the image.

Chapter 4

The **Safari.psd** document is now complete. You should save it and print it.

▸ **File - Save**
▸ Depending on your printer, adjust the page setup with **File - Page Setup**.
▸ **File - Print**
▸ Activate the **Printer Color Management** (or **PostScript Color Management**) and click **OK**.
▸ Close this document and open **Kilimanjaro.jpg**.

---

15 In this section, you are going to be using a similar technique to the one you used for colour duplication to select the sky. The selection you make will come in useful later.

SELECTING A RANGE OF COLOURS

[a] If necessary, select the layer on which you wish to make the selection.

▸ Here, the document only contains a **Background** layer.

[b] Select
Color Range

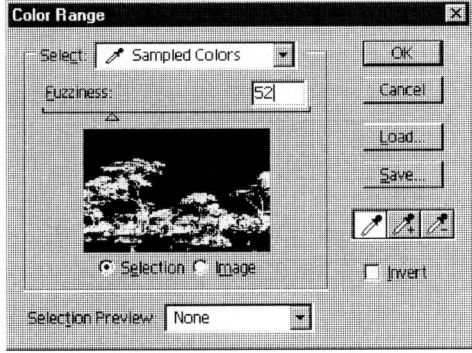

[c] Use the following options from the **Select** drop-down list:

Sampled Colors	To select an area on the image in relation to the colours of your choice.
Reds/Yellows/Greens/Cyans/Blues/Magentas	To select an area on the image in relation to a precise colour. The image must have a high colour contrast if you wish to obtain an interesting result.
Highlights/Midtones/Shadows	To select in relation to the image luminosity. As for the preceding options, the image needs to be highly contrasted.

Chapter 4

Out of Gamut — To select all the colours that fall outside the CMYK colour spectrum. This option can be used in order to select this type of colour and modify them to make them printable.

Only the Sampled Colors option can be used on a selected area.

➤ Here, leave the **Sampled Colors** option active.

[d] To help you when selecting, choose your desired type of **Selection Preview** in the corresponding text box:

None — No selection preview will be shown in the document.

Grayscale — Allows you to see on the image the selected areas in the same way as in the dialog box when the **Selection** option is active.

Black Matte/ White Matte — The selected areas appear normally on the image and the others are filled in black or white.

Quick Mask — The selected areas appear on the image as if you were using Quick Mask mode. By default, the selected areas are displayed normally in the picture and the others are shown with a red film over them. If the Quick Mask options have been modified the display could be inverted or another colour could be used.

➤ Here, select the **Quick Mask** option.

[e] To make your selection, use one of the following options:

Selection — Shows you the image areas that have been selected. The white pixels will be selected while the black pixels will not be. Grey pixels will be partially selected.

Image — Shows you a miniature version of the complete image in the dialog box. This can be interesting when you are looking at a document with a high zoom level. If you use this option, think of checking the **Selection** result with the corresponding option.

➤ Here, use the **Selection** option.

[f] Using the ![] tool, click on a place in the image, or a place on the preview in the dialog box, corresponding to the colour you want to select. You can spread out the selection by activating the ![] tool and clicking another place on the image. You can reduce it in the same way with the ![] tool. You can also hold down [⇧ Shift] when using the ![] tool to use the ![] tool momentarily or [Alt] to switch to the ![] tool.

➤ Here, click the sky then activate the ![] tool and click to select the volcano and the blue clouds too.

g   Vary the **Fuzziness** value so as to take into account more or less similar colours.

➤   Here, set the **Fuzziness** so as to obtain a result similar to this in the preview frame in the dialog box:

h   You can activate **Invert** if you wish to invert the selection.

➤   Here, that is not necessary.

i   Click **OK**.

The selection appears on the image. If some of the pixels of the foreground of the picture have also been selected, hold down [Alt] and surround them with the [lasso] tool to remove them from the selection.

☑ This method tends not to produce very precise selections, so you should confine it to highly contrasted images, whether contrasted in colour or in brightness.

☑ You can *Save* the adjustments applied and use them on another image by clicking the *Load* button.

Save this selection.

➤   **Select - Save Selection**

➤   Enter **Blue Sky** in the **Name** box and click **OK**.

You will use this selection later on but for the moment you can deselect.

➤   **Select - Deselect**

Chapter 4

16

You know how to cancel one command or retouch. Photoshop offers you the opportunity to cancel several successive commands or to go back and work with the image in one of its previous states. Look now at how this is possible.

MANAGING THE HISTORY PALETTE

ACCESSING THE HISTORY PALETTE

[a] **Window** Click the **History** tab
Show History

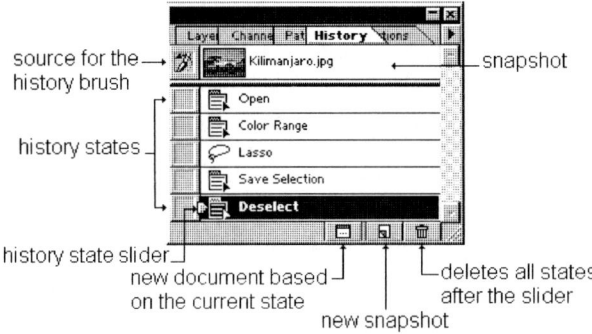

The states correspond to the different actions made. Next to the name of each state, the 📄 icons symbolise a menu command. If you use a retouch or drawing tool the tool icon will appear. To see all the states and all the snapshots, click the ▣ button on the palette title bar.
The list of history states, like the list of snapshots, is shown in chronological order. The oldest state or snapshot is the highest in the list and the lowest one is the most recent.
The palette contents are not saved with the document and only changes made since the document was last opened appear in the list. This limitation applies to both the snapshots and the states. Each open image has its own history; the commands applied to each image are not mixed on one single palette. They are shown in relation to the active document.

Check how each history is separated.

➠ Open the **Mask.jpg** document.

➠ **Image - Adjust - Auto Levels**

The history palette should look like this:

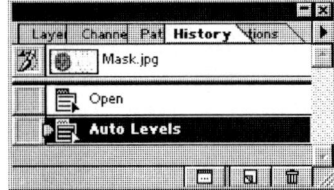

Chapter 4

▶ Now activate the **Kilimanjaro.jpg** document by clicking its window or by using **Window - Kilimanjaro.jpg**.

The history palette should look like this:

This shows that the history palette is specific to each individual image.

Close the mask without saving the changes made.

▶ Activate the **Mask.jpg** document by clicking its window or with **Window - Mask.jpg**.
▶ **File - Close** then click the **No** button to close without saving.

> ✓ To use the history palette's retouch possibilities on work that is long and cannot be completed in one work session, you will have to create documents corresponding to individual states with the ▭ button. In this case, you could replace the 🖌 tool with the 🖫 tool, making your sampling point for duplication on the document that corresponds to a specific state.

Make some interventions on the Kilimanjaro document before continuing.

▶ **Image - Adjust - Curves**
▶ Create a point on the curve with an input value of **100** and an output value of **140** then click **OK**.

The image should be much lighter.

▶ **Image - Adjust - Hue/Saturation**
▶ Select **Reds** in the **Edit** list, set the **Hue** slider at **+90**, the **Saturation** slider at **+40** and the **Lightness** slider at **+20** then click **OK**.

The parts of the image showing the bare earth have now become green.

▶ **Filter - Sketch - Water Paper**
▶ Set the **Contrast** slider at **50** then click **OK**.

The image's colours now appear to run like ink on wet paper.

▶ **Filter - Texture - Texturizer**

Adobe Photoshop 5.5

Chapter 4

▸ Select the **Canvas** texture, set the **Relief** at **4** then click **OK**.

UNDOING SEVERAL ACTIONS

a If the **History** palette is hidden, click its tab or show it with **Window - Show History**.

b Point to the earliest of the actions which you wish to cancel, or to the snapshot you wish to preserve.

▸ Here, point to the **Curves** manoeuvre.

c Click the action or snapshot. You can also drag the palette's selection slider (▷) to position it on the operation in question.

▸ Here, click the **Curves** action.

The selection slider moves and the image is transformed, reverting to the state corresponding to your Curves adjustment, that is the original image in a lightened form. The three cancelled operations are still visible but are greyed-out. As long as you do not do any new work, you can still move the selection slider on any cancelled actions to redo them.

Chapter 4

✓ Using the palette menu (▶), you can also use the following commands:

| Step Backward | Ctrl Alt Z | To cancel the last action made. |
| Step Forward | Ctrl ⇧Shift Z | To redo the previously cancelled action. |

DELETING HISTORY STATES

[a] If the **History** palette is hidden, click its tab or show it with **Window - Show History**.

[b] Select the history state you wish to delete. All the states that follow it will also be deleted.

➠ Here, select the **Water Paper** state that should currently be greyed-out.

[c] Click the 🗑 button on the palette or use the **Delete** command on the palette menu (▶).

➠ Here, click the 🗑 button.

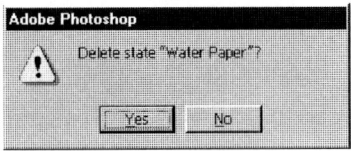

Photoshop prompts you for a confirmation.

[d] Click **Yes** to delete the state.

The **Water Paper** state and the **Texturizer** one that follows it are deleted from the palette.

✓ Contrary to undoing work, these deleted states are permanently removed and you will have to do the work all over again. You can always use *Edit - Undo* to undo your deletion!

Cancel the Hue/Saturation command.

➠ On the **History** palette, place the selection slider on the **Curves** state.

EMPTYING THE HISTORY PALETTE

[a] If the **History** palette is hidden, click its tab or show it with **Window - Show History**.

[b] In the palette menu (▶), activate the **Clear History** command or Ctrl-click the 🗑 button on the palette.

There is only one state left in the palette. In this example, it is the *Curves* state.

➠ **Edit - Undo**

✓ Only states are deleted, snapshots are saved.

✓ If you clear the history by mistake, you can retrieve it with *Edit - Undo*.

Adobe Photoshop 5.5   211

Chapter 4

☑ You can partially clear the history. Make sure that the slider is placed on a more recent state than the one that will be deleted. This is essential to ensure the operation works properly. Drag the last state you want to delete onto the 🗑 button on the palette. This state and all those before it will be erased.

☑ To remove items permanently, so as to free memory space, use the following options of the **Edit - Purge** command:

History   This command is similar to *Clear History* but there is no chance of reversing it because the data contained in *Edit - Undo* is also erased.

Undo   Removes from the memory all the data corresponding to the last work performed, which makes it impossible to use *Edit - Undo*.

All   Removes the history from the memory, and in addition removes the pattern and the clipboard contents.

MODIFYING THE HISTORY PREFERENCES

[a]   If the **History** palette is hidden, click its tab or show it with **Window - Show History**.

[b]   In the palette menu (▶), activate the **History Options** command.

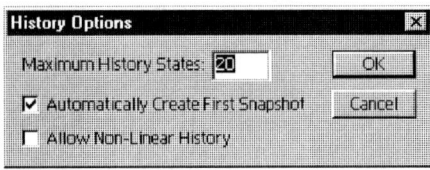

[c]   Use the **Maximum History States** option to set the maximum number of undos. You can specify any value from 1 to 100. The higher the value, the more possibilities you have for undoing work and retouching, but this consumes a considerable amount of memory. A high value, especially when working on large images, can seriously impede the application's speed.

[d]   The **Automatically Create First Snapshot** option when activated creates a snapshot of the image at the moment of opening. This can be very useful if you wish to return rapidly to the original image or to work on a small part of it.

[e]   If you activate the **Allow Non-Linear History** option, any cancelled operations are not definitively erased. You saw that cancelled work in the history appears in grey and that when new commands are used, these operations disappear. If this option is active, the cancelled operations appear normally and are kept in the palette even when new modifications are made to the image. This option can be useful if you want to go back to old cancellations.

➤ Here, leave the default options as they are.

[f]   Click **OK**.

Chapter 4

Before seeing how to create snapshots, modify the image.

➠ **Image - Adjust - Curves**

➠ Place a first point on the curve whose input value equals **51** and whose output is **118**, then a second with an input of **165** and an output of **239**. Click **OK**.

The image is now excessively lightened.

➠ **Image - Adjust - Hue/Saturation**

➠ Set the **Hue** slider to **+30**, the **Lightness** slider to **+10** and click **OK**.

The image becomes green and purple and lighter still!

---

17 *From the History palette, you are going to create a snapshot and a new document.*

CREATING SNAPSHOTS OF IMAGES

DEFINING A SIMPLE SNAPSHOT

[a] If the **History** palette is hidden, click its tab or show it with **Window - Show History**.

[b] Click the [📷] button on the **History** palette.

If you do not see the top part of the palette reserved for snapshots, increase the height of the palette.

The top part of the palette now contains a new snapshot. By default, new snapshots are numbered, as Snapshot 1 (and so on). If the default name suits you, you can skip the following steps.

[c] You can rename a snapshot by double-clicking its thumbnail.

➠ Here, double-click the **Snapshot 1** thumbnail.

Adobe Photoshop 5.5   **213**

Chapter 4

|d| Enter the new **Name** in the corresponding text box.

⟹ Here, enter **Light Green**

|e| Click **OK**.

The snapshot is renamed but all the states are cancelled, because they appear greyed-out. However, the image is not modified because the selection slider is positioned on the renamed snapshot called Light Green.

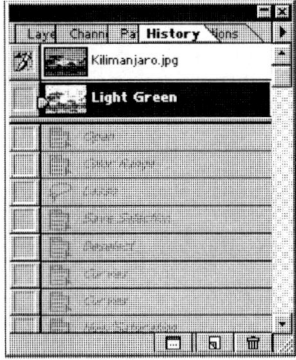

|f| If the states that have just been cancelled may still be of some use to you, click the last state in the **History** palette or drag the slider to the bottom of the list.

⟹ Here, you are going to keep the **Light Green** snapshot but undo the same effect on the original image. Click the first **Curves** command so the second **Curves** command can be seen in grey:

The image reverts to normal colours.

Chapter 4

- ✓ You can create as many snapshots as you wish. This allows you to create elaborate effects and to be able to compare similar effects.
- ✓ To delete a snapshot, simply drag it onto the 🗑 icon on the palette.

DEFINING A SPECIFIC SNAPSHOT

[a] If the **History** palette is hidden, click its tab or show it with **Window - Show History**.

[b] Activate the **New Snapshot** command in the palette menu (▶) or [Alt]-click the 📷 button on the palette.

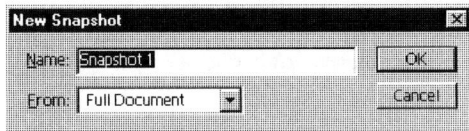

[c] Enter the **Name** of the new snapshot in the corresponding text box.

➤ Here, type in **Lighter**

[d] In the **From** list, choose between:

Full Document Takes the snapshot with all layers separately memorised. This is the default option applied if you simply click the 📷 button on the palette.

Merged Layers Takes a snapshot of the flattened image, that is without taking into account the various layers, which are treated as one single image.

Current Layer Takes a snapshot of the active layer only. The other layers in the image are not saved in the snapshot.

➤ Here, select **Merged Layers**.

[e] Click **OK** to save the new snapshot.

CREATING A DOCUMENT FROM A STATE OR A SNAPSHOT

[a] If the **History** palette is hidden, click its tab or show it with **Window - Show History**.

[b] Select the state or snapshot you want to use to create the new document.

➤ Here, the **Curves** state is selected.

[c] Click the 📷 button in the **History** palette.

A new document appears in a new window. This document takes by default the name of the state from which it was created. In this example, it is called *Curves*.

- ✓ This document could be used at a later time, either because it presents an interesting effect or to replace a snapshot if you have closed and opened the document from which it was made.

Adobe Photoshop 5.5   **215**

Chapter 4

☑ You can also create a new document from a current state using the command **Image - Duplicate**.

☑ You can replace the contents of this document quickly. To do this, display the document containing the image you wish to reproduce, and drag the state or snapshot from the palette onto the window of the document you are replacing.

Try out this last tip.

➤ Display the **Kilimanjaro.jpg** document by clicking its window or activating **Window - Kilimanjaro.jpg**.

➤ **Filter - Render - Difference Clouds**

You have already used the **Clouds** filter. This is a similar filter to that one, except that it is applied with a Difference blending mode instead of a Normal one.

➤ If the **Kilimanjaro.jpg** window is completely covering the **Curves** document, move the window so both documents are partially visible.

➤ Drag the **Difference Clouds** state onto the **Curves** document window as shown below:

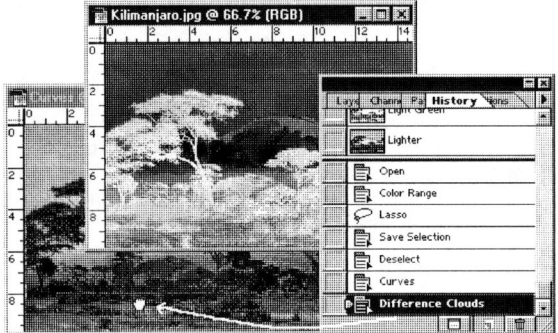

The **Difference Clouds** state is copied onto the **Curves** document. This document is now identical to the one called **Kilimanjaro.jpg**. The same operation could have been performed from the snapshot.

➤ Close the **Curves** document without saving it.

*You are back in the **Kilimanjaro.jpg** document. You can cancel the clouds effect.*

➤ Click the **Curves** state located just above the **Difference Clouds** state in the **History** palette.

You are now going to create a comic strip effect on this image. The snapshot you previously created will now come in handy.

➤ **Layer - Duplicate Layer**
➤ Enter **Comic Book Effect** in the As text box and click **OK**.

*A new layer is created above the **Background** layer.*

➤ **Image - Adjust - Desaturate**

The image is converted to grayscale.

➤ **Image - Adjust - Posterize**

➤ Set the number of **Levels** to **6** and click **OK**.

The original 256 levels of grey are replaced by 6, which creates a very flat result. In the top corners of the image, there are flat areas which are not suitable: you can remove them.

➤ Activate the [tool icon] tool and click a light grey area on the sky.

➤ Activate the [tool icon] tool. In the **Options** palette, check that the **Painting Mode** is **Normal**, that **Opacity** equals **100%** and that the **Fade** option is set to **0**. Select the 65 diameter brush type in the **Brushes** palette. Point to one of the corners which are a slightly darker grey and drag to paint over these corners of the sky. Be careful not to touch the volcano or the trees.

➤ **Filter - Stylize - Trace Contour - OK**

The outside edges of all the items in the picture stand out and the rest of the picture appears in white.

➤ **Image - Adjust - Threshold**

➤ Set the **Threshold Level** at **75** and click **OK**.

The contours are streamlined, less scattered and darker.

➤ In the **Layers** palette, apply the **Multiply** blending mode to the **Comic Book Effect** layer.

As white is a neutral colour for this mode, these zones are transparent. Black is not modified and remains black. The result is a dark image. The clouds retain a photographic aspect.

➤ Activate the **Background** layer.

➤ **Image - Adjust - Curves**

➤ Create a first point on the curve with an input value of **75** and an output value of **126**, then a second point with an input value of **134** and an output value of **204** and finally a third point with an input value of **228** and **250** for the output value. Click **OK**.

The comic book effect is almost complete, as the background is now considerably lightened.

---

18 *Use the history palette's retouch possibilities.*

REPRODUCING A PREVIOUS STATE OR SNAPSHOT

USING THE HISTORY BRUSH

[a] If the **History** palette is hidden, click its tab or show it with **Window - Show History**.

[b] Point to the first column on the palette to define which state or snapshot will be the reference for your duplication then click.

Chapter 4

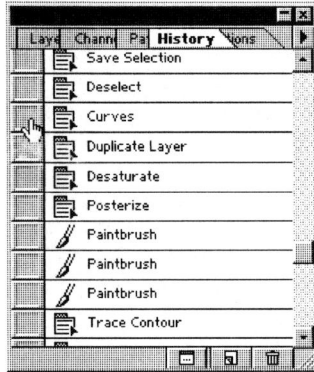

▸ Here, click in the first column at the **Curves** state located above **Duplicate Layer**.

When you click, this icon appears in the first column next to the state. This indicates where the source material is for the tool. The selection slider on the palette should not be moved.

|c| Activate the tool.

|d| If the **Options** palette is hidden, click its tab or show it by double-clicking the tool icon in the toolbox.

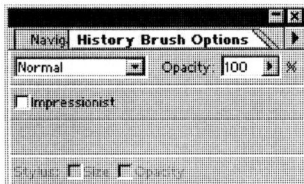

|e| Set the **Blending Mode** and **Opacity** for the tool.

|f| Activate the **Impressionist** option to create an effect similar to that of an impressionist painting.

The effect obtained by this is often radically different. If the option is active, you work as if using the tool but with no notion of pressure. Due to this, the paint is spread out continuously and not just to a certain distance as is the case with the tool.

▸ Here, leave the default options as set.

|g| If the **Brushes** palette is hidden, click its tab or show it using **Window - Show Brushes** then select a brush type.

▸ Here, select the type whose diameter equals **65**

|h| Drag over the areas of the image you wish to replace.

▶ Here, drag over the sky, taking care not to go over onto the trees or the volcano. Leave a slim white halo around these elements, the effect will look slightly more realistic. For thinner areas, choose a smaller tool.

The sky becomes bluer: it takes on its original colour.

✓ *The ⌘ tool is not always available. In this case, the mouse pointer shows a no-go sign ⊘ when you want to use it on the image. This usually happens if you try to reproduce a state with a lower number of layers than the current state. This problem does not occur when working with snapshots.*

✓ *If you click the ⌘ tool in the first column of the History palette, you can no longer use the ⌘ tool. To reactivate it, click the first column of a state or snapshot.*

✓ *If you use the eraser ⌘ tool with the Erase to History option active, this is the equivalent of using the ⌘ tool but also allows you to access certain properties of the ⌘ or ⌘ tools. The ⌘ tool only has properties similar to those of the ⌘ tool.*

Finish creating your effect.

▶ Place the history brush source on the **Light Green** snapshot.

▶ Select a medium-sized brush type, such as the one located above the 100 diameter brush.

▶ Drag over the foliage of the highest trees on the left and right and also over the one in the centre.

The comic book effect is complete with trees much lighter and greener.

▶ Save this image under the name **Kilimanjaro Comic**

USING THE FILL COMMAND

|a| If the **History** palette is hidden, click its tab or show it with **Window - Show History**.

|b| Click the first column on the palette to define the source state or snapshot for the reproduction.

▶ Here, click the **Kilimanjaro.jpg** snapshot.

Chapter 4

- [c] If necessary, make a selection to limit the areas filled.
- ➟ Here, load the **Blue Sky** selection: **Select - Load Selection**, select the **Blue Sky Channel** then click **OK**.
- [d] **Edit**
  Fill ⇧ Shift ⟵
- [e] Select **History** in the **Use** list.
- [f] If necessary, adjust the **Opacity** and blending **Mode**.
- [g] Activate the **Preserve Transparency** option to limit the fill to the visible pixels on the layer.
- ➟ Here, the **Preserve Transparency** option is not available, as you are working on the **Background** layer.
- [h] Click **OK**.

  The entire selection is filled with the initial version of the image. The sky is much darker.

  The result is not very satisfactory. It would be just as well to go back to the Kilimanjaro document saved on your disk.

- ➟ Close the current document without saving it then open **Kilimanjaro.jpg** again and make some changes.
- ➟ **Image - Adjust - Curves**
- ➟ Create a point on the curve with an input value of **100** and an output value of **140** then click **OK**.

  The image becomes lighter.

19

You can create a stylised painting effect based on a state or snapshot from the History palette.

CREATING AN ART REPRODUCTION OF AN EARLIER STATE OF THE IMAGE

- [a] If the **History** palette is not visible, click its tab or use **Window - Show History** to display it.
- [b] Choose the source state or snapshot for the reproduction in the same way as you would if you were going to use the 🖌 tool.
- ➟ Here, click the first column of the **Curves** state.

  The 🖌 symbol should appear next to the first column.

- [c] Activate the 🖌 tool.

Chapter 4

[d] If the **Options** palette is not on screen, click its tab or double-click the tool.

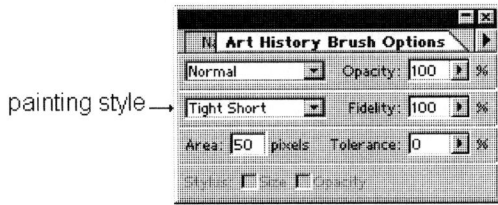

painting style →

[e] Set the **Painting Mode** and **Opacity** for the tool.

➟ Here, leave the default values.

[f] Choose which sort of line the tool will draw by defining a **Painting style**.

➟ Here, choose the style called **Dab**.

[g] Adjust the colour **Fidelity**. If you choose a low **Fidelity**, the colours in the reproduction might differ from those in the state or snapshot. A high fidelity guarantees the colours.

➟ Here, leave the value at **100**

[h] Define the width of the **Area** covered by the tool, by entering a value between 0 and 500. On a low-resolution image, it is advisable to define a narrow area.

➟ Here, enter **10** for the **Area**.

[i] Set a **Tolerance** to limit the parts of the image affected by the tool. If the **Tolerance** is high, the tool will only work on parts of the image where the colour is very different from the state or snapshot. If the **Tolerance** is low, the tool will affect any part of the image to which it is applied.

➟ Here, leave the default value of **0**.

[j] If the **Brushes** palette does not appear on screen, show it by clicking its tab or by **Window - Show Brushes** then select a brush.

➟ Here, select the brush underneath the one with a diameter of 35.

[k] Drag over the areas of the picture to which you want to apply the art effect.

➟ Here, apply the effect to the whole image.

The scene looks more or less as if it had been painted.

> ✓ *For a more marked effect, you could apply a filter to the image before using the Art History Brush on it. You could also fill the image with solid colour then use a snapshot of the original as the source of your art reproduction.*

➟ Save this image under the name **Kilimanjaro art**

Adobe Photoshop 5.5

Chapter 4

PRACTICE EXERCISE 4

- Open the **Elephant.jpg** document.
- Create a pattern from the elephant's head, choosing an area between its eyes. This pattern can be copied into a new document.
- Make sure there is no checkered effect on the texture (the document should not contain any layers).
- Save this new document as **Elephant Texture.psd**.
- Before closing the document, retrieve the image as a pattern then close both open documents.
- Open the **Giraffe.jpg** document.
- Using the color range, select as precisely as possible all the spots on the giraffe. Refine this selection with other tools.
- Copy this selection into a new layer called **Spots** (create the new layer via copy).
- Create a new layer over the **Spots** layer that you call **Elephant Pattern**.
- Fill this layer with the pattern.
- Select a foreground colour whose components are **R**= 177, **G**= 153 and **B**= 110 then apply a **Clouds** filter to this layer.
- Fade the filter effect with 40% opacity.
- From the **Layers** palette, apply a **Hard Light** mode to the **Elephant Pattern** layer.
- Take a snapshot of this image, using merged layers.
- Remove the blending mode, the softening and the cloud filter to return to the original pattern.
- Create a clipping group between the **Spots** and **Elephant Pattern** layers.
- The spots should be a little redder and also duller, apply an appropriate adjustment layer on the Elephant Pattern only.
- Use the **Snapshot 1** snapshot to paint the very bottom of the **Background** layer with the history brush. Leave the highest grass visible, but the ground should take on a light elephant skin effect.
- Save this document as **Giraffe Elephant.psd** and leave Photoshop.

Corrected versions of these documents have been created under the names **Elephant Texture Chapter 4.psd** and **Giraffe Elephant Chapter 4.psd**.

CHAPTER 5

1 - CHANGING THE DEPTH OF COLOURS 224
2 - CONVERTING A COLOUR IMAGE FROM ONE COLOUR MODEL TO ANOTHER 225
        CONVERTING AN RGB OR CMYK IMAGE INTO LAB MODE 225
        CONVERTING AN RGB OR LAB MODE IMAGE INTO CMYK 226
        CONVERTING A CMYK OR LAB IMAGE INTO RGB 229
3 - CONVERTING AN IMAGE INTO GRAYSCALE 230
4 - CONVERTING A GRAYSCALE IMAGE TO BITMAP 231
5 - CONVERTING AN IMAGE TO DUOTONE 234
6 - CONVERTING AN RGB IMAGE INTO INDEXED COLORS 238
7 - MANAGING AN IMAGE'S COLOR TABLE 242
        LOADING ANOTHER COLOR TABLE 242
        MODIFYING THE EXISTING COLOR TABLE 243
8 - COLORIZING A GRAYSCALE IMAGE 245
        USING DRAWING TOOLS OR THE FILL COMMAND 245
        MODIFYING HUE AND SATURATION 246
        USING A DUOTONE 247
        USING INDEXED COLORS 248
9 - MODIFYING THE SIZE OF THE CANVAS 249
10 - APPLYING A TRANSFORMATION TO A SELECTION BORDER 251
11 - CHANGING THE SIZE AND/OR RESOLUTION OF AN IMAGE 252
12 - CROPPING AN IMAGE 257
13 - SAVING A DOCUMENT IN A SPECIFIC FORMAT 259
        DEFINING A SAVING FORMAT 259
        JPEG FORMAT 261
        COMPUSERVE GIF FORMAT 263
        GIF89A FORMAT 264
        TIFF FORMAT 267
        PHOTOSHOP EPS FORMAT 268
        PHOTOSHOP DCS 1.0 AND 2.0 FORMATS 270
        PHOTOSHOP PDF FORMAT 271
        BMP FORMAT 272
        OTHER FORMATS RECOGNISED BY PHOTOSHOP 273
14 - SAVING AN IMAGE FOR USE ON THE WEB 274
        PRACTICE EXERCISE 5 282

Chapter 5

During this chapter, you look at functions that can be applied to the image as a whole, such as switching from one colour model to another, changing size or resolution and also saving in different formats.

➟ If you previously left Photoshop, restart it now.

➟ Open the **Lion.jpg** document in the **ENI Photoshop 5.5** folder.

1 *Start by modifying the depth of the colours in the image.*

CHANGING THE DEPTH OF COLOURS

[a] If the image is not in RGB, CMYK or Grayscale mode, convert the image to one of these modes.

➟ Here, your image is in a correct mode as it is in RGB mode.

[b] If the image contains layers, flatten it with **Layer - Flatten Image**.

➟ Here, that is not necessary.

[c] **Image**
    Mode

[d] Select one of the following options:

8 Bits/Channel	This is the most frequently used mode. It allows you to obtain a standard photographic quality. For example, a CMYK image would contain 32 bits, because it has 4 channels and 8 bits per channel.
16 Bits/Channel	This mode allows you to obtain a higher quality with a much better distinction of colours. To see a visible difference in relation to an 8 bits per channel image, the image has to be scanned in 16 bits per channel, which few scanners support. This mode has two major disadvantages: some tools and commands (mostly filters) cannot be used and more importantly, you cannot use layers. This creates a much bigger document than for 8 bits per channel pictures so you should reserve this mode for documents requiring extremely high print quality.

A tick can be seen next to the current colour depth.

➟ Here, leave the image in **8 Bits/Channel**.

Chapter 5

2 *The different colour models available in Photoshop have already been described. Here is how to change from one to another.*

CONVERTING A COLOUR IMAGE FROM ONE COLOUR MODEL TO ANOTHER

CONVERTING AN RGB OR CMYK IMAGE INTO LAB MODE

[a] If the image is in **16 Bits/Channel** convert it to **8 Bits/Channel**.

➤ Here, that is not necessary.

[b] If necessary, merge the adjustment layers so as not to lose their effects.

➤ Here, the image only contains a **Background** layer.

[c] **Image**
Mode
Lab Color

Lab mode encompasses the colour spectrums of both RGB and CMYK, so the image will show no modification.

[d] If you are trying to convert an image with more than one layer, Photoshop asks you how to proceed.
— If the image still contains an adjustment layer:

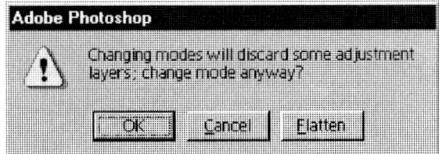

Click:

OK	To convert the image and delete the adjustment layers (the adjustments will not be applied before being deleted).
Flatten	To keep the adjustment effects made. However, the conversion will merge all existing layers onto the image's background layer.
Cancel	To stop the conversion.

— If the image contains a normal layer:

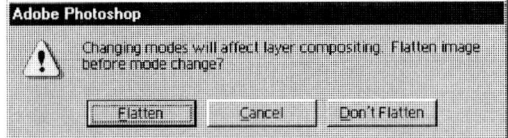

Chapter 5

Click:

Flatten	To convert while merging all layers onto the background layer.
Don't Flatten	To make the conversion and preserve all the layers.
Cancel	To stop the conversion.

☑ *Some commands cannot be used when an image is in Lab mode. This is notably the case for certain filters.*

☑ *You can freely convert another type of image, such as a grayscale, into Lab mode. Only Bitmap mode cannot be converted into Lab mode.*

Cancel this conversion.

➤ **Edit - Undo**

CONVERTING AN RGB OR LAB MODE IMAGE INTO CMYK

[a] If the image is in **16 Bits/Channel**, you should switch to **8 Bits/Channel** if you want to adjust the conversion. The RGB and Lab spectrums contain non-printable colours, that is colours for which there is no CMYK equivalent. Most hues have shades which cannot be printed but blue is the colour most affected by a CMYK conversion.

➤ Here, the image is in **8 Bits/Channel**.

[b] To make the most accurate conversion possible, by viewing the out-of-gamut colours beforehand, use this command:
View   Ctrl ⇧Shift **Y**
Gamut Warning

This command determines which areas of the image will be altered by the conversion. If there are very few out-of-gamut colours, the conversion can go ahead with no adjustment, using black point compensation.

On this example, most of the sky becomes grey, except for a small patch at the bottom. This means that the sky is made up of colours that cannot be printed, which will be distorted if you proceed directly with the conversion.

[c] If considerable areas of the image appear as out-of-gamut, select these colours:
Select - Color Range
Choose **Out Of Gamut** in the **Select** list and click **OK**.

➤ Here, select the colours in this way.

Chapter 5

[d] To avoid making too obvious a correction, feather the selection:
Select - Feather
Set a **Feather Radius**, which is generally between 5 and 15, depending on the resolution of the image, then click **OK**.

➤ Here, choose a feather radius of **5**, because the image resolution is low.

[e] Adjust the saturation slightly (as well as the hue, if necessary) by means of a **Hue/Saturation** adjustment layer situated in the foreground, that is, on top of all the other layers. To avoid corrections which are too harsh and would give a worse result than a direct conversion, you may need to perform these three steps several times. To make more precise saturation retouches, use the ▦ tool with a low pressure.

➤ Here, create an adjustment layer with **Layer - New - Adjustment Layer**.
Select **Hue/Saturation** in the **Type** list and click **OK**.
Set the **Hue** slider at **-4** and the **Saturation** slider at **-16** and click **OK**.

At least half of the out-of-gamut colours disappear.

➤ Select the non-printable colours again then create a new adjustment layer, feather the selection, using a radius of **5** and set the **Hue** and **Saturation** at the same values as for the previous adjustment (here, this works but that may not always be the case).
Make yet another new selection and adjustment and use **-1 Hue** and **-14 Saturation**.

Most of the colours can now be printed. There are still a few small areas in out-of-gamut colours but it is not necessary to correct those.

In the interets of speed, only three adjustment layers have been created for this example. For a better result, you could have desaturated the colours more gradually, by creating intermediate adjustment layers.

[f] If necessary, merge the adjustment layers to preserve their effects.

➤ Here, activate the **Layer - Flatten Image** command.

[g] Deactivate the display of non-printing colours by choosing **View - Gamut Warning**.

[h] To preview the image as it will appear after conversion, use:
View [Ctrl] **Y**
Preview
CMYK

Some areas are a little blurred, particularly at the bottom of the image where there were still a few out-of-gamut colours present.

The title bar on the document window indicates that you are looking at a preview by naming the current colour mode and the CMYK mode.

Chapter 5

[i] If the colour distortion is too noticeable, deactivate the preview by repeating **View - Preview - CMYK** then make further corrections.

⟹ Here, the result seems to be correct.

[j] If necessary, deactivate the preview:
View - Preview - CMYK

⟹ Do this here.

[k] Make the conversion:
Image
Mode
CMYK Color

The image is converted to CMYK colours. It can now be printed without suffering colour distortion.

- ✓ As for a conversion to Lab colour, Photoshop offers to delete or flatten any existing adjustment layers or to merge or keep any normal layers.

- ✓ If you make a conversion without taking into account the out-of-gamut colours, you risk finding a result very far removed from your original image. It is often preferable to retouch the colours yourself rather than let Photoshop do the job for you. This is mainly the case when the out-of-gamut colours are spread over a wide area, as they were in our example. You will obtain an optimum correction by feathering slightly the selection of out-of-gamut colours before making your retouches.

- ✓ Some commands, mainly certain filters, cannot be used on images in CMYK mode.

- ✓ You can freely convert Grayscale or Duotone images to CMYK mode. For Indexed Color images, you will not be able to run a check on the out-of-gamut colours. In this case, convert firstly to RGB in order to make your verifications.

- ✓ You can change the colour used to highlight the out-of-gamut colours with the command *File - Preferences - Transparency & Gamut*. Select a colour that really stands out in relation to the image. The ideal would be a very bright out-of-gamut colour.

☑ There are other pre-conversion previews that you can use to make very specific colour checks. Only a more experienced user would be able to take full advantage of the possibilities they offer. Activate *View - Preview* and choose one of the following:

Cyan/Magenta/ Yellow/Black	To view separately the various CMYK channels. This preview occurs in grayscale. The darker the grey is, the more ink there is of the corresponding colour.
CMY	Allows you to see how these three primary colours would merge without the addition of black.

➥ Save the lion under the name **Four Colour Lion** and open the original **Lion.jpg** document again to return to the image in RGB.

To prepare for the next step, you should convert the image to Lab mode.

➥ **Image - Mode - Lab Color**

CONVERTING A CMYK OR LAB IMAGE INTO RGB

[a] If necessary, flatten the adjustment layers to preserve their effects.

➥ Here, that is not necessary.

[b] **Image**
Mode
RGB Color

The image is converted into RGB.

☑ As for a conversion to Lab colour, Photoshop offers to delete or flatten any existing adjustment layers or to merge or keep any normal layers.

☑ The CMYK and Lab spectrums are very different to that of RGB mode. The image can therefore suffer from colour distortion. Contrary to a conversion into CMYK mode, Photoshop does not offer any previews allowing you to correct these potential distortions before they occur. You can however see a preview of the converted image on different platforms to check how it is rendered. Choose one of the following options in *View - Preview*:

Macintosh RGB	To view the image as it would appear on a Macintosh. This option is only useful if you are working under Windows.
Windows RGB	To view the image as it would appear under Windows. This option is only useful if you are working on a Macintosh.
Uncompensated RGB	To view the image with no colour adjustment. This is equivalent to not displaying a preview.

Chapter 5

✓ You can freely convert other image modes such as Indexed Color into RGB.

---

3 After the colour conversion, try converting your image into grayscale.

CONVERTING AN IMAGE INTO GRAYSCALE

[a] If necessary, flatten the adjustment layers to preserve their effects.

[b] **Image**
Mode
Grayscale

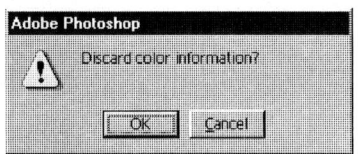

If the image contains no other layers than the **Background** layer, Photoshop prompts for confirmation before removing the colours.

If the image contains several layers, Photoshop offers to delete or flatten any existing adjustment layers or to merge or preserve any ordinary layers (cf. Converting an RGB or CMYK image into Lab mode).

[c] Click **OK** to make the conversion.

➔ Here, click **OK**.

The image is converted into grayscale.

✓ For a high quality conversion, you can prepare the image beforehand by mixing channels. You will look at this in greater detail in chapter 7, which deals with channels.

Chapter 5

☑ If you are converting an image in Bitmap mode to grayscale, Photoshop prompts you for the size ratio, the factor by which to reduce the image's size.
The higher the ratio, the smaller the image produced, but the more shades of grey used. Photoshop creates new levels of grayscale by interpolation and the number of levels that it can create depends on the size ratio. If you leave the ratio at 1, the image will only have two grayscale levels: pure black and pure white. The actual number of levels created when you scale down varies from image to image. The histograms below represent an image concerted to grayscale using different size ratios.

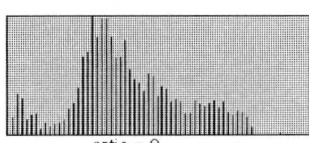
ratio = 2

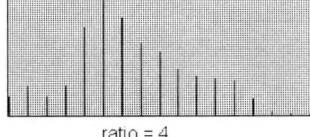
ratio = 4

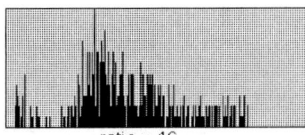
ratio = 8

ratio = 16

4 When an image is in grayscale, you can convert it either to Bitmap or Duotone. Start by making a conversion to Bitmap to change the grey tones to pure black and white.

CONVERTING A GRAYSCALE IMAGE TO BITMAP

[a] Merge the adjustment layers before converting. Conversion cannot take place if adjustment layers are present in the document. To save time, you can simply flatten the image or delete these layers if you do not wish to keep them. A Bitmap image cannot manage layers.

➤ Here, this is not necessary.

[b] **Image**
Mode
Bitmap

If you have not flattened the image, Photoshop prompts you to do it.

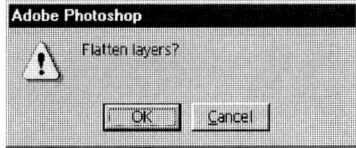

Adobe Photoshop 5.5

Chapter 5

[c] If required, flatten the layers.

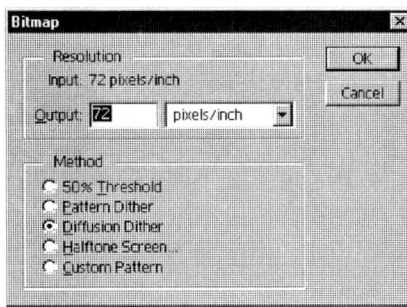

A dialog box appears, to allow you to set the conversion parameters.

[d] Use the **Output** option to set the resolution used. By default, an identical value to the one on the grayscale image is used. Using a higher **Output** resolution limits the loss of grey tones in the picture. The higher the resolution used, the smaller the surface used to print the black and white dots, which gives a more realistic impression of grey.

original grayscale image

image converted to bitmap with a resolution of 72 ppi

image converted to bitmap with a resolution of 300 ppi

➨ Here, leave the **Output** option at 72 ppi.

[e] Select the desired conversion method:

50% Threshold All the pixels containing more than 50% black are converted to black and all the rest become white. This method produces a highly contrasted result similar to the **Image - Adjust - Threshold** command.

Pattern Dither Simulates shades of grey by creating geometric shapes made up of black and white dots.

Diffusion Dither Simulates shades of grey by error-diffusion. The error margin is determined when the first pixel in the top left corner is converted. This method produces results close to the original image. It is often used to create images that will be viewed on black and white monitors.

Halftone Screen Simulates shades of grey by using halftone dots. These dots are linked to a screen. This is defined when you click **OK**. Like any screen, it functions in relation to the screen ruling, the screen angle and the dot shape used. Ask your print shop for the information needed to obtain a quality result. An office printer, like an ordinary monitor, will not be able to suitably reproduce the information supplied for the halftone screen.

Chapter 5

Custom Pattern — This method is an intermediate solution between **50% Threshold** and **Pattern Dither**. It applies a texture to the screen, using the pattern defined with the **Edit - Define Pattern** command. The result is highly contrasted, while taking into account the shape of the pattern. This method can be used to obtain a particular texture within an image.

original grayscale image

bitmap image with 50 % threshold

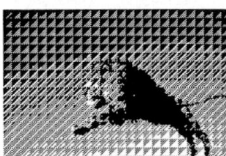
bitmap image with pattern dither

bitmap image with diffusion dither

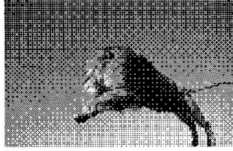
bitmap image with halftone screen (default screen settings)

bitmap image with custom pattern (hard linear grain texture)

➽ Here, select **Halftone Screen**.

[f] Click **OK**.

[g] If you selected the **Halftone Screen** option, define the screen:

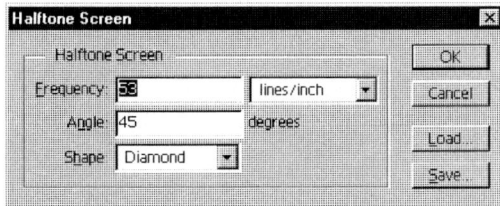

Frequency — This varies between 1 and 999 **lines/inch** (or **lpi**). The screen ruling determines the number of lines on the halftone screen per inch. You may use a lines/centimetre measure, but it is perhaps preferable to keep the lines/inch measure which is more common in printing. The higher the **Frequency**, the better the printing quality. For example, a newspaper uses on average a 85 lpi screen while a magazine uses a frequency between 130 and 150 lpi. For a very large image, the frequency is often low as the image is designed to be viewed from afar. The choice of **Frequency** depends not only on the required quality but also on the equipment and paper used for printing.

Adobe Photoshop 5.5

Chapter 5

Angle	Lets you determine the angle of the screen ruling and therefore the angle of the screen orientation. You can specify a value between -180 and +180.
Shape	Use this to define the shape of the dots on the screen. You can choose between a **Round**, a **Diamond**, an **Ellipse**, a **Line**, a **Square** or a **Cross**.

➠ Here, leave the default options as your screen will not be able to reproduce the halftone screen correctly anyway.

[h] Click **OK**.

The image is converted to Bitmap and contains only pure black or white points. The 45° angle used for the halftone screen can be seen at the top of the image.

- ✓ If your printer has supplied the required information to define the halftone screen, use the *Save* button on the *Halftone Screen* dialog box when you first define the screen characteristics. You can click the *Load* button to activate these parameters automatically when you use this function at a later time.

- ✓ A large number of commands cannot be used when an image is in Bitmap.

- ✓ Only Grayscale and Multichannel images can be converted into Bitmap mode. If you convert a Multichannel image, only the active channel will be used and all others will be deleted.

Cancel this conversion to return to the grayscale image.

➠ **Edit - Undo**

---

5 *Now you can make a duotone from this grayscale picture.*

CONVERTING AN IMAGE TO DUOTONE

[a] If the image is not in grayscale, convert it to grayscale using **Image - Mode - Grayscale** (cf. Converting an image into grayscale).

[b] **Image**
Mode
Duotone

Chapter 5

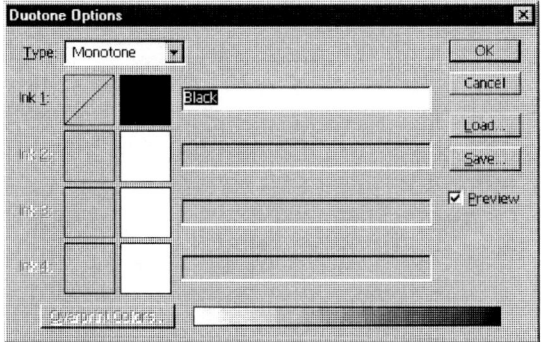

|c| Select the desired **Type** of image. You can print the image with one type of ink in **Monotone**, which will produce a variety of shades of the same colour (if that colour is black, the image will appear as if it was in grayscale); with two inks in **Duotone**, with three in **Tritone** or with four inks in **Quadtone**. **Duotone** is used for example to create "old photograph" effects by combining yellow and black.

⇒ Here, select **Tritone**.

|d| Depending on what **Type** was chosen, click the different colour samples to define what colour ink to use. By default Photoshop prompts you to use spot colours such as the Pantone custom colours. If this is not the case and the Color Picker is displayed, click **Custom** to use this type of colour.

It is preferable to use spot colours rather than colours chosen from the Color Picker. The reason for this is that if you choose a colour from the picker, there is a good chance that several different inks will have to be used to produce that colour. In this case, if you were making a monochrome, printing would use several inks where one would have been sufficient, increasing the cost.

⇒ Here, click the first colour box, click if necessary the **Custom** button and select **Pantone Coated** in the **Book** list.
Select the **Pantone Process Black CVC** colour.
Click **OK**.
Click the **Ink 2** colour box.
Select the **Pantone Orange 021 CVC** colour.
Click **OK**.
Click the **Ink 3** colour box.
Select **Pantone Process Yellow CVC** and click **OK**.

Each time you choose spot a colour, its name is automatically given. If you use the Color Picker, you will have to enter a name for the colour.

|e| Set the duotone curves by clicking the corresponding boxes to the left of the ink colour boxes.

⇒ Here, click the curve box for **Ink 1**.

Adobe Photoshop 5.5

Chapter 5

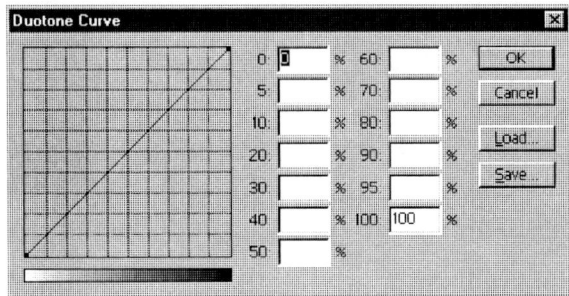

The curves are similar to those used for retouching brightness and contrast, but in this case they act on the density of ink used:

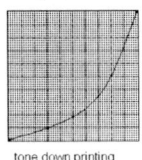 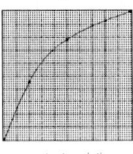 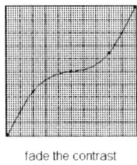 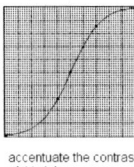 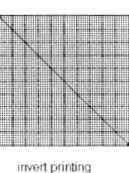

tone down printing with this ink (lighter)   accentuate printing with this ink (darker)   fade the contrast of this ink   accentuate the contrast of this ink   invert printing of this ink (negative)

The most frequently used curves are those used to lighten or darken colours.

[f] To add a point, click the text box corresponding to the input value then type the required density (or output) value.

You can add points at every 10% mark plus two extra points at 5 and 95%. You can also define the density (or output) value by vertically dragging a point on the curve.

➧ Here, click in the **50** text box and type **35** to add a point at input value 50 for an output value of 35.

The curve sags down and the image becomes lighter.

[g] To delete a point, erase the percentage entered or drag the point out of the curve box.

➧ Here, you do not need to delete any points.

[h] Click **OK** to confirm your duotone curve.

➧ Here, click **OK** then set the curve for orange by adding a point at 50% with an output of 60%.
Click **OK** then set the curve for yellow by adding a point at 50% with an output value of 70%.
Click **OK**.

Chapter 5

[i] If necessary, click the **Overprint Colors** button to adjust the screen display in order to simulate the printed result correctly.
Click the sample boxes corresponding to the various inks mixed at 100% to correct the colour.

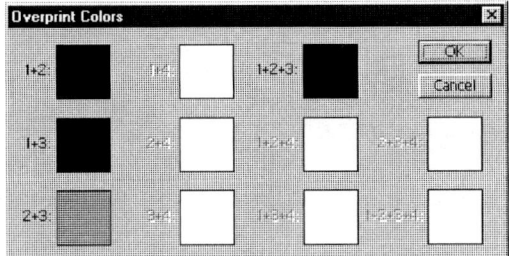

This step is not a must but it can give you a better perception of the final result. Be careful, this does not change anything in relation to printing the image. It is purely a correction on the screen display. To make a correct adjustment, use a printed sample of the overprinted inks.

➤ Here, click **OK** without making any changes to the display.

[j] Click **OK**.

The image appears in a yellowish orange colour.

- ✓ If the original grayscale image contains adjustment or ordinary layers, you do not have to flatten these before converting to Duotone because they will be preserved.

- ✓ If the result is unsatisfactory, you do not have to cancel the Duotone. You can return to a Duotone mode at anytime you wish by changing the colours or the curves. This is of no consequence to the image because Duotone is based on the original image in grayscale.

- ✓ You can *Save* the adjustments made and apply them to another image later by clicking *Load*.

Save the duotone information and modify it.

➤ **Image - Mode - Duotone**

➤ Save the settings under the name **Tri Pantone Black - 021 - Yellow**

As a general rule, use a name which will remind you of the duotone type and the colours used. This will allow you to retrieve the information more easily.

➤ Select **Duotone** in the **Type** list. Replace the orange by the yellow called **Pantone 109 CVC** (type **109** in the dialog box to obtain the colour more rapidly).

Chapter 5

▸ Adjust the two curves identically, adding a point at 50% with an output value of 40%. Click **OK** to confirm your duotone.

The image resembles an old sepia photograph.

▸ Save the image under the name **Duotone Lion**, close it and open **Lion.jpg**.

6

Sometimes it is useful to limit the number of colours used in the image to 256.

CONVERTING AN RGB IMAGE INTO INDEXED COLORS

[a] If the image is in **16 Bits/Channel**, convert it to **8 Bits/Channel**.

▸ Here, that is not necessary.

[b] **Image**
Mode
Indexed Color

If you have not flattened the image, Photoshop prompts you to do so.

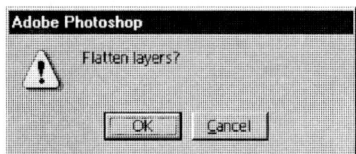

[c] Click **OK** if necessary to flatten the image and proceed with the conversion.

In this case, there is no layer present so no message will be displayed.

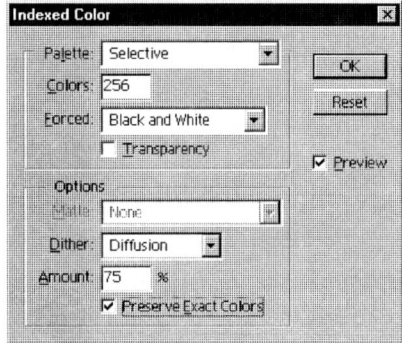

Chapter 5

|d| Select the type of **Palette** that you wish to apply:

Exact
This option is available if the image does not contain more than 256 colours: if this is the case, it is offered as the default. The image undergoes no changes, and all the colours can be integrated into the colour table.

System (Macintosh)
Uses the Macintosh system palette to make the conversion. If the image is to be used on a Macintosh, you can use this option to ensure an optimum display in 256-colour mode. This avoids unpleasant colour transitions when you move from displaying the image to displaying another window. This can be useful when creating multimedia applications in 256 colours. If you are sure of using the image on a Macintosh with a thousands or millions of colours display, you may wish to use another palette.

System (Windows)
Palette similar to **System (Macintosh)** but designed for computers using Windows. Its conditions of usage are identical to that of the Macintosh.

Web
Converts with a palette of 216 colours used by most Internet browsers to display 8 bit images. Although this palette is theoretically optimised for images included in Web pages, you can use other palettes, notably the **System** palettes. In this case, images will not always be correctly viewed on a computer using 256 colours.

Uniform
Uses a palette based on a uniform colour sample of the image's whole colour spectrum. Photoshop takes between 2 and 6 levels for each of the red, green and blue components and combines them to make a uniform palette. This palette is limited to 216 colours. Depending on the image, it can produce good results if you want to limit the number of colours to 8. For a higher number of colours, it is generally a better idea to use the **Adaptive** palette.

Perceptual
Converts using a palette made up of the colours in the image, with priority given to the colours most easily perceived by the eye. If the **Exact** palette is not available, this palette is one of your best hopes of reproducing the original image faithfully (the **Selective** and **Adaptive** palettes also produce satisfactory results). If you make a selection before conversion, the colours of the pixels in the selection will influence the resulting colour table.

Selective
This palette is similar to **Perceptual**, but gives priority to large areas of colour and preserves Web colours.

Adaptive
This palette is similar to **Perceptual**, in that it is made up of the colours in the image. It does not, however, give priority to any particular colour.

Chapter 5

Custom	Lets you apply a special palette. When you choose this palette, Photoshop opens the **Color Table** dialog box to allow you to create your own palette or to load one. This allows you to use a specific palette over several images, which can be useful for multimedia applications. You can save your palette when you create it or after the conversion to Indexed Colors. You will see more about the **Color Table** dialog box a little further on.
Previous	Lets you apply the palette used to make the last conversion, providing it was made with the **Perceptual, Selective, Adaptive** or **Custom** palettes. This could be useful when working on multimedia applications to ensure that each image has the same colour table.

➟ Here, choose **Adaptive**.

[e] If you have selected a **Uniform, Perceptual, Selective** or **Adaptive** palette, you can define the exact number of **Colors** you want to use for the image in the corresponding text box.

➟ Here, leave the **256** option entered by default.

[f] If you have selected a **Perceptual, Selective** or **Adaptive** palette, you can ensure that particular colours are used in the picture. To do this, select an option from the **Forced** list:

None	You do not require any particular colour in the palette.
Black and White	The palette contains pure black and pure white.
Primaries	Adds the primary CMY and RGB colours to the palette, along with pure black and pure white.
Web	Adds the 216 colours from the Web palette (cf. the information on palettes given above). This leaves no more than 40 colours for colours specific to the image.
Custom	The **Forced Colors** dialog box appears for you to select your own required colours.

➟ Here, select **None**.

[g] Activate the **Transparency** option to preserve the transparent areas of the image. This option is only useful if the image has no **Background** layer. If the option is deactivated, the transparent areas are filled with the colour selected in the **Matte** option, or by white, if no particular colour has been defined.

➟ Here, make sure that the option is not active: the image has a **Background** layer.

[h] In **Matte**, select the colour with which to fill the transparent areas. If the **Transparency** option is active, the image's semi-transparent edges will be filled with a gradient to the **Matte** colour. You will find this option very useful if you have to transfer an image to an HTML page with a solid-colour background.

Chapter 5

matte = None   matte = White

*Notice the pixelation effect, especially visible on the tail, back legs and belly when no **Matte** is selected.*

» Here, the option is not available, as the image has no transparent areas.

[i] If you use a different palette from **Exact**, the palette generally does not contain all the colours of the image. Select a **Dither** option to simulate the colours that do not appear:

None No dithering will occur and the missing colours are replaced by the closest colours in the colour table. Colour transition will be stronger and you will obtain a posterized effect.

Diffusion Produces a simulation by error-diffusion. Pixels of different colours are juxtaposed to replace missing colours. This method produces result close to the original, especially when used with the **Adaptive**, **Selective** and **Perceptual** palettes.

Pattern Simulates the missing colours with a pattern of juxtaposed colours. This method is only available in conjunction with the **System (Macintosh)**, **Web** and **Uniform** palettes.

Noise Similar to the **Diffusion** dither, this simulation is particularly useful if you are extracting an image to place it in an HTML table. If minimises the number of stray pixels on the edges of the extracted object.

original RGB image

indexed color dithering none

indexed color diffusion dithering

indexed color pattern dithering

indexed color noise dithering

*This illustration shows the image being converted to 16 colours so that you can see the dither effects, and in particular the difference between **Diffusion** and **Noise**, more clearly.*

» Here, leave **Diffusion** active.

Chapter 5

[j] If you have chosen a **Diffusion** dither, set the **Amount** to define the density of the dither effect. A high **Amount** value ensures correct colour simulation, but creates a large document.

➤ Here, leave the default value.

[k] If you have chosen a **Diffusion** dither, activate the **Preserve Exact Colors** option to avoid carrying out a simulation on palette colours which exactly match the colours from the original image. This option is particularly useful for preserving fine lines or text.

➤ Here, keep the **Preserve Exact Colors** option active.

[l] Click **OK**.

The image is converted to 256 colours. Using a perceptual, selective or adaptive palette and diffusion dithering ensures a minimum loss of visual quality for the image.

✓ *Many commands are unavailable when an image is in Indexed Color mode.*

✓ *Grayscale and Duotone images can be converted to Indexed Color. In this case, no choice needs to be made concerning the palette because these images are in 256 levels and require no palette optimisation.*

✓ *If you select a number of colours less than 256, you will obtain a smaller document of inferior quality. Photoshop is capable of handling colour tables of under 256 colours and adapts to take account of the exact number of colours. You can edit the table to change this number.*

7 *How should you manage the color table of an image in Indexed Color?*
MANAGING AN IMAGE'S COLOR TABLE

LOADING ANOTHER COLOR TABLE

[a] **Image**
Mode
Color Table

Chapter 5

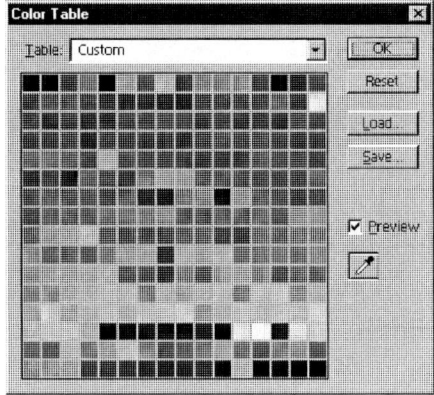

|b| Select a predefined **Table** in the corresponding list box or click the **Load** button to open a saved palette. If you load a palette, you can retrieve one of three different palette **Types**:

Color Table   This is Photoshop's default format when saving color tables.

Swatches   You can load Photoshop swatch palettes to use in the color table. If the swatch palette contains more than 256 colours, only the first 256 will be imported into the color table.

Microsoft Palette®   This is the standard Microsoft format used to save 256-colour palettes. If you wish you can choose this format rather than the Photoshop format. Files in this format do take up a little more disk space than those in Photoshop format.

➡ Here, select the **Black Body** palette in the **Table** list and click **OK**.

A curious result occurs. This is because colour matching has already taken place. If you had selected this palette at the time of the conversion (using the Custom palette in the Indexed Colors dialog box), the result obtained would have been quite different.

This result is not suitable, so cancel it and return to the color table.

➡ Here, cancel your result with **Edit - Undo**.

MODIFYING THE EXISTING COLOR TABLE

|a| Image
Mode
Color Table

|b| To modify a colour in the palette, click the corresponding swatch in the dialog box: the **Color Picker** is displayed. Set new components for this colour and click **OK**.

➡ Here, click the last colour (in the bottom right corner) select a bright red then click the **OK** button on the **Color Picker** then on the **Color Table**.

The darkest areas on the lion have turned red.

Adobe Photoshop 5.5

Chapter 5

Modify this colour again.

▶ For this example, undo the last action and open the **Color Table** again (**Image - Mode - Color Table**).
Click the last colour, set its components at **C= 60**, **M= 54**, **Y= 51** and **K= 76** then click the **OK** button on the **Color Picker** then on the **Color Table**.

The change is much less noticeable.

[c] To modify a range of colours, create a gradient between two distant colours in the table by dragging from the start colour to the finish colour.

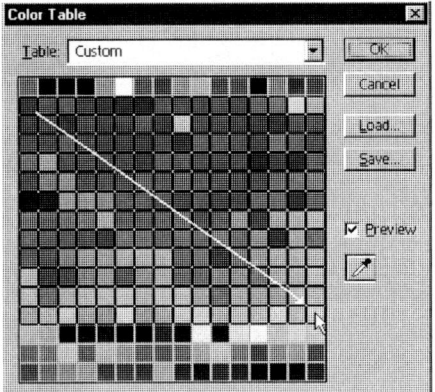

Photoshop will show the Color Picker twice, to define in succession the start colour and the end colour for the gradient.

▶ Here, open the **Color Picker** using **Image - Mode - Color Table** then drag over the swatches as shown in the illustration above. Click **OK** on the first **Color Picker** then set the components of the second colour to **C= 44**, **M= 0**, **Y= 10** and **K= 0** then click **OK** on the **Color Picker**.

*The **Preview** option is active, and you can already see the changes to the image: the sky has been changed, as have a few pixels on the lion. If the colours appear more uniform in the colour table, it is not the case on the picture. As for the previous modification made with **Black Body**, this is due to the fact that the colour matching has already been done.*

[d] Activate the dialog box's [icon] tool if you want to make one of the palette colours transparent then click the colour concerned in the palette.

▶ You do not need to create any transparent colours here.

[e] If the result obtained with this new palette is satisfactory, you can save it in order to use it with other images. To do this, open the **Color Table** again using **Image - Mode - Color Table** then click the **Save** button. Choose a **File name** for your palette and click **Save**.

▶ Here, you do not need to save this palette.

[f] Click **OK**.

Cancel all these modifications then reconvert the image to grayscale.

⟹ In the **History** palette, click the **Open** state to return to the initial image in RGB.

You are going to colorize this image, but beforehand, make a selection and save it as you will need it later on.

⟹ Use the ▨ tool to select the sky then invert the selection with **Select - Inverse**. Save the selection using **Select - Save Selection**.

⟹ Enter **Lion** in the **Name** box and click **OK**.

⟹ **Select - Deselect**

⟹ **Image - Mode - Grayscale**

⟹ Click **OK** to confirm removing all colour information.

8

You are going to see how to add colour to a grayscale image.

COLORIZING A GRAYSCALE IMAGE

USING DRAWING TOOLS OR THE FILL COMMAND

[a] Convert the image to RGB, CMYK or Lab mode. RGB and Lab produce the best results on a colorization. You can convert the image to CMYK at a later stage.

⟹ Here, activate the **Image - Mode - RGB Color** command.

[b] Select a foreground colour and if necessary a background colour.

⟹ Here, select a foreground colour whose components are **R= 244**, **G= 157** and **B= 9** then a background colour similar to the foreground colour whose components are **R= 255**, **G= 190** and **B= 2**.

[c] Activate one of the following drawing tools: ▨, ▨, ▨, ▨, ▨ (or other gradient tools), ▨ or use the **Edit - Fill** command. Using this command or the ▨ tool, you can make a selection beforehand to limit the colorization to a particular area.

⟹ Here, activate the ▨ tool.

[d] Select the image area concerned if necessary.

⟹ Here, load the **Lion** selection.

[e] Set the tool **Options** as you wish but do not forget to set **Color** as the **Painting Mode**.

⟹ Here, use a **Foreground to Background** gradient and set the **Painting Mode** to **Color**.

Adobe Photoshop 5.5

Chapter 5

[f] If you activated the ▦, ▦ or ▦ tool, select a **Brush** for the tool in the corresponding palette.

[g] If using the **Edit - Fill** command, click **OK**. If using a tool, apply it to the image.

➤ Here, drag from the lion's head down to the bottom of its back legs.

As the Color mode has no effect on brightness, the image's relief is preserved. In this example, the lion's head becomes orange. This orange changes progressively to a more yellow shade on the lion's legs.

[h] You can complete the colorization by changing tool or drawing colour and modifying as many areas of the image as you wish.

Colorize the sky now.

➤ **Select - Inverse**

The sky should now be selected.

➤ Select a foreground colour whose components are **R= 47**, **G= 69** and **B= 142**.

➤ **Edit - Fill**

➤ Select **Foreground Color** in the **Use** list, **100% Opacity** and **Color Mode** then click **OK**.

➤ **Select - Deselect**

The image has been colorized. The result is not too far removed from the original image, which had a fairly limited colour range. On most images, a very precise colorization would take a lot longer to complete.

Take a snapshot to compare the different methods.

➤ Click the ▦ button on the **History** palette.

➤ Go back to the **Load Selection** state in the **History** palette.

MODIFYING HUE AND SATURATION

[a] Convert the image into RGB, CMYK or Lab mode.

➤ Here, the image has returned to RGB mode.

[b] If required, make a selection to limit the colorization.

➤ Here, the selection is already active.

[c] **Image**
   Adjust
   Hue/Saturation

[d] Activate the **Colorize** option and adjust the **Hue** and **Saturation** sliders.

▸ Here, activate the **Colorize** option and set the **Hue** slider at **34** and the **Saturation** at **56**.

[e] Click **OK**.

The lion takes an orange-yellow shade.

[f] If necessary, complete the colorization by applying **Hue/Saturation** adjustments to other selections.

▸ Here, use **Select - Inverse**
Image - Adjust - Hue/Saturation
Activate the **Colorize** option: set the **Hue** slider to **216** and **Saturation** at **68** then click **OK**.
Select - Deselect

The image is colorized.

Take a snapshot to make a comparison between the various results.

▸ Click the [▣] button on the **History** palette.

▸ Return to the **Grayscale** state on the **History** palette then deselect the lion.

USING A DUOTONE

[a] **Image**
Mode
Duotone

The previously defined parameters of the last duotone are put forward.

[b] Set the duotone parameters.

▸ Here, select a **Duotone**. For the first colour, make sure the selected colour is **Pantone Process Black CVC** and check that the curve has an input value of 50% set to output at 40% (these parameters correspond to those of the last duotone applied). For the second colour, select a **Pantone 137 CVC** and modify the curve so the input value of **50%** has an output value of **60%**.

[c] Click **OK** to close the **Duotone** dialog box.

You obtain a standard duotone.

[d] Convert this image into a RGB, CMYK or Lab mode.

▸ Here, select **Image - Mode - RGB Color**.

✓ *This is a partial method of colorization, it has the advantage of being easy to apply. You may wish to complete it with the other methods you have just seen.*

Adobe Photoshop 5.5

Chapter 5

Take a snapshot for the purposes of comparison then return to your grayscale image.

⇒ Click the [⎙] button on the **History** palette.

⇒ Return to the **Grayscale** state on the **History** palette then deselect the lion.

USING INDEXED COLORS

[a] If necessary, make an initial conversion to duotone.

⇒ Here, that is not necessary.

[b] **Image**
Mode
Indexed Color

The image is automatically converted to colours indexed to the 256 levels of grey in the image.

[c] **Image**
Mode
Color Table

[d] Modify the colour table by using a predefined palette or loading a custom palette. The **Black Body** palette can produce interesting results for colorization. You can also create your own table. In this case, take care that the first colour is black or a very dark colour then progressively lighten the colours to finish with white or another very light shade. If you do not follow this method, the results are rarely very good.

⇒ Select the first six rows in the table. For the gradient start colour, click **OK** directly, and for the end colour, use components of C= **0**, M= **59**, Y= **96** and K= **0**.
Make a second selection starting with the last shade of orange then drag over the next six rows. Click **OK** directly for the start colour and for the end colour, use components of C= **0**, M= **0**, Y= **100** and K= **0**.
Make a final selection from the last yellow down to the last colour on the table. Leave the start as is by clicking **OK** and choose components C= **0**, C= **0**, Y= **0** and K= **0** for the end colour.

[e] Click **OK**.

The sky is coloured with a gradient from orange towards yellow and the lion's colour appears more natural.

[f] Convert the image to RGB, CMYK or Lab colour mode.

⇒ Here, select **Image - Mode - RGB Color**.

> ✓ *This is a partial method of colorization, which has the advantage of allowing you to use certain colour effects automatically. To complete it, you may use the other methods explained.*

Chapter 5

☑ To make colorizations with special effects or very precise colorizations, you can combine all these different methods.

To make your comparison, take a snapshot now.

➤ Click the ▣ button in the **History** palette.

➤ View all the different snapshots in succession.

Snaphots 1 and 2 which correspond to the first two methods are the ones that are closest to the original image. The last two are the most far removed, especially in relation to the sky. For the lion, Snapshots 2 and 3 give an equivalent result. On a more complex image, with more objects and different colours, the first two methods provide a rapid initial colorization.

➤ If you wish, save the snapshots in different documents.

Return to the original version of the document.

➤ **File - Revert**

---

9 *In some cases, an image can be too small and you may need extra space to add new elements or to enlarge part of the image by duplication. The size of the canvas can be modified.*

MODIFYING THE SIZE OF THE CANVAS

[a] If necessary, choose a background colour to fill the new areas of the document. This is only useful if your image contains only layers and no **Background**.

➤ Here, invert the foreground and background colours by clicking the ⇅ icon on the toolbox.

The blue colour should now be the background colour and the orange, the foreground.

[b] **Image**
Canvas Size

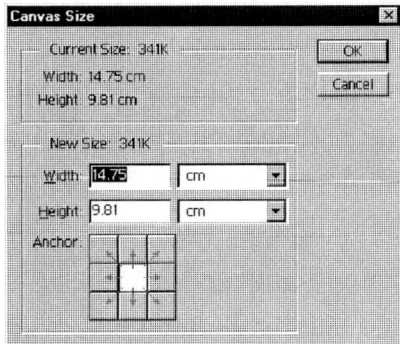

Adobe Photoshop 5.5

Chapter 5

- c) Determine the new **Width** and **Height** of your document, specifying the desired unit of measurement. The **%** option allows you to increase the canvas size by a percentage of its actual size.

➟ Here, enter **17 cm** (about 6.7 inches) for the **Width** and leave the **Height** as set.

- d) Specify the **Anchor** position for your image by clicking one of the nine buttons displayed, as shown below:

➟ Here, click the centre right button.

- e) Click **OK**.

The work space is increased to the left of the image. This new area is filled by the background colour where there is a **Background** (for layers, this area would be transparent).

✓ *The default dimensions offered correspond to the image size before using this command. Generally you would specify higher values than these dimensions. If you use lower values, Photoshop offers to clip your image by removing the parts that correspond to the areas surrounding the position chosen in Anchor. This can allow you to reframe an image to a particular size or to clip a particular part of the image.*

Before continuing, make a selection with one of the type tools.

➟ Activate the tool.
➟ Click the lion to place text on it.
➟ Select a **Times New Roman Font** in **Bold** and with a **Size** of **72**. Type **Lion** in the text box and click **OK**.

A selection in the shape of a text appears.

➟ If necessary, move this selection border by dragging it from its interior to place the letter **L** on the lion's head.
➟ Check that the **Info** palette is visible.

Chapter 5

 You have seen how to transform a selection but the same work can be done on a selection border.

APPLYING A TRANSFORMATION TO A SELECTION BORDER

[a] Make your selection with the tools of your choice.

▣▶ Here, the selection is active.

[b] Select
Transform Selection

Move handles appear on the selection's bounding box, in the same way as when you are making a free transformation on a layer.

Selection transformation allows you to apply the same commands as when using **Edit - Free Transform**. However only the selection border is modified, not its contents. For all transformations you can point inside the rectangle (the pointer takes this shape ▶) and drag to move the border.

[c] Scale the border by dragging one of the handles. To keep the selection's proportions, hold down [⇧ Shift] then start dragging.
Perform a rotation by pointing outside the rectangle then dragging. To constrain the rotation to 15 angles, hold down [⇧ Shift] then start dragging.
Skew by holding down [Ctrl] and [⇧ Shift] and dragging one of the side handles. To make a symmetrical skew in relation to the centre of the rectangle, hold down [Alt] while you drag.
Distort by pressing [Ctrl] and dragging a handle.
To make a symmetrical distortion in relation to the centre of the rectangle, hold down [Alt] while you drag.
Create a perspective effect by holding down [Ctrl][⇧ Shift][Alt] and dragging a handle.

▣▶ Here, rotate the selection border through a 26° angle. Use the **Info** palette to help you see the rotation angle being applied. Note the precise angle applied (the closest you can get might be **25.7°**, for example).

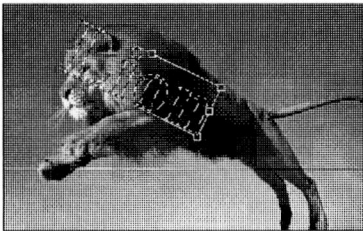

[d] Press [Enter] to apply the transformation and [Esc] to cancel it.

▣▶ Here, press [Enter] to confirm your rotation.

The selection border rotated but the image has not been modified.

Adobe Photoshop 5.5

Chapter 5

☑ For additional information on transforming selection borders, refer to the section in chapter 2 on transforming selections and layers.

☑ As with a selection or layer, you can also apply a numeric transformation (cf. Applying a transformation to a selection or a layer in chapter 2).

Continue with the exercise.

➡ Move the selection border, by pointing inside it so the selection is completely over the lion.

➡ **Layer - New - Layer Via Copy**

The selection can no longer be seen. Photoshop has created a layer containing the Lion text, but filled with a "lion texture": check this on the *Layers* palette.

➡ **Edit - Transform - Numeric**

➡ Activate only the **Rotation** option and use an angle of -116° (-90° + -26°). If you were not able to make a rotation of exactly 26°, replace 26° by the value of your rotation in order to achieve a perfectly vertical text. Click **OK** to confirm the rotation.

➡ Activate the [tool icon] tool and move the contents of the type layer into the new blue area of the image.

The *Lion* text is perfectly vertical and filled with the colour and texture from the lion.

➡ If you want to keep this result, save the picture under another name.

➡ Close this image then and open the **Elephant.jpg** document.

11 *You now know how to change the size of your canvas, but it can also be useful to know how to change the size and resolution of an image.*

CHANGING THE SIZE AND/OR RESOLUTION OF AN IMAGE

[a] **Image**
Image Size

Chapter 5

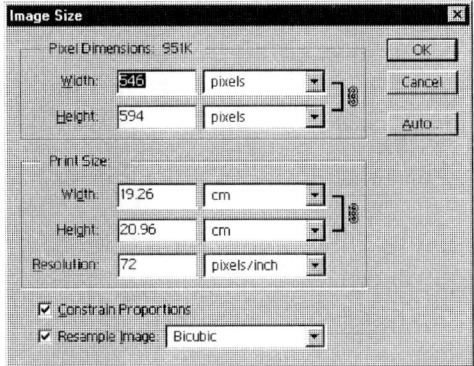

[b] Leave the **Constrain Proportions** option active to automatically adjust the **Height** when you change the **Width** and vice versa. This avoids the image being distorted when it is resized.

When this option is active a link symbol appears between the Width and Height. Unless you have particular needs, it is better to leave this option active.

[c] Leave the **Resample Image** option active if you wish to authorise Photoshop to increase or decrease the number of pixels when you modify the size or resolution. Adding pixels is referred to as resampling up, while taking pixels away is called downsampling. You can indicate an interpolation (or approximation) method to be used when pixels are added or taken away:

Nearest Neighbor This is the fastest method, but also the least precise. The image will appear more jagged and the colour transition will be more marked.

Bilinear Produces a medium-quality interpolation. This is an intermediate method between **Nearest Neighbor** and **Bicubic** in terms of speed and quality.

Bicubic Produces a better quality result with colour transitions closer to those of the original image. However this method requires more work and time to apply.

When you downsample or sample up by modifying only the Resolution, the size of the printed image stays the same. On the other hand, the screen size of the image changes.

image with 200 ppi resolution

image with 72 ppi resolution

Adobe Photoshop 5.5

Chapter 5

The illustration above shows the same document printed using two different resolutions after resampling. Notice how on the picture at lower resolution you can see jagged edge pixels and a lack of picture detail. Below you have the same documents as seen on screen with an identical zoom of 50%.

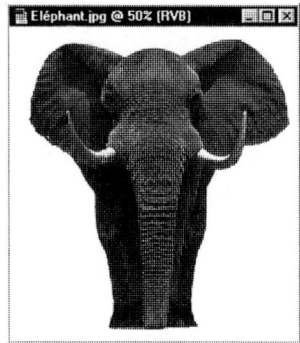

image with 200 ppi resolution

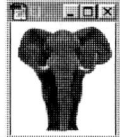

image with 72 ppi resolution

The size difference on screen is due to the fact that the two images do not contain the same number of pixels. The size of a pixel on the screen is fixed and the screen resolution is generally 72 ppi. However, during printing, the printed pixels get smaller as the image resolution increases. This explains why a low-resolution image has a pixelation effect as the pixels printed are bigger and suffers from a lack of detail as the image has fewer pixels.

If you wish to change the size using the **Resample Image** option, the result obtained may be a little blurry. This can be corrected with the **Filter - Sharpen - Sharpen** option to retrieve more picture detail and sharpen the image (cf. Extra Information).

You should in fact avoid resampling if you wish to retain an optimal picture quality. Try instead to scan or create your pictures again in the correct resolution.

[d] Deactivate the **Resample Image** option if you do not want Photoshop to change the number of pixels when you modify the **Width, Height** or **Resolution** (under Print Size). If you alter one of these three values, the other two are adjusted proportionally and the number of pixels in the image does not change. If you increase the image size, the resolution will be reduced and vice versa. This can be especially useful. Take an example:

You have a photo measuring 10 x 13 cm. You want to obtain a good quality print of this picture using a resolution of 300 ppi. To print an image which is:

Half the size of the original (5 x 6.5 cm)	Scan the image at 150 ppi. In Photoshop, change the image **Resolution** to 300 ppi without resampling. The number of pixels stays the same but they are twice as small when printed.

Chapter 5

The same size (10 x 13 cm)	Scan the image directly at 300 ppi. No change of size will be necessary in Photoshop.
Twice the size of the original (20 x 26 cm)	Scan the image at 600 ppi. In Photoshop, change the **Resolution** to 300 ppi without resampling. The pixels are twice as big when printed.

[e] Depending on your needs and how the picture will ultimately be used, choose the correct **Resolution**. The size of a document on the hard disk (and the amount of memory used to work with it) vary considerably depending on the image resolution. An RGB image 10 x 13 cm takes up 306 Ko at 72 ppi, 5.2 Mo at 300 ppi and 20.8 Mo at 600 ppi. If the document contains layers, this will increase even more.

The 72 ppi resolution corresponds to the resolution of a monitor and works perfectly well for images that will be seen on-screen (photos for CD ROMs, Web pages...). For images that you intend to print, choose a resolution of between 150 and 600 ppi depending on the quality required (150 ppi is the minimum resolution you can use to obtain a decent printing result). Except for deluxe professional printing jobs, it is not necessary to exceed a resolution of 300 ppi.

➧ Here, deactivate the **Resample Image** option, check that the measurement unit for the **Resolution** is **pixels/inch** and enter **300** in the corresponding text box.

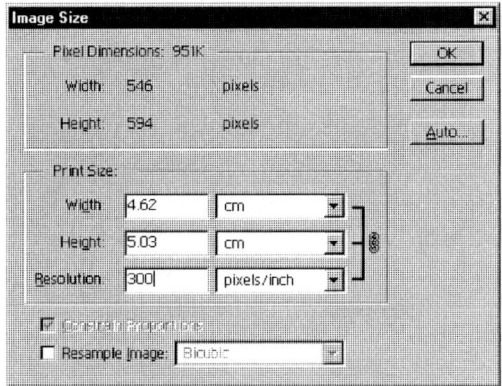

*The brackets and link icon next to the **Width**, **Height** and **Resolution** options show that these are linked.*

➧ Here, the width and height were adjusted at the same time as the resolution. They have changed respectively from 19.26 to 4.62 cm and from 20.96 to 5.03 cm respectively.

[f] Click **OK**.

The image on the screen remains unchanged as it was not resampled.

✓ *If you change the size and/or the resolution of an image with* **Resample Image** *a progress bar will appear on the status bar because the process can take some time.*

Adobe Photoshop 5.5

Chapter 5

- ☑ The default *Interpolation* method for the *Resample Image* option can be set in the *File - Preferences - General* dialog box.

- ☑ You can also define the image resolution automatically by clicking the *Auto* button in the *Image Size* dialog box (cf. Extra Information).

- ☑ To make a quick check on an image's size and resolution, [Alt]-click the position on the status bar where the document size is listed in Kb or Mb:

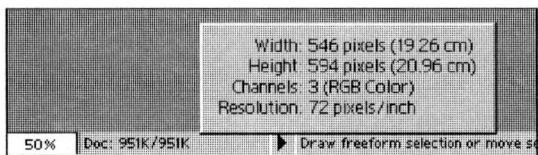

- ☑ If you wish to reduce the size of an image and resample it, you can also use the *File - Automate - Fit Image* command. Specify a new *Width* and *Height* to adjust the image to a precise number of pixels. The image will be reduced while keeping its proportions but will lose some information during sampling. This command has no effect if you specify a value larger than the current size.

- ☑ You can change the size of the image easily by resampling it with the help of the *Resize Image Wizard (Help - Resize Image)*.

Highlight the resolution change that occurs with resampling.

➡ **View - Actual Pixels**
The image is displayed at 100% zoom.

➡ **View - Print Size**
The image becomes smaller with a zoom of 24% corresponding to the size of the printed image.

Cancel the resolution changes.

➡ **Edit - Undo**

➡ **View - Actual Pixels**
The image is displayed at 100% zoom, the pixels are identical to those seen in the previous 100% zoom because the change in resolution was made without resampling.

➡ **View - Print Size**
The image is still at 100% zoom. You have returned to a resolution of 72 ppi which is the same as for the monitor's screen.

Chapter 5

12 *You can also crop your image to display only part of it.*

CROPPING AN IMAGE

[a] Activate the ⛶ tool (it is in the group of selection tools).

[b] If necessary, show the **Options** palette by clicking its tab or double-clicking the ⛶ tool.

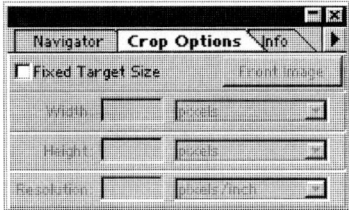

[c] Activate the **Fixed Target Size** option to determine the **Width**, **Height** and **Resolution** of the image once it has been cropped. You can also click the **Front Image** button to automatically use the **Width**, **Height** and **Resolution** of the current image. The cropped image will then have the same values.

Be careful, if you choose the Fixed Target Size option, Photoshop will resample the cropped image.

➣ Here, do not activate this option.

[d] If you want to see more information during cropping, show the **Info** palette.

➣ Here, click the **Info** palette tab.

[e] Drag a marquee around the image area that you want to keep.

➣ Here, drag around the elephant's right tusk.

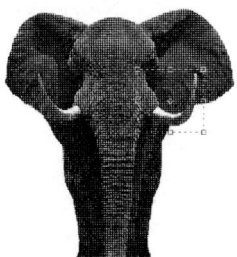

A bounding box with handles appears.

Adobe Photoshop 5.5

Chapter 5

|f| You can rotate the crop marquee to produce a turned-around image. To do this, point outside the crop marquee and drag. You can also move the rotation axis by dragging this icon ✦ located by default at the centre of the marquee.

Cropping without rotation

Cropping with -45° rotation

This rotation can be made between -45° and +45°.

⇒ Here, rotate the marquee through approximately -45°.

|g| If necessary, move the crop marquee by pointing inside it then dragging or resize it by dragging one of the handles.

⇒ Here, enlarge the marquee a little if the tusk is cut off.

|h| Press [Enter] to confirm your crop or [Esc] to cancel.

⇒ Here, press [Enter].

The image now shows just the right tusk. The rotation made has also been applied and the image is now wider than it is high.

- ✓ You can also crop an image from a selection made with the [▢] tool. Once the selection is made, activate the *Image - Crop* command. This command is only available if you have enlarged or reduced the selection or if you have transformed the selection border.

- ✓ You can also use a third method that you have already seen, by using the *Image - Canvas Size* command and specifying smaller *Width* and/or *Height* values.

Chapter 5

13 *You know how to save a document simply, using the standard Photoshop PSD format. But you may find the other formats managed by Photoshop useful as well.*

SAVING A DOCUMENT IN A SPECIFIC FORMAT

DEFINING A SAVING FORMAT

[a] Select one of the following, depending on your image:

File Ctrl ⇧ Shift S This command does not always allow you to save in every image format. If your image contains layers, you will have to flatten them before saving in a different format to Photoshop format. In addition to this, some formats cannot manage images in CMYK, duotone, images with alpha channels or drawn objects. This is why it is preferable to set aside this command for saving in Photoshop format.

Save As

File Ctrl Alt S This command lets you save in various formats even if the image contains layers or alpha channels. Only the image mode may restrict the number of formats available: a duotone only gives access to three formats. This command offers another advantage: it preserves the image you have been working on in Photoshop format while saving a "final" copy in another format. This is the command you will be looking at in detail here.

Save a Copy

➔ Here, choose the **File - Save a Copy** command.

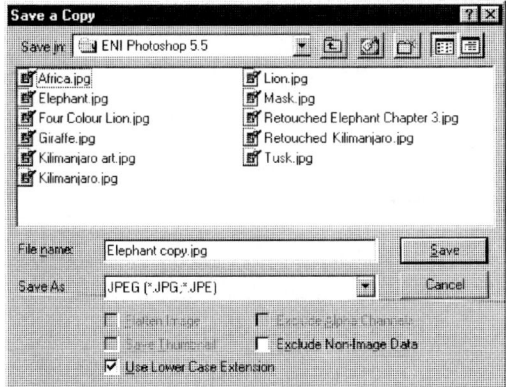

[b] Access the folder into which you are saving then enter the **File name** in the corresponding text box.

➔ Here, enter **Cropped Tusk**

Adobe Photoshop 5.5

Chapter 5

[c] Select the saving format from the **Save As** list.

The different formats are described over the next few pages.

⟹ Here, keep the **JPEG (*.JPG;*.JPE)** format.

[d] Activate the **Save Thumbnail** option if possible to show a thumbnail of the image instead of a standard icon when in the **Windows Explorer** or in **My Computer** and using large icons. This option is only available if you modify the saving preferences with **File - Preferences - Saving Files**. By default, the **Image Previews** option is set to **Always Save** but some formats cannot manage thumbnail previews.

⟹ Here, the option is not accessible.

[e] If you save in **Photoshop (*.PSD;*.PDD)** format and the document contains several layers, you can activate the **Flatten Image** option so the saved document only contains one layer. For other formats, this option is automatically activated.

⟹ Here, the option is not accessible.

[f] If you save in a format that manages alpha channels and if the document contains alpha channels, activate the **Exclude Alpha Channels** option so the document is saved without these channels. If the saving format does not manage alpha channels, this option is automatically activated.

⟹ Here, the option is not accessible.

[g] Activate the **Exclude Non-Image Data** to avoid saving drawing objects, guides, grids, thumbnails, colour or printing ink profiles or the image file information, if the saving format cannot manage this type of information. This option also allows you to slightly reduce the document size.

[h] Click the **Save** button.

Depending on the document selected, a second dialog box opens to set the specific saving parameters for the chosen format.

[i] Set the saving parameters relative to the chosen format.

These parameters are described in detail below.

☑ When you save a copy, Photoshop considers that the active document is not saved and will prompt you to do so when you close the image.

JPEG FORMAT

This format is often used for images made for publishing on the Internet or for multimedia applications. It has the advantage of considerably reducing the document size. On the other hand, the image quality tends to be poorer because this format eliminates data by creating more or less visible flat areas of colour. For this reason, do not save your image in this format until the last moment and avoid saving many times because with each save the image quality is diminished. Also, do not use this format for images that are to be printed. To avoid any incompatibility, it is recommended not to save a thumbnail with the document.

[a] **File**
Save a Copy
Select **JPEG (*.JPG;*.JPE)** in the **Save As** list.
Set the other saving parameters and click **Save**.

▸ Here, you have just performed this task.

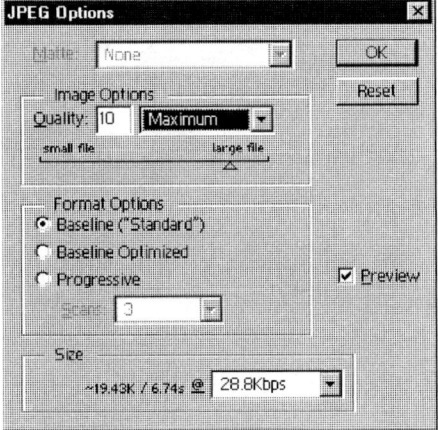

[b] Choose a **Matte** colour to fill the transparent areas of the image. If the image has a **Background** layer, this option is not available.

▸ Here, the option is not available.

[c] Set the required **Quality** for the image. This can vary from 0 (**Low** quality) to 10 (**Maximum** quality). The lower the quality, the more the image is compressed and vice versa. Depending on the image, the document can be 10 times larger on maximum quality than on low quality. You can also use the slider to set the **Quality**.

▸ Here, set the **Quality** at **6**.

Chapter 5

d Select one of the JPEG Format Options:

Baseline ("Standard")	This is the traditional format recognised by most Internet browsers.
Baseline Optimized	This format optimises the image's colour quality and creates a smaller document. It is not recognised by all browsers.
Progressive	The image is displayed in 3 to 5 Scans. As it is downloaded, the image appears gradually, in a more and more detailed form. The created document is a little bigger and uses more memory. This format is not recognised by all browsers, nor by various other applications.

➟ Here, select a **Baseline Optimized** format.

e Select a **Size** to so that some indication can be given of the size of the document and the time it will take to download at various modem speeds. This information is approximate and will only appear if the **Preview** option is active.

➟ Here, leave the default value.

f Click **OK**.

The image is saved, the active document is still **Elephant.jpg** because what you have just saved is simply a copy.

✓ You could also use the *File - Save for Web* command to set an image up for the Web (more details are given later in this chapter).

Return to the initial version of the document and prepare the image to be saved again.

➟ Click the **Elephant.jpg** snapshot in the **History** palette.

➟ Activate the default colours by clicking the ▇ icon on the toolbox.

➟ Activate the ▨ tool.

➟ Set the **Tolerance** to 32 in the **Options** palette and click the white area surrounding the elephant.

➟ **Edit - Clear**

The image background is now perfectly white.

➟ **Select - Deselect**

Chapter 5

COMPUSERVE GIF FORMAT

*This is a frequently used format for online display, especially picture bullets or images for multimedia applications. This format has a high compression capacity without information loss. However, the image has to be in **Bitmap**, **Grayscale** or **Indexed Color** mode. For colour images in particular, do not use this format on documents you intend to print.*

[a] If your image is in CMYK or Lab colour, convert it to indexed color using the **Image - Mode - Indexed Color** command.

▶ Here, this is not necessary.

[b] **File**
Save a Copy
Select the **CompuServe GIF (*.GIF)** format in the **Save As** list.
Set the other saving parameters and click **Save**.

[c] If your image is in RGB, set up a conversion to Indexed Color mode. Only the copy you are saving will be converted, not the original image.

▶ Here, select an **Adaptive** palette, **256 Colors**, **None** as the value of **Forced**, a **Diffusion Dither** with an **Amount** of **75%** and Preserve Exact Colors then click **OK**.

[d] Select the type of format:

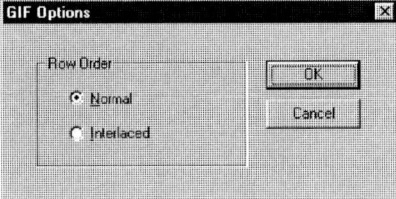

Normal	This is the standard format.
Interlaced	As it is downloaded, the image appears gradually, in a more and more detailed form. The document created is a bit bigger.

▶ Here, leave the **Normal** option active.

[e] Click **OK**.

▶ Here, click **Cancel** because you are going to use a variation of the GIF format.

☑ *You could also use the File - Save for Web command to set an image up for the Web (more details are given later in this chapter).*

Chapter 5

Before trying out the new format, convert your image to a Indexed Color format:

➟ **Image - Mode - Indexed Color**

➟ Select an **Adaptive** palette, **256 Colors**, **None** as the value of **Forced**, a **Diffusion Dither** with an **Amount** of **75%** and **Preserve Exact Colors** then click **OK**.

GIF89A FORMAT
This format has the same characteristics as the standard GIF format (see above) with the possibility of defining transparent colours to simulate Photoshop layers. This function can be very useful for certain HTML documents used on the Internet. Furthermore you can export an image in RGB mode without converting to indexed colors because the image will be converted at the time of exporting. Photoshop can also save an images made up of layers which will be flattened at the time of saving.

[a] If needed, convert your image into RGB or Indexed Color mode.

➟ Here, this image is already in indexed color mode.

[b] If your image contains several layers, mask layers that are not to be exported. This is often the case with the **Background** layer. You can also isolate a part of the image on a layer before exportation. The transparent areas on the layer will continue to be on the final result.

➟ Here, this image contains no layer because it is in indexed color.

[c] **File**
Export
GIF89a Export

If your image is in RGB (which is not the case here) this dialog box will appear.

264 Adobe Photoshop 5.5

Chapter 5

[d] If the image is in RGB, set the conversion options to indexed color. You have four palettes available:

Exact	When the image contains a maximum of 256 colours this option is available. If that is the case, it is a good idea to use this palette.
Adaptive	Coverts with a palette made from the image's real colours. If the **Exact** palette is not available, this palette is the closest to the original. You can reduce the number of colours to limit further still the document size. This will also limit the image quality and does not have much impact on small images.
System	Uses the palette of your operating system, so if you are using Windows, the Windows palette is used, and if you are using a Macintosh, the Macintosh palette will be used. Activate the **Use Best Match** option for a better quality conversion.
Custom	Use the **Load** button to open a specific palette. Contrary to the standard indexed color conversion, you cannot create your own palette. Activate the **Use Best Match** option for a better quality conversion.

The **Preview** button lets you view the palette and the image before the conversion. The dialog box shown is similar to the one displayed for indexed color images.

➤ Here, as the image is in indexed color, you see the following dialog box:

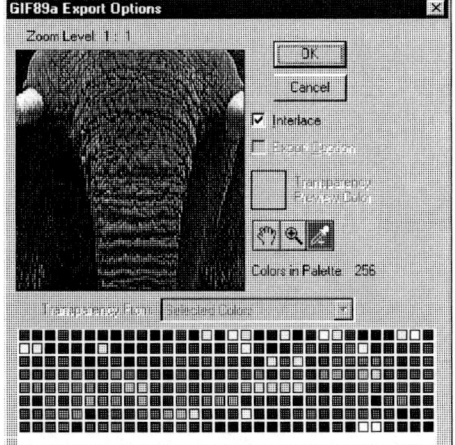

[e] If the image is in indexed color, define the area of the image that should be transparent in this way:
— if a selection has been saved, select it in the **Transparency From** list and all the areas not in this selection will be considered as transparent (the ✎ tool in the dialog box will no longer be available).

Adobe Photoshop 5.5

Chapter 5

- if no selection has been saved or you do not want to create transparency with one of these selections, activate the ![] tool then click in the palette or on part of the image for each colour that should be made transparent.

You can zoom in on the image preview by activating the ![] tool (hold down [Alt] to zoom out). Use the ![] tool to drag the preview contents.

➤ Here, activate the ![] tool and move the image until you see the white outline surrounding the elephant then activate the ![] tool and click this white colour on the preview.

The image background becomes grey which is the colour used to represent transparent areas.
The colour on the palette that corresponds to this white is highlighted in a black square (in the last row of the palette).

|f| Define the colour used to represent the transparency:
 - if the image is in RGB and if it is on a layer, click the **Transparency Index Color** box.
 - if the image is in indexed color, click the **Transparency Preview Color** box.

It is a good idea to leave the default color as this corresponds to the background colour of most Internet browsers.

➤ Here, do not change anything.

|g| Whatever the image mode, activate the **Interlace** option to ensure the image appears gradually when it is downloaded.

This creates a slightly larger document.

➤ Here, leave this option active.

|h| Click **OK**.

|i| Enter the image's **File name** in the appropriate text box.

➤ Here, enter **Transparent Elephant**

|j| Click Save.

The document is saved. Depending on the GIF format used, two different results could be obtained from an HTML document intended for Internet publication:

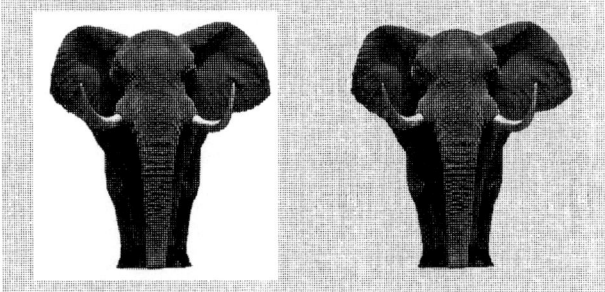

GIF image with no transparent colour on an HTML document

GIF 89a image with transparent colour on a HTML document

☑ You could also use the *File - Save for Web* command to set an image up for the Web (more details are given later in this chapter).

☑ The Wizard will guide you through the creation of an image on a transparent background (Help - Export Transparent Image).

Before continuing, return to the initial image.

➠ Click the thumbnail of the **Elephant.jpg** snapshot on the **History** palette.

The section that follows gives a more theoretical description of the various formats you can use. If you wish, read briefly through the introductions to have an idea of the function of each format. You can always refer to this section if you need to use one of these formats, some of which are important.

TIFF FORMAT

This format is primarily used for images that will be printed, either directly from Photoshop or after integration in a desktop publishing application such as Xpress. Contrary to the other formats you saw, this one does not suffer colour information loss. It can also save alpha channels and spot colours but cannot manage multichannel images (which you will see later), duotones and drawing objects. It also offers good document compression. In addition to this it ensures easy exchanges between PC and Macintosh systems.

[a] **File**
Save a Copy
Select **TIFF(*.TIF)** format in the **Save As** list.
Set the saving parameters and click **Save**.

Chapter 5

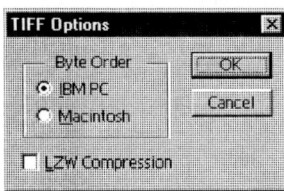

|b| Select either **IBM PC** or **Macintosh** byte order depending on which type of computer will be used to work on the image.

|c| Activate the **LZW Compression** option to obtain a smaller document. The time it takes to open and save the document will be longer because the compression or expansion has to be taken into account.

|d| Click **OK**.

➤ Here, click the **Cancel** button.

✓ *LZW Compression is handled by most applications but not all.*

PHOTOSHOP EPS FORMAT

This format is even more useful than TIFF for printing or exporting to a desktop publishing application. It can manage photographic images as well as Vector graphics. In Photoshop, this format can save duotones and drawing objects. This last possibility lets you integrate an image with transparent areas while preserving colour quality, contrary to the GIF89a format. The EPS format is a PostScript format which optimises the printing quality produced by this type of printing but also for professional printing purposes. On the other hand, it cannot save alpha channels or spot colours.

|a| **File**
Save a Copy
Select **Photoshop EPS(*.EPS)** format in the **Save As** list.
Set the saving parameters and click **Save**.

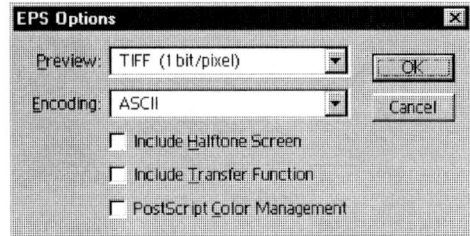

268   Adobe Photoshop 5.5

Chapter 5

[b] Select a **Preview** option:

None — No preview is saved and the image will not have any preview when integrated into a desktop publishing application. It is preferable not to use this option if you are going to use the same image both with Windows and on a Macintosh.

TIFF (1 bit/pixel) — In the desktop publishing application the document preview will be in black and white but the image will be printed in colour.

TIFF (8 bits/pixel) — The image will be previewed in colour. The document will be much larger.

[c] Specify the **Encoding** option that will be used during printing:

ASCII — This is the basic encoding. Use it if you experience printing errors or difficulties. You should use it if printing under Windows.

Binary — This is a more compact and more rapid encoding than ASCII. Some applications and some print drivers cannot manage this encoding. This is generally the encoding used for separating films before sending to a print shop.

JPEG — This is the fastest type of encoding. But as with the standard JPEG format, some colours are lost. Printing quality is subsequently altered. Avoid this encoding especially if the image will be sent to a print shop as the colours cannot be separated.

[d] Activate the **Include Halftone Screen** and **Include Transfer Function** options if you wish these two parameters to be saved with the document. In that case, they will have to be defined beforehand with the **File - Print Setup** command. Generally you can leave these options deactivated because the imagesetter will specify them.

[e] Activate the **PostScript Color Management** option if you are printing on a PostScript printer and you have not converted the image to the printer's colour mode. If your image is in CMYK you will only be able to activate this option if you have a level 3 PostScript printer. For a level 2 PostScript printer, convert to Lab color before saving the document.

[f] Click **OK**.

➠ Here, click the **Cancel** button.

✓ *A certain number of applications do not recognise EPS documents in CMYK or including drawn graphics. This is the case with most word processing programmes.*

Chapter 5

PHOTOSHOP DCS 1.0 AND 2.0 FORMATS

This is a variation of the EPS format. In addition to this format's advantages (see above) the DCS 2.0 format allows you to save multichannel images for specific printing work as well as spot channels and an alpha channel. The DCS 1.0 format is equivalent to the EPS format except it creates five files instead of just one for the EPS format.

[a] If the image is not in CMYK, convert it with **Image - Mode - CMYK Color** (remember the problem of out-of-gamut colours).

➔ Here, convert the image if you wish to look at this saving method.

[b] **File**
Save a Copy
Select **Photoshop DCS 1.0(*.EPS)** or **Photoshop DCS 2.0 (*.EPS)** format in the **Save As** list.
Set the saving parameters and click **Save**.

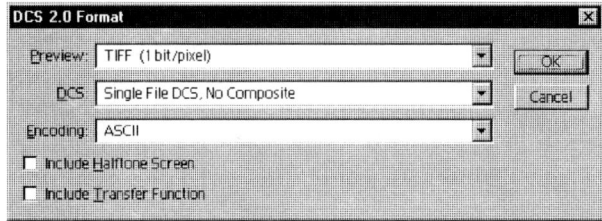

[c] Work on the **Preview, Encoding, Include Halftone Screen** and **Include Transfer Function** options as when saving in EPS format. Refer to the previous section for further details.

[d] Depending on the saving format, select one of the available DCS formats:
— if the format is **DSC 1.0**, the image is saved in five different files: one for the master document and four others for the individual C, M, Y and K channels. Select the **Grayscale Composite (72 pixels per inch)** or **Color Composite (72 pixels per inch)** options to integrate a composite image into the master document. This will let you print a low resolution draft to test the result. If you wish to print directly, or reduce the size of the master document, select the **No PostScript Composite** option.
— if the format is **DSC 2.0**, the options are similar to those for DSC 1.0. However DSC 2.0 can save an image in a single file if you select one of the **Single File...** options. If you select a **Multiple File...** option, at least five files will be saved as for the DCS 1.0 format but if the image has spot channels or an alpha channel, these will also have separate files. The **Single File** choices save disk space and limit the risk of losing one of the files.

[e] Click **OK**.

➔ Here, click the **Cancel** button.

Chapter 5

✓ If you save the image as multiple files, the different files generated will have to be in the same folder to be correctly viewed and printed.

PHOTOSHOP PDF FORMAT

This format is more universal than the others. It can be read by a PC, a UNIX workstation or a Macintosh without any problems. It is an electronic publishing format which can save not only photographic images but also vector graphics, text, video, sound and can also create hyperlinks. Of course in Photoshop, this is limited to images. This format saves drawn areas which lets you create transparencies but does not save spot colours or alpha channels. Documents in PDF format can be viewed with Adobe Acrobat Reader. This format is still in a state of flux, for although it was originally created for electronic publishing, it will probably become indispensable for printing in future versions.

|a| **File**
Save a Copy
Select **Photoshop PDF(*.PDF)** format in the **Save As** list.
Set the saving parameters and click **Save**.

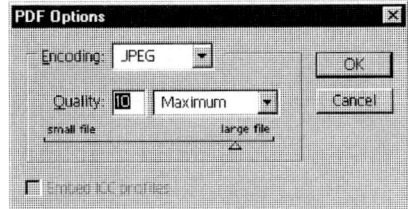

|b| Select the type of **Encoding**:

ZIP   Compresses the image without loss of colour information.

JPEG   Compresses the image according to the JPEG format, so with some loss of information. You should specify a **Quality** as with the standard JPEG format.

|c| If the original image is in CMYK, you can activate the **Embed ICC profiles** option to include the image's ICC profile in the PDF document. This profile ensures that the image's colour space is reproduced correctly when the document is opened in another application which manages ICC profiles.

|d| Click **OK**.

➠ Here, click the **Cancel** button.

Adobe Photoshop 5.5   271

Chapter 5

BMP FORMAT

This is the traditional Windows environment format. It is recognised by most applications working under Windows. It saves images in RGB, grayscale and indexed color. It cannot save alpha channels or spot colours or drawings.

[a] Make sure the image is in **RGB, Grayscale** or **Indexed Color** mode.

▶ Here, activate if necessary **RGB** mode.

[b] **File**
Save a Copy
Select **BMP (*.BMP;*.RLE)** format in the **Save As** list.
Set the saving parameters and click **Save**.

[c] Select **OS2** if the image is to be exported to a computer equipped with an OS/2 system, or if not, leave **Windows**.

[d] If necessary select the colour **Depth**.

The default option equals the current image resolution.

[e] For images in grayscale or indexed color (8 bits maximum), you can activate the **Compress (RLE)** option to reduce the document size.

This compression does not lose any information but some application cannot manage it.

[f] Click **OK**.

▶ Here, click the **Cancel** button.

▶ Use **File - Save a Copy**.

Chapter 5

OTHER FORMATS RECOGNISED BY PHOTOSHOP

[a] When opening or saving a document, select one of the following formats:

Amiga IFF (*.JFF) This is the standard format for Amiga computers. It is also used for the Deluxe Paint application on PC. This format cannot manage CMYK images, alpha channels, spot colours or drawn objects.

EPS TIFF or EPS PICT Preview This format can only be used to open documents. It allows you to open documents whose format is not supported but which contain low resolution preview files. This is the case with XPress documents. **EPS PICT Preview** can only be used on Macintosh.

RAW (*.RAW) This is an image format which allows you to transfer files to other systems or specific applications. It will save alpha channels on RGB, CMYK and grayscale images. Other modes are managed except Bitmap but the alpha channels are not saved. Drawn items are not saved. Be careful, the size and color mode of an image are not saved, so you should note them for any future opening.

PICT Resource (*.PCT;*.PIC) This is a format from the Macintosh environment. It can memorise photographic images and also vector graphics. This format can provide an interesting platform for exchanging images with a Macintosh. You should specify the colour resolution you wish to use (16 or 32 bits per pixel). This format only manages RGB, indexed color or grayscale images and does not save drawn items.

Filmstrip (*FLM) This format is used to open film files from the Adobe Premiere video editing application. If you change the image size, its colour mode or if you delete an alpha channel, you will no longer be able to save the image in this format. You can only use this format to save existing Filmstrip documents.

FlashPix (*.FPX) This format was conceived to speed up the transfer of large, high-resolution files in applications supporting the FlashPix technology. This format manages RGB and grayscale images. It does not save alpha channels or spot colours or drawn paths. You could encode the image in JPEG if required.

Kodak Photo CD (*.PCD) Lets you open images from a Kodak Photo CD disk. You cannot save a file in this format.

PCX (*.PCX) This format is often recognised by PC applications. It manages RGB, grayscale, indexed color and bitmap images. It does not save alpha channels or spot colours or drawn paths.

Adobe Photoshop 5.5

Chapter 5

PIXAR (*.PXR) This format was designed to exchange images with PIXAR workstations, which use high-end 3D graphics programmes.

PNG (*.PNG) This format is used to publish images on the Internet. It can save an alpha channel with RGB and grayscale images to obtain a result equivalent to GIF89a but in millions of colours. No alpha channel is memorised with Bitmap or indexed color images. Some Internet browsers do not recognise this format. Choose an **Adam7** interlace if you wish the image to display progressively when downloading. To optimise compression, select a type of **Filter**. Opt for **None** on Bitmap or indexed color images. For other modes, you can also choose another filter. The **Adaptive** filter will select from those on offer the most appropriate filter for your image.

Scitex CT (*.SCT) This format is used to process high-end images on Scitex computers. It manages RGB, CMYK and grayscale images. It does not support alpha channels, spot colours or drawn paths. The documents created are often very large. The Scitex system produces few moiré images and is often used for professional colour printing.

Targa (*.TGA;*.VDA; *.ICB;*.VST) This format is recognised by many PC applications. It supports RGB 32 Bit modes with an alpha channel and RGB 16 and 24 bit modes without alpha channels. When saving an image in this format, you can select the desired colour **Resolution**.

[b] Click the **Save** button.

➠ Here, click **Cancel**.

Certain formats offer extra options before the final save.

➠ Close this image without saving it.

---

14 *When you want to save an image that will be used on the Internet, there is a specific command you can use that will obtain the optimum result based on the image size and quality.*

SAVING AN IMAGE FOR USE ON THE WEB

[a] **File**
Save for Web Ctrl Alt ⇧Shift S

➠ Here, open the **Lion.jpg** document before using this command.

Chapter 5

|b| Show several preview thumbnails in order to make a comparison between the original image and the different formats. To do this, click the **2-Up** or **4-Up** tab at the top of the dialog box. You can change each thumbnail by clicking it to activate it.

➤ Here, click the **4-Up** tab.

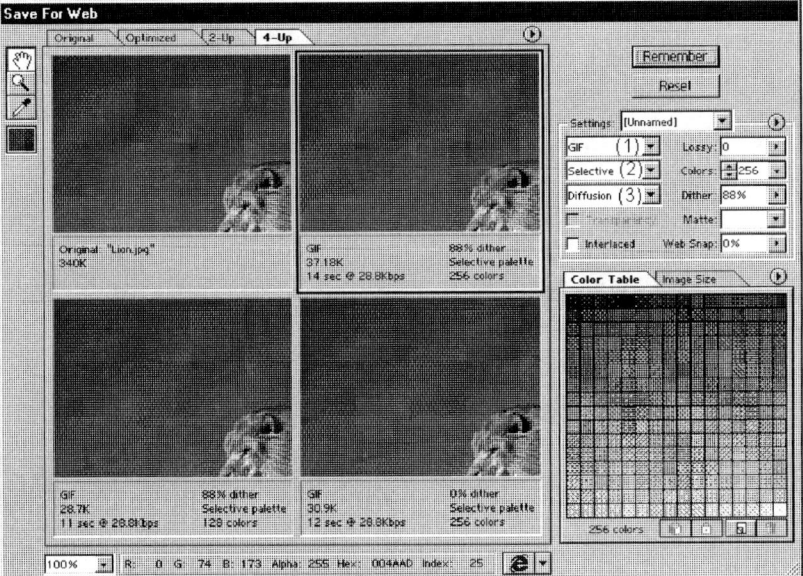

|c| Select one of the predefined **Settings** to adjust quickly most of the format options. You can also use this option to go back to the **Original** image in the active thumbnail.

➤ Here, leave the **[Unnamed]** setting to define the options individually.

|d| Select the **Optimized file format** (1) that you wish to use.

➤ Here, keep the **GIF** format.

The options available vary depending on the file format chosen.

Adobe Photoshop 5.5

Chapter 5

[e] Set up the conversion to indexed colours if you select **GIF** or **PNG-8** format. While the **JPEG** and **PNG-24** formats keep all the colours, they have respectively one and two mutual options concerning transparency. Go to the Converting an RGB image into Indexed Colours section to see the details:

Dialog box option	Corresponding in the indexed color conversion dialog box option
Color reduction algorithm (2)	Palette
Colors	Colors
Transparency	Transparency
Matte	Matte
Dithering algorithm (3)	Dither
Dither	Amount

➟ Here, select **Adaptive** as the **Color reduction algorithm** (**2**), **Diffusion** as the **Dithering algorithm** (**3**) and leave the other default options.

[f] Activate the **Progressive** option with **JPEG** format or the **Interlaced** option for other formats to ensure that the images are displayed gradually, with overlaying layers of higher and higher resolution. The created document is slightly larger and will require more RAM to display.

➟ Here, do not activate this option.

[g] Specify **Lossy** quantity when selecting **GIF** format. This allows the **GIF** format to lose some colour information, as JPEG format does, which makes the image size smaller. You can often give a value between 5 and 10 without affecting picture quality. This option is not available if you activate the **Interlaced** option or select **Noise** or **Pattern** as the dithering algorithm (**3**).

➟ Here, take note of the current image size, located beneath the preview (44.19 kb) and set the **Lossy** option at **10**.

The preview is regenerated: the image changes little but the size is reduced to 33.24 kb making a 25% reduction.

[h] Set the **Web Snap** in the colour palette if you select **GIF** or **PNG-8** format. The higher the value, the higher the number of colours used for the conversion that will be compatible with the 256 colour palette of the browsers. This option is only useful for computers whose display is configured at 256 colours. A high value necessarily reduces the number of colours used and thus the image quality. If you leave a value less that 100%, you can see the preview on a screen in 256 colours by activating the **Browser Dither** option in the **Preview Menu** (click the arrow above the thumbnails).

➟ Here, leave the option at **0%**.

Chapter 5

[i] Activate the ![eyedropper] tool in the dialog box if you wish to apply one of the following effects:

Forcing a colour from the **Original** image into the palette of a **GIF** or **PNG-8** image	To do this, click the **Original** tab, at the top of the dialog box, then click the required colour and return to the **Optimized** image by clicking the corresponding tab. The colour has been memorised but has not yet been applied to the palette (see the next point).
Defining a colour from the image as the **Matte** list	To do this, click a colour in the image and select **Eyedropper Colour** in the **Matte** list.

➧ Here, do not select any colour with the ![eyedropper] tool.

[j] If required, redefine one or more colours in the **Color Table** if you select the **GIF** or **PNG-8 Format**. To do this, double-click a colour in the table or use one of the following options:

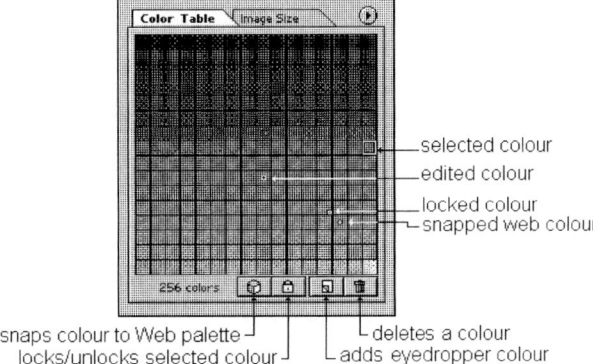

➧ Here, do not redefine any colour.

Before going on, try with another image format.

➧ Activate another thumbnail and select **JPEG** in the file format list (**1**).

The activated thumbnail is modified, the previous thumbnail stays in GIF format, which allows you to compare the two.

[k] Set the required **Quality** for the image, if you have chosen **JPEG** format. This can vary from **0** (**Low** quality to **100** (**High** quality. The lower the quality, the more the image is compressed and vice-versa. Depending on the image, the document can be ten times bigger in high quality mode than in low quality mode.

➧ Here, set the **Quality** to **60**.

The preview is regenerated: the image is modified only slightly but its size shrinks to 17.19 kb or 50% less than in GIF format.

Chapter 5

- Activate the **Optimized** option in **JPEG** format to improve the quality of the image colours and create a smaller document. Be careful, not all Web browsers handle this option.

➡ Here, leave this option active.

- Activate the **ICC Profile** in **JPEG** format to conserve this profile in the image. These profiles are used by certain browsers for colour correction, by describing the image's colour space. Using this option makes the document a little larger.

➡ Here, activate this option.

The preview stays the same. The visual difference would have been more noticeable if the image had been in CMYK.

- Determine the **Blur** to apply to the image in **JPEG** format. This option applies a gaussian blur to the image to eliminate stray pixels. The resulting document will be smaller but less clear. The blur value can vary between **0** and **2** but the blur may be excessive if you go over **0.5**.

➡ Here, leave this value at **0**.

- If necessary, rework the **Image Size** by clicking this tab, next to the **Color Table** tab. See the title Changing the size and/or resolution of an image for further details. The **Quality** option corresponding to the **Resample Image** option.

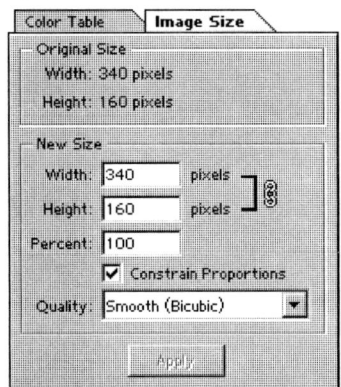

*The image is automatically resampled. Notice that you can change the size according to a certain **Percent** value.*

➡ Here, leave the image at its current size.

- If you choose to resize the image, click the **Apply** button.

➡ Here, that button is not accessible.

Chapter 5

|q| Check the image quality using one of the following commands in the **Preview Menu** (click the arrow over the top of the thumbnails):

Uncompensated Color	To see the image without any colour adjustment. This is equivalent to not showing a preview.
Standard Windows Color	To view the image as under Windows. This is only useful if you are working on a Macintosh.
Standard Macintosh Color	To view the image as on a Macintosh. This is only useful if you are working under Windows.
Photoshop Compensation	To view the image using its ICC Profile.

➟ Here, activate **Photoshop Compensation**.

The preview remains unchanged as you integrated the ICC Profile to the image.

|r| Check how quickly the image will download by selecting a **Download Rate** from the Preview Menu.

➟ Here, leave the **28.8 Kbps Download Rate** option.

|s| You may wish to click the button corresponding to the selected browser to view the image in that browser. You should close the browser window to return to Photoshop.

➟ Here, you do not need to view the image in this way.

|t| Activate the thumbnail that corresponds to the format in which you want to save the image.

➟ Here, leave the thumbnail in **JPEG** format with a **Quality of 60**.

|u| Click **OK**.

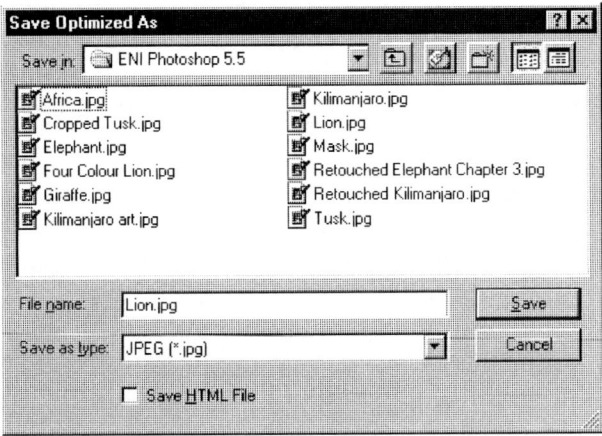

|v| Go into the folder where you wish to save the picture and enter the **File name** in the corresponding text box.

➟ Here, enter **Internet Lion**

Adobe Photoshop 5.5

Chapter 5

☞ Activate the **Save HTML File** option if you wish to create an HTML page containing the image automatically.

➡ Here, activate this option.

☒ Click the **Save** button.

*Two documents are created: the **Internet Lion.jpg** image, which is an optimised copy of the original **Lion** picture and an HTML page called **Internet Lion.html**.*

- ✓ *Generally speaking, you should select image formats according to the following criteria:*

    JPEG   *For rather large photos on which no transparent background needs to be applied.*

    GIF   *For drawings, smaller images or those for which you wish to add a transparent background. This format is also useful if you wish to retain a consistent image quality regardless of the number of colours displayed by the computer, by using Web compatible colours.*

    PNG-8   *Respects the same guidelines as the GIF format but is used for larger images.*

    PNG-24   *For large photos on which a transparent background is to be applied.*

- ✓ *You can also ask Photoshop to set the save options appropriate to the size of the document by selecting the* Optimize to File Size *command in the* Optimize Menu *(click the arrow in the* Settings *frame). Give the Desired File Size in Kb and click OK.*

- ✓ *The* Optimize Menu *also contains a* Save Settings *option which allows you to save the current parameters and add them to the* Settings *list for use with another image.*

- ✓ *To zoom the image preview in the dialog box, activate the* 🔍 *tool in the dialog box.*

- ✓ *If the zoom is too high, you can use the* ✋ *tool in the dialog box to move the preview around.*

- ✓ *To make it easy to customise the color table on GIF or PNG-8 images, you can use the* Select *or* Sort *commands in the* Color Palette *menu.*

- ✓ *You can* Save *or* Load *the specific color table with the appropriate options in the* Color Palette *menu.*

Chapter 5

☑ To optimise an image for the Internet, especially to slice it for an HTML table, to animate it, create an image map or various Web effects, you can also transfer the current image to ImageReady. To do this, save the image then click the ▦ button at the bottom of the toolbox.

⇉ Close the picture.

Chapter 5

PRACTICE EXERCISE 5

- *Open the **Kilimanjaro.jpg** document.*
- *Select the sky with as much precision as possible without including the volcano or the clouds.*
- *Invert the selection and create a layer via cut.*
- *Delete the **Background** layer.*
- *Create a Duotone on this image use **Pantone Process Black CVC** and **Pantone 306 CVC**.*
- *Lighten the image considerably by modifying the Duotone curves.*
- *Extend the canvas by 0.5 cm towards the bottom.*
- *Fill this new area using the rubber stamp tool to reproduce the bottom of the picture which will give the image more perspective.*
- *Change the image size by resampling to obtain an image height of 9.5 cm.*
- *Convert the image to RGB color mode.*
- *Save the image in GIF89a format calling the document **Kilimanjaro No Sky**.*
- *Change the colour of the image to make it look like an old sepia photo.*
- *Save a copy of this image in EPS format as **Old Kilimajaro** with a colour preview (8 bits/pixel) and leave Photoshop.*

Corrected versions of these documents have been saved under the names **Kilimanjaro No Sky Chapter 5.gif** and **Old Kilimanjaro Chapter 5.eps**.

CHAPTER 6

- 1 - USING THE FREEFORM PEN 284
- 2 - SAVING A WORK PATH 286
- 3 - DELETING A PATH 286
- 4 - CREATING A PATH 287
- 5 - RENAMING A PATH 287
- 6 - USING THE MAGNETIC PEN TOOL 288
- 7 - USING THE PEN TOOL 290
  - DRAWING STRAIGHT LINES 290
  - EXTENDING AN EXISTING PATH 291
  - DRAWING CURVES 292
- 8 - EDITING A PATH 296
  - SELECTING ANCHOR POINTS AND SEGMENTS 296
  - MOVING A SEGMENT OR AN ANCHOR POINT 297
  - ADDING OR DELETING ANCHOR POINTS 298
  - MODIFYING A CURVE 298
  - CONVERTING A SMOOTH POINT TO A CORNER POINT AND VICE VERSA 299
  - OPENING A CLOSED PATH 300
- 9 - SHOWING /HIDING PATHS 301
- 10 - CONVERTING A SELECTION BORDER INTO A PATH 302
- 11 - CONVERTING A PATH INTO A SELECTION BORDER 303
  - USING THE DEFAULT OPTIONS 303
  - BY DEFINING THE OPTIONS 304
- 12 - APPLYING COLOUR TO A PATH OUTLINE 306
- 13 - APPLYING FILL COLOUR INSIDE A PATH AREA 307
  - USING THE DEFAULT OPTIONS 307
  - BY DEFINING THE OPTIONS 307
- 14 - DUPLICATING A PATH 309
  - ONTO A NEW PATH 309
  - BY COPYING AND PASTING 309
  - ONTO ANOTHER IMAGE 310
  - ONTO THE SAME PATH 310
- 15 - CLIPPING AN IMAGE 312
- 16 - EXPORTING PATHS TO ILLUSTRATOR 314
- 17 - IMPORTING AN ILLUSTRATOR IMAGE 315
  - OPENING AN ILLUSTRATOR DOCUMENT 315
  - PLACING AN ILLUSTRATOR DOCUMENT ONTO AN EXISTING IMAGE 317
  - COPYING/PASTING AN ILLUSTRATOR OBJECT 318
- PRACTICE EXERCISE 6 319

Chapter 6

*During this chapter you are going to look at **paths**, or line drawings. These elements are not quite the same as the other Photoshop elements as you create them with vector drawing tools, as you would use in Illustrator or CorelDraw. These tools can be used to draw or retouch but also to make complex and precise selections quickly. Paths also offer several very specific possibilities for your work.*

⋙ If you have left Photoshop, restart it.

⋙ Open the **Mask.jpg** document.

1 *Start by drawing a simple path.*

USING THE FREEFORM PEN

[a] Activate the tool.

This is in the same tool group as the tool.

[b] If the **Options** palette is hidden, show it by clicking its tab or double-clicking the tool.

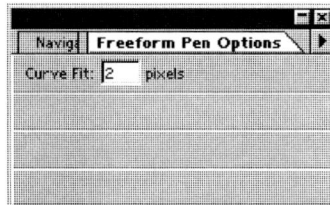

[c] Set the **Curve Fit** option to between 0.5 and 10. The higher the value set, the smoother and simpler the path will be with few anchor points. A low value ensures a more faithful reproduction of your freeform drawing but will not correct any "shakiness" seen on the drawing.

 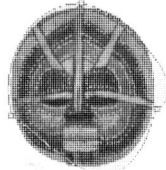

The path surrounding the mask on the left was made with a **Curve Fit** of *1*; the one on the right was drawn with a **Curve Fit** of *10*.

⋙ Here, set the **Curve Fit** to **1.5**.

Chapter 6

|d| Drag around the image to draw your path as you would with the [lasso] tool. If you release the mouse button before returning to your starting point, you create an open-ended path. If you return to the beginning, the pointer takes this form: [pointer] and you create a closed path.

➤ Here, drag around the top half of the mask.

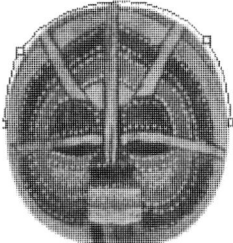

When you finish drawing the path, its line appears. But it is not necessarily exactly like the dragged path you followed, due to the smoothing effect linked to the **Curve Fit** *option. Anchor points along the path can be seen. These can be modified, as you will see a little further on.*

|e| If necessary, continue the path by pointing to one of its ends. Depending on the pointer preferences, the pointer can take one of these forms: [pointer] or [pointer]. Drag again from the chosen point.

➤ Here, continue the path in order to close it.

When you continue a path in this way, it is possible that this is not very faithful to what you dragged. This is normal because of the smoothing effect but also because taking up the path again creates a corner point.

A path created in this way is called a work path (like a draft). You can check this by looking in the **Paths** *palette, by clicking its tab or using* **Window - Show Paths**.

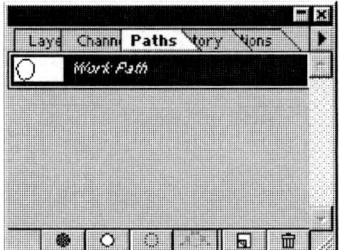

✓ This tool is the simplest drawing tool to use. It is also the least precise.

✓ When you continue a path, this automatically creates a corner point. These are used to make abrupt direction changes to a path. The different types of points that make up a path are discussed further on.

✓ A vector graphic does not actually contain any pixels. It is completely distinct from the image and will not be seen when the image is printed.

Adobe Photoshop 5.5

Chapter 6

2 *A work path is only temporary. To be sure of keeping it you must save it.*

SAVING A WORK PATH

a Show the **Paths** palette, by clicking its tab or using **Window - Show Paths**.

➠ Here, use **Window - Show Paths** if the palette is not displayed.

b Double-click the **Work Path** thumbnail or activate the **Save Path** option in the palette menu (▶).

➠ Here, double-click the thumbnail.

 *A dialog box appears.*

c Enter the path's **Name** in the corresponding text box.

➠ Here, enter **Encircle Mask** in the **Name** box.

d Click **OK**.

The saved path is displayed in the palette and replaces **Work Path**.

3 *This path is not precise. You could modify it, but here you are going to cancel it.*

DELETING A PATH

a Show the **Paths** palette, by clicking its tab or using **Window - Show Paths**.

b Select the path you wish to delete by clicking its thumbnail.

➠ Here, the **Encircle Mask** path is the only one in the document so it is already active.

c Click the 🗑 button on the palette or activate the **Delete Path** command on the palette menu (▶).

➠ Here, click the 🗑 button.

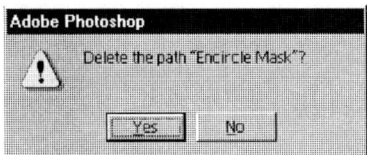 *You are prompted to confirm your deletion.*

Chapter 6

[d] Click the **Yes** button to delete the path or **No** to cancel your deletion.

➤ Here, click the **Yes** button.

✓ Using the *Delete Path* command directly deletes the path without prompting for confirmation.

✓ You can also delete a path without having to confirm by dragging the thumbnail onto the 🗑 button on the palette.

4

You can now create a new path.

CREATING A PATH

[a] Show the **Paths** palette, by clicking its tab or using **Window - Show Paths**.

[b] Click the 📄 button on the **Paths** palette.

*A new path called **Path 1** is created in the palette. This path is automatically activated.*

✓ It is preferable to create a new path before drawing it. As you saw previously, if you just begin drawing on the image, your path is considered to be a *Work Path*. This can be easily lost if you do not remember to save it.

✓ You can also activate the *New Path* command on the palette menu (▶) or [Alt]-click the 📄 button on the palette. This lets you name your path straight away by opening the *Path Name* dialog box for you.

5

You can give a specific name to your path.

RENAMING A PATH

[a] Show the **Paths** palette, by clicking its tab or using **Window - Show Paths**.

[b] Double-click the thumbnail of the path you wish to rename.

➤ Here, double-click the **Path 1** thumbnail.

Adobe Photoshop 5.5

Chapter 6

A dialog box appears.

|c| Enter the new **Name** in the corresponding textbox.

➤ Here, enter **Encircle Mask** in the Name box.

|d| Click **OK**.

The path has been renamed.

6

Now you are now going to draw a path around the mask using another tool.

USING THE MAGNETIC PEN TOOL

|a| Activate the ![] tool.

This tool functions in a similar way to the ![] tool.

|b| If the **Options** palette is hidden, click its tab or double-click the ![] tool.

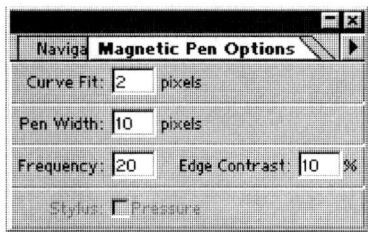

|c| Set the **Curve Fit** option between 0.5 and 10. The higher the value set, the smoother and simpler the path will be with fewer anchor points. A low value ensures a more faithful reproduction of your freeform drawing.

➤ Here, set the **Curve Fit** to **1.5**.

|d| Use the **Pen Width** to determine the automatic edge detection width. This can vary between 1 and 40. Use a small pen width if the object you are drawing around contrasts little with its surrounds and use a large pen width if the object is highly contrasted. You can modify the **Pen Width** while you are drawing by using the [→] and [←] keys to respectively decrease or increase the width by a pixel.

➤ Here, set the **Pen Width** at **6**.

[e] Use the **Frequency** option to define how frequently fastening points are created. You can choose a value between 5 and 40. This option works in the opposite way to the [icon] tool. For images with low contrast or complex forms, use a low frequency.

➤ Here, set the **Frequency** at **40**.

[f] Modify the **Edge Contrast** to define how sensitive the "magnet" is to the image edges. If the edges are soft, use a high value. If the edges need to abruptly change direction, set a lower value.

➤ Here, leave the **Edge Contrast** at **10%**.

[g] Click to start the path then drag along the path you wish to draw. While dragging, you can drag the pointer backwards if you are not satisfied with the last sections drawn. Press the [Del] key to delete the last fastening point. You can also click to create an extra fastening point.

➤ Here, make a path around the mask by dragging over its edges.

[h] To complete your path, click back at the starting point. The mouse pointer takes this form: [icon]. You can also double-click to close the path with a magnetic segment or [Alt]-double-click to close the path with a straight segment. Although this tool is not really adapted to creating open paths, you can create one by pressing [Enter], which ends the path where the pointer is.

➤ Here, return to the starting point and click when the pointer takes this form: [icon].

This path is now part of the active **Encircle Mask** path. The result is more accurate than with the [icon] tool and quicker to obtain. It is however not perfect as some parts of the mask have been cut.

✓ This tool is almost as easy to use as the [icon] tool. The results obtained are often sufficient for drawing paths around objects. When you need to obtain a very precise result when drawing or to use paths to draw and retouch, it is preferable to use the [icon] tool.

✓ You can temporarily deactivate the magnetic properties of this tool. To do this, hold down [Alt] and drag to draw a segment of the path as with the [icon] tool, or proceed by a series of clicks to draw the path with straight segments. Release the key to bring the magnetic properties back.

Chapter 6

Before continuing, open another image without closing the mask.

➤ Open the **Giraffe.jpg** document.

7 *Now you should create a new path by using the most important drawing tool, the Pen tool.*

USING THE PEN TOOL

[a] Activate the ✒ tool.

[b] If the **Options** palette is hidden, click its tab or double-click the ✒ tool.

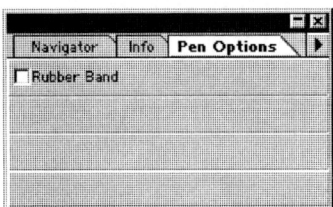

[c] Activate the **Rubber Band** option to preview the next segment that will be drawn when you click or drag. This can be useful when you want to get your drawing right in a short space of time. If you are not used to handling this tool or vector graphics in general, it would be a good idea to activate this command.

➤ Here, activate the **Rubber Band** option.

DRAWING STRAIGHT LINES

[a] Click the place on the image where you want your path to begin.

➤ Here, zoom in on the giraffe and click the bottom of the underside of its neck.

The path's first anchor point appears.

[b] Click the place where the other end of the line should appear. If you want to draw a perfectly horizontal or vertical line, or a line along a 45° angle, hold down ⇧ Shift before you click.

➤ Here, click the top of its neck, near its head to create a straight line that slides up the neck.

Chapter 6

A straight line appears with an anchor point on each end.

|c| Continue this path by clicking the place where the end of the next segment should fall.

➭ Here, draw a rough border part of the way around the giraffe, without worrying about small details like its horns, but do not close the path yet.

|d| To close the path, click the first anchor point. The mouse pointer should take this form: . If you wish to make an open path, Ctrl-click anywhere on the image except on the path itself, or click the tool again.

➭ Here, Ctrl-click to leave the path open.

EXTENDING AN EXISTING PATH

|a| If necessary, activate the path you wish to extend by clicking its thumbnail in the **Paths** palette.

➭ Here, the path is already active.

|b| Activate the tool.

|c| Point to one of the path's ends, the mouse pointer taking either this form: or this one: depending on the pointer preferences in use. Where the pointer looks like , place the centre of it precisely on the end of the path or you risk creating a new path.

➭ Here, point to the end which corresponds to the last anchor point you defined.

|d| Click to continue drawing with a straight line or drag to continue with a curve.

➭ Here, click without dragging.

If you have taken up the path again correctly, all the anchor points will be displayed.

|e| Continue your drawing by defining all the anchor points you think necessary.

➭ Here, continue drawing around the giraffe.

Adobe Photoshop 5.5

Chapter 6

[f] Close the path by clicking or dragging on the first anchor point. The pointer should look like this: 🖊︎. Leave the path open by Ctrl-clicking elsewhere on the image or clicking the 🖊︎ tool again.

⇒ Here, click the first anchor point.

The path is closed.

The giraffe is not made up of as many straight lines as this path! Delete this attempt and create a new path using curves.

⇒ Click the 🗑 button on the **Paths** palette then **Yes** to confirm deleting the path.

DRAWING CURVES

[a] If necessary, activate the 🖊︎ tool.

Before starting to draw your first curves, you should become familiar with the various elements that will make up your drawing. Paths can be very complex objects, especially when you use the 🖊︎ tool.

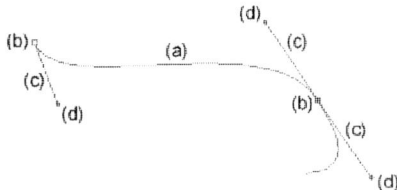

You saw in the last exercise that a **segment** (*a*), straight or curved, is defined by two **anchor points** (*b*). In the case of a curve, **direction lines** (*c*) determine the curve's direction and slope. The direction lines are tangents to the curve at the anchor points. The shorter the direction line, the straighter the curve will be, whereas a long direction line produces a more generous curve. At each end of the direction line there is a **direction point** (*d*). This is the point that you will work with to act upon the direction line when you want to modify the curve. The direction points are sometimes called **handles**.

To define a curve, you proceed by clicking and dragging: The first click defines the anchor point position and as you drag you move the direction lines arising from that point.

[b] Click without releasing the mouse button the place on the image where your curve should start and drag the pointer in the direction that the path should take. Hold down ⇧ Shift as you drag to constrain the direction lines to move horizontally or vertically or at a 45° angle.

You are going to start with a little training exercise, because the 🖊︎ tool is difficult to master if you are using it for the first time. For now, concentrate on the giraffe's body, without worrying about its neck, head or legs.

292 Adobe Photoshop 5.5

Chapter 6

▸ Here, zoom in on the giraffe's back, where it has a slight hump, click just above this hump and drag from the first anchor point towards the right to define the direction line:

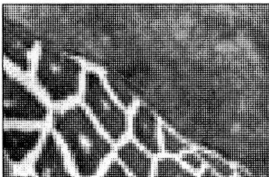

|c| Click, without releasing the mouse button, the place where the other extremity of the curve will be and drag the pointer so that the curve is correctly defined. Depending on where you dragged the first anchor point and the direction in which you are now dragging, you will obtain very different curves.

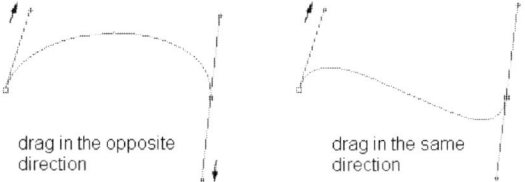

drag in the opposite direction

drag in the same direction

|d| If you are not satisfied with the result produced by an anchor point, you can press [Ctrl] **Z** to delete the last point.

You can also modify a point once the path is finished, as a path can be freely modified.

▸ Here, click after the little hump and drag down so the path follows the hump:

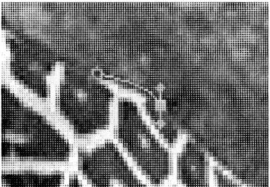

Adobe Photoshop 5.5

Chapter 6

[e] If necessary, drag the anchor point that you have just defined to increase or decrease the length of the direction line defining the next curve. By default, the two direction lines on an anchor point are identical. Changing the length of a direction line alters the roundness of each curve. Be careful to redefine the direction line from the anchor point and not from the direction point or you will just create another anchor point.

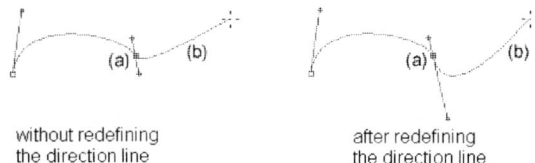

without redefining the direction line

after redefining the direction line

On the example on the left, the selected anchor point (a) and its direction lines have been defined by one drag. On the example on the right, a second drag has been made from point (a) to extend the direction line. This means that the second curve (b) will be more marked.

➟ Here, correct the length of the direction line from the anchor point only if it seems necessary then continue the path until you have drawn around the hindmost leg and are ready to start on the second hind leg.

The path must change direction abruptly here.

[f] Continue the path by clicking where the new anchor point should be or dragging the pointer to define the curve. To suddenly change the curve's direction, hold down [Alt] and drag the anchor point to modify the direction line. Continue making the path.

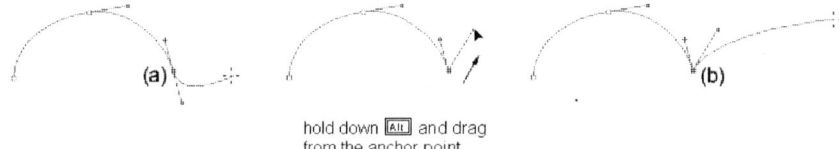

hold down [Alt] and drag from the anchor point

The anchor points created along the path are called **smooth corners** *(a). The direction lines that extend from them are always opposite to each other which gives a smooth curve (as the curve follows the same slope). When direction lines are "folded back", in other words, follow the same direction, the anchor points created are called* **corner points** *(b). A corner point is always made from a smooth point that you convert along the path using* [Alt]

If you [Alt] *-click and not* [Alt] *-drag the anchor point you will change the curve into a straight line.*

➟ Here, drag around the giraffe's body and front legs using corner points on bends (such as the intersection between the legs and the belly). Do not close the path.

Chapter 6

[g] To close the path, drag to the first anchor point. The pointer should take this form: ![pen]. Hold down [Alt] if this point should be a corner point. For the last curve on a closed path, you should drag in the opposite direction to the direction line that needs to be redefined. This is specific to the first/last point on the path:

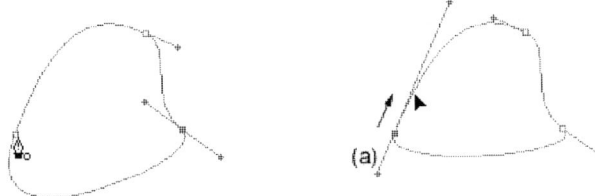

On the example on the left, the curve on the bottom was made by a simple click. On the example on the right, the curve has been made sharper by dragging upwards. This drag works on the direction line *(a)* contrary to the other points.

[h] If you wish to make an open path, [Ctrl]-click elsewhere on the image or click the ![pen] tool again.

➨ Here, finish dragging round the giraffe then close the path. If the path is not satisfactory, delete it by clicking the ![trash] button on the **Paths** palette then start again. Try to be quite precise (or very precise if you can). You will fix the imperfections in this path later on.

- ✓ The ![pen] tool is undoubtedly one of the hardest drawing tools to master. But it is very precise once you have learnt how to use it. If you find difficulties using it, try not to lose patience and force yourself to practise with it. After a while you will use it with ease. You will then find it very useful to make precise selections or to create clipping paths, when you want to export to other applications. You will be looking at that later on.

- ✓ Try to space out anchor points as much as possible in order to create very smooth curves. A path containing too many points takes up more space in the memory.

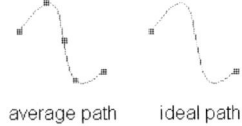

average path   ideal path

- ✓ While you are drawing, if you are not satisfied with the anchor point you have just placed, press [⌫] to delete it and place a new point in the right position.

At this point, you should save you work before continuing with the exercice.

Adobe Photoshop 5.5

Chapter 6

8 *You can now see how to modify a path.*

EDITING A PATH

a Activate the path you wish to modify by clicking its thumbnail in the **Paths** palette.

➤ Here, the path is already selected.

SELECTING ANCHOR POINTS AND SEGMENTS

You make selections of this kind when you need to move anchor points or segments or to modify curves. Here you will just select items to see how each method works.

a Activate the [tool] tool (in the same group as the [tool] tool).

b To select a segment, click the segment.

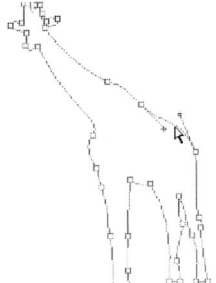

If a curved segment is selected, the direction lines controlling the curve are also shown.

➤ Here, click the curved segment shown on the above illustration.

c To select an anchor point, click it.

➤ Here, click one of the anchor points on the path.

The square representing the point becomes solid: any direction lines also appear.

d To select several points press [⇧ Shift] and click each anchor point you wish to select. You can also drag diagonally to draw an invisible rectangle around all the points to be selected.

➤ Here, select a few points along the path.

e To select all the anchor points, press [Alt] and click the path (the pointer should take this form: ⬚+).

➤ Here, select all the points on the path.

✓ *You can deselect selected points by [⇧ Shift]-clicking the point concerned or by clicking outside the path to deselect all the anchor points.*

Chapter 6

✓ You can temporarily activate the [tool] tool while any other drawing tool is active by holding down the Ctrl key.

MOVING A SEGMENT OR AN ANCHOR POINT

[a] Activate the [tool] tool.

[b] To move a straight segment plus the anchor points defining it, point to the segment and drag it.

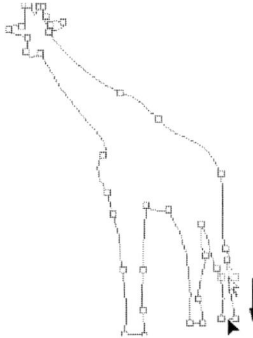

▸ Here, drag a straight segment, if you have one along your path.

[c] To change the roundness of a curve, point to the curve and drag.

▸ Here, modify one of the curves so it fits the giraffe's outline better.

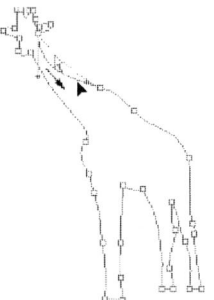

The anchor points do not move when you modify a curve, only the direction lines are altered.

[d] To move an anchor point, select it and drag it. If several points are selected, you can move them all simultaneously. Moving anchor points will affect the curves attached to these points.

▸ Here, drag one of the points to position it correctly in relation to the giraffe.

✓ You can also move a curved segment, without changing its magnitude, by selecting the two anchor points that define the curve and dragging one of them.

Adobe Photoshop 5.5

Chapter 6

ADDING OR DELETING ANCHOR POINTS

[a] To add an anchor point, activate the ▣ tool then point to the segment to which you wish to add a point. Click to add a point without changing the existing curve or drag to modify the direction lines associated with this new point.

▸ Here, add an anchor point to a part of the path that needs another point (you can always delete it afterwards if necessary).

[b] To delete an anchor point, activate the ▣ tool then point to the point you wish to remove. Click to delete the point (the curve will adapt itself to the remaining anchor points) or drag to delete the point and correct the way the path is restructured.

▸ Here, delete an anchor point that seems superfluous to you. If all the anchor points seem correctly placed, add one then delete it.

✓ When the ▣ tool is active, the ▣ tool automatically becomes available when you point to an anchor point or direction point. This also applies when the ▣ tool is active. This allows you to modify the path without first having to activate the ▣ tool.

✓ You can momentarily activate the ▣ tool while using the ▣ tool (or vice versa) by holding down the [Alt] key.

MODIFYING A CURVE

[a] Activate the ▣ tool.

[b] Click the curved segment you wish to modify or one of the anchor points to display the curve's direction lines.

▸ Here, click one of the curves in order to modify it.

[c] Drag one of the direction points. To modify the roundness of the curve, move the direction point to bring it closer to or push it away from the anchor point, trying not to modify the way the associated direction line is pointing. To change the slope of the curve, move the direction point while changing the orientation of the direction line.

Depending on the type of anchor point, changing a curve can have very different effects. If you change the orientation of a direction line on a smooth point, the opposite direction line will also change direction, as is shown by a grey arrow on the figure below. For a corner point, only the direction line you are working on will be modified.

Chapter 6

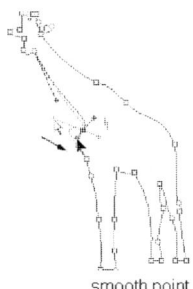 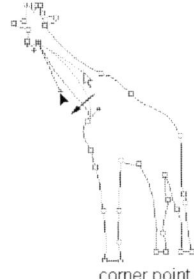

smooth point   corner point

➠ Here, move one of the direction points to adjust the curve.

CONVERTING A SMOOTH POINT TO A CORNER POINT AND VICE VERSA

|a| Activate the ▧ tool.

|b| Click the anchor point you wish to convert to display the direction lines that are attached to it.

➠ Here, click any point you wish to convert.

This may be a point on which the roundness and slope of the curve are unsatisfactory.

|c| Activate the ▧ tool.

|d| To convert a smooth point into a corner point, drag one of the direction points to "fold" the direction lines associated with the anchor point.

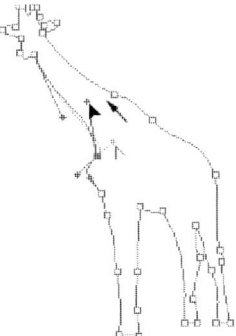

➠ Here, drag a direction point to create a corner point.

Adobe Photoshop 5.5

Chapter 6

[e] To convert a corner point into a smooth point, drag from the anchor point to place the direction lines opposite to each other again.

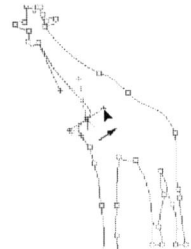

This conversion also works on points that have no direction lines. This allows you to create these lines.

➤ Here, convert a corner point to a smooth point. If all your corner points are needed, transform any one into a smooth point, you can convert it back again later.

[f] To delete the direction lines from an anchor point, click the anchor point once. If the next anchor point has no direction lines either, a straight segment will be created.

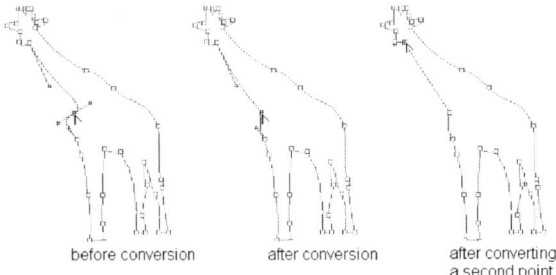

before conversion   after conversion   after converting a second point

On the middle figure, the converted point does not have any direction lines, but the two segments attached to it stay curved as the other anchor points defining these segments do have direction lines. On the last example, the point under the giraffe's head has been converted to a point with no direction lines, which means that the neck segment has been straightened.

➤ Here, click one of the points that make up the base of the feet.

☑ You can activate the ⬚ tool momentarily while the ⬚ tool is active by holding down [Ctrl][Alt].

OPENING A CLOSED PATH

[a] Activate the ⬚ tool.

[b] Select the anchor point where you want to open the path.

➤ Here, select any point on the path.

Chapter 6

[c] Press either the [Del] or [←] keys.

The path is open, the selected anchor point and the two segments attached to it all disappear.

☑ *If you do not want to create a large opening on the path, add two anchor points to fence off the opening before deleting the space in between the new points.*

☑ *You can also use this method to split an open path in two.*

You can now finish adjusting the giraffe's outline then that of the mask.

➔ Press [Ctrl] **Z** to cancel the last action.
➔ Adjust the giraffe's path as precisely as possible so it is perfectly outlined.
➔ Save the **Giraffe.jpg** document.
➔ Access the **Mask** document:
  Window - Mask.jpg
➔ Proceed in the same way to outline the mask and save the document.

9

The mask path needs to be temporarily hidden.

SHOWING /HIDING PATHS

[a] To hide all existing paths, use: [Ctrl][⇧ Shift] **H**
  View
  Hide Path

The path is hidden.

[b] To display the path again, use: [Ctrl][⇧ Shift] **H**
  View
  Show Path

The path reappears. If the document contains several paths, only the active path is visible.

[c] To deactivate a path, [⇧ Shift]-click the active path's thumbnail or use the **Turn Off Path** command on the palette menu (▶).

*Unlike the **Hide Path** command, turning off the path only hides the active path and not all existing paths.*

➔ Here, [⇧ Shift]-click the **Encircle Mask** thumbnail.

The path is no longer selected.

Adobe Photoshop 5.5

Chapter 6

[d] To make the path reappear, simply click it.

▸ Here, you do not need to do this.

Before continuing, select the mask again.

▸ Activate the ▨ tool.
▸ Set the **Tolerance** to **32** in the **Options** palette.
▸ Click the pale background.
▸ **Select - Inverse**

---

10 *You can create a path using another method. This one is especially interesting for simple shapes or objects with a homogenous background, as is the case with the mask.*

CONVERTING A SELECTION BORDER INTO A PATH

[a] If a selection is active, click the ▨ button on the **Paths** palette to convert the selection, attributing the default tolerance value.

▸ Here, click the button as described.

A path corresponding to the selection border is created and the flashing border disappears. This type of new path is always created as a Work Path.

▸ For this example, type **Ctrl Z** to cancel the conversion.

[b] To make the most accurate path in relation to the selection, you should specify a **Tolerance** which will best adapt the path to the selection border. To do this, activate the **Make Path** command on the palette menu (▶) or **Alt**-click the ▨ button on the **Paths** palette.

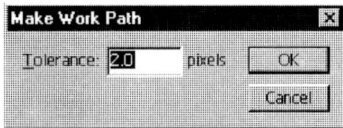

[c] Set the **Tolerance** between 0.5 and 10 pixels. The higher the value, the smoother the path will be, with less anchor points, but this path may not exactly fit the initial selection border. On the other hand, a smaller value creates a path with more anchor points which will be a more faithful reproduction of the initial selection border. Be careful though, as too small a value can produce a very bumpy path. In general, a value between 1.0 and 2.0 produces good results.

Chapter 6

The example below is based on the giraffe and not on the mask as the mask is too round to demonstrate correctly the results obtained with different tolerance values:

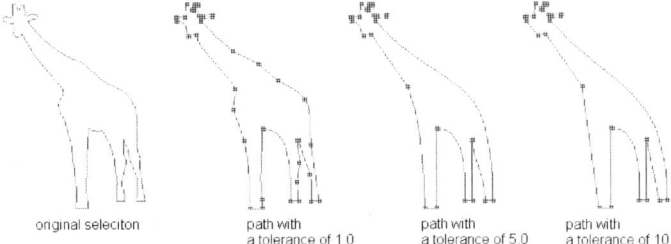

original seleciton | path with a tolerance of 1.0 | path with a tolerance of 5.0 | path with a tolerance of 10

▶ Here, set the **Tolerance** to **1.0**.

[d] Click **OK**.

The path is created.

[e] As a general rule, you should modify the path to correct any gaps between the selection border and the new path.

▶ Here, this is not necessary.

You already have a path surrounding the mask, so you do not need to correct this new path. In fact, you can delete it.

▶ Click the 🗑 button on the **Paths** palette then click **Yes** to confirm your deletion.

11

You are now going to proceed in the opposite way by making a selection from a path.

CONVERTING A PATH INTO A SELECTION BORDER

USING THE DEFAULT OPTIONS

[a] Activate the path you want to convert by clicking its thumbnail.

▶ Here, activate the **Encircle Mask** path.

The path becomes visible again.

[b] Click the ⚪ button on the **Paths** palette or [Ctrl]-click the path thumbnail.

▶ Here, click the ⚪ button.

*A selection border corresponding to the previous path appears. The conversion options used for the selection are those in the **Make Selection** dialog box.*

Adobe Photoshop 5.5 303

Chapter 6

- ✓ To add the selection made from a path to an existing selection, hold down [Ctrl][⇧ Shift] then click the path thumbnail.

- ✓ To remove the selection made from a path from an existing selection, hold down [Ctrl][Alt] then click the path thumbnail.

- ✓ To pick up a selection that corresponds to the intersection between the path and an existing selection, hold down [Ctrl][Alt][⇧ Shift] then click the path thumbnail.

BY DEFINING THE OPTIONS

[a] Activate the path you wish to convert by clicking its thumbnail.

➤ Here, the **Encircle Mask** path is active (leave the existing selection active too).

[b] Activate the **Make Selection** command in the **Paths** palette menu (▶) or [Alt]-click the ⬚ button.

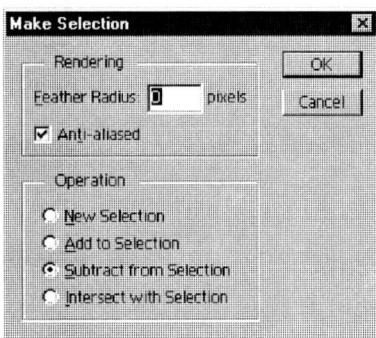

[c] Determine a **Feather Radius** between 0 and 250. This lets you define the sharpness of the selection border.

➤ Here, set the **Feather Radius** to **10**.

[d] Activate the **Anti-aliased** option to prevent a pixelation effect on the border.

➤ Here, leave this option active.

[e] If a selection already exists on the image, use the **Operation** options to determine how to combine the existing selection and the one you are creating:

New Selection	Replaces the existing selection with the selection made from the path.
Add to Selection	Combines the existing selection with the selection made from the path.
Subtract from Selection	Deletes the area that corresponds to the new selection from the existing selection.

Chapter 6

Intersect with Selection   Preserves the intersection between the new selection and the existing one.

⟫ Here, select **New Selection**.

[f] Click **OK**.

The selection border is slightly offset from the path, due to the use of a feather radius.

✓ *If you make a selection border from an open path, the selection border will follow the shape of the path and the two open ends will be linked by a straight segment.*

✓ *When a path is active, you can also define a New Selection with a Feather Radius of 0 by pressing the* [Enter] *key on the numeric keyboard while any drawing tool is active.*

Try now to create a halo effect around the mask.

⟫ Without deselecting the current selection, activate the **Make Selection** command on the **Paths** palette menu.

⟫ Set the **Feather Radius** to **0** and select **Subtract from Selection** then click **OK**.

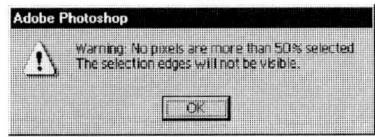

Photoshop displays a message to warn you that too few pixels have been selected.

⟫ Click **OK** to continue without seeing the selection border.

The original selection with a feather radius minus the selection with no feather radius lets you obtain an equivalent selection to the figure on the right. The selection border cannot be seen but it is nonetheless present.

⟫ **Image - Adjust - Hue/Saturation**

⟫ Set the **Saturation** to **+100** and the **Lightness** at **50** then click **OK**.

A slight halo effect appears. By filling in this area with a light colour, you could have produced an effect similar to that obtained with the **Outer Glow** *effect but without using a layer.*

The selection border cannot be seen but is still there so you can cancel it.

⟫ **Select - Deselect**

Adobe Photoshop 5.5   **305**

Chapter 6

12 *You can reinforce this halo effect by applying a colour to the path outline. This technique can also be used to make retouches.*

APPLYING COLOUR TO A PATH OUTLINE

a Activate the layer on which you wish to apply the colour or retouch.

➠ Here, the image does not have any layers, so only the **Background** layer can be activated.

b Activate the path that you want to use for the drawing or retouching.

➠ Here, the **Encircle Mask** path should be active.

c Select the drawing or retouching tool to be applied along the path. You can activate one of the following tools: ▨, ▨, ▨, ▨, ▨, ▨, ▨, ▨, ▨, ▨, ▨, ▨, ▨, ▨ and ▨. If you select the ▨ tool, a starting point for the reproduction has to have been previously defined, or Photoshop will show an error message and the effect will not be carried out. If another tool other than those above is activated, Photoshop will use the ▨ tool by default.

➠ Here, activate the ▨ tool.

d If necessary, show the **Options** palette to modify the tool parameters.

➠ Here, select **Hard Light** mode with a **Pressure of 50%** and a **Fade** option of **0**.

e Select one of the **Brushes** in the corresponding palette.

➠ Here, select the brush type located above the 100 diameter type.

f If you have selected a drawing tool, choose a foreground colour for the application.

➠ Here, select a colour whose components are R=248, G=200 and B=112.

g Click the ▨ button in the **Paths** palette.

➠ Here, click this button then deactivate the path to see the result more clearly: activate the **Turn Off Path** command in the **Paths** palette menu.

The halo effect is very accentuated in the selected colour outside as well as inside the mask. That is due to an even distribution of the brush on either side of the path:

Adobe Photoshop 5.5

Chapter 6

✓ To outline a path, you can also activate one of the following commands on the Paths palette menu (▶) or [Alt]-click the ⬚ button.

Stroke Path   If no anchor point or segment is selected.

Stroke Subpath   If at least one anchor point is selected.

✓ This method uses the current tool type and options. If you have not set these correctly, the result will not be satisfactory.

---

13 *You have just applied colour around a path, now you can fill the inside area of the path.*

APPLYING FILL COLOUR INSIDE A PATH AREA

USING THE DEFAULT OPTIONS

[a] Activate the layer to which you wish to apply the fill colour.

➠ Here, there are no layers.

[b] Activate the path you wish to fill in.

➠ Here, activate the **Encircle Mask** path.

[c] Select a foreground colour for the fill.

➠ Here, leave the previously selected colour.

[d] Click the ⬚ button on the **Paths** palette.

*The inside of the path is filled with the foreground colour. The fill options correspond to those of the **Fill Path** or **Fill Subpath** dialog box.*

This result is not suitable, so you should cancel it.

➠ **Edit - Undo**

BY DEFINING THE OPTIONS

[a] Activate the layer to which you wish to apply the fill colour.

[b] Activate the path you wish to fill in.

➠ Here, you are working on the **Encircle Mask** path.

[c] Select a foreground colour for the fill.

➠ Here, leave the current foreground colour.

Adobe Photoshop 5.5

Chapter 6

|d| Alt-click the ⬤ button or activate one of these commands from the **Path** palette menu (▶):

Fill Path   To apply a background colour to a path of which no anchor point or segment is selected.

Fill Subpath   To apply fill to a path of which at least one anchor point is selected.

➭ Here, the **Fill Path** option is available.

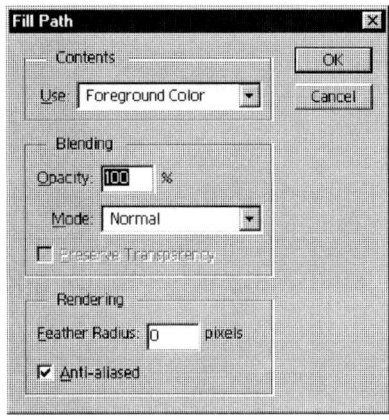

|e| Define the **Use, Opacity, Mode** and **Preserve Transparency** options as you would for the **Edit - Fill** command.

➭ Here, select **Color** for the blending **Mode** and leave the other options as set by default.

|f| Specify a width for the **Feather Radius** of between 0 and 250 to control the sharpness of the fill's edges.

➭ Here, leave **0**.

|g| Activate the **Anti-aliased** option to soften any jagged edges on the fill edge.

|h| Click **OK**.

➭ Here, click **OK** then deactivate the path.

The mask is filled with the foreground colour but the relief of this has not been modified, as you used the *Color* mode. This gives a rather mystical effect to the mask!

> ✓ If you fill an open path, the various meanders of the path will be filled in, and the path will be closed off by a straight segment joining the two ends.

Chapter 6

14 *To strengthen this effect, you can duplicate the path.*

DUPLICATING A PATH

ONTO A NEW PATH

|a| Drag the thumbnail of the path you want to duplicate onto the ▭ button on the **Paths** palette.

⇒ Here, drag the **Encircle Mask** path thumbnail onto the ▭ button.

*The path is duplicated onto a path called **Encircle Mask copy**. You can modify or move this path according to your needs.*

> ✓ To duplicate a path and give it a specific name, activate the path and duplicate it with the Duplicate Path command on the Paths palette menu (▸).

You are going to use another method instead, so cancel this attempt.

⇒ **Edit - Undo**

BY COPYING AND PASTING

|a| Activate the path you wish to duplicate.

⇒ Here, activate the **Encircle Mask** path.

|b| Activate the ▭ tool (which is in the same tool group as ▭).

|c| [Alt]-click the path to select all the anchor points. If not all the anchor points are selected, only part of the path will be copied.

|d| **Edit** [Ctrl] **C**
    Copy

|e| Create if needed a new path to take the copy. If no path is created, the copy will be pasted on the active path. If no path is active, the copy will be pasted on a **Work Path**.

The path can also be pasted onto another image.

⇒ Here, click the ▭ button on the **Paths** palette.

A new path called Path 1 is created.

|f| **Edit** [Ctrl] **V**
    Paste

The path is pasted in the middle of the image.

> ✓ It is possible to paste a copied path into an Illustrator document. The item will be pasted from Photoshop without any fill or stroke colour.

Adobe Photoshop 5.5

Chapter 6

For now, cancel this new Path 1.

▸ Click the 🗑 button in the **Paths** palette then click **Yes** to confirm the deletion.

ONTO ANOTHER IMAGE

[a] Drag the thumbnail of the path you want to duplicate onto the window of the document where you wish to place the copy:

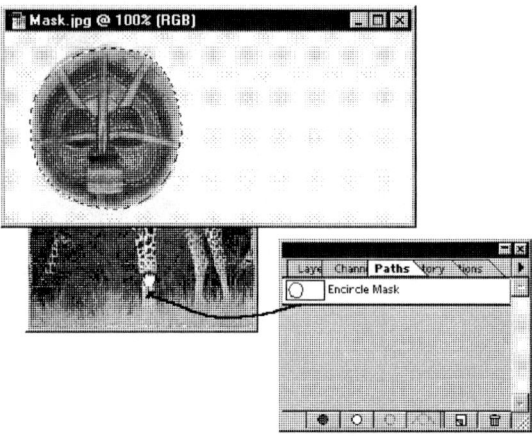

▸ Here, drag the **Encircle Mask** path onto the **Giraffe.jpg** document.

*The **Encircle Mask** path is duplicated onto the giraffe image as a **Work Path**.*

> ✓ *This technique may be interesting when different images contain the same objects and you do not wish to create several different paths for objects which are identical.*

Cancel this copy and show the Mask document again.

▸ **Edit - Undo**
▸ **Window - Mask.jpg**

ONTO THE SAME PATH

[a] Activate the path you wish to duplicate.

▸ Here, activate the **Encircle Mask** path.

[b] Activate the ▸ tool.

Chapter 6

|c| Select all the anchor points by [Alt]-clicking the path.

All the anchor points on the path must be selected.

➤ Here, [Alt]-click the path and move the path slightly to the left so that the left edge of the path is on the left edge of the halo surrounding the mask.

|d| Hold down [Alt] and drag the path to the place where you wish to put the copy.

➤ Here, hold down [Alt] (which copies your path) and drag across to position the copy to the right of the mask: the right edge of the copied path should line up with the right edge of the surrounding halo.

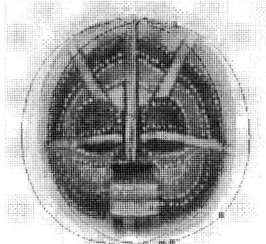

*The two paths make two crossed circles, the copy is situated on the same path as the original, that is the **Encircle Mask** path.*

You can finish off this effect.

➤ Deselect the anchor points by clicking elsewhere on the image, outside the path.

➤ Click the [ ] button on the **Paths** palette.

The retrieved selection corresponds to the two paths minus the area where they intersect.

➤ Activate the **Turn Off Path** command on the **Paths** palette menu ([▶]).

➤ **Select - Feather**
Set the **Radius** to **5** and click **OK**.

➤ **Image - Adjust - Hue/Saturation**
Set the **Hue** at 10 and click **OK**.

The edges of the mask have a slight red tinge.

➤ **Select - Deselect**

➤ Save this image under the name **Mystic Mask** then close it to continue working with the giraffe.

Chapter 6

15 *You can now prepare the image of the giraffe so that when the image is exported to a desktop publishing application such as QuarkXPress, only the giraffe is visible.*

CLIPPING AN IMAGE

[a] Activate the path that will be used to make the clipping path. This must be a saved path.

➠ Here, if the path has not been saved: double-click **Work Path** and click **OK** to save it as **Path 1**.

[b] Activate the **Clipping Path** command on the **Paths** palette menu (▶).

[c] Select the required **Path** from the corresponding list.

➠ Here, select **Path 1**.

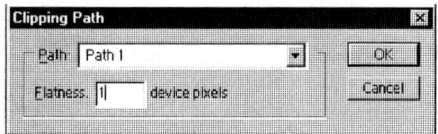

[d] Determine the **Flatness** of the clipping path. This defines how precisely curves are reproduced during printing. A curve is interpreted by a printer as a series of straight segments. When a low value is set, very small straight lines will be used to represent a curve and a precise result will be obtained. Excessive precision on a complex path can lead to memory saturation problems with your printer. The flatness value can vary between 0.2 and 100. Leave this value blank if you wish to use the printer's default value. If you prefer to define your own value, specify a value between 1 and 3 for printing using between 300 and 600 ppi and a value between 8 and 10 for high resolution printing (between 1200 and 2400 ppi). Remember, this is the print resolution, not that of the image itself.

The higher the *Flatness* value is, the less precise the path created will be, and the giraffe will subsequently have an angular appearance, especially around the neck, legs and tail.

➠ Here, set the **Flatness** at 1.

[e] Click **OK**.

Chapter 6

The clipping path is created.
When no path is active, the path used for the clipping path is indicated in bold type:

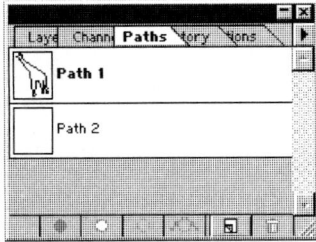

[f] Generally this type of document that contains a clipping path is destined for a desktop publishing application and consequently for printing. If the image is not in CMYK mode, convert the image taking the necessary precautions to avoid losing too much colour quality.

⟹ Here, make a quick conversion: **Image - Mode - CMYK Color**.

[g] Save the image in **Photoshop EPS** format. If you converted to CMYK colours, you can also use **Photoshop DCS 1.0** and **Photoshop DCS 2.0** formats.

⟹ Here, use **File - Save As**.
Enter **Clipped Giraffe** in the File name box.
Select **Photoshop DCS 2.0 (*.EPS)** in the Save As list and click the **Save** button.
Select **TIFF (8 bits/pixel)** in the Preview list.
Choose **Single File with Color Composite (72 pixel/inch)** for the **DCS** option and leave the **Encoding** as **ASCII** then click **OK**.

The document is saved and can be imported into a desktop publishing application. The results obtained with and without the clipping path are quite different:

image without clipping path   image with clipping path

✓ *If you make a clipping path from an open path, the contours of the path will be followed but the two open ends will be joined by a straight segment.*

Adobe Photoshop 5.5

Chapter 6

☑ If the image contains a hole or empty space, for example the handle on a teacup, you can create two paths on a single saved path in the palette to create a transparency effect on the hole:

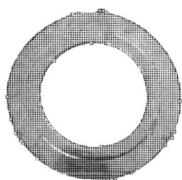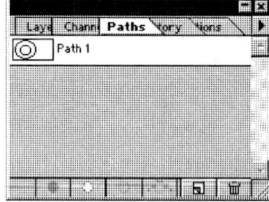

The image above contains only one saved path but two paths are drawn onto it. This allows the central part of the image to become transparent as well as any areas outside the largest path.

☑ Some applications do not recognise EPS images containing clipping paths. This is the case with the Microsoft Word ® word processing application, for example.

16
You are going to export this path to use it in Illustrator, or another vector graphics application, such as CorelDRAW ®.

EXPORTING PATHS TO ILLUSTRATOR

[a]   **File**
   Export
   Paths to Illustrator

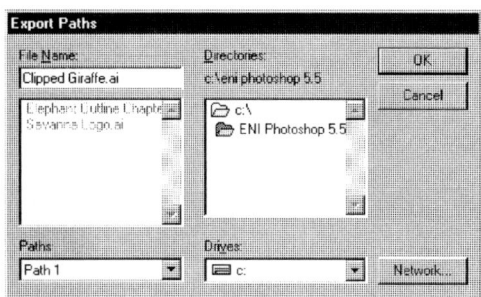

[b]   Select in the **Drives** list a disk drive on which to save the paths. If necessary, double-click the c:\ icon to access all the folders of the selected drive. Double-click the folder in which you want to save the paths.

➠ Here, go into the **ENI Photoshop 5.5** folder in C: drive (or whatever drive you have saved it onto).

Chapter 6

|c| Select the path that you wish to export in the **Paths** list. If your document contains several paths, you can save them by selecting **All Paths**.

The ***Document Bounds*** *option lets you retrieve in Illustrator the crop marks corresponding to the size of the image but does not let you retrieve the paths.*

➨ Here, make sure **Path 1** is selected.

|d| Enter the document name that will contain the paths in the **File Name** box.

➨ Here, leave the name set by default.

The .ai extension refers to an Illustrator document.

|e| Click **OK**.

The path is exported.

> ✓ *When you open the document in Illustrator or another vector graphics application, the paths will be invisible because they are exported without any fill or stroke colour.*
>
> ✓ *You can also export a path to Illustrator by copying and pasting. This possibility is not correctly managed by other vector graphics application because the copy of the Photoshop path is recognised as an image and not as a path.*

➨ Before continuing, close this image and open **Kilimanjaro.jpg**.

---

17 *You can also import into Photoshop a drawing created in Illustrator.*

IMPORTING AN ILLUSTRATOR IMAGE

OPENING AN ILLUSTRATOR DOCUMENT

|a| **File**   Ctrl **O**
    Open

|b| Select the Illustrator document you wish to open.

➨ Here, select the **Savanna Logo.ai** document in the **ENI Photoshop 5.5** folder.

Chapter 6

|c| Click **Open**.

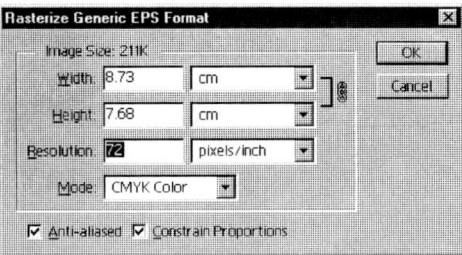

Photoshop gives you the opportunity to set the parameters for converting the vector drawing into an image.

|d| Depending on your needs, adjust the **Width**, **Height** and **Resolution** that you wish to obtain. As no notion of resolution is associated with vector graphics, you can modify the different parameters as you wish. For a better reproduction of the drawing, you should leave the **Anti-aliased** and **Constrain Proportions** options active.

➧ Here, set the **Width** to **5** cm.

|e| Select the colour **Mode** that should be used.

➧ Here, leave **CMYK Color**.

|f| Click **OK**.

*It sometimes occurs that Photoshop cannot retrieve all the character fonts used. In this case, an error message will appear, prompting you either to **Continue** opening the document or to **Cancel**. This font problem is often of no consequence to the result.*

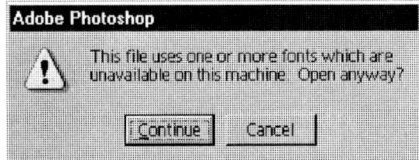

|g| As a general rule, when this message appears, click the **Continue** button if only to see the result obtained.

➧ Here, click **Continue** if necessary.

The Illustrator drawing is placed in a new Photoshop document. This drawing is on a layer. You can now apply to it all the retouches or transformations available in Photoshop.

➧ Close this document without saving it.

Chapter 6

PLACING AN ILLUSTRATOR DOCUMENT ONTO AN EXISTING IMAGE

[a] **File**
Place

[b] Select the document you wish to import.

▸ Here, select the **Savanna Logo.ai** document situated in the **ENI Photoshop 5.5** folder.

[c] Click the **Place** button.

You can also double-click the document.

[d] If there is a font problem (cf. Opening an Illustrator document), click the **Continue** button.

The drawing is placed in a rectangle. It is located on a layer bearing the document name with the .ai extension.

[e] Before rasterizing the drawing (or converting it into pixels), you can transform the placed image using one of the **Free Transform** options. The only transformation that cannot be applied is **Perspective**.

▸ Here, reduce the size of the drawing by about half, holding down [⇧ Shift] to conserve its proportions then press [Enter] to confirm the placement.

Photoshop rasterizes the drawing and the result is placed on a new layer, whose name is taken from the original Illustrator document.

☑ *You can also place images or drawings contained in an Acrobat document (.PDF).*

Now you can move this logo, save your image and then close it.

▸ Activate the [move] tool.

▸ Move the logo to the top right corner of the image.

▸ Save the image under the name **Savanna** and close it.

Adobe Photoshop 5.5

Chapter 6

COPYING/PASTING AN ILLUSTRATOR OBJECT

Unless you have the Illustrator application installed, you will not be able to carry out the instructions that follow. They will be useful if you ever have to use Illustrator in conjunction with Photoshop.

[a] In Illustrator, select the path you want to copy.

➤ Here, open for example, the **Savanna Logo** document then select all.

[b] Activate the **Edit - Copy** command in Illustrator.

[c] Access the Photoshop document into which you wish to paste your Illustrator item then activate the **Edit - Paste** command.

➤ Here, open any document.

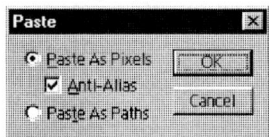

[d] Select one of the following options:

    Paste As Pixels   To paste a rasterized image of the drawing. Leave the **Anti-Alias** option active to avoid pixelation effects on the edges. The image will be pasted on a new layer as for a placed item.

    Paste As Paths   To paste the path on a work path or the active path. The path preserves all its vector graphic properties and you can modify it in Photoshop with the ⬚ tool.

[e] Click **OK**.

The path is pasted in the form of an image or a path depending on the choice you have made.

✓ *This function is not correctly managed by other vector graphics applications because Photoshop only recognises Illustrator paths.*

Chapter 6

PRACTICE EXERCISE 6

- Open the **Elephant.jpg** document.
- Using the ✒ tool, draw a precise outline around the elephant. If necessary, make some retouches in order to achieve a perfect result.
- Save the path as **Outline** or rename the path if you have already saved it.
- Convert the path into a selection border with a feather radius of 1.
- Lighten this selection using curves, adding an 128 input point on the curve with an output of 144.
- Create a clipping path for this image using the **Outline** path. The image should be printed at 600 ppi.
- Export the **Outline** path in order to use it in Illustrator.
- Save the image in EPS format as **Clipped Elephant** then quit Photoshop.

The corrected versions of these documents are called **Elephant Outline Chapter 6.ai** and **Clipped Elephant Chapter 6.eps**.

Chapter 6

CHAPTER 7

1 - ACCESSING CHANNELS 322
2 - USING ALPHA CHANNELS 324
        CREATING A NEW ALPHA CHANNEL 324
        CREATING AN ALPHA CHANNEL FROM A SELECTION 325
        LOADING A SELECTION FROM AN ALPHA CHANNEL 325
3 - MODIFYING ALPHA CHANNEL OPTIONS 326
4 - MODIFYING A CHANNEL 327
5 - DUPLICATING A CHANNEL 330
        ON A NEW CHANNEL ON THE IMAGE 330
        ONTO ANOTHER IMAGE 330
6 - DELETING A CHANNEL 331
7 - COMBINING TWO CHANNELS 332
8 - COMBINING CHANNELS FROM TWO IMAGES 335
9 - SELECTING WITH QUICK MASK MODE 337
        DEFINING THE QUICK MASK MODE PREFERENCES 337
        MAKING A SELECTION IN QUICK MASK MODE 338
10 - MIXING COLOUR CHANNELS 339
11 - USING SPOT CHANNELS 342
        CREATING A NEW SPOT CHANNEL 342
        CONVERTING AN ALPHA CHANNEL INTO A SPOT CHANNEL 343
        MANAGING OVERPRINTING AND TRAPPING IN A SPOT COLOUR CHANNEL 344
        MERGING A SPOT CHANNEL WITH THE IMAGE 347
12 - CONVERTING AN IMAGE INTO MULTICHANNEL MODE 349
13 - SPLITTING CHANNELS INTO SEVERAL DOCUMENTS 351
14 - MERGING CHANNELS INTO A SINGLE DOCUMENT 351
        PRACTICE EXERCISE 7 354

Chapter 7

During this chapter you are going to learn about working with channels. Channels can be used to make special selections and also to create special effects for advanced retouching or to prepare specific printing jobs.

➠ If you have left Photoshop, restart it.
➠ Open the **Kilimanjaro.jpg** document.
➠ **Image - Adjust - Curves**
➠ Create one point on the curve with an input value of **84** and an output value of **141** and a second point with an input value of **164** and an output value of **212** and click **OK**.

---

1 *To start learning about channels, the first thing to do is to open the **Channels** palette.*

ACCESSING CHANNELS

[a] **Window**   Click the **Channels** tab
    Show Channels

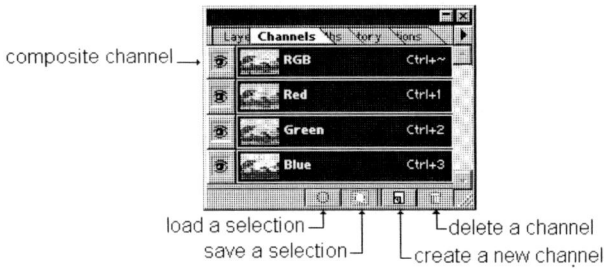

To view all the existing channels in a palette, click the ▬ button on the palette's title bar.

The channel at the top of the list corresponds to the **Composite Channel**, that is the channel that regroups all the colour information. This channel is only present if your image is in RGB, CMYK or Lab mode.

[b] To activate a channel, click its thumbnail or name. All the selections, transformations or retouches as well as any moves made will be made on this channel and will not change the others. If your image is composed of several layers, only the active layer will be modified. If you activate the composite channel, all the colour channels are activated; this is the case by default. You can also activate several channels by holding down ⇧Shift and clicking each of the channels that you want simultaneously to modify.

The visible channels are represented by the 👁 icon.

Chapter 7

|c| You can hide a channel by clicking the 👁 icon that corresponds to it. To hide all the channels except the one that you wish to work on, simply activate that channel.

➟ Here, click the 👁 icon that corresponds to the **Blue** channel.

The sky takes on a yellow colour.

➟ Click the 👁 icon on the **Blue** channel again.

The image is displayed normally again.

> ✓ An image can contain special channels such as Alpha channels and spot channels. These two types of channels will be discussed in detail in the pages coming up.
>
> ✓ You can change the size of the thumbnails on this palette by activating *Palette Options* on the palette menu (▶).
>
> ✓ As for layers, you can change the stacking order of Alpha and spot channels. This does not alter the appearance of the image on the screen. For spot channels, changing the order can have an influence on how the printed image looks. In any case, the colour channels stay at the head of the list.
>
> ✓ The colours channels are by default displayed in the palette in grayscale. You can display them in colour by using the *File - Preferences - Display & Cursors* command and then activating the *Color Channels in Color* option. This option is not recommended for images in CMYK mode because you will not accurately perceive the result that would be printed on a film for a print shop.

Try this last possibility on the image of Kilimanjaro which is in RGB mode.

➟ **File - Preferences - Display & Cursors**

➟ Activate the **Color Channels in Color** option then click **OK**.

The colour channels are now displayed in their corresponding colour in the **Channels** *palette.*

➟ Click the **Green** channel thumbnail.

You can now see only this colour and the image is displayed in levels of green.

➟ **File - Preferences - Display & Cursors**

➟ Deactivate the **Color Channels in Color** option then click **OK**.

The **Green** *channel is again displayed in grayscale as are all the other channels on the* **Channels** *palette.*

➟ Click the thumbnail of the composite channel to display the image in colour and activate all the colour channels.

Adobe Photoshop 5.5

Chapter 7

2

You may remember that in the first chapter you learnt how to save and load a selection. Selections saved in this way are saved on Alpha channels. You can now learn how these Alpha channels work and how to use them.

USING ALPHA CHANNELS

CREATING A NEW ALPHA CHANNEL

[a] Click the [📄] button on the **Channels** palette. If you wish to define the new channel's options directly, [Alt]-click this button or select the **New Channel** command in the **Channels** palette menu (▶).

➤ Here, click the [📄] button.

*A new Alpha channel appears in the Channels palette. This channel is activated automatically, which explains why the image has suddenly gone black! This new channel is called **Alpha [number]** because you did not define its options when you created it.*

[b] Make any necessary modifications to this channel.

You will see how to select options and modify channels a little later on in this chapter.

✓ You can have up to 24 channels in an image. The colour channels are included in this number.

✓ You can activate the composite channel quickly (and consequently all the colour channels) by [⇧ Shift]-clicking the thumbnail of the selected Alpha channel.

Now, you need to display your image normally again then select the sky.

➤ Hold down the [⇧ Shift] key and click the Alpha channel thumbnail to activate all the colour channels.

324   Adobe Photoshop 5.5

Chapter 7

▸ **Select - Color Range**
Select the sky so that it is entirely white in the preview screen on the dialog box:

All blue areas in the image background are also selected.

▸ Click **OK**.

CREATING AN ALPHA CHANNEL FROM A SELECTION

[a] Create a selection with the tool of your choice.

▸ Here, the selection is in the process of being made.

[b] Save the selection by clicking the [▫] button on the **Channels** palette. To directly define the channel options, [Alt]-click this button.

▸ Here, click the [▫] button on the **Channels** palette then if necessary click the [▫] button on the palette to view all the channels.

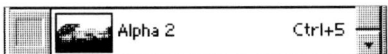

A new channel corresponding to the selection appears in the palette.

✓ *As you already know, you can also save a selection using* Select - Save Selection.

For now, you do not need to keep the sky selected, so you can cancel your selection.

▸ **Select - Deselect**

LOADING A SELECTION FROM AN ALPHA CHANNEL

[a] Activate the Alpha channel containing the selection you wish to retrieve then click the [▫] button on the **Channels** palette or [Ctrl]-click the channel thumbnail.

▸ Here, activate the **Alpha 2** channel then click the [▫] button.
The selection is loaded.

[b] If required, show the image in colour again by clicking the composite channel thumbnail or by [⇧ Shift]-clicking the Alpha channel thumbnail.

▸ Here, [⇧ Shift]-click the **Alpha 2** channel's thumbnail.

Adobe Photoshop 5.5

Chapter 7

- ✓ As you saw previously, you can also use the *Select - Load Selection* command.
- ✓ You can also drag the channel's thumbnail onto the [icon] button. This avoids activating the Alpha channel then reactivating the composite channel.
- ✓ To add the Alpha channel selection to an existing selection, hold down [Ctrl][⇧ Shift] then click the Alpha channel thumbnail.
- ✓ To subtract the Alpha channel selection from the existing selection, hold down [Ctrl][Alt] the click the Alpha channel thumbnail.
- ✓ To load a selection corresponding to the intersection between the Alpha channel and the existing selection, hold down [Ctrl][Alt][⇧ Shift] then click the Alpha channel thumbnail.

Your next task is to modify the Alpha channel before loading a selection that you need to work on. First, deselect what is currently selected.

➤ **Select - Deselect**

---

3 The options of the Alpha channel containing the sky selection need modifying.

MODIFYING ALPHA CHANNEL OPTIONS

[a] Activate the channel that needs modifying then either select the **Channel Options** command in the **Channels** palette menu (▶) or double-click the channel thumbnail.

➤ Here, double-click the **Alpha 2** thumbnail.

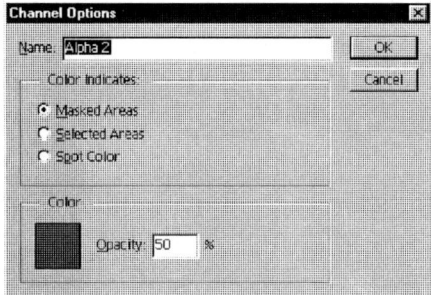

[b] Enter a **Name** for the saved channel in the corresponding text box.

➤ Here, enter **Sky** in the **Name** box.

|c| Activate one of the following options:

> Masked Areas   The selected areas are white on the Alpha channel, the non-selected ones are black and partially selected areas are grey. If you are viewing the Alpha channel with another channel, this is shown in the **Color** sample box in the dialog box. The white areas on the channel are considered as transparent, and the black areas displayed in the **Color** and **Opacity** selected for that channel.
>
> Selected Areas   This is the opposite of the **Masked Areas** option. The black areas on the Alpha channel correspond to the selected areas and the white areas to non-selected parts. The idea of showing the selection with several channels is identical to that used in **Masked Areas**.

➤ Here, leave the **Masked Areas** option active.

|d| Select a display **Color** for the channel by clicking the sample box.

➤ Here, leave the default colour as it is set.

|e| Define what **Opacity** the display colour will use for the black areas on the Alpha channel.

➤ Here, do not change the proposed **Opacity** value.

|f| Click **OK**.

The channel has been renamed in the palette.

4 *You can now begin to modify the Sky channel.*

MODIFYING A CHANNEL

|a| Activate the channel you wish to modify.

You can work directly on a colour channel as on an Alpha or spot channel.

➤ Here, activate the **Sky** channel.

|b| Activate a drawing or retouching tool or use one of the retouch commands from the menus. You can also apply filters to the channel to create special effects.

➤ Here, activate the ✏ tool.

|c| If you have used a tool, adjust its **Options** by double-clicking the tool you have just activated.

➤ Here, check that the blending **Mode** used is **Normal** and that the **Opacity** equals 100%.

Chapter 7

- [d] Show the **Brushes** palette by clicking its tab or using **Window - Show Brushes** and select the tool type you want to use.

➨ Here, select the **65** diameter tool to do the roughest work, you can progressively reduce the tool size as your work needs to become more precise.

- [e] If you activated a drawing tool, select a drawing colour (foreground colour). If the channels are displayed in grayscale, use the following colours depending on the type of channel:

RGB color channels, Lightness channels in Lab mode, and Alpha channels with **Masked Areas** option	**Black**	Removes colour from the areas drawn on or filled. For Alpha channels, the modified areas will be removed from the selection.
	White	Applies 100% of the drawing colour on the corrected areas. For Alpha channels, the modified areas will be added to the selection.
CMYK color channels, spot channels and Alpha channels with **Selected Areas** option	**Black**	Applies 100% of the drawing colour to the corrected areas. For Alpha channels, the modified areas will be added to the selection.
	White	Removes colour from the areas drawn on or filled. For Alpha channels, the modified areas will be removed from the selection.
All colour, spot and Alpha channels	**Grey**	Applies a certain level of colour to the channel. For Alpha channels, the filled areas will be partially included in the selection.

➨ Here, select black so you can remove some areas from your selection (remember that the **Masked Areas** option is active for the **Sky** channel).

Chapter 7

- [f] Drag over the image if you are using a drawing or retouch tool. Set the parameters if you are using a menu command.
- Here, fill in all the areas that are not part of the sky in black. As these areas get smaller, choose a finer tool type so as to be more precise.

initial selection
all the background area is selected

modified selection
only the sky is selected

The initial selection made with the **Color Range** command allowed you to pick up all areas of the sky including all the very small parts, such as those seen through the tree branches. By modifying the Alpha channel, you can easily retrieve just the sky without any of the parts of the background being included.

You can now load this sky selection and correct its colour.

- Click the [ ] button.
- [⇧ Shift]-click the **Sky** channel thumbnail to activate the composite colour channel.
- **Image - Adjust - Hue/Saturation**
- In the **Edit** list, choose **Blues** then click the sky in the top right corner of the image. Set the **Hue** at **+16**, the **Saturation** at **+45** and the **Lightness** at **11** then click **OK**.

The sky is a darker, more intense blue which even has violet overtones.

- **Select - Deselect**

You need to change the image's colour mode.

- **Image - Mode - Lab Color**

Adobe Photoshop 5.5

Chapter 7

5 *Sometimes you may want to create special effects which require you to create a temporary copy of an image. An interesting way of doing this may be to duplicate a channel.*

DUPLICATING A CHANNEL

ON A NEW CHANNEL ON THE IMAGE

[a] Drag the thumbnail of the channel you wish to duplicate onto the 🔲 button on the **Channels** palette.

➤ Here, drag the **Lightness** channel onto the 🔲 button then, if required, click the 🔲 button on the **Channels** palette.

*The channel is duplicated onto a channel called **Alpha 2**. You can always modify this channel if you need to do so.*

For now, you are going to look at a different method, so you can cancel what you just did.

➤ **Edit - Undo**

ONTO ANOTHER IMAGE

[a] To duplicate the channel onto an existing document, open this document.

The document should be as many pixels wide and high as the image currently containing the layer.

➤ Here, you do not need to open another document.

[b] Activate the channel you want to duplicate.

➤ Here, activate the **Lightness** channel.

[c] Use the **Duplicate Channel** command in the **Channels** palette menu (▶).

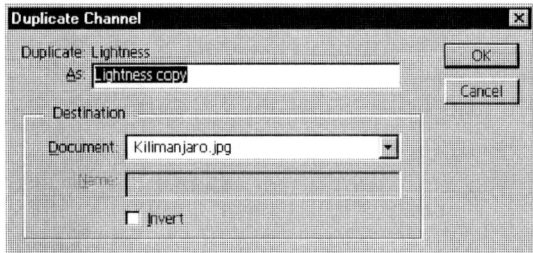

[d] Enter the new channel's name in the **As** text box.

➤ Here, enter **Outline Effect**

[e] Use the **Document** list to select the open document into which you want to copy the channel or a **New** document (in this case, enter a **Name** for this document).

➤ Here, you are going to copy into the same document: leave **Kilimanjaro.jpg** active.

330 Adobe Photoshop 5.5

Chapter 7

[f] Activate the **Invert** option if you want to duplicate a negative of the channel.

➤ Here, make sure that the option is not active.

[g] Click **OK**.

The **Outline Effect** channel appears in the **Channels** palette. This new channel is active by default.

> ✓ You can also duplicate a channel onto another document by dragging the channel thumbnail onto the window of the other document. This method also lets you duplicate a channel when two documents do not have the same number of pixels.

6 *When some channels are no longer useful for you, you can delete them to free memory in your computer and create smaller documents. Try doing this now.*

DELETING A CHANNEL

[a] Show the **Channels** palette by clicking its tab or with **Window - Show Channels**.

[b] Activate the channel you wish to delete.

➤ Here, activate the **Alpha 1** channel.

[c] Click the 🗑 button on the **Channels** palette or use the **Delete Channel** command on the **Channels** palette menu (▶).

➤ Here, click the 🗑 button.

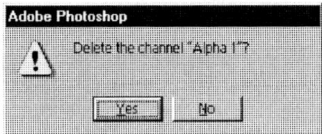

A message prompting for confirmation appears.

[d] Click **Yes** to delete the channel.

The channel is no longer seen in the palette and the composite channel is again activated.

> ✓ You can also drag the channel thumbnail onto the 🗑 button. In this case, it will be deleted without any confirmation being required.

> ✓ If you delete a colour channel, the image will be automatically converted to Multi-channel mode. If it is an *RGB* image, the remaining channels will be converted into *CMYK* components complementary to the deleted colour. For example, if you delete a *Green* channel, the *Red* channel will be converted into *Cyan* and the *Blue* channel into *Yellow*.

Adobe Photoshop 5.5

Chapter 7

*Before continuing, you can apply an effect to the **Outline Effect** channel you previously created.*

▸ Activate the **Outline Effect** channel.

▸ **Filter - Brush Strokes - Ink Outlines**

▸ Leave the default options as set (**Stroke Length** at **4**, **Dark Intensity** at **20**, **Light Intensity** at **10**) then click **OK**.

A drawing effect is applied. You will later use this to make an oil painting effect on this image.

---

7 *Other interesting effects can be made with channels. For example, it is possible to combine two channels and create a third. You are going to try this right now.*

COMBINING TWO CHANNELS

[a] Open, if necessary, another document to combine two channels coming from two distinct images.

This requires the two documents to be the same number of pixels wide and high.

▸ Here, this is not necessary.

[b] **Image**
Calculations

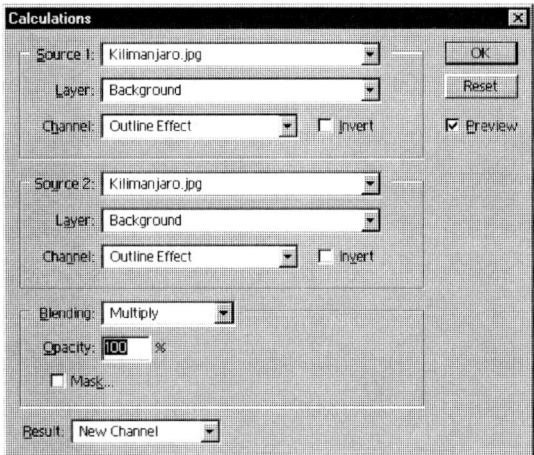

[c] For each of the channels you wish to mix, provide the following information:

Source   Indicate the name of the document that contains the channel to be mixed.

Layer   Indicate on which layer the channel that you want to mix is located. You can choose **Merged for Layer** to use all the layers in the image.

	Channel	Specify the channels that you wish to combine. On an RGB or CMYK image you can select **Gray** to work on a channel that would correspond to the colour image in grayscale (or to the **Lightness** layer for a Lab image).
	Invert	Lets you combine the negative of the channel in question.

➟ Here, specify **Kilimanjaro.jpg** for both **Source 1** and **Source 2**. For the **Channel** of **Source 1**, select the **Outline Effect** channel and for the **Source 2** channel, **Lightness**.

[d] Select the **Blending** mode that you wish to use to combine the two channels. The options on offer are the same as the blending modes used for layers or for drawing tools. They work in the same way, so you can refer back to chapter 4 if you need to refresh your memory on the effects produced. Two **Blending** modes are specific to this command:

Add	The values of the pixels in both channels are added together. If you use this calculation, you will have to specify two options: **Offset** and **Scale**. The **Offset** varies between -255 and +255. If its value is negative, the result is darkened; if it is positive the result is lightened. The **Scale** option allows you to divide the addition result by any value between 1.000 and 2.000. If you leave the **Scale** at 1, the addition will not modify the black areas that are common to both channels; they will remain black. The white areas too will stay white on the result. This value could be useful if you were combining Alpha channels with 0 **Offset**. If you specify a **Scale** value of 2, the two channels will be perfectly combined if the **Offset** is left at 0.
Subtract	The pixel values in the source channel are subtracted from the corresponding target channel pixels. As with the add mode, you will have to specify the **Scale** and **Offset**. These options work in the same way as for **Add**.

➟ Here, select **Lighten** as the **Blending** mode.

[e] Set the **Opacity** value. If it is less than 100%, the calculation result will be toned down and the **Source 2** will be more dominant.

➟ Here, leave the **Opacity** at **100%**.

[f] If required, attribute a **Mask** for the calculation. In this case you will have to supply the same information for this **Mask** as for the **Source** channels. The white areas on the **Mask** channel will be modified by the calculation. The black areas will be protected and the corresponding pixels will only be applied with those from **Source 2**.

➟ Here, activate the **Mask** option, select the **Kilimanjaro.jpg** image and the **Sky Channel**. The calculation will only be applied to the sky but in fact you need to apply the effect to the rest of the image only. Activate the **Invert** option under **Mask** so that the calculation is not applied to the sky, just to the rest of the image.

Chapter 7

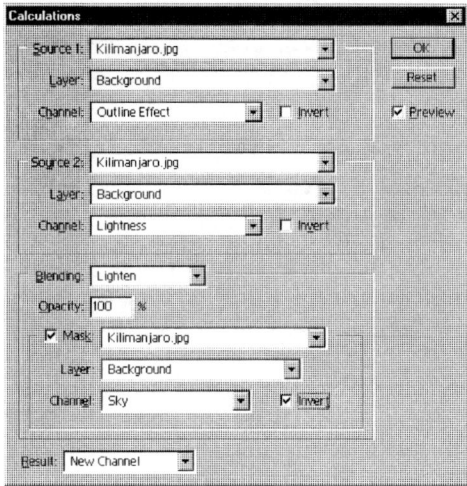

- [g] Indicate how the **Result** will be managed using the list of the same name:

    New Document   Creates a new document in Multichannel mode. This contains the result of the calculation, made up into a single channel in grayscale.

    New Channel   The result of the calculation is placed on a new channel in the active document.

    Selection   The result is not placed in a channel but in the form of a selection in the active document.

- Here, leave the **New Channel** option.
- [h] Click **OK**.

A new channel called *Alpha 1* is displayed, containing the results of the calculation.

> ☑ Combining channels in this way does not allow you to combine composite channels. To do that, use the layers by adjusting the blending mode or use the *Image - Apply Image* command.

Now that that is done, you can rename your new channel and continue with your oil-paint effect.

- Double-click the **Alpha 1** channel thumbnail and enter **Painting Draft** in the **Name** box and click **OK**.
- Activate the **Lightness** channel.
- **Filter - Brush Strokes - Spatter**
- Leave the default values (**Spray Radius** = **10** and **Smoothness** = **5**) as set and click **OK**.

Chapter 7

8 *Two channels can be combined using another method. This method also allows you to combine the composite channels of two images. What about trying out that method now?*

COMBINING CHANNELS FROM TWO IMAGES

a) If necessary, open a second image in order to combine two channels coming from two separate images or to combine a composite channel from both images.

As you saw previously, the two images have to contain the same number of pixels across and down. You cannot combine the composite channels of two images if they are not both in the same colour mode.

➤ Here, you are going to use this technique to combine two channels from the same image.

b) Activate the layer and the channel where your result should eventually be placed. These also correspond to the second source used for the operation. Depending on your needs you can also activate the composite channel.

➤ Here, the document only contains a **Background** layer and the result should apply to the **Lightness** channel which is already active.

c) **Image**
   Apply Image

d) For the channel that you want to combine, give the following information:

   Source   Indicate the name of the document.

   Layer   Indicate the layer whose channel should be combined. You can select **Merged for Layer** to use the channel corresponding to all layers.

   Channel Specify the channels that will be combined. On a RGB, CMYK or Lab image, you can select the composite channel.

   Invert   Use this to combine the negative of the corresponding channel.

➤ Here, specify **Kilimanjaro.jpg** as the **Source** and for the **Channel** option, use **Painting Draft**.

You are going to use this command to combine the Lightness channel and the Painting Draft channel.

e) Select the **Blending** mode you wish to use to combine the two channels. The options on offer are the same as for layer blending modes. They function in the same way (look back to chapter 4 for extra details). You also have the **Add** and **Subtract** modes, which you looked at in the last section: Combining two channels.

➤ Here, select the **Add Blending** mode with and **Offset** of **0** and a **Scale** of **2**.

Adobe Photoshop 5.5

Chapter 7

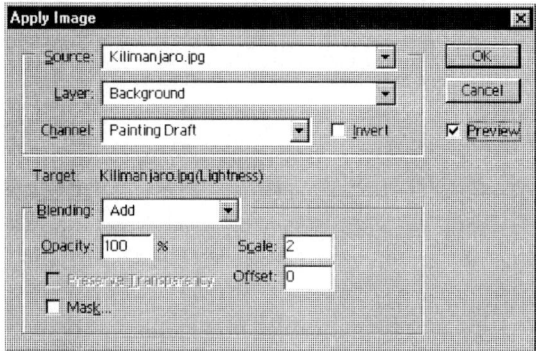

[f] Set an **Opacity** value. If it is inferior to 100%, the result of the operation will be toned down and the destination channel will be dominant.

➡ Here, leave the **Opacity** at **100%**.

[g] Activate the **Preserve Transparency** option if you do not wish the transparent areas on the destination layer to be modified. This option works a little like a mask.

➡ Here, your image only contains one layer so this option is not available.

[h] If required, attribute a **Mask** for the operation. If you do, you will have to specify the same information for this mask as for the **Source** channel. The white areas on the **Mask** channel will be modified by the operation. The black areas will be protected and the corresponding pixels will only be applied with those of the destination channel.

➡ Here, you are not going to use any mask this time.

[i] Click **OK**.

The result of the operation is shown in the destination channel.

In order to see the final result, you need to activate the composite channel.

➡ Click the **Lab** channel thumbnail.

*Well, you are really an artist! The sky looks a little unrealistic, but you could always correct that by applying the [tool] tool with the **Impressionist** option active.*

➡ Save this image under the name **Kilimanjaro Painting** then close it and open **Lion.Jpg**.

Chapter 7

9 *You are already familiar with the various Photoshop selection techniques. There is another method that you are about to discover which you may find very interesting. This is the Quick Mask mode.*

SELECTING WITH QUICK MASK MODE

DEFINING THE QUICK MASK MODE PREFERENCES

Before making your selection, you need to determine the method to be used.

[a] Double-click either the ⬚ button or the ⬚ button on the toolbox.

➤ Here, double-click the ⬚ button.

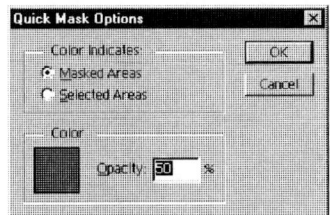

[b] Activate one of the following options:

    Masked Areas   If you draw in white on a mask, your selection is extended. If you use black, you remove pixels from your selection. Using grey, you make a partial selection. The **Edit in Quick Mask mode** tool takes this form on the toolbox: ⬚. This method allows you to perceive the selected areas more clearly.

    Selected Areas   This works in the opposite way to the **Masked Areas** option. The areas drawn in white are removed from the selection and those drawn in black are added to the selection. The **Edit in Quick Mask mode** tool takes this form on the toolbox: ⬚. This method favours the visual aspect of the non-selected areas.

➤ Here, leave the **Masked Areas** option active.

[c] Select a mask **Color** for the channel by clicking the sample box. It is preferable to use a colour that is not present on the parts of the image that you want to select.

➤ Here, select a bright green as the mask colour.

[d] Define what **Opacity** you want to use with the mask colour on the black areas of the mask.

➤ Here, leave **50% Opacity**.

[e] Click **OK**.

If you had activated the Selected Areas option, the Edit in Quick Mask Mode tool would have looked different on the toolbox.

Adobe Photoshop 5.5

Chapter 7

MAKING A SELECTION IN QUICK MASK MODE

a) Check that the **Selection** mode is active on the toolbox: the ▣ button (Standard Mode) should be pressed in. You can make an initial selection to reduce the selection work you will need to do in Quick Mask mode.

➤ Here, activate the ◩ tool and specify a **Tolerance** of 120 in the **Options** palette. Click bottom left corner of the image then inverse the selection with **Select - Inverse**.

b) Activate the Quick Mask mode by clicking the ▣ button on the toolbox (this button can also look like this: ▣).

The non-selected areas are overlaid with a film of the colour chosen in the Quick Mask mode options. In the **Channels** palette, you can see a new, temporary Alpha channel called **Quick Mask**. In the **Layers** palette, the active layer is selected in light grey instead of blue. The **Quick Mask** channel is the only active channel but all the other colour channels are visible.

c) Activate a drawing tool to modify the selected area.

➤ Here, activate the ◩ tool.

d) Adjust the tool **Options** by double-clicking the tool you have just chosen.

➤ Here, leave the options as they are.

e) Show the **Brushes** palette by clicking its tab or with **Window - Show Brushes** then select the type of tool you want to use.

➤ Here, select a **35** diameter tool to remove from the selection quickly the area under the lion's tail.

f) Select a drawing colour depending on the Quick Mask mode preferences:

Mask in Masked Areas	Black	The painted areas are taken from the selection.
	White	The painted areas are added to the selection.
Mask in Selected Areas	Black	The painted areas are added to the selection.
	White	The painted areas are taken from the selection.
Any Mask	Gray	The filled areas will be partially included in the selection.

Chapter 7

→ Here, select black to remove these areas of sky from the selection.

[g] Drag to paint the areas you wish to add to or take from the selection.

→ Here, fill all the remaining areas of sky in black. Reduce the tool size when you need to paint very precisely.

When you drag the pointer, green colour is added to the screen, because this is the colour you chose to represent the painting colour on-screen. However in this instance the "real" colour perceived by the mask is black.

If any areas on the lion have not been included in the selection, you can include them now.

→ Select white as the foreground colour.

→ Add to the selection any areas of the lion that have been badly selected.

[h] Once the selection is correctly made, click the ▢ button on the toolbox to return to **Selection** mode.

*The selection is active and the **Quick Mask** channel disappears. You can always save this selection if you want to use it at a later time.*

✓ *Paths and mask selections are the two most useful selection techniques available in Photoshop.*

Save this selection then deselect for now.

→ Click the ▢ button on the **Channels** palette.

→ **Select - Deselect**

---

10 *In the previous chapters, you learnt how to retouch an image. There are more retouch possibilities that you can use. On RGB and CMYK images, you can make colour corrections by mixing channels.*

MIXING COLOUR CHANNELS

[a] If necessary, activate the layer on which you wish to make a correction or make a selection to limit the areas retouched.

→ Here, you are going to correct the entire image.

[b] **Image**
Adjust
Channel Mixer

Adobe Photoshop 5.5 339

Chapter 7

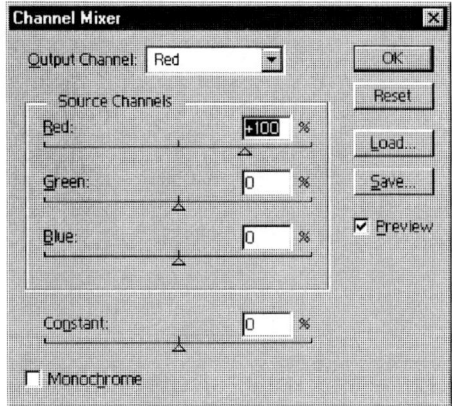

|c| If necessary, activate the **Monochrome** option to prepare a high quality grayscale conversion or create specially tinted images. In this last case, you can use the **Channel Mixer** command again without activating the **Monochrome** option.

⇒ Here, leave this option deactivated for now. You will be able to use it later on.

|d| Select the **Output Channel** to which the channel mix will be applied.

The options available depend on the image mode: RGB or CMYK.

⇒ Here, select the **Green** channel.

|e| Set the values on the **Source Channels** by dragging the sliders or entering a value in the text box. The values allowed vary between -200 and +200%. A negative value inverts the source channel before mixing it with the output channel. The **Source Channels** available depend on the image mode (RGB or CMYK).

⇒ Here, set the **Red** slider to **+24**, the **Green** to **+42** and the **Blue** to **+36** to give the lion a more tawny colour and lighten the sky.

|f| If required modify the **Constant** option by dragging the slider to mix the output channel with a uniformly black or white channel. The value allowed varies between -200 and +200%. The negative values equal a black channel while positive values equal a white channel.

⇒ Here, leave this option at **0**.

|g| Click **OK**.

The sky is lighter and the lion is a more intense tawny colour, with less yellow especially on the lion's head.

> ✓ *Apart from classic colour retouching and preparing images for grayscale and colour tints, you can use this command to make more creative adjustments or to exchange or duplicate channels.*

Chapter 7

> ✓ You can Save any adjustments that you apply to use them on another image by clicking the Load button.

You can also swap channels: try it on this image.

▶ **Image - Adjust - Channel Mixer**

▶ Select **Red** as the **Output Channel**, set the **Red** slider at **0%** and the **Blue** slider at **+100%**. Next, select **Blue** as the **Output Channel**, set the **Red** slider at **+100%** and the **Blue** slider at **0%** and click **OK**.

The sky becomes orange and the lion blue.

That is a startling effect, but you do not need to keep it for the moment, as you will be able to recreate it with another method a little further on.

▶ **Edit - Undo**

To further exploit the channel mixing possibilities, you are now going to create an image in grayscale with an optimal conversion.

▶ **Image - Adjust - Channel Mixer**

▶ Activate the **Monochrome** option. Set the **Red** slider to **+50%**, the **Green** slider to **+30%** and the Blue to **+40%** then click **OK**.

The image appears in grayscale but is still in RGB mode.

▶ **Image - Mode - Grayscale**

▶ Click **OK** to confirm.

If you had converted the image directly into grayscale, it would have lost a number of shades in the lighter parts of the image. By first preparing it with the Channel Mixer, there are many less lost shades. The result, of course, would vary from image to image:

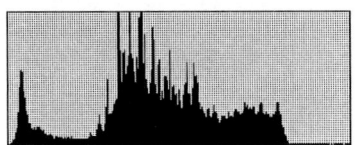

histogram of the image converted directly into grayscale

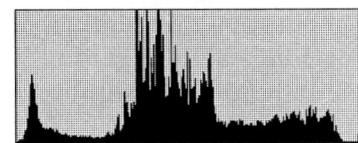

histogram with a pre-conversion preparation using the **Channel mixer**

Adobe Photoshop 5.5

Chapter 7

11 *You have seen how Alpha channels work, but Photoshop also lets you create spot channels, which you can use to print custom colours.*

USING SPOT CHANNELS

CREATING A NEW SPOT CHANNEL

[a] If necessary, make a conversion to CMYK mode, grayscale or even multichannel mode. You may have guessed that these channels are used for special printing jobs that will eventually be processed by a professional printer. Unless you wanted to create unusual colour effects, you would not need to use this type of channel on an RGB or Lab image.

➤ Here, the image is already in grayscale.

[b] If the **Channels** palette is not visible, click its tab or use **Window - Show Channels**.

[c] If needed, make a selection so that the future spot channel only recognises the selected areas as areas containing the spot colour.

➤ Here, use **Select - Load Selection**.
Choose **Alpha 1** as the **Channel**.
Activate the **Invert** option then click **OK**.

[d] Choose the **New Spot Channel** option in the **Channels** palette menu or [Ctrl]-click the [icon] button on the palette.

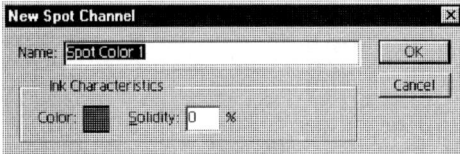

[e] Click the **Color** sample box to determine the spot colour you want to use. By default, Photoshop gives you the opportunity to select the colour using the **Color Picker**. Click the **Custom** button to choose a predefined custom colour, such as one of the Pantone colours. These usually produce a higher quality print result.

➤ Here, click the colour box, click the **Custom** button, select the **Pantone 293 CVC** colour from the **PANTONE Coated** swatches then click **OK**.

[f] Specify the colour **Solidity** between 0 and 100%. This option merely allows a visual simulation of the spot colour on the screen and does not affect the printed result. A 0% value simulates a transparent ink (overprinted) which would allow all the colours underneath to show through, like a clear varnish. A 100% value simulates opaque ink that would cover up all the inks situated under it (which would be the case with traditional Pantone colours or metallic inks).

➤ Here, choose a **100% Solidity**.

Chapter 7

|g| If required, choose a **Name** for your spot channel in the corresponding text box. If you use a Pantone colour, a **Name** is automatically attributed.

➠ Here, leave the **Name** as PANTONE 293 CVC.

|h| Click **OK**.

A new channel appears in the palette. This channel is not really any different from an Alpha channel, except that its name will often describe a colour, such as Pantone. This type of channel can automatically be seen with the rest of the image which is not the case with an Alpha channel. Black areas on a spot channel are printed in the selected colour and the white areas are left empty.

☑ If you want to keep any spot channels in the final document in order to send it to a desktop publishing application and eventually to a professional print shop, you should save the image in *Photoshop DCS 2.0* format. For some applications, you will have to save the Pantone colour names in an abbreviated form so they can be recognised. To do this, go into *File - Preferences - General*, activate the *Short PANTONE Names* option then click *OK*.

☑ You can modify the spot colour by accessing the channel options as for an Alpha channel.

☑ If you must use a selective varnish that will only cover part of the image, create a spot channel using any colour and name this channel *Varnish*.

☑ You can use the drawing tools to retouch a spot channel exactly as you would for an Alpha channel.

CONVERTING AN ALPHA CHANNEL INTO A SPOT CHANNEL

|a| If the **Channels** palette is hidden, show it by clicking its tab or using **Window - Show Channels**.

|b| Activate the Alpha channel you want to convert.

➠ Here, activate the channel **Alpha 1**.

|c| Double-click the channel thumbnail or select the **Channel Options** command in the **Channels** palette menu ▶.

➠ Here, double-click the **Alpha 1** channel thumbnail.

Chapter 7

|d| Activate the **Spot Color** option then set the desired **Color** and **Solidity** for the spot channel.

➭ Here, activate the **Spot Color** option and leave the other options as set by default.

|e| Click **OK**.

The Alpha channel is converted into a spot channel. It is called *Spot Color 1*.

☑ It is not possible to convert a spot channel into an Alpha channel, although you can copy the contents of a spot channel and paste them onto an existing Alpha channel.

You can now cancel this conversion and display the image again with the spot channel.

➭ **Edit - Undo**

➭ Click the thumbnail of the **Black** channel to activate it.

➭ Click the square on the **PANTONE 293 CVC** channel in order to show the 👁 icon and thus display the channel.

MANAGING OVERPRINTING AND TRAPPING IN A SPOT COLOUR CHANNEL

When you use several spot channels, you need to ensure that the colours do not mix. To do this, you should remove one (or more) of the colours from the areas of the image where they overlap. You may, however wish to leave a trap (a slight overlap of the colours) to avoid gaps appearing between them. Of course, in cases where you actually want certain colours to overprint others creating a varnish effect, you do not need to worry about this.

image printed with
the spot colour overprinted

image printed with the underlying
colour removed and a trap defined

Without any preparation, the Pantone colour will be overprinted onto the black channel and the two inks are mixed, as with a duotone. In order to obtain a single background colour, some preparation is necessary.

Chapter 7

|a| If the **Channels** palette is hidden, show it by clicking its tab or using **Window - Show Channels**.

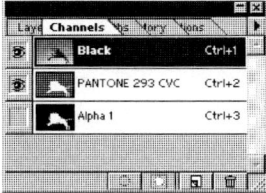

|b| Activate the spot channel whose colour you wish to print correctly.

➤ Here, activate the **PANTONE 293 CVC** channel.

|c| Click the ⬚ button on the **Channels** palette to load this channel's selection.

|d| Use the **Modify** command in the **Select** menu then activate one of the following options to define the trap:

Expand   Use this if the underlying spot colour is lighter than the active spot colour. The underlying colour is situated over the active channel in the **Channels** palette, considering the first colour on the list is the first one printed and the last one on the list is printed last.

Contract   Use this if the underlying spot colour is darker than the active spot colour.

➤ Here, use the **Select - Modify - Contract** command.

|e| Set the value to expand or contract the selection. This value is equivalent to the width of the overlap (trap) you are creating and should be specified by your print shop. This overlapping avoids white areas appearing on the printed result between the spot colour and the rest of the image:

image printed with no expansion or contraction of the selection   image printed with expansion or contraction of the selection

Notice the white outline that appears around the lion if no contraction or expansion value has been specified.

➤ Here, set the value to **1**

|f| Click **OK**.

Adobe Photoshop 5.5   345

Chapter 7

|g| Activate the underlying channel that contains areas which have to be removed if you want to avoid overprinting. This channel can be another spot colour or a CMYK channel. For a four-colour image you will have to activate the various CMYK channels. For a grayscale image, proceed in the same way, selecting the black channel.

➠ Here, activate **Black**.

|h| Check that the background colour is pure white. If this is not the case, select white for the background.

➠ Here, select white as the background colour.

|i| **Edit**
 Clear   [Del]

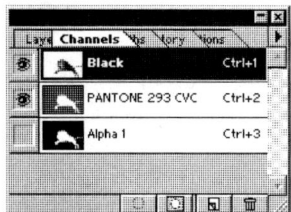

*It would appear that nothing has happened to the image. You can however see the modification in the **Channels** palette (compare this illustration to the previous one of the **Channels** palette). Even though the image you see on the screen does not appear to have changed, the printed result will be completely different.*

|j| If several spot channels are superimposed, repeat this operation for any other channels on which you do not wish to have overprinting.

✓ *This method is only important if you are using one or more spot channels should not be overprinted and mixed (in other words, several colours have to be juxtaposed). You do not have to use this method if the spot colour contains more than 95% black.*

✓ *For CMYK images, Photoshop offers automatic trap management with the Image - Trap command. This command should only be used with images using pure cyan, magenta or yellow colours. To avoid bad quality print results, do not use this command on photographic images or those containing colour gradients.*

*In this case, you do not need to keep the modification you have just made to the **Black** channel as the spot colour will be overprinted.*

➠ **Edit - Undo**

➠ **Select - Deselect**

To see what result overprinting a spot colour would give, you can set up a simulation of this on your screen.

➠ Activate the **PANTONE 293 CVC** channel.

Chapter 7

▸ Select the **Channel Options** command in the **Channels** palette menu (▶).

▸ Set the **Solidity** at **0%** then click **OK**.

You can now save your lion image.

▸ **File - Save As**

▸ Enter **Special Tritone Lion** in the **File name** box, select the **Photoshop DCS 2.0 (*.EPS)** format and click **Save** (the image is not a tritone yet, but you will transform it a little further one). Select **TIFF (8 bits/pixel)** in the **Preview** list, choose **Single File with Color Composite (72 ppi)** then click **OK**.

Now that your image is saved, you can make some other temporary modifications to the image.

▸ If the **PANTONE 293 CVC** channel is not active, activate it now.

▸ Click the 🗑 button on the **Channels** palette then the **Yes** button to delete the channel.

▸ Activate the ⬚ tool.

▸ Make a rectangular selection on the left side of the image.

▸ Select the **New Spot Channel** command in the **Channels** palette menu (▶).

▸ Select the **PANTONE 144 CVC** colour and set the **Solidity** at **0%** then click **OK**.

▸ **Image - Mode - CMYK Color**

MERGING A SPOT CHANNEL WITH THE IMAGE

[a] If the **Channels** palette is hidden, show it by clicking its tab or using **Window - Show Channels**.

[b] Activate the spot channel you want to merge with the colour channels of the image.

▸ Here, activate the **PANTONE 144 CVC** channel.

Adobe Photoshop 5.5

Chapter 7

[c] Select the **Merge Spot Channel** command in the **Channels** palette menu (▶).

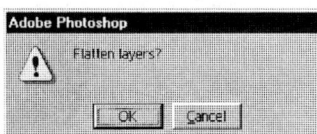

[d] If the image contains layers, you will have to flatten the image. Click **OK** to flatten the layers and merge the spot channel, or **Cancel** if you do not want to merge the spot channel yet.

➜ Here, this message does not appear.

The spot channel is merged with the colour channels. This merging preserves the *Solidity* parameter of the spot channel. The result will be different if the spot channel has a 0 or 100% *Solidity*.

✓ The printed result from a print shop is generally different from that obtained by using a spot channel. For the most part, Pantone colours do not have a perfect match in the four-colour range.

✓ You cannot merge a spot channel with a grayscale image.

You are now going to revert to the previously saved version of the document and from that create a duotone image.

➜ **File - Revert**

➜ **Image - Mode - Duotone**

➜ Select a **Duotone Type**. For the first ink, select **PANTONE Process Black CVC** and, if necessary, modify its curve to add a point with an input value of **50%** and an output of **40%**. For the second ink, select **PANTONE 144 CVC** then, if necessary, modify its curve so it has an input value of **50%** with an output value of **60%**. Click **OK** to confirm your duotone.

Chapter 7

12 *You are going to prepare a special print job. The first step you need to perform is to convert your image into multichannel mode. Try doing this now.*

CONVERTING AN IMAGE INTO MULTICHANNEL MODE

[a] If your image is an RGB or CMYK image in **16 bits/channel**, convert it to **8 bits/channel**.

⟹ Here, this is not necessary.

[b] **Image**
Mode
Mulitchannel

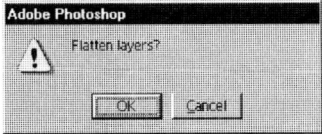

[c] If your image contains layers, you will have to flatten the image. If this dialog box appears, click **OK** to confirm the conversion.

⟹ Here, the image only has a single layer.

The colour channels are converted into spot channels. In the case of a duotone, the two inks are separated onto different channels.

✓ On a colour image, the conversion to multichannel deletes the composite channel. The remaining channels vary depending on the colour mode:

RGB Color	Three channels are created, *Cyan, Magenta* and *Yellow*, to replace the *RGB* channels. The visual aspect can be noticeably changed. The channels are spot channels.
CMYK Color	The four channels, *Cyan, Magenta, Yellow* and *Black* are preserved and become spot channels.
Lab Color	The three original channels are converted into three *Alpha* channels and there is no longer any notion of colour.

Adobe Photoshop 5.5

Chapter 7

☑ If you wish to export a multichannel image to a desktop publishing application, with a view to printing by a print shop, you should save the image in Photoshop DCS 2.0 format. If you use Pantone colours, it may be necessary to save the shortened names of these colours so they are easily recognised. To do this, select the *File - Preferences - General* command, activate the Short PANTONE Names and click OK.

☑ You can use multichannel mode to export images towards specific systems or to create special printing effects.

You are now going to create a special tritone by working on how the various colour channels will be printed in relation to each other.

➤ Activate the **PANTONE 293 CVC** channel.
➤ Click the [○] button in the **Channels** palette to load the selection.
➤ Activate the **PANTONE 144 CVC** channel.
➤ **Select - Modify - Contract**
➤ Set the **Contract By** value to **1** and click **OK**.
➤ **Edit - Clear**
➤ **Select - Deselect**

You now have a specific tritone that in fact corresponds to two duotones: one between the **PANTONE Process Black CVC** channel and the **PANTONE 293 CVC** channel for the sky and another between **PANTONE Process Black CVC** and **PANTONE 144 CVC** for the lion.

Your next task is to delete the Alpha channel and save the image. After that you will close the image and open another.

➤ Activate the **Alpha 1** channel.
➤ Click the [🗑] button on the **Channels** palette and click **Yes**.
➤ **File - Save**
➤ **File - Close**
➤ Open the **Lion.jpg** document.

Chapter 7

13 For some specific tasks, you need to separate the channels in an image so that each channel forms a distinct document. This could be particularly useful when you wish to use a file format that does not support certain channel types but still keep the information in each individual channel, especially Alpha channels. You are now going to do this on the document you have just opened.

SPLITTING CHANNELS INTO SEVERAL DOCUMENTS

[a] If your image contains layers, activate the **Layer - Flatten Image** command because layers are not managed when channels are split.

➡ Here, this is not necessary.

[b] Select the **Split Channels** command on the **Channels** palette menu (▶).

Photoshop creates a distinct document for each channel in the image. The original document is closed without any changes (especially the flattening of the layers) being saved. Each document created is in grayscale and takes the name of the original document followed by the letter representing the name of the original channel (for example, here, Lion_R, Lion_G and Lion_B).

14 As you now have a series of documents in grayscale, you can regroup them to make a colour image.

MERGING CHANNELS INTO A SINGLE DOCUMENT

[a] If you have not done so already, open all the documents that you wish to merge. These documents must be in grayscale, have the same number of pixels across and down and possess no layers. The number of open documents determines which colour modes you could use for the merge. For example, if you only have three documents, you could not merge them into a CMYK document, although a subsequent conversion would remain a possibility.

➡ Here, the images you wish to merge are already open.

Adobe Photoshop 5.5   351

Chapter 7

b   Select the **Merge Channels** command in the **Channels** palette menu (▶).

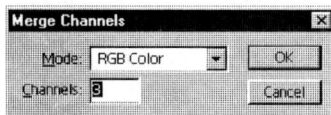

c   Select the type of image you want to create. If you modify the **Channels** option by putting in a value which is incompatible with the suggested **Mode**, the **Multichannel** mode will automatically be chosen.

⟶   Here, leave the **Mode** as **RGB Color**.

d   Click **OK**.

e   Select the name of the document that will be associated with each channel. If the image mode is not satisfactory, you can go back to the previous step in the process by clicking the **Mode** button.

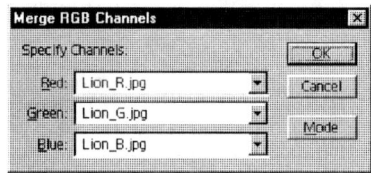

If you opt for a multichannel image, select the document name associated with the first channel then click the **Next** button to select the other channels. You will have to repeat this operation as many times as you want to add channels in the next step:

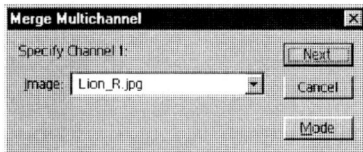

⟶   Here, you are going to take advantage of the merge process to create another effect on this image. You are going to invert two channels, in the same way as with the Channel Mixer. Select the **Lion_B.jpg** document for the **Red** channel, the **Lion_G.jpg** document for the **Green** channel and the **Lion_R.jpg** document for the **Blue** channel.

f   Click **OK**.

Chapter 7

A new image regrouping all the channels is created. This corresponds to the colour mode you selected. Photoshop automatically closes the original documents.

- ✓ If you select a multichannel image, all the channels will be Alpha channels and the image will be in grayscale.

- ✓ You cannot separate then merge an image containing spot channels. The spot channel will either be omitted during the merge or, in the case of a multichannel image, inserted as an Alpha channel.

- ✓ You can use this technique to merge a image digitised in grayscale using red, green and blue filters to make a colour image.

- ✓ If you use documents in DCS 1.0 or DCS 2.0 format and save them as multiple files, the links between the files may sometimes be lost: this means the document can not be printed or opened. In this case, open the documents as split channels and merge them in a CMYK document.

➠ Save the image under the name **Blue Lion** and close it.

Chapter 7

PRACTICE EXERCISE 7

- *Open the **Giraffe.jpg** document.*
- *Select the giraffe using **Quick Mask** mode.*
- *Save the selection and deselect.*
- *Rename the **Alpha 1** channel as **Giraffe Selection**.*
- *Using the calculations method, combine the inverted **Giraffe Selection** channel and the **Green** channel onto a new channel, applying a soft light blending mode.*
- *Apply the **Alpha 1** channel to the **Green** channel, using a mask that corresponds to an inverted **Giraffe Selection** channel.*
- *Delete **Alpha 1**.*
- *Invert the **Red** and **Blue** channels using the **Channel Mixer**.*
- *Load the **Giraffe Selection** channel again.*
- *Create a spot channel with a **Pantone 420 CVC** colour with **0% Solidity**. Name this channel **Varnish**.*
- *Delete the **Giraffe Selection** channel.*
- *Convert the image to **CMYK Color**.*
- *Save the image under another name using **Photoshop DCS 2.0** format in a single file with color composite and a preview. Leave Photoshop once you have saved your document.*

*The corrected version of this file is called **Psychedelic Giraffe Chapter 7.eps**!*

CHAPTER 8

1 - CREATING A CONTACT SHEET 356
2 - CREATING A WEB PHOTO GALLERY 359
3 - CREATING A PICTURE PACKAGE 363
4 - CONVERTING AN IMAGE WITH CONDITIONAL MODE CHANGE 365
5 - WORKING WITH THE ACTIONS PALETTE 366
6 - USING RECORDED ACTIONS 367
7 - CREATING AN ACTION SET 369
8 - CREATING AN ACTION 370
9 - INSERTING A STOP 372
10 - INCLUDING A PATH IN AN ACTION 374
11 - INSERTING A MENU ITEM INTO AN ACTION 375
12 - DUPLICATING AN ACTION OR A SET 377
13 - DELETING AN ACTION/AN ACTION ITEM/A SET 378
14 - MODIFYING AN ACTION'S OPTIONS 378
15 - MODIFYING AN ACTION 380
      RECORDING A COMMAND OR ACTION AGAIN 380
      ADDING COMMANDS 381
16 - MODIFYING THE PLAYBACK OPTIONS ON AN ACTION 384
17 - SAVING A SET OF ACTIONS 385
18 - PLAYING AN ACTION ON A GROUP OF IMAGES 386
    PRACTICE EXERCISE 8 389

Chapter 8

During this chapter, you are going to look at how you can automate some Photoshop tasks. This can be particularly useful as it can help you perform some onerous tasks in one operation.

1

When a folder contains a number of images, you may like to create a catalogue of these images in the form of thumbnails. As you would with a photographic film, you can create a series of miniature prints called a contact sheet.

CREATING A CONTACT SHEET

[a] Close the documents that you want to include in the contact sheet.

▶ Here, no document is open just now.

[b] **File**
Automate
Contact Sheet II

[c] Click the **Choose** button to choose the folder containing the images you wish to display on your contact sheet.

▶ Here, click the **Choose** button.

[d] Click the + icons to the right of each disk drive name to show the folders it contains. If the folder you are looking for is inside another folder, click the + icon corresponding to that folder to see the subfolders it contains. When you have located it, click the folder name to select it.

▶ Here, select the **ENI Photoshop 5.5** folder.

356 Adobe Photoshop 5.5

Chapter 8

|e| Click **OK**.

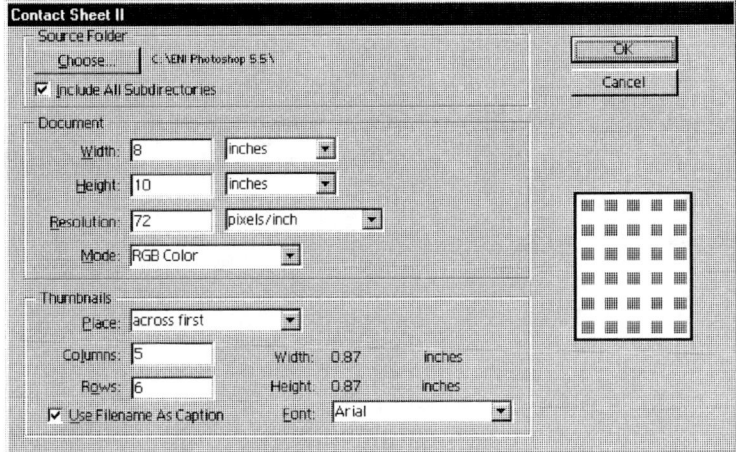

The name of the selected folder appears in the Contact Sheet II dialog box.

|f| Leave the **Include All Subdirectories** option active if you intend to create a contact sheet for all the images in the selected folder and its subfolders.

➠ Here, leave the option active.

|g| Define the **Width**, **Height** and **Resolution** in the corresponding text boxes. For the resolution, it is better to use **pixels/inch** instead of **pixels/cm**.

➠ Here, leave the default options offered.

|h| Select the colour **Mode** for the contact sheet. You can choose from **Grayscale**, **RGB Color**, **CMYK Color** and **Lab Color**.

➠ Here, leave **RGB Color Mode**.

|i| Select **across first** or **down first** from the **Place** list depending on whether you want to read the contact sheet in rows or columns.

➠ Here, leave the **Place across first** option active.

|j| Determine the number of **Columns** and **Rows** that you wish to appear on the contact sheet. Depending on the size of the document and the number of thumbnails, Photoshop will specify on the right of the dialog box the size of the thumbnails. If the number of thumbnails specified (number of **Columns** multiplied by the number of **Rows**) is insufficient to show all the image in the selected folder, Photoshop will create as many contact sheets as is necessary to show them all.

➠ Here, leave the values as set because this folder probably contains at least thirty images.

Adobe Photoshop 5.5

Chapter 8

[k] If you leave the **Use Filename As Caption** option active, the name of each image will appear under its thumbnail.

➡ Here, leave this option active.

[l] Choose a **Font** for the captions. This option is only available if **Use Filename As Caption** is active. The list of fonts does not necessarily include all those on your computer, just the most legible ones.

➡ Here, select **Times New Roman**.

[m] Click **OK** to make the contact sheet.

The images are resampled then placed in a new document with a single layer for all the thumbnails. Depending on the number of documents in the ENI Photoshop 5.5 folder, it is possible that two contact sheets have been made.

- ✓ You cannot update a contact sheet. When images are removed from or added to the folder, you simply make a new contact sheet.

- ✓ Images in multichannel mode are often misrepresented since they have been converted to the colour mode selected for the contact sheet.

- ✓ EPS or DCS images including clipping paths will be shown in their entirety without any masked areas.

- ✓ Gif 89a and PNG images with a transparent background are shown on a background of solid colour.

➡ Save the contact sheet under the name **Contact Sheet** then close it.

Chapter 8

2
You can create a photo gallery so as to publish it on the Internet.
CREATING A WEB PHOTO GALLERY

a Close the documents you wish to include in the gallery.

➽ Here, there are no documents open.

b **File**
   Automate
   Web Photo Gallery

c Click the **Choose** button on the **Source** option to define which folder contains the images for your Web gallery.

➽ You can do that now.

Photoshop displays the folder selection box, which you already used when you created the contacts sheet.

d Click the + icons to the right of the disk drives to see the folders. If the folder you seek is a subfolder of another, click the + sign until you see the folder you want. Click the folder name to select it.

➽ Here, select the **ENI Photoshop 5.5** folder.

e Click **OK**.

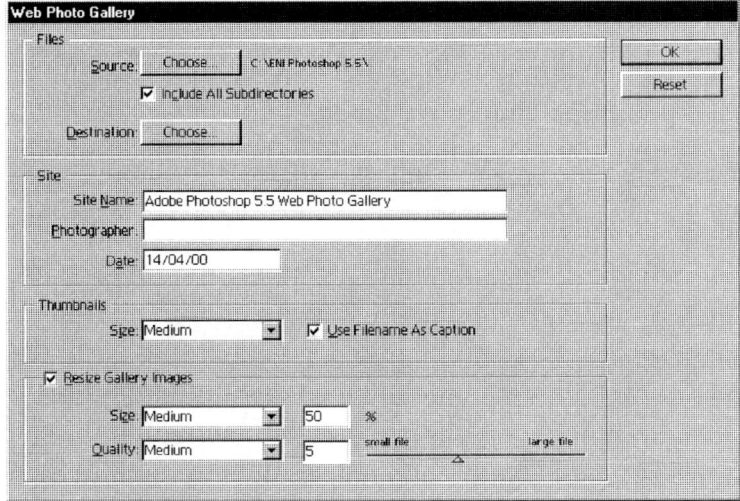

*The selected folder appears in the **Web Photo Gallery** dialog box.*

Adobe Photoshop 5.5

Chapter 8

[f] Leave the **Include All Subdirectories** option active if you want to create a gallery from all the images in the selected folder <u>and</u> all its subfolders.

➟ Here, leave the option active.

[g] Click the **Choose** button on the **Destination** option to define the folder where the Web gallery will be saved. This should not be the same folder as that chosen in **Source**.

➟ Here, open the Windows Explorer and create a subfolder of C:, calling it **Web Gallery**. Close the Explorer.

➟ Click the **Destination** frame's **Choose** button.

The folder selection box appears, as it did when you defined the **Source**.

[h] Select the name of the folder that will contain the Web gallery.

➟ Here, select your **Web Gallery** folder.

[i] Click **OK**.

The selected folder appears in the **Web Photo Gallery** *dialog box.*

[j] Enter the **Site Name** of the site you want to create in the corresponding text box.

➟ Here, use the name **My Photo Gallery**

[k] Enter the **Photographer** name in the next text box.

➟ Here, use the name **ENI**

[l] Enter the **Date** that should appear on the Web site. Photoshop enters by default the day's date, that is, the day the gallery was created.

➟ Here, leave the current date.

[m] Select the **Size** of the **Thumbnails** that will appear in the gallery index. You should avoid large images on the index as the page may take too long to display if the gallery is put on the Internet.

➟ Here, choose **Small**.

[n] Leave the **Use Filename As Caption** option active to display the image names under the thumbnail in the index.

➟ Here, leave the option active.

[o] If you want to publish in the gallery images smaller than their original size, leave the **Resize Gallery Images** option. Even if you want to leave images in their original size, you can leave this option active if you wish to adjust the image quality.

➟ Here, leave the option active.

Chapter 8

|p| Select a **Size** for displaying the images in the gallery or enter a reduction percentage. You cannot make images larger by giving a figure higher than 100%.

➡ Here, choose **Large**.

|q| Select a **Quality** for saving the gallery images in **JPEG** format. You can also move the slider between a **small file** and a **large file**. The **Quality** can vary from **0** (**Low** quality) to **12** (**Maximum** quality). The lower the quality, the more the image will be compressed, and vice versa. Depending on the image, a document can be 10 times bigger in maximum quality than in low quality.

➡ Here, select **High** quality.

|r| Click **OK** to create the gallery.

The images are resampled then placed in subfolders within the destination folder. Once the gallery is finished, it is displayed in the default browser.

|s| Click the image or its name to show it as large size.

➡ Here, click any image in the gallery.

Adobe Photoshop 5.5   361

Chapter 8

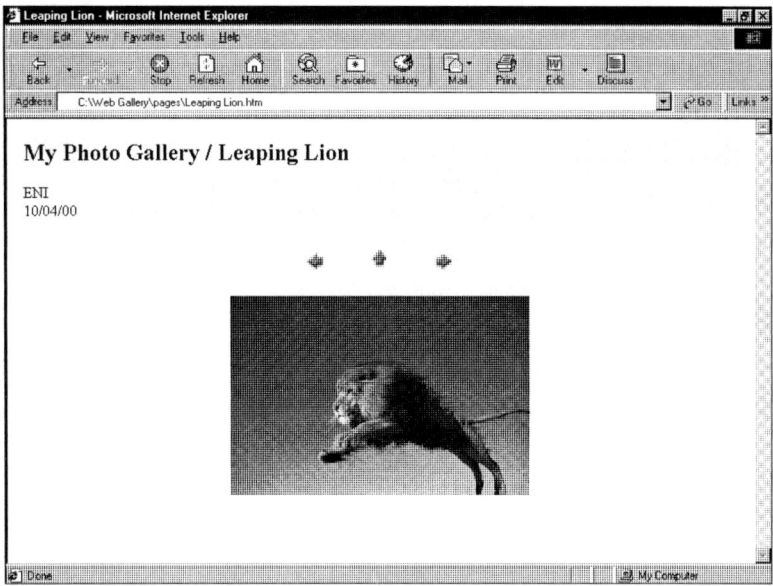

The image appears and its name is indicated at the top of the window.

t   Use the arrows:

> To display the previous image.
>
> To return to the gallery index.
>
> To display the next image.

» Here, take a look at some of the images, if you would like to.

u   Click the ⊠ button on the Web browser window to leave the browser and return to Photoshop. You can display the gallery at a later date by double-clicking the **Index.htm** file in the gallery's destination folder.

» Try that now.

✓ *The only way to update a gallery, if images have been deleted from or added to the folder, is to create it all over again.*

✓ *The colours in multichannel images may be misrepresented as they will be converted to RGB before being added to the gallery.*

✓ *EPS or DCS images including a clipping path will appear as a whole image, without any masked areas.*

Chapter 8

☑ GIF89a and PNG images with transparent backgrounds will appear as whole images, the transparent background filled with a single colour.

☑ You can customise your gallery by modifying the HTML pages created by Photoshop.

3

As well as creating a catalogue in the form of a contact sheet and a photo gallery, you can also duplicate an image in different formats on the same page; this picture package is based on a similar practice used by professional photo studios.

CREATING A PICTURE PACKAGE

[a] **File**
Automate
Picture Package

[b] Click the **Choose** button to choose the image that will be used in the picture package. If the image is already open in Photoshop, activate the **Use Frontmost Document** option. Be careful, this option takes the active photo as the source; if several documents are open, make sure you activate the image that interests you before creating the picture package. If you activate the **Use Frontmost Document** option, you can skip the next stage.

➠ Here, there is no image open. Click the **Choose** button.

A dialog box appears, which is similar to the one used to open an image.

[c] Select the image name and click **Open**.

➠ Here, select the **Lion.jpg** image from the **ENI Photoshop 5.5** folder, then click **Open**.

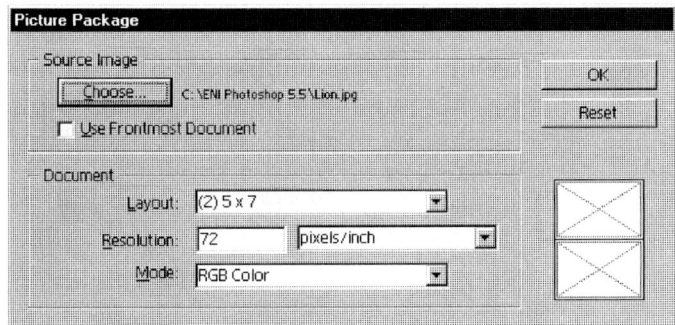

The selected document appears in the Picture Package dialog box.

Chapter 8

[d] Select the image **Layout** you wish to use for the picture package. Depending on the layout chosen, the preview in the lower right of the dialog box may differ.

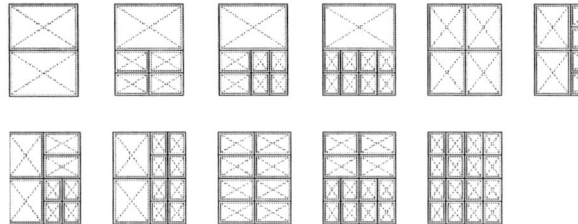

Layouts are available for displaying anything from two to sixteen images per page.

➜ Here, select the (2) 4 x 5 & (4) 2.5 x 3.5 layout to create 2 large copies of the image and 4 small ones.

[e] Define the **Resolution** for the picture package. It is preferable to use the **pixels/inch** measurement unit to the **pixels/cm** unit.

➜ Here, leave the default value.

[f] Select the colour **Mode** for the picture package. You have the choice of **Grayscale**, **RGB**, **CMYK** and **Lab** colours. Generally, a picture package is made to be printed so it is customary to use **Grayscale** or **CMYK** colours. If the source image is in another mode, especially **RGB** or **Lab**, it is preferable to convert the image in preparation for the picture package (cf. Chapter 5).

➜ Here, leave the **RGB Mode**.

[g] Click **OK**.

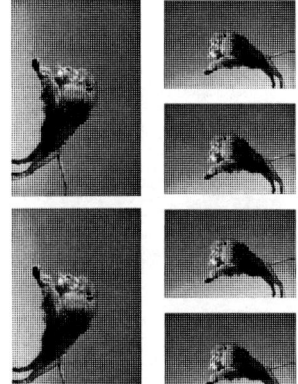

The picture package is created: in this example, there are two large photos and four small ones.

✓ The size of the thumbnails indicated in the *Layout* box is measured in inches.

➜ Close this document without saving it and open **Giraffe.jpg**.

Chapter 8

4

*When you automate tasks by creating **scripts** that perform **actions**, you may use commands that require an image to be converted to another colour mode. To avoid error messages appearing during execution of the script, you can indicate whether or not to convert the image into the correct mode.*

CONVERTING AN IMAGE WITH CONDITIONAL MODE CHANGE

[a] **File**
Automate
Conditional Mode Change

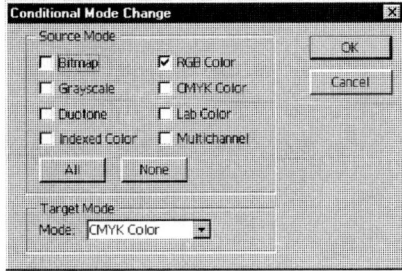

[b] In the **Source Mode** frame, activate the colour modes that are to be converted. If you click the **All** button, all the image modes will be activated. If you click the **None** button, no mode will be active.

➟ Here, **RGB Color** is already activated.

[c] In the **Target Mode** frame, select the **Mode** into which the image will be converted.

➟ Here, select **Lab Color**.

[d] Click **OK**.

The image is converted into Lab Color, because it was in RGB. Had it not been in RGB, it would not have been converted.

✓ *This function is only useful if you use it in an automated action.*

✓ *This command flattens images containing layers before converting them.*

✓ *You might prefer to make a systematic conversion with* Image - Mode, *but that is not always advantageous. Say for example your script creates layers as part of its actions; you could convert an indexed colour image into RGB. But if the image is in CMYK, you would not want to convert it because this mode supports layers and converting it could produce out-of-gamut colours. Using* Conditional Mode Change *ensures that a conversion only occurs when the relevant mode is active.*

Adobe Photoshop 5.5

Chapter 8

Cancel this command for now, you will have an opportunity to use it later on.

➤ **Edit - Undo**

5 *Before creating your first action, turn your attention to the **Actions** palette.*

WORKING WITH THE ACTIONS PALETTE

[a] **Window**   Click the **Actions** tab
Show Actions

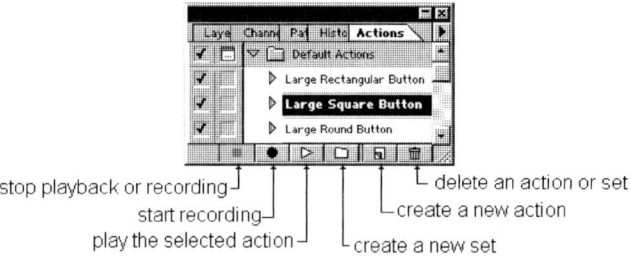

stop playback or recording ⏌
    start recording ⏌   ⌐ delete an action or set
                                ⌐ create a new action
        play the selected action ⏌ ⌐ create a new set

The actions are placed together in sets symbolised by this icon: 📁.

[b] To show the actions in a set, click the ▷ icon that corresponds to the set.

➤ Here, click the ▷ icon located to the left of the **Default Actions** set.

The icon will change its shape: ▽, indicating that the list has been opened out. The list of actions offered by default appears. These icons are also present for each action. They allow you to show all the commands saved in each action. You can click the ▽ icon to hide an opened list again.

The ✓ icon seen in the first column indicates that the action or action command is active.

[c] To deactivate an action, click this icon, the corresponding action or command are deactivated and will not be executed. If you deactivate an entire action, you can still run it but it will have no effect. To reactivate an action or command, click the corresponding square again in the first column.

When the ✓ icon appears in red, this signifies that some commands in the action have been deactivated.

Chapter 8

|d| When recording actions, you will make use of the menu commands. Most of these commands produce dialog boxes. You can choose if the action will use the values already indicated in the dialog box or if you wish to reset the parameters each time the action is played.

In the second column on the palette, the ▭ icon indicates that a **modal control** is in place, which means simply that the dialog box will be shown each time the action is played. If you click this modal control icon, you will deactivate this function and the values set in the dialog box previously will be used. Click an empty square in this column to show the modal control icon and thus display the dialog box for the corresponding command whenever the action is played.

When the ▭ icon is red, some commands use default values and others will require you to set options while the action is running.

|e| To move an action from one set to another, drag its name towards the destination set. This method is similar to that used to change the order of layers or Alpha channels.

✓ *You can also display actions without sets. To do this, activate the Button Mode option in the Actions palette menu (▶). If you use this display mode, you will not be able to modify the properties of an action or the commands used in one. This mode only allows you to play the actions as they are. To return to the standard display mode, deactivate the Button Mode option on the Actions palette.*

6

To familiarise yourself with how an action works, you should try using an existing one before creating one yourself.

USING RECORDED ACTIONS

|a| If the **Actions** palette is hidden, click its tab or show it with **Window - Show Actions**.

|b| If necessary, click the ▷ icon on the set containing the action you want to play to show the list of actions available.

➠ Here, if you did not click the ▷ icon on the **Default Actions** set earlier in the exercise, open that set now then click the ▭ button on the palette to display all the actions it contains.

|c| Select the action you want to play by clicking its name in the **Actions** palette.

➠ Here, select the **Wood Frame - 50 pixel** action.

Chapter 8

|d| Click the ▷ button on the **Actions** palette or activate the **Play** command on the palette menu (▶).

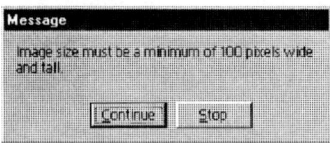

A message appears, warning you that a minimum image size is required here. Depending on the action, you can obtain various messages, or none at all. These messages help you to avoid errors occurring while an action is being played.

|e| If a message appears, click the **Continue** button to keep playing the action. If you are unsure of the conditions stated in the message, click **Stop** to check them before continuing.

➟ Here, click the **Continue** button.

The action is played and the image is modified accordingly. In this example, it is placed inside a wood frame.

➟ To continue with this example, show the **Layers** palette.

Playing the action has created several layers automatically, associated with the various effects.

- ☑ When you play actions, you should always save any open documents, because, due to the intense work it is undertaking, Photoshop often completely blocks your computer! This is especially the case when you play several actions one after another.

- ☑ An action can be associated with a shortcut key to play it more quickly. If you know what this shortcut key is you can use it without having to select the action first.

- ☑ You can add new actions in the palette using the *Load Actions* command in the Actions palette menu (▶). Seven extra action sets are provided with Photoshop. You can load them from the *Programs Files\Adobe\Photoshop 5.5\Goodies\Adobe Photoshop Only\Actions* folder. In the same way, you can replace existing action sets with other sets using the *Replace Actions* command on the palette menu.

Chapter 8

✓ *If you make any modifications to these predefined actions, and these are unsatisfactory, you can use the Reset Actions command on the Actions palette menu (▶) to retrieve the default action sets. This command is only useful if you have not saved the actions again with the modifications.*

You are not going to keep this wood frame effect, although if you like it, you now know how easy it is to apply and you can use it on another image if you wish.

➟ **File - Revert**

---

7 *You will create an action of your own soon but first it would be a sensible idea to create a set into which you can place your action.*

CREATING AN ACTION SET

[a] If the **Actions** palette is hidden, click its tab or show it with **Window - Show Actions**.

[b] Click the ☐ button on the **Actions** palette or activate the **New Set** command on the palette menu (▶).

➟ Here, click the ☐ button on the **Actions** palette.

[c] Enter the **Name** of your new set in the corresponding text box.

➟ Here, enter **Personal Actions**

[d] Click **OK**.

A new set appears in the palette. This set is automatically activated.

Adobe Photoshop 5.5   **369**

Chapter 8

You can now create an action; for example one that will produce an impressionist painting effect on an image.

CREATING AN ACTION

[a] If the **Actions** palette is hidden, click its tab or show it with **Window - Show Actions**.

[b] Click the ⬛ button on the **Actions** palette or activate the **New Action** command on the palette menu (▶).

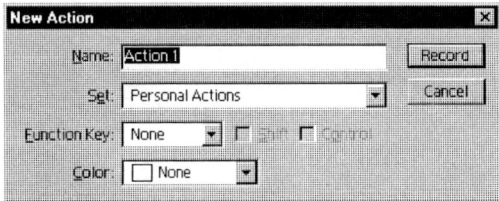

[c] Enter the **Name** of the new action in the corresponding text box.

➤ Here, enter **Impressionist Effect**

[d] Specify in which **Set** the action will be created.

By default, Photoshop proposes the active set.

➤ Here, leave the **Set** as **Personal Actions**.

[e] If you wish, attribute a **Function Key** to the action. If you leave the option as **None**, no key will be attributed. If you define a **Function Key**, you can combine it with ⇧Shift by activating the **Shift** command or with Ctrl by activating **Control**.

➤ Here, leave the **None** option active.

[f] Select the colour in which you wish to display the action. This colour will only be visible if you have activated the **Button Mode** mode in the palette menu.

➤ Here, leave the colour option as **None**.

[g] Click the **Record** button to start saving the script.

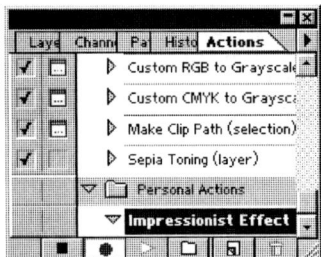

The *action* is created and recording begins automatically (the ⬤ button appears pressed-in).

Chapter 8

[h] Go through all the commands necessary for the action you are recording. Most commands can be recorded. Only drawing and retouching tools, except for the gradient tools, tool options, view commands (such as the zoom) and preferences cannot be recorded. Selection and type tools, free transformations, cropping, drawing paths and menu commands (apart from the exceptions already stated) can be recorded. For commands that require using a specific background or foreground colour, you can define the colour during recording and it will be memorised.

[i] When you have finished performing your action, stop recording by pressing the ■ button on the **Actions** palette.

▸ Here, do not stop recording at this point.

You have started recording so you can partially create your impressionist painting effect.

▸ **File - Automate - Conditional Mode Change**

▸ Activate **Indexed Color**, **RGB Color** and **CMYK Color** under **Source Mode** then choose **Lab Color** as the **Target Mode** and click **OK**.

▸ If the **Channels** palette is hidden, click its tab or show it with **Window - Show Channels**.
Duplicate the **Lightness** channel by dragging its thumbnail onto the ■ button on the **Channels** palette.

▸ **Select - All**
Edit - Copy
Select - Deselect

▸ **Image - Adjust - Levels**
Set the output level for shadows at **63** and the output level for highlights to **191** (this channel has to lose a lot of its contrast) then click **OK**.

▸ Activate the **Lightness** channel.

▸ **Filter - Stylize - Trace Contour - OK**

▸ **Filter - Noise - Add Noise**
Set the **Amount** at **120** with a **Uniform** distribution and deactivate the **Monochromatic** option then click **OK**.

▸ **Select - Load Selection**
Select **Alpha 1** as the **Channel** then click **OK**.
Edit - Paste Into
Select - Deselect

▸ Activate the **Lab** composite channel.

Your effect is deliberately missing a step, which you will add later on in the exercise.

▸ Click the ■ button on the **Actions** palette.

Adobe Photoshop 5.5

Chapter 8

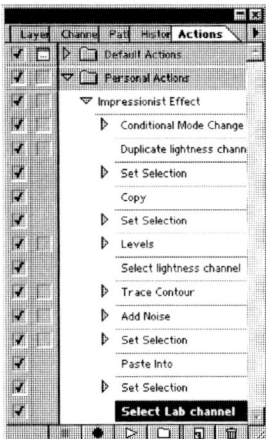

The action is recorded and the commands used are listed under its name in the palette.

☑ While recording an action, you can play another action if you want to integrate it into your new action.

☑ If you save *Image Size* or *Canvas Size* commands in an action, make sure that you adjust the *Width* or *Height* as a percentage of the current size. If you do not respect this rule, any image to which you apply the action will be changed to a fixed size and not in relation to its actual size.

☑ If you save a document as part of an action, it is preferable to use the *Save a Copy* command, leaving the *File name* offered by default in the corresponding text box. This ensures you will avoid accidentally replacing other images already processed in the action.

---

9 *You are now going to add a stop at the beginning of this action in order to limit it to colour images.*

INSERTING A STOP

[a] If the **Actions** palette is hidden, click its tab or show it with **Window - Show Actions**.

[b] If necessary, click the ▷ icon on the action to display all the commands that are defined in it.

▸ Here, the commands in the **Impressionist Effect** action are already shown.

[c] Select the command after which you want to insert the stop. If the stop is to be the first command in the action, you will have to move the command after you have inserted it. If you select the action name, the stop will be inserted at the end of the action.

▸ Here, select the first command in the action by clicking **Conditional Mode Change**.

Chapter 8

|d| Select the **Insert Stop** command in the **Actions** palette menu (📋).

|e| In the corresponding text box, enter the **Message** you want to display.

➽ Here, enter **The image must be in colour**

|f| Activate the **Allow Continue** option if the message is not to constitute a definite stop in the action process. If this option is not activated, you will only be able to click the Stop button on the message box.

➽ Here, activate the **Allow Continue** option.

|g| Click **OK**.

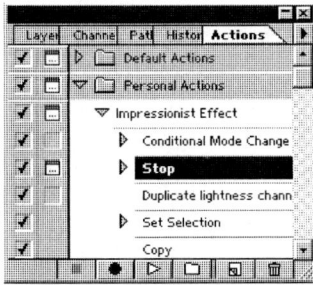

The stop is inserted.

|h| If you want to place this stop at the beginning of the action, drag the Stop command up to insert in between the action name and the first command.

➽ Here, drag the **Stop** command as shown.

The command is now placed at the start of the action.

Adobe Photoshop 5.5

Chapter 8

☑ You can insert a stop during the recording of an action.

Before continuing with this exercise, you are going to see how to create a path from a piece of text.

➤ Activate the [T] tool.

➤ Click at the top right of the image to place the text in that corner.

➤ Use an angular type of font, such as **Matisse** (or a similar font: see the example below to guide you) with a **Bold** style (activate **Faux Bold** if your font does not have a **Bold** Style), 32 point **Size** and click the [≡] button to align the text on the right.

➤ Enter **SAVANNA** in the area set aside for your text and click **OK**.

SAVANNA

➤ If necessary, move the selection until the text fits neatly into the top right corner.

➤ Show the **Paths** palette by clicking its tab or using **Window - Show Paths**.
Activate the **Make Work Path** command on the **Paths** palette menu ([▶]).
Set the **Tolerance** to **0.5** and click **OK**.

➤ Double-click the **Work Path** thumbnail to save it.
Enter **Savanna Text** in the **Name** box and click **OK**.

10 When you have a path at your disposal, you can include it in an action so that it is automatically created on any image on which you play the action. This is what you are going to do with the path you have just created.

INCLUDING A PATH IN AN ACTION

[a] If the **Paths** palette is hidden, click its tab or show it with **Window - Show Paths**.

[b] Activate the path that you want to insert into the action.

➤ Here, the **Savanna Text** path is already active.

[c] If the **Actions** palette is hidden, click its tab or show it with **Window - Show Actions**.

[d] If necessary, click the ▷ icon on the action to display all the command it contains.

➤ Here, the commands on the **Impressionist Effect** action can already be seen.

[e] Select the command after which you want to insert the path. If you select the action name, the path will be added at the end of the action.

➤ Here, select the **Conditional Mode Change** command by clicking its name.

Chapter 8

|f| Select the **Insert Path** command on the **Actions** palette menu (▶).

The path is inserted and can be used in the habitual manner in the context of the action, that is as a drawing, retouch or selection tool, or as a clipping path.

☑ You can insert a path while you are recording the action.

☑ The path will always be created as a *Work Path* in the image on which you are playing the action. If you use a path in an action without inserting it into the action, you will have to create a path with the same name whenever you play the action on another image.

☑ The path saved in an action preserves its starting position. On each image you will find the path in the same place. In this example, the path has been recorded in the top right corner. The path will be always up the top on other images but it could be placed in the centre or on the left depending on the image width. The only way to ensure a path is always placed in exactly the same spot is to position it in the top left corner which corresponds to the starting point of the image.

---

11 *When you create or modify an action, you can use menu commands in the usual way. You can also use another more precise method, that you are going to look at now.*

INSERTING A MENU ITEM INTO AN ACTION

|a| If the **Actions** palette is hidden, click its tab or show it with **Window - Show Actions**.

|b| If necessary, click the ▷ icon on the action to display all the commands it contains.

➤ Here, the commands for the **Impressionist Effect** action can still be seen.

|c| Select the command after which you want to insert a menu item. If you select an action name, the command will be added at the end of the action.

➤ Here, select the **Add Noise** command by clicking its name.

Chapter 8

|d| Select the **Insert Menu Item** command in the **Actions** palette menu (▶).

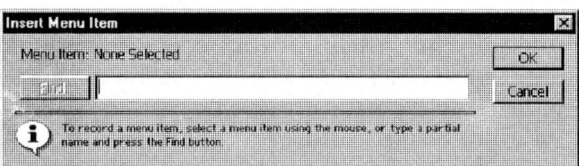

|e| Define which menu command you want to insert by either selecting the command in the menu as you normally would or by entering its name in the text box if the menu command is not currently available. You can check that the name you have entered is correct by clicking the **Find** button. This prompts Photoshop to look for the closest command name to the one you have indicated.

➤ Here, open the **Image** menu and choose **Adjust - Hue/Saturation**.

The command name appears in the dialog box, in this example Hue/Saturation comes up.

|f| Click **OK**.

*The command appears in the action. The ⬚ icon is automatically displayed for this command. This **dialog on** icon is greyed-out and cannot be deactivated.*

- ✓ You can insert a menu item in this way while you are recording the action.

- ✓ This method allows you to insert menu items without taking the context into account. For example, you may make a selection during the recording of an action but forget to copy it into the clipboard. You can insert the *Copy* command after you have finished recording the action, without having to reselect anything or record the action again.

- ✓ When you insert a command with this method, no value is recorded. The image will not be modified when the command is inserted (contrary to a normal command recording) but can be when the action is played.

Chapter 8

☑ If the inserted command is associated with a dialog box, you cannot stop the dialog box being displayed, contrary to commands inserted during a normal recording, where the ▭ dialog on icon can be activated or deactivated depending on your requirements.

12 When you work with two effects which are created in a similar way, you can duplicate an action, adding or modifying the steps between them that differ. Try this method now.

DUPLICATING AN ACTION OR A SET

[a] If the **Actions** palette is hidden, click its tab or show it with **Window - Show Actions**.

[b] Activate the action or set that you want to duplicate by clicking its name.

➤ Here, activate the **Impressionist Effect** action.

[c] Drag the action you want to duplicate onto the ▭ button on the **Actions** palette or activate the **Duplicate** command on the palette menu (▶).

If you want to duplicate an entire set, dragging onto the ▭ button will not work, you will have to use the **Duplicate** command instead.

➤ Here, activate the **Duplicate** command on the palette menu.

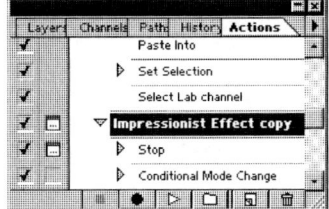

The action or set is duplicated. Here, an action called **Impressionist Effect copy** appears in the palette.

☑ If you duplicate a set, all the actions in it are also copied.

☑ You can select several actions by holding down ⇧Shift and clicking each of their names.

Adobe Photoshop 5.5

Chapter 8

13 *Some actions may outlive their usefulness. If you have actions that you no longer need, you can delete them.*

DELETING AN ACTION/AN ACTION ITEM/A SET

a If the **Actions** palette is hidden, click its tab or show it with **Window - Show Actions**.

b Activate the action, the action command or the set you wish to delete by clicking its name.

➤ Here, activate the **Impressionist Effect copy** action.

c Click the 🗑 button on the **Actions** palette or select the **Delete** command on the palette menu (▶).

➤ Here, click the 🗑 button on the palette.

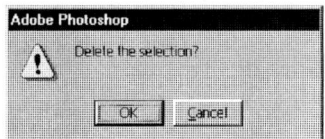

Photoshop prompts you to confirm your decision.

d Click **OK** to confirm deletion of the action, command or set.

The action or set is deleted.

✓ You can also drag the name of the action or set you wish to delete onto the 🗑 button. With this method, no confirmation will be sought and deletion is instantaneous.

✓ If you delete a set, all the actions in it are also deleted.

✓ You can also delete all the sets and action saved on the palette by using the **Clear Actions** command on the **Actions** palette menu (▶).

✓ You can select several actions or commands by ⇧Shift - clicking their names.

14 *When you created your action, you had the opportunity to define a shortcut key, and other options. If you need to, you can still modify these options.*

MODIFYING AN ACTION'S OPTIONS

a If the **Actions** palette is hidden, click its tab or show it with **Window - Show Actions**.

b Activate the action whose options you wish to modify by clicking its name.

➤ Here, activate the **Impressionist Effect** action.

Chapter 8

- [c] Double-click the action name or activate the **Action Options** command in the **Actions** palette menu (▶).
- ⟹ Here, double-click the **Impressionist Effect** action.

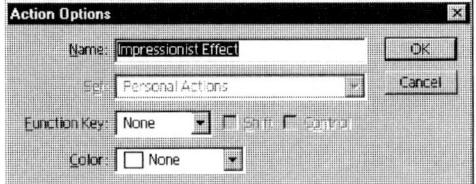

- [d] Modify the action options. You can change the action **Name**, the **Function Key** associated with it, and its **Color** when you are in **Button Mode**.
- ⟹ Here, select [F5] as the **Function Key** and check the **Control** box to combine the [Ctrl] key with the [F5] key.
- [e] Click **OK**.

The options are modified, you can now play the Impressionist Effect action by pressing [Ctrl][F5].

> ✓ You cannot use this method to modify the set to which the action belongs. The only way to do that is to drag the action into another set:

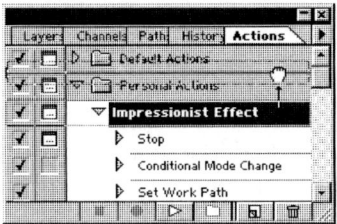

In the example on the left, you can see how the Impressionist Effect action could be moved from the Personal Actions set to the Default Actions set.

> ✓ You can also rename a set by proceeding in a similar way. Double-click the set name or activate the *Set Options* command in the *Actions* palette menu (▶).

Before continuing with the next task, duplicate this image's Alpha 1 channel.

- ⟹ Drag the **Alpha 1** channel thumbnail onto the ▣ button on the **Channels** palette.
- ⟹ Double-click the **Alpha 2** thumbnail.
- ⟹ Enter **Copy Lightness** in the **Name** box and click **OK**.
- ⟹ Activate the **Alpha 1** channel.

Chapter 8

15 *Once you have recorded an action, you can remodel it, adding new commands or modifying a recorded command. Look now at several ways of doing this.*

MODIFYING AN ACTION

RECORDING A COMMAND OR ACTION AGAIN

[a] If the **Actions** palette is hidden, click its tab or show it with **Window - Show Actions**.

[b] If necessary, click the ▷ icon on the action to display all the commands it contains.

➤ Here, the commands in the **Impressionist Effect** action can already be seen.

[c] Select the command that you want to record again. If you have used similar commands several times throughout the action, click the ▷ icon on the command to see its details just to be sure you have chosen the correct command. To record a whole action again, select the action name.

➤ Here, select the **Set Selection** command located just above the **Paste Into** command (its details should read **To: channel "Alpha 1"**).

[d] Double-click the command name or activate the **Record Again** command in the Actions palette menu (▶).

➤ Here, double-click the command name you have just selected.

[e] Set the parameters of the recorded command. If it is a transformation or a crop, modify it. If you are recording a whole action again, you will have to go through steps **e** and **f** for each command in the action.

➤ Here, select **Copy Lightness** as the **Channel** option instead of **Alpha 1**.

[f] If the newly-recorded command causes a dialog box to appear, click **OK**. If you are working on a transformation or a crop, press [Enter]. If you are recording an entire action again, you can click the **Cancel** button or press [Esc] to keep the values already recorded in the action.

➤ Here, click **OK**.

The command has been recorded again. For this example, it was necessary to use a channel called ***Copy Lightness*** *because the* ***Lightness*** *channel had already been copied in the action by dragging it on the palette. However the next time Photoshop plays the action, it will duplicate the channel using the* ***Duplicate*** *command on the* ***Channels*** *palette. This command will create a copy of the channel called* ***Lightness copy*** *and not* ***Alpha 1*** *as is the case when you duplicate by dragging.*

Chapter 8

✓ Photoshop might refuse to record some commands again. This means that the current context does not permit it. In the example used here, you could not have recorded the command again simply by renaming the Alpha 1 channel Lightness copy. As the Alpha 1 channel was used in the action command, had it been renamed or deleted, Photoshop would consider that it was absent in the current context and would show a message indicating that the command was not available.

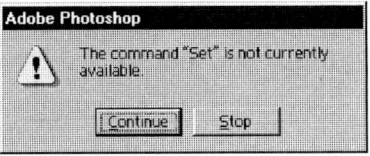

Click the *Continue* button or *Stop* to cancel the recording.

ADDING COMMANDS

[a] If the **Actions** palette is hidden, click its tab or show it with **Window - Show Actions**.

[b] If necessary, click the ▷ icon on the action to display all the command it contains.

➤ Here, the commands from the **Impressionist Effect** action are already displayed.

[c] Select the command after which you want to insert an extra command. If you want to add it to the end of the existing commands, select the action name, or the last command.

➤ Here, select the **Add Noise** command by clicking its name.

[d] Click the ● button on the **Actions** palette or use the **Start Recording** command in the palette menu (▶).

[e] Make the series of commands corresponding to what you want to add. You can look back over the information that describes how actions can be created if you want to know what commands can be recorded.

➤ Here, add several commands: **Image - Adjust - Invert**
Filter - Noise - Add Noise
Leave the values as set and click **OK**.
Image - Adjust - Invert

[f] When you have added the commands to the action, stop recording by clicking the ■ button on the **Actions** palette.

➤ Here, click the ■ button.

The commands are now added to the action.

Adobe Photoshop 5.5   **381**

Chapter 8

There is a command that you no longer need: you can delete it.

➡ Select the **Hue/Saturation** command in the action.

➡ Click the [🗑] button in the **Actions** palette and click **OK** to confirm deleting the command.

Your impressionist effect is complete, but you still need to add new commands to the end of the action in order to use the path that you inserted. This will act somewhat like a logo which will be automatically placed on the image.

➡ Select the **Impressionist Effect** action by clicking its name.
Click the [●] button on the **Actions** palette.

➡ Show the **Paths** palette.
If the **Savanna Text** path is active, go on to the next step. If not, activate it now.
Click the [○] button on the **Paths** palette.
Select the **Turn Off Path** command in the **Paths** palette menu.

➡ **Image - Adjust - Invert**
Select - Deselect

➡ Show the **Actions** palette then click the [■] button.

➡ If you had to activate the **Savanna Text** path, select the **Select Path "Savanna Text"** command in the action and click the [🗑] button on the **Actions** palette then click **OK**.

*This step is necessary because the path will be inserted into the action as a **Work Path** and not as **Savanna Text**. Inserting a path during an action automatically activates that path anyway.*

You are now going to test your action, but before playing it, you need to revert to the original version of your document and then verify your action.

➡ **File - Revert**

Chapter 8

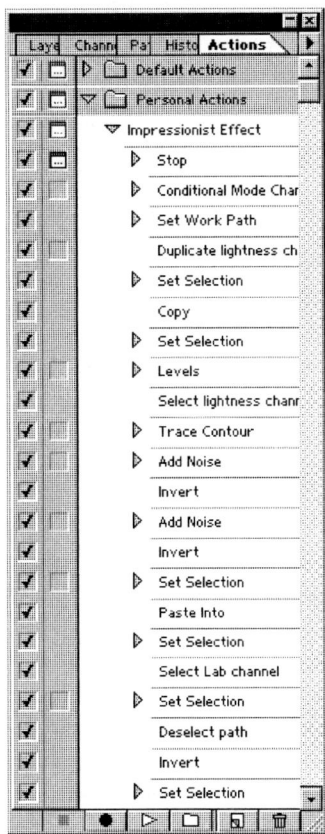

The commands listed in your action should be the same as those seen here. If that is not the case, modify your action until it exactly matches this one.

The time has come to test your action!

➤ Click the name of the **Impressionist Effect** action to select it.

➤ Click the ▷ button on the **Actions** palette.

A message appears due to the stop that you inserted into the action.

➤ For this example, click the **Continue** button.

The action is played and you obtain an impressionist painting effect, more or less, on the giraffe: a negative of the Savanna *"logo" is embedded in the image. You can use this effect on any image, but you will find that it works best on landscapes that do not contain too many dark areas.*

Adobe Photoshop 5.5   383

Chapter 8

16 Once you have created an action and you go on to test it, problems can arise and it is often difficult to tell which step in the action is producing them. To try to find the source of this type of problem, you can change the way the action is played.

MODIFYING THE PLAYBACK OPTIONS ON AN ACTION

[a] The **Actions** palette is not visible, click its tab or show it with **Window - Show Actions**.

[b] Choose the **Playback Options** command on the **Actions** palette menu (▶).

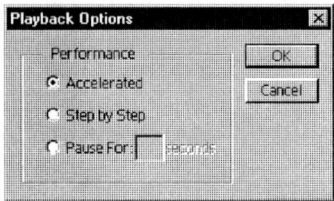

[c] Activate one of the following options:

Accelerated This is the normal playing speed. The image display is not changed after each command in the action is performed, but only at the end of the action to show the final result.

Step by Step Each command is executed and the image display is updated before the next command is started. This is a slower playing mode than the accelerated mode but still may be too fast to allow you to determine the cause of the problem.

Pause For Each command is carried out and the display refreshed, then a pause occurs, whose duration you can specify in the accompanying text box, before the next command is performed. The default value for this pause is 3 seconds.

➠ Here, leave the **Accelerated** option active.

[d] Click **OK**.

> ✓ If you modify the playback options in order to find a malfunction in an action, do not forget to change the options back once the problem is identified and corrected. The default option is *Accelerated* and should be activated to avoid all your actions being played in slow motion.
>
> ✓ If you find that you encounter frequent blockages in Photoshop while playing actions, you should select a *Step by Step* playback mode. This may help you avoid problems of this kind.

✓ When you change the playback options to detect errors in the action, replay the action on an image that has not already been modified by the action in question. To do this on the image with which you are working, revert to the last saved version of the image or use the *History* palette to return to the state preceding execution of the action.

17 Now that your action is complete and correct, you can save the **Personal Actions** set that you created.

SAVING A SET OF ACTIONS

[a] If the **Actions** palette is not visible, click its tab or show it with **Window - Show Actions**.

[b] Select the set you wish to save by clicking its name.

➡ Here, select the **Personal Actions** set.

[c] Activate the **Save Actions** command in the **Actions** palette menu (▶).

[d] Preferably, access the **\Program Files\Adobe\Photoshop 5.5\Goodies\Adobe Photoshop Only\Actions** folder so that any sets you create are kept in the same folder as those supplied with the Photoshop application.

➡ Here, access this folder.

[e] If you wish, you can change the **Name** of the document containing the set in question. To find a set more easily, leave the name suggested by default.

The file carries an .atn extension.

➡ Here, leave the name **Personal Actions**.

[f] Click the **Save** button.

The set is saved as well as the actions it contains. If you clear the actions in the application window, you can always reload this set at another point in time.

✓ You cannot save an action independently. You can only save a whole set.

Chapter 8

18 You have now mastered the technique of creating and playing an action on a single image. However, Photoshop also gives you the possibility of playing an action on a group (or batch) of images.

PLAYING AN ACTION ON A GROUP OF IMAGES

[a] **File**
Automate
Batch

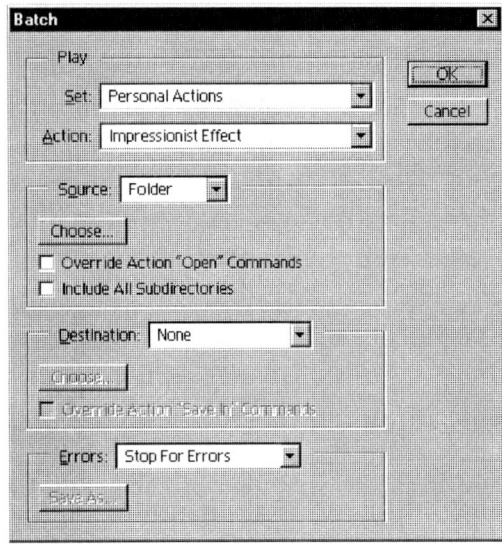

[b] Select the **Set** containing the action to be played from the corresponding list box.

➠ Here, the **Personal Actions** set is already selected in the **Set** list.

[c] Select the action that you want to apply to the images.

➠ Here, the **Impressionist Effect** action is already selected.

[d] Select one of the following options in the **Source** list:

    Folder   The action will be played on images already saved in a folder on the hard disk.

    Import   If you have a scanner with a document feeder or a digital camera, you can use this option to digitize images before playing the action on each of them. The scanner or digital camera needs to have a plug-in that can support actions and be able to import several images.

➠ Here, leave the **Folder** option which should be selected by default.

Chapter 8

[e] If you select the **Folder** option, click the **Choose** button to define which folder contains the images you want to process.

➡ Here, do this to choose a folder.

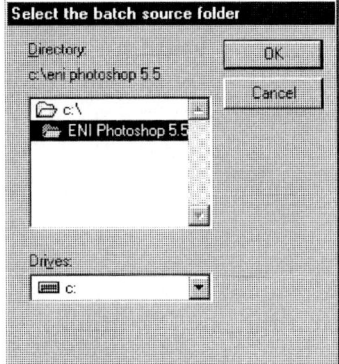

[f] In the **Drives** list, select the disk drive that contains the folder in question. If necessary, double-click the c:\ icon to access the principal group of folders on the selected drive. Double-click the folder containing the images on which you wish to work. Click **OK** to confirm your choice.

➡ Here, access the **ENI Photoshop 5.5** folder and click **OK**.

The name of the selected folder appears to the right of the Choose button.

[g] If you select the **Import** option in the **Source** list, choose where to import **From**:

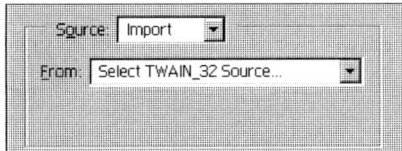

Generally you would select the TWAIN_32 option. Look at the Extra Information chapter for more details about digitization options.

[h] Activate the **Override Action "Open" Commands** option to be sure to open the images in the specified folder. Any **Open** commands integrated in the action are thus ignored.

➡ Here, leave this option deactivated because no **Open** command is included in the action used.

[i] Activate the **Include All Subdirectories** option to process images contained in the subfolders of the selected folder. If you wish to process different folders that are not embedded, create shortcuts to these folders inside the selected folder and activate this option.

➡ Here, leave this option deactivated.

Adobe Photoshop 5.5

Chapter 8

[j] Select the **Destination**:

None   The processed documents remain open and are not saved unless a **Save** command is part of the action used. You should not use this option if the folder used contains many images.

Save and Close   The processed documents are saved, replacing the previous versions and then closed.

Folder   The processed documents are saved into another folder then closed. This option allows you to preserve the original documents as they are. If the processed image is not saved in Photoshop format, Photoshop will prompt you to do so by opening the **Save As** dialog box. If you select this option, click the **Choose** button to specify a destination folder in the same way you chose the **Source**. You can also choose to **Override Action "Save In" Commands** to be sure that any **Save In** commands in the action, which may specify another destination folder, are ignored and ensure the images are saved in the specified **Folder**.

⟹ Here, leave the **None** option active.

[k] Choose how you want action errors dealt with from the choices in the **Error** list:

Stop For Errors   The batch processing will be interrupted until you confirm the error message that will be displayed. If you give a negative reply to the error message, the processing will be stopped indefinitely.

Log Errors to File   The errors are saved in a file without processing being suspended. If any errors have occurred an error message will inform you of this at the end of processing. You can click the **Save As** button to choose the name of the file in which the errors will be recorded.

⟹ Here, leave the **Stop For Errors** option active.

[l] Click **OK**.

The batch processing begins.

⟹ For the first two images, click the **Continue** button on the warning that appears. On the third image, click **Stop**.

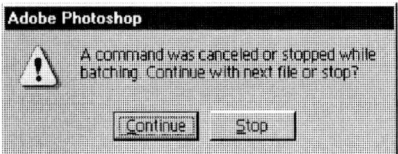

Photoshop displays another warning.

Chapter 8

☐ When this message appears, either click **Continue** to stop applying the action to this particular image but continue applying it to the other images in the folder, or click **Stop** to put an end to the batch processing.

➡ Here, click **Stop**.

> ✓ *To avoid wasting time during batch processing, duplicate the action that you want to use and delete all the Stop commands in the copy. You will not have to wait for each image to be treated to click the Continue button, which means you can do other work while waiting for the batch to be processed.*
>
> ✓ *To process a batch of images using several actions, create an action in which you insert an Automate - Batch command for each action you wish to use.*

➡ Close all the open images without saving them. You can always recreate this effect at another time if you so desire.

PRACTICE EXERCISE 8

- Open one of the images in the **ENI Photoshop 5.5** folder.
- Convert the image to indexed color mode.
- In the **Personal Actions** set, create an action called **Image Button**.
- For this action, make a conditional mode change. If the image is in indexed color, have it converted to RGB.
- Select the entire image then cut the selection onto a new layer.
- Apply a bevelled edge effect to this new layer using an inner bevel 10 pixels deep.
- Stop recording the action.
- Duplicate the **Image Button** action and call the copy **Pressed-in Image Button**.
- On the **Pressed-in Image Button** action, record the **Set Layer Effects of current layer** command again and choose **Down** in the **Bevel and Emboss** dialog box this time.
- Record the following commands at the end of the **Image Button** action.
- Insert a stop and enter **Click Stop to obtain a simple button**. and authorise continuing with the action.
- Select all of **Layer 1** then make a new selection consisting of the outer edges of the previous one, to a depth of 10 pixels.
- Cut this selection onto a new layer then apply to it a bevel effect using a pillow emboss 5 pixels deep.

Chapter 8

- *Test both actions then save the **Personal Actions** set if they work correctly. A normal error may occur at the beginning of the action if you have opened an image that is not in indexed color. If any other errors appear, correct them before saving the set.*
- *Leave Photoshop without saving the image (you can always use these actions at another point in time).*

EXTRA INFORMATION

1 - SELECTING A DIGITISATION SOURCE 392
2 - SCANNING AN IMAGE 392
3 - MANAGING THE BRUSHES PALETTE 394
        CREATING A STANDARD TOOL BRUSH 394
        CREATING A BRUSH FROM A DRAWING 396
        MODIFYING BRUSH OPTIONS 398
        DELETING A BRUSH 398
        SAVING OR OPENING A BRUSH PALETTE 399
4 - SMOOTHING A SELECTION 399
5 - USING SEVERAL VIEWS ON AN IMAGE 400
6 - CONVERTING AN ACROBAT DOCUMENT INTO A PHOTOSHOP IMAGE 401
7 - DEFINING DOCUMENT INFORMATION 402
8 - DELETING DISSIMILAR PIXELS 403
9 - INCREASING IMAGE SHARPNESS 404
10 - APPLYING A 3D EFFECT TO AN IMAGE 404
11 - DEFINING THE RESOLUTION AUTOMATICALLY 406
12 - AUTOMATICALLY MODIFYING AN IMAGE'S BRIGHTNESS AND CONTRAST 407
13 - THROWING LIGHT ONTO PART OF AN IMAGE 408
14 - USING THE ▨ TOOL 410
15 - USING THE ▨ TOOL 411
16 - AUTOMATICALLY SELECTING A LAYER WITH THE ▨ TOOL 412
17 - SETTING THE GENERAL PHOTOSHOP PREFERENCES 412
18 - SETTING PREFERENCES FOR SAVING FILES 413
19 - SETTING PREFERENCES FOR THE WORK DRIVES 414
20 - SETTING MEMORY PREFERENCES 414
21 - CONFIGURING COLOUR MANAGEMENT 415

Extra information...

1 SELECTING A DIGITISATION SOURCE

[a] **File**
Import
Select TWAIN_32 Source

[b] Select one of the **Sources** proposed. You may see two similar names, but choose the one ending with **32** (or **32 bits**).

[c] Click the **Select** button.

☑ You can only digitise in Photoshop if your scanner or digital camera has a TWAIN compatible plug-in. You can check this by checking your equipment's user manual.

☑ If you only have a single plug-in you will not have to choose a digitisation source. However, it will be necessary if you have a scanner and a digital camera which are both TWAIN compatible.

2 SCANNING AN IMAGE

[a] **File**
Import
TWAIN_32

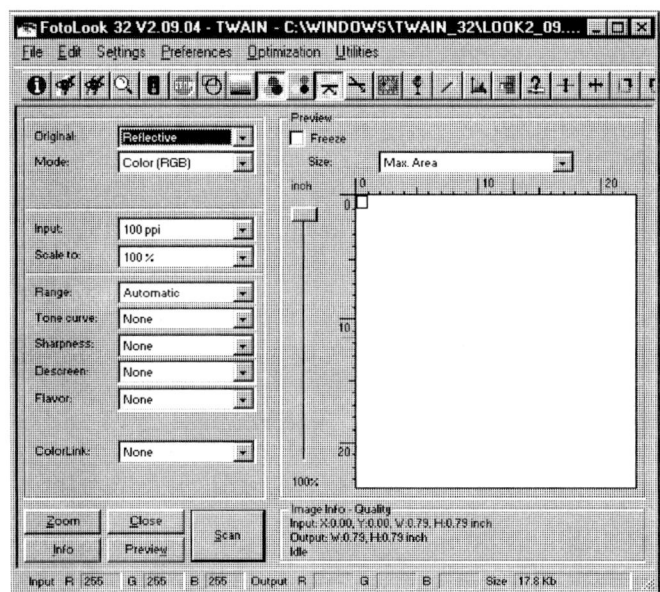

This screen is simply an example. Each scanner or digital camera has its own plug-in.

Extra information...

[b] Before adjusting the various scan parameters, make a preview scan by clicking the button usually called **Preview**.

The image is scanned rapidly and appears in the preview box.

[c] If the image you are scanning is smaller than the scan area, reduce the area, or in the opposite case, enlarge it. You do not need to digitise areas that do not contain any images as the process will be unnecessarily long and the image size too large.

[d] Select an **Input** resolution (this option may be called **Resolution**). As you have seen previously, this is an important step. Always digitise at the required resolution and avoid increasing this resolution once the image is in Photoshop. If you want to obtain an image twice as large as the scanned picture, you should digitise the image at twice the resolution you require for the result and change the **Image Size** in Photoshop. This will avoid having to resample the image (see the section Changing the size and/or resolution of an image in Chapter 5).

[e] Set the scanning mode. Most plug-ins allow you to choose from RGB mode, grayscale and black and white (or Bitmap). With a top-of-the-range scanner, you can also digitise directly in CMYK. In this case, carry out a few tests, as with some scanners it is not advantageous to scan directly into CMYK. It would be better to scan in RGB and convert to CMYK in Photoshop.

[f] Most scanner plug-ins have settings optimised for certain types of documents. Select the document type from the list offered (the names will vary between different types of equipment):

A black and white drawing	Select the **Line Art** or **Black and White** option or similar.
A colour drawing	Select **Coloured Art** or **Colour Drawing**. If a similar option is not offered, choose **Colour Photo**.
A black and white photo	Select the **Grayscale Photo** or **Black and White Photo** or **Grayscale** option.
A colour photo	Select the **Colour Photo** option.
A text document	Select the **Text** or **Line Drawing** or **Black and White** option.

[g] If necessary, adjust the **Brightness** and/or **Contrast** settings.

[h] If necessary, adjust the **Range** for grayscales. Changing the **Range** may affect the **Brightness** of the image.

[i] Depending on the scanning application, you may have some retouch functions, similar to the **Levels** and **Curves** commands in Photoshop. In this case you can adjust these settings for optimal image quality. Check your retouches in the preview screen. You can still use the retouch commands in Photoshop but there will be less work to do and the result will be clearer.

Extra information...

[j] Other functions may be available, such as filters to improve image quality. Some of these may be useful, such as **Descreen** or **Demoiré** filters, which remove printing screens. Use these filters when reproducing an image from a magazine for example.

[k] If your scanner has a transparent back, you can also digitise slides or negatives. If you digitise a negative, ask the scanner plug-in to invert the scanned image to obtain a positive. Be careful, for a colour negative, the plug-in must include an option to remove the orange filter from the negative. If this is not available, you will have to correct the orange dominant in Photoshop.

[l] When the settings appear correct, click the **Scan** button to scan and digitise the image.

When the image is digitised, it appears in a new window in Photoshop.

[m] Quit the scan application to return to Photoshop and work on the image as required.

> ✓ *It is essential to configure your scanner to avoid colour distortions between the original image and the digitised image. To do this, make several scans of a test image with different settings and compare the results on screen. This however relies on your monitor screen being correctly calibrated as well!*

> ✓ *For optimum results, do not exceed the scanner's optical resolution when digitising. If you exceed this resolution, the plug-in will interpolate by "inventing" extra pixels based on the ones that were actually scanned. For example, if your scanner has a optical resolution of 600 x 1200 ppi, it is a good idea not to go over 600 ppi for the resolution, even if you can digitise at 9600 ppi.*

3 MANAGING THE BRUSHES PALETTE

CREATING A STANDARD TOOL BRUSH

[a] If the **Brushes** palette is hidden, click its tab or show it with **Window - Show Brushes**.

[b] Select the **New Brush** command on the **Brushes** palette menu (▶) or click an empty place on the palette.

Extra information...

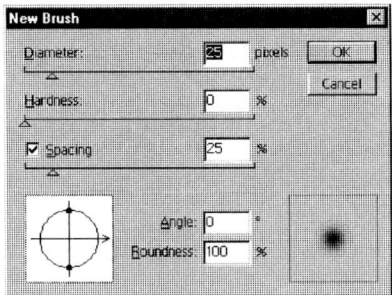

[c] Set the brush **Diameter** in the corresponding text box (or use the slider). The diameter can vary from 1 to 999 pixels.

[d] Set the **Hardness** value. The higher this is, the more the brush has a contrasted edge. Inversely, the lower the hardness, the more blurred the edges will be.

0% hardness   50% hardness   100% hardness

*You can see how three different **Hardness** values affect a brush of the same diameter.*

[e] Set the **Spacing** to determine the various brush marks in a stroke will be spaced when you draw or retouch with it. This value can vary between 1 and 999%. If you deactivate the **Spacing** option, the speed with which the stroke is drawn will be proportional to how fast you drag.

25% spacing
75% spacing
100% spacing
150% spacing
proportional spacing

*In this illustration, the same stroke is drawn with different **Spacing**. The last stroke was made with the **Spacing** option deactivated. When dragging began, it was slow and the **Spacing** is almost non-existent, but near the end, the mouse was dragged faster and the spacing is more significant.*

[f] Specify the brush **Roundness**. You can also change the shape of the brush by dragging the black handles on the circle in the bottom left corner of the dialog box. This allows you to create elliptical brush shapes. A 100% **Roundness** gives a circular shape. Use a 0% **Roundness** to make a straight line shape.

25% roundness   50% roundness   75% roundness

Adobe Photoshop 5.5

Extra information...

[g] Set the offset **Angle** for the brush shape. You can also drag the arrow on the circle in the bottom left corner of the dialog box. This option has no value if you choose a 100% **Roundness** for the brush.

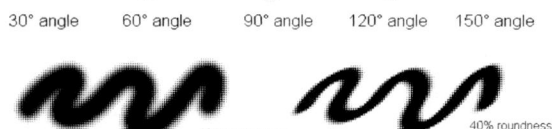

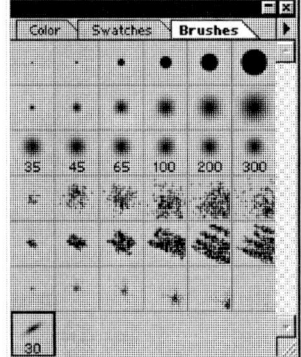

This options lets you draw with upstrokes and downstrokes, as with calligraphy.

➡ Click **OK**.

The new brush appears in the palette.

CREATING A BRUSH FROM A DRAWING

[a] Activate the drawing tool of your choice.

[b] Set the **Options** for the tool. If you want to manage opacity correctly with the new brush shape, select a 100% **Opacity**.

[c] Again, in order to manage opacity correctly, select black as the foreground colour.

[d] If the **Brushes** palette is hidden, click its tab or show it with **Window - Show Brushes**.

[e] Select the tool shape you want to use for the drawing.

[f] Draw your shape with the selected tool. Draw on a new layer or on a white background so Photoshop can make out easily the edges of the shape.

Extra information...

|g| Activate a selection tool and select the drawn object. Do not try and select the object down to the last pixel, on the contrary, make a fairly large selection around it. Photoshop will only use the non-white and non-transparent pixels in the selection to create the shape.

|h| Select **Define Brush** in the **Brushes** palette menu ( ).

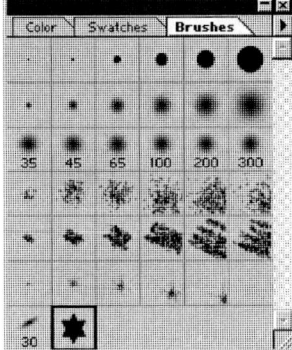

The brush is added to the palette.

- ✓ To create very regular drawn shapes, create a path and apply a black stroke or fill to it.

- ✓ To create square or rectangular shapes, make a selection with the tool. Add a feathered edge to the selection if you want to create a brush with blurred edges then fill the selection in black.

- ✓ If your drawn shape is too voluminous, the brush shape may not fit in the tiny display space on the *Brushes* palette. Contrary to standard brushes, Photoshop does not shrink drawn brushes to fit them on the palette, nor does it supply any information about their size. In some cases the drawn brush may seem completely invisible on the palette but will be correctly defined:

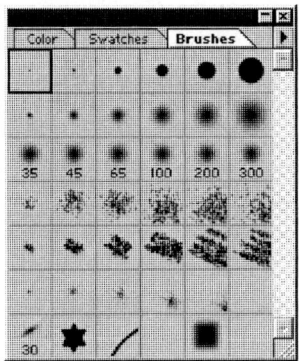

The third brush on the last line is cut off and the fourth space appears blank.

Adobe Photoshop 5.5

Extra information...

In fact, these spaces contain, respectively, these two brushes.

MODIFYING BRUSH OPTIONS

[a] If the **Brushes** palette is hidden, click its tab or show it with **Window - Show Brushes**.

[b] Activate the brush type whose options you wish to modify.

[c] Double-click the brush or select the **Options** command in the **Brushes** palette menu (▶).

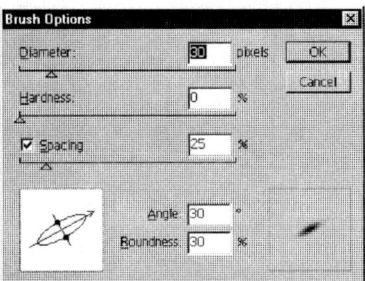

The options for standard brushes

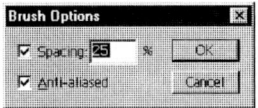

The options for drawn brushes

[d] Set the various parameters for the brush, in the same way as for creating a standard brush type. The **Anti-aliased** option is specific to drawn brushes, to avoid pixelation effects on the edges of the brush. If the shape naturally has pixelated edges, this option is not available.

[e] Click **OK**.

DELETING A BRUSH

[a] If the **Brushes** palette is hidden, click its tab or show it with **Window - Show Brushes**.

[b] Activate the brush type you want to delete.

[c] Hold down [Ctrl] then click the brush or select the **Delete Brush** command from the **Brushes** palette menu (▶).

Extra information...

SAVING OR OPENING A BRUSH PALETTE

[a] If the **Brushes** palette is hidden, click its tab or show it with **Window - Show Brushes**.

[b] Click the **Brushes** palette menu (▶) and select the command **Save Brushes** or **Load Brushes**.

Go into the folder containing the extra brush types. By default, these are placed in the \Program Files\Adobe\Photoshop 5.5\Goodies\Brushes folder. You do not have to save extra brushes in this folder, but it is recommended, so all the brush types are grouped together in the same place on the hard disk.

[c] Click the name of the brush palette that you want to load or give a **Name** to your palette if you are saving one.

[d] Click **Load** to open a palette or **Save** to save one.

☑ *In the palette menu (▶), you can also use the Replace Brushes command. Unlike the Load Brushes command which adds the extra brushes onto the existing palette, Replace Brushes erases the current palette and replaces it with the loaded one.*

☑ *To return to the default brush set, use the Reset Brushes command on the Brushes palette menu (▶).*

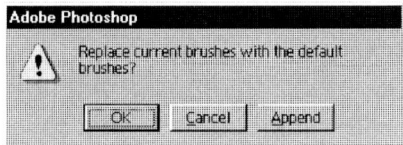

Click OK to replace the brushes currently in the palette with the basic set of brushes. Click Append to add the current brushes to the default set.

☑ *The last brushes palette used is left in place when you leave Photoshop.*

4 SMOOTHING A SELECTION

[a] Make a selection with the ✶ tool or using the **Select - Color Range** command.
In some cases, the selection may contain many "holes", or tiny areas of unselected pixels.

[b] **Select**
Modify
Smooth

Adobe Photoshop 5.5

Extra information...

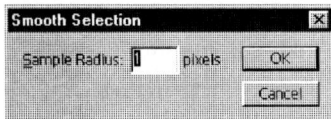

|c| Specify a **Sample Radius** between 1 and 16 pixels. For each pixel in the selection, Photoshop analyses the neighbouring pixels within the chosen **Sample Radius**. If most pixels are selected, the unselected pixels in this radius are added to the selection. Pixels selected in otherwise unselected areas are removed from the selection.

|d| Click **OK**.

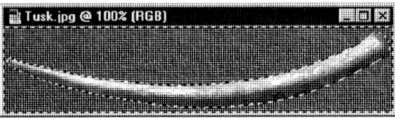

The red background was dotted with unselected pixels: these unselected areas are now included in the selection.

5 USING SEVERAL VIEWS ON AN IMAGE

|a| Open the document of your choice.

|b| **View**
New View

A new window for this document is displayed.

☑ *A new view does not create a new document. If you change the image on one view, all the other views are altered in turn.*

☑ *You can use different views with higher or lower zoom values. For example, in one window you could have a highly zoomed picture of one part of an image and a global display of the same image in the other window.*

☑ *When you wish to make a conversion to CMYK Color, use an extra view to show the CMYK Preview in one window and the other to show the image in its current mode.*

☑ *These different views can be very useful when working on large images so you can work simultaneously on different areas of the image which are far from each other.*

☑ *When you are working on a layer, use another view to show the composite colour channel.*

Extra information...

6 **CONVERTING AN ACROBAT DOCUMENT INTO A PHOTOSHOP IMAGE**

[a] File
Automate
Multi-Page PDF to PSD

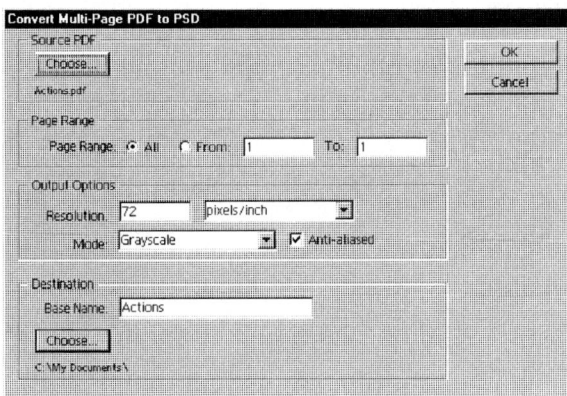

[b] Click the **Choose** button under **Source PDF** to determine which Acrobat document is to be converted.

[c] Using the **Page Range** option, specify which pages of the Acrobat document you wish to convert. You can choose to convert **All** the pages or only those **From** page x **To** page y.

[d] Select the output **Resolution** you wish to obtain after converting the Acrobat document (which is a Post Script document).

[e] Select the colour **Mode** for the image. You can choose from **Grayscale, RGB Color, CMYK Color** or **Lab Color**.

[f] Activate the **Anti-aliased** option to avoid a pixelation problem on the converted pages.

[g] If necessary, select a **Base Name** for the created documents. By default, this name is the same as the Acrobat document.

[h] Click the **Choose** button under **Destination** to determine in which folder the converted images will be placed.

[i] Click **OK**.

Each page of the Acrobat document is converted from a vector graphic to a Photoshop image then saved in the destination folder. It will be called Base Name 0001 for the first page, Base Name 0002 for the second page and so on. If the document contains several pages, the conversion may take quite some time.

Adobe Photoshop 5.5

Extra information...

7 DEFINING DOCUMENT INFORMATION

[a] **File**
File Info

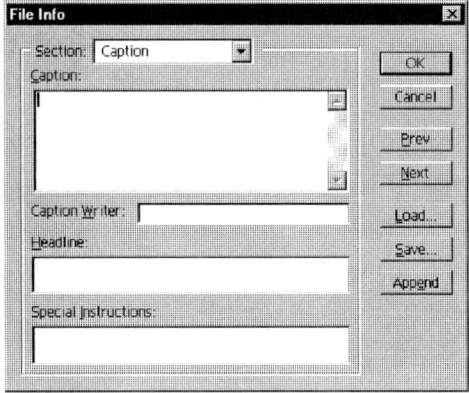

[b] Fill in the required information, clicking **Next** to move through each of the six **Sections** available:

Caption — Lets you add a **Caption**, a **Headline** and **Special Instructions** to the image. You can print the **Caption** by activating the corresponding option in the **Page Setup** dialog box.

Keywords — Lets you define keywords for the image. These can be used by certain image browsers to search for a document. Enter a keyword of a maximum of 31 characters then click **Add**. To delete a keyword, select it then click **Delete**.

Categories — Enter a **Category** using a three-character code. A list of categories can be obtained in a press agency. You can also add extra categories using the **Supplemental Categories** option. The **Urgency** option lets you choose a priority level for publication, but not for processing.

Credits — Use these entries for images protected by copyright.

Source — You can enter details of the context in which the photograph was taken.

Copyright & URL — This section is used to enter extra copyright information, as an appendix to that already entered in the **Credits** section. If you activate the **Mark as Copyrighted** option, the © symbol will be shown in the title bar of the image window. Enter a copyright notice and a URL if the information concerning an image is on an Internet site. Whenever Photoshop detects a Digimarc watermark in an image, this section will be automatically updated.

Extra information...

[c] Click **OK**.

✓ You can *Save* the information entered in order to use it on another image. Click the *Load* button to use the information saved or the *Append* button to add the saved information to that already defined on the image.

8 DELETING DISSIMILAR PIXELS

[a] **Filter**
Noise
Dust & Scratches

[b] Set the **Threshold** option to **0** to take into account all the pixels in the selection. This option is equivalent to the **Tolerance** option used for the ▨ tool, but in the other direction.

[c] Define a **Radius** between 1 and 16. This determines the perimeter for searching for differences among pixels.

[d] Progressively increase the **Threshold** value until the unwanted pixels reappear. Choose at that point the **Threshold** value immediately before the current one so that the pixels are deleted.

[e] Click **OK**.

✓ This filter is especially useful for digitised images containing defects such as dust or tiny scratches (hence its name). You can also use it to correct screening problems on images digitised from a magazine.

✓ This filter produces a slight blur on the areas treated. The image sharpness can be improved with the *Sharpen* filter.

✓ You can also use the *Filter - Noise - Despeckle* or *Filter - Noise - Median* depending on the image. On drawn pictures, (less so on photographs), the *Filter - Blur - Smart Blur* filter may also give good results.

Extra information...

9 INCREASING IMAGE SHARPNESS

[a] **Filter**
Sharpen
Unsharp Mask

[b] Set how much you want the sharpness increased using the **Amount** option. For high resolution images, use a value between 100 and 200%.

[c] Set the **Radius** surrounding the edge pixels that will be affected by the sharpening. Specify between 1 and 2 for high resolution images.

[d] Define the **Threshold**, that is the level of luminosity before the filter is applied that will be used for the contrast. This avoids an exaggerated accentuation on areas of solid colour, such as sand or skin, while accentuating other areas on the image. For images with areas of solid colour, set a value between 2 and 20. A value of 0 sharpens the whole of the image.

[e] Click **OK**.

✓ You can use this filter systematically after resampling to improve the sharpness of the result.

10 APPLYING A 3D EFFECT TO AN IMAGE

[a] Activate the layer on which you wish to make the transformation.

[b] **Filter**
Render
3D Transform

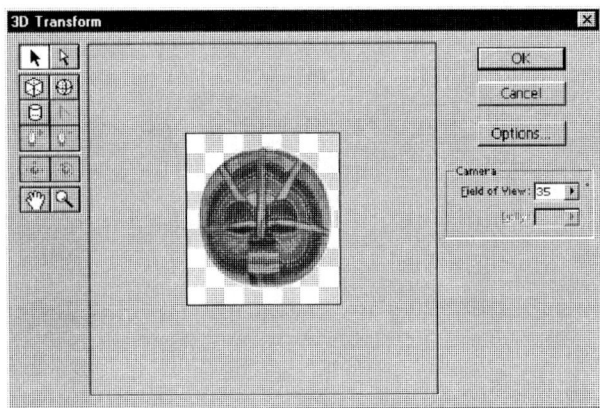

This filter allows you to manipulate a two-dimensional image as though it were a 3-D image. Essentially you can manipulate cubic, spherical or cylindrical objects.

Extra information...

|c| Select one of the following tools in the dialog box:

- To transform the image onto a cubic surface. Use this tool to create objects such as a die, a box, ...
- To transform the image onto a spherical surface. Use this tool to create objects such as a ball, a globe, ...
- To transform the image onto a cylindrical surface. This surface could also be distorted to obtain an irregular cylinder. Use this tool on objects such as a tin can or irregular cylinders such as a bottle, an hourglass, ...

|d| Drag around the image in the preview box to draw the structure, or wire frame, for the selected shape.

|e| Activate the ▶ tool to move the whole wire frame or the ▶ tool to move an anchor point on it.

|f| Drag a segment to move the whole structure or an anchor point with the ▶ tool to adjust an individual point. For an optimal result, the wire frame should perfectly encircle the image you want to transform. If the wire frame turns red, the 3D transform cannot be applied. In that case move one or more anchor points until the wire frame turns green.

|g| If you are creating an irregular cylindrical structure, activate the ▶ tool in the dialog box to add anchor points. Click the right side of the wire frame to add a point. When you are moving this point, the left side will be symmetrically distorted in accordance with the right side.

Here, the outline has been deliberately drawn in this way so you can view more clearly the anchor points and the outline shape. When you are doing it yourself, you will draw the outline as close as possible to the object.

|h| If required, convert some of the smooth points into corner points using the ▶ tool from the dialog box. Click to convert the smooth point into a corner point and vice versa.

|i| You can delete superfluous anchor points by activating the ▶ tool on the dialog box and clicking them.

|j| The **Field of View** option lets you increase or decrease the outlined area, especially in places where you could not place anchor points.

|k| Activate the ▶ tool to make a panoramic view. Drag the outline to move the outlined area and/or use the **Dolly** option to increase or decrease this area.

Adobe Photoshop 5.5

Extra information...

|l| Activate the ▣ tool to rotate the object. Drag the outline to turn the outlined area on the 3D shape and/or use the **Dolly** option to increase or decrease this area.

An image that has undergone a rotation on a 3D sphere.

|m| Click the **Options** button to define the result quality options.

|n| Specify the quality required for the result with the **Resolution** option. This is most effective with a transformation on a cube.

|o| Use the **Anti-aliased** option to reduce any pixelation that may occur.

|p| Activate the **Display Background** option if you wish to preserve parts of the layer that are not affected by the transformation. If you deactivate this option, the areas of the layer that have not been outlined in the **3D Transform** dialog box will be erased from the final result.

|q| Click **OK** to confirm the quality options.

|r| Click **OK** to apply the filter.

- ✓ To delete a wire frame, select it with the ▣ tool and press the [Del] key.
- ✓ To increase or reduce the size of the image preview in the dialog box, activate the ▣ tool in the dialog box and click the image.
- ✓ If the zoom is too high, you can activate the ▣ tool and move the image around with it.
- ✓ 3D transformations can only be performed on RGB images.

11 DEFINING THE RESOLUTION AUTOMATICALLY

|a| **Image**
Image Size

|b| Determine whether or not you want to **Resample Image**.

Extra information...

[c] Click the **Auto** button.

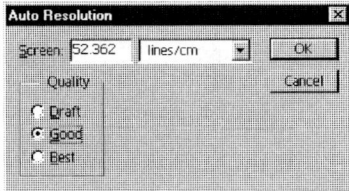

[d] Preferably select a **Screen** frequency in **lines/inch** (or lpi) and enter the value in the corresponding text box.

The resolution will thus be determined by the screen frequency used for printing images with halftone screens. This frequency depends on the output device. Depending on the print (or display) quality of this device, you could use a higher or lower frequency. If the image is to be sent to a print shop, you should find out what screen frequency will be used.

[e] Select the required **Quality**:

Draft   The resolution will equal the screen frequency to a maximum of 72 ppi.
Good   The resolution will be 1.5 times higher than the frequency.
Best   The resolution will be 2 times as high as the frequency.

[f] Click **OK** twice.

> ✓ *Be careful, the frequency that you indicate here is only used by Photoshop to calculate the resolution. This frequency does not affect the actual output frequency that is defined using the Screens option in the File - Page Setup dialog box.*

12 AUTOMATICALLY MODIFYING AN IMAGE'S BRIGHTNESS AND CONTRAST

This command is especially useful for images with a strong light or dark dominant, because it distributes brightness in a more homogenous manner.

[a] **Image**
   Adjust
   Equalize

[b] If a selection has been made, you should select how the equalizing is to be carried out.

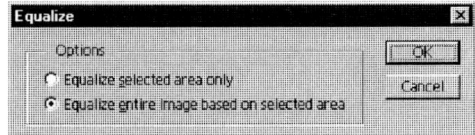

Adobe Photoshop 5.5

Extra information...

Equalize selected area only	To only equalize the selected area based on the brightness of the pixels in the selection.
Equalize entire image based on selected area	To equalize the whole image based on the brightness of the pixels in the selection and not with all the pixels on the image or layer.

13 THROWING LIGHT ONTO PART OF AN IMAGE

[a] **Filter**
Render
Lighting Effects

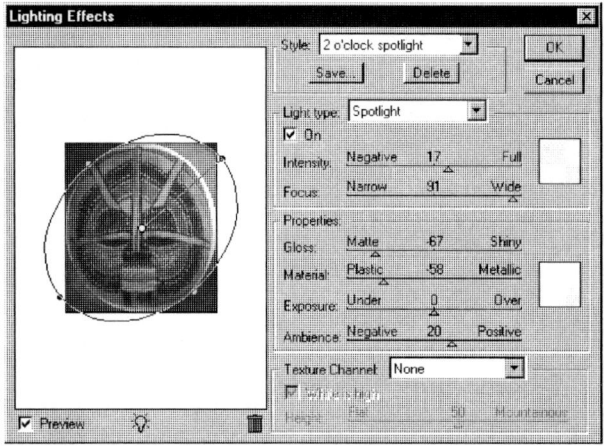

[b] If required, select a predefined **Style** for the effect. If the result is satisfactory, any additional adjustments to the settings will be minimal, if not entirely unnecessary.

[c] If using several light sources, select the one you want to adjust. To do that, click its white circle or press the ⇄ key successively to scroll through the different lights.

[d] Select a **Light type** for the selected lighting effect:

Directional	Projects a far-off light source, like that of the sun.
Omni	Projects light outwards from a central point, like a light bulb.
Spotlight	Projects lights in one direction with an elliptical beam, like a spotlight.

[e] To move the light source, drag the central point of the ellipse in the dialog box preview screen.

Extra information...

[f] Depending on the **Light type**, adjust the light source:

Directional — Drag point (a) to modify the angle and/or the distance of the light. Hold down [⇧ Shift] to change direction without changing the angle. Hold down [Ctrl] to modify the angle without changing the distance.

Omni — Drag one of the four handles to modify the size of the light beam, as if the light bulb were moving closer or further away.

Spotlight — Drag point (a) to modify the light angle. Drag one of the four handles to modify the shape of the beam. Hold down [⇧ Shift] to change the shape of the beam without changing its angle. Hold down [Ctrl] to modify the angle without changing the shape of the beam.

[g] If several light sources are present, you can deactivate the selected source with the **On** option.

[h] Set the **Intensity** of the selected source, that is its luminosity value. The normal value is 50. A negative value diminishes the luminosity and a positive value increases it.

[i] For **Spotlight** lights, set the width of the **Focus**. This determines what quantity of light is emitted from the beam.

[j] Change the colour of the light by clicking the sample box in the **Light type** frame. The **Color Picker** appears so you can define the new colour.

[k] Define the **Properties** of the selected light source:

Gloss — Determines if the surface of the image is matte or glossy. If the image is glossy, the light will be reflected.

Material — Determines whether the light source reflects more light than the image (**Plastic**) or if the image reflects more (**Metallic**) in the final reflection. If the **Gloss** option is set to **Matte**, this option will have little effect on the result.

Exposure — This allows you to increase or decrease the luminosity. If the option is set to 0, it has no effect.

Ambience — Defines the impact of ambient light on the light sources. You can define the colour of this light by clicking the sample box in the **Properties** frame.

Adobe Photoshop 5.5

Extra information...

<u>l</u> If required, use a **Texture Channel** to modify the way in which the light is reflected. This gives a relief effect to the image. Select an Alpha channel in the list. You can copy a texture from another image onto an Alpha channel before applying this filter.
To give the image an embossed effect, you can convert the image to Lab Color, duplicate the Lightness channel then convert the image back to RGB before applying the filter.

<u>m</u> If you are using a texture channel, activate the **White is high** to increase the relief on light areas of the texture. Deactivate this option to accentuate the dark areas on the texture.

<u>n</u> If you use a texture, set the **Height** option to accentuate or tone down the texture's relief.

<u>o</u> You can add an extra light source by dragging the 💡 icon onto the preview screen. You can also duplicate an existing light source by pressing [Alt] and dragging the central point of the light to copy it. You can use up to 16 light sources.

<u>p</u> To delete a light, drag its central point from the preview screen to the 🗑 icon on the dialog box.

<u>q</u> Click **OK**.

    ✓ *This filter can only be applied to RGB images.*

    ✓ *Click the Save button on the Lighting Effects dialog box to create a new Style from the current parameters.*

    ✓ *For more specific lighting effects, such as adding a highlight, you can also use the filter Filter - Render - Lens Flare.*

14 USING THE 📏 TOOL

This tool allows you to calculate the distance between two points on an image but also to measure angles.

<u>a</u> Activate the 📏 tool.

<u>b</u> Point to the place on the image where you want to take a measurement.

<u>c</u> Drag to make the measurement. Hold down [⇧ Shift] while you drag if you want to measure on a horizontal, vertical or 45° angle.

The measurement is displayed in the **Info** palette.

<u>d</u> To modify the measure, drag one of its ends. To move it without changing its length, drag the measuring segment.

Extra information...

|e| To measure a specific angle or make two measurements simultaneously, press down [Alt] and drag from one of the ends to draw a second measuring line.

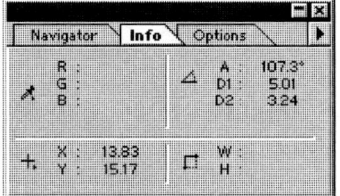

*The angle is indicated in the **Info** palette and the two distances are specified in **D1** and **D2**.*

|f| To delete a measurement, drag the line segment out of the limits of the document window.

15 USING THE TOOL

*This tool supplies you with vital information about the colour components of four points on the image. You can choose these points according to different criteria such as white point/black point... This information can be used essentially in conjunction with the **Image - Adjust** commands.*

|a| Activate the tool.

|b| Click an area on the image to define the first sample. As required, define three other samples.

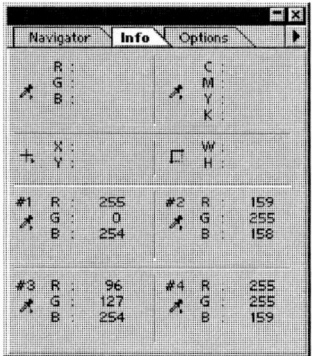

*The information concerning the samples appears in the **Info** palette.*

|c| If needed, move the sample points by dragging them. The mouse pointer must take this form: .

Adobe Photoshop 5.5

Extra information...

[d] To delete a sample point, hold down [Alt] and click the point.

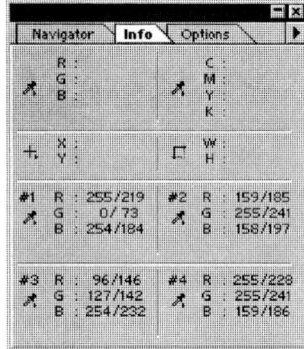

When you are making a colour adjustment with the *Image - Adjust* commands, the samples indicate the current pieces of colour information then those resulting from the adjustment.

✓ To hide the colour samples without deleting them, select the *Hide Color Samplers* command in the *Info* palette menu (▶).

16 AUTOMATICALLY SELECTING A LAYER WITH THE ⊕ TOOL

[a] Double-click the ⊕ tool to show the **Options** palette.
[b] Activate the **Auto Select Layer** option.

Now when you want to move a layer, you will not have to activate it beforehand. Simply click a non-transparent area on the layer and it will be automatically activated.

✓ This option only functions with the ⊕ tool.

17 SETTING THE GENERAL PHOTOSHOP PREFERENCES

Only the preferences that have not already been explained are set out here.

[a] **File**
    Preferences [Ctrl] **K**
    General

[b] Depending on your needs, activate or deactivate the following options:

Anti-alias PostScript Used to remove pixelation effects on selections pasted or imported into Photoshop. If you import a line drawing, you can deactivate this option if you want to produce clearly defined contours.

Export Clipboard Activate this option so that a copied image can be pasted into another application after you have left Photoshop.

Extra information...

	Show Tool Tips	Activate to display ScreenTips when you point to a tool.
	Auto-update open documents	Activate this option if you wish to have an automatic update when you wish on Photoshop and ImageReady simultaneously. In this case, if the image is altered in one application, it will be automatically updated when you go into the second application. If the option is not active, the second application will ask if you wish to update the image manually. If the image is not updated, you risk having two different versions of the one image and one may be overwitten when you save the document. If you require two versions of the same image, save one of the versions under a different name.
	Beep When Done	Activate this option so that Photoshop makes a beeping sound at the end of an operation. This option is useful when you are working on large images and you are applying complex effects that take a long time.
	Dynamic Color Sliders	Lets you modify the colour sliders in the **Color** palette. If you move one of the sliders, the others change colour. This indicates to you what colours could be made by moving the other sliders to strategic positions. If you deactivate this option, the other sliders do not provide this "preview". Photoshop's performance may be better when the option is deactivated.
	Save Palette Locations	Activate this option if you want to the final palette positions to be saved when you leave Photoshop. This allows you to return to your previous working environment every time you open the application again.

[c] Click **OK**.

18 SETTING PREFERENCES FOR SAVING FILES

[a] **File**
Preferences
Saving Files

[b] If required, modify these options:

Image Previews	Saves a thumbnail whenever the file is saved. If you select the **Ask When Saving** option, you can activate or deactivate the **Save Thumbnail** option on the **Save As** or **Save a Copy** dialog boxes.
File Extension	Allows you to **Use Lower Case** or **Use Upper Case** to save the file extensions on documents.
Include Composited Image With Layered Files	Activate this option in order to use images in applications recognising Photoshop 2.5 format.

[c] Click **OK**.

Adobe Photoshop 5.5

Extra information...

19 SETTING PREFERENCES FOR THE WORK DRIVES

[a] **File**
Preferences
Plug-Ins & Scratch Disks

[b] If required, select another folder for the plug-ins, which are special features added to Photoshop, such as filters and certain import and export commands. To do this, click the **Choose** button. Be careful, if you change the folder used by Photoshop, you will no longer have access to the standard filters and certain other commands.

[c] If you have several hard disks or partitions on your computer, you can select up to four working disks. If the first disk is saturated, Photoshop will use the second and so on. This lets you avoid memory saturation. Photoshop can handle up to 200 Gb of virtual memory. You should use you fastest disk drives as the first scratch disks. You cannot use a network drive or any extractable drive.

To optimise you work, place high-volume documents on a different disk to the disk used for the Photoshop virtual memory. You should also defragment your hard disks regularly, as Photoshop only uses areas of continuous space on the disks.

[d] Click **OK**.

20 SETTING MEMORY PREFERENCES

[a] **File**
Preferences
Memory & Image Cache

[b] Define the number of **Cache Levels** used for the memory cache. This allows you to update high-resolution images more quickly by using versions at a lower resolution to refresh display. Enter a value between 1 and 8. The higher the value, the faster the display will be updated, but more RAM and disk space will be required to do it. Select a value of 1 to deactivate the cache memory and a value of 4 to work on high-resolution images.

Be careful, for low-resolution images, the dialog box previews can be inaccurate, as well as the image display itself if the **Cache Levels** option is higher than 1 and the image is not displayed at 100%.

[c] Activate the **Use cache for histograms** option to display histograms more quickly. They will however be less accurate in relation to the image.

Extra information...

[d] Define the percentage of RAM used by Photoshop. To obtain optimal working conditions, it is essential to have a maximum of memory available. To determine how much memory should be allocated to Photoshop, open a high-volume document, one that represents more or less the largest document you will be working on. Once the document is open, look at the status bar to see the amount of memory used by the image:

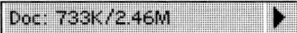

The first value indicates the size of the flattened image, the second value indicates the amount of memory actually used. Layers, channels and paths are all elements that can increase the amount of memory used by an image.
Set the **Used by Photoshop** option according to the second value, leaving a working margin of 5 to 10 Mb minimum.

[e] Click **OK**.

21 CONFIGURING COLOUR MANAGEMENT

[a] Help
Color Management

The *Adobe Color Management Wizard* dialog box opens.

[b] Click the **Open Adobe Gamma** button to calibrate your monitor.

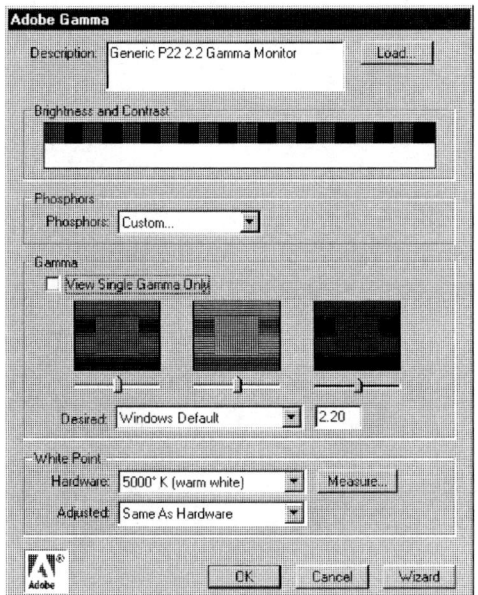

The dialog box may differ as some systems under Windows cannot control the monitor.

Adobe Photoshop 5.5

Extra information...

[c] If necessary, enter a **Description** of your monitor in the corresponding text box.

[d] Set your monitor's contrast level to maximum.

[e] Set the brightness level on your monitor so that the grey and black bands in the **Brightness and Contrast** frame are almost intermingled. Greys should remain slightly visible.

[f] Select the **Phosphors** that correspond to your monitor. If you do not know this information, consult the user manual for your monitor or better still, obtain an ICC profile from the manufacturer. These profiles can generally be downloaded from the Internet. These profiles will not necessarily let you avoid setting the contrast and gamma details but can at least serve as a base as the **Phosphors** are usually configured correctly. An ICC profile must be located in the **\Windows\System\Color** folder to be managed correctly. If you cannot obtain certain pieces of information, leave the default setting as is.

[g] Activate the **View Single Gamma Only** option to define the colour balance according to a combined grayscale. For a more precise setting, you should deactivate this option and define this balance colour by colour (Red, Green, Blue).

[h] If this option is available, select the required gamma in the **Desired** box or enter a value between **0.75** (very light) and **3.75** (very dark). As a general rule, it is better to use the gamma corresponding to your work platform.

[i] Adjust the slider(s) under each or all of the colour boxes. The difference between the striped square (the large one) and the coloured square (the small one) should be as little as possible, so the two squares blend together as best they can:

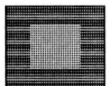
gamma too light

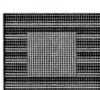
correct gamma

gamma too dark

[j] If you cannot manage to obtain the right gamma, change the **Desired** gamma. A substantial modification in the gamma affects the brightness and you will have to readjust it to ensure that the **Brightness and Contrast** setting is correct.

[k] Define the temperature of your monitor's white point in the **Hardware** box. Some monitors allow you to set this temperature, in this case, select the same temperature. A high temperature produces cool tones (more blue) and a low temperature produces warm tones (more red). If you do not know the white point temperature of your monitor, or if you wish to check its configuration, click the **Measure** button. Three coloured squares appear. Click the one with the most neutral grey. When you click the central square, the white point temperature is defined.

[l] If you have an **Adjusted** setting available, choose **Same As Hardware**.

Extra information...

[m] Click **OK**.

A save dialog box for the ICC profile appears.

[n] Enter the profile's name and click **Save**.

The monitor is correctly calibrated, you find yourself back in the Adobe Color Management Wizard window.

[o] Click **Next** to configure the way Photoshop manages colours.

[p] Select an option depending on the type of work you usually do in Photoshop. If you create documents for a wide variety of media, select the **Use default Photoshop 5 settings (5)** option.

[q] Click **Next**.

Only the Customize for prepress and other uses option will require more details on the subsequent screen. The other options do not have any specific parameters. If you use one of them, simply click the Next button as many times as necessary then click Finish.

[r] Click the **Next** button.

[s] Select the RGB colour space that will determine the colour range that can be represented in your documents:

sRGB	This is the space used when you choose the Photoshop default settings. Select this option if you create images for the Web, for multimedia applications or for printing on office printers optimised for sRGB images.
Adobe RGB (1998)	Choose this option for images that will be converted to CMYK and for printing. Be careful, some monitors cannot reproduce these colours correctly.
ColorMatch RGB	This colour space is close to the one achieved with **Adobe RGB (1998)**; select this option if you have a Radius ® ColorMatch TM monitor or if you wish to obtain a similar colour match.
Monitor RGB	This option is not recommended; it uses the colour range of your monitor which may misrepresent colours when they are displayed on other computers. This was the option used by Photoshop 4.0.

[t] Click **Next**.

[u] Specify whether or not Photoshop should convert an image's colour space on opening if it does not correspond to the colour space you have defined:

Always convert mismatched files	If all the images have an exact ICC profile, use this option to preserve image appearance by modifying the colour values.

Adobe Photoshop 5.5

Extra information...

Never convert mismatched files	If you create Web images, use this option to keep the exact colour values. The appearance of mismatched images will be modified.
Ask me what to do with mismatched files	Used by the Photoshop default settings: select this if you want Photoshop to prompt you on opening a mismatched image. You can then decide whether or not to convert the file.

 Click **Next**.

Specify whether or not Photoshop should convert "untagged" files or files containing no information about their colour space:

Never convert untagged files	Used with the Photoshop default parameters: select this option to keep the precise colour values as they are in the image. The image's appearance may be modified.
Assume untagged files use my monitor's color space	Select this option if the untagged images were created on a computer with a correctly configured monitor. The colour values will be changed but the look of the image should not vary.
Assume untagged images were created in Photoshop 4.0	Use this option to convert the image from the Photoshop 4.0 RGB color space to the RGB space previously defined. Colour values can be modified and the image's appearance need not change.
Assume untagged files use the sRGB color space	Use this option to convert the image from the sRGB colour space to the RGB space previously defined. The colour values may be changed but the image appearance may not change if it comes from the sRGB space.
Ask me what to do when opening untagged files	Choose this option if you want to be prompted by Photoshop when it opens an untagged file. You can then decide the type of conversion you wish to apply.

 Click **Next** then click the **Finish** button.

> ✓ If the monitor needs calibrating, the same thing applies to the printer and scanner. Generally speaking, a printed picture should be a true reproduction of the screen image (the digital image), which should itself be a true copy of the original document. Calibrating the scanner should be done from the Twain drivers of the scanner and the calibration will be specific to the scanner.
>
> As far as the printer goes, you can save corrections made in Photoshop by clicking the *Transfer* button in the *File - Page Setup* dialog box. In *Transfer Functions*, the *All Same* option allows you to adjust the inks separately as you would for a duotone. Once you have achieved a suitable result, click the *Save* button; you then only have to *Load* the saved transfer functions for the images you wish to print.
>
> You should always calibrate your printer and scanner with a test image containing swatches of CMYK, RGB, a neutral grey (50% black) and a correctly-balanced CMYK photograph.

Appendix

SHORTCUT KEYS FOR TOOLS

ACTIVATING TOOLS

M   [marquee]
C   [crop]
V   [move]
L   [lasso]
W   [magic wand]
J   [airbrush]
B   [paintbrush]
S   [stamp]
Y   [history brush]
E   [eraser]
N   [pencil]
R   [blur]
O   [dodge]
P   [pen]

[Shift] + [dodge+]
[Shift] - [dodge-]

A   [arrow]
T   [type]
U   [measure]
G   [gradient]
K   [paint bucket]
I   [eyedropper]
H   [hand]
Z   [zoom]
X   Switch foreground and background colours (⇆)
D   Default colours (■)
Q   [icon] or [icon]
F   [icon] or [icon] or [icon]

Press [Shift] and the tool's shortcut key to see the hidden tools it contains.

Double-click a tool to display the **Options** palette.

Press the [Caps Lock] key to use a cross hair as the pointer.

SELECTION/MOVING TOOLS

Any selection tool + [space] and drag	Moves the current selection.
Any selection tool + [Shift] and drag	Expands the selection.
Any selection tool + [Alt] and drag	Contracts the selection.
Any selection tool + [Shift] + [Alt] and drag	Creates an intersection between two selections.
[Shift]-drag	Draws a selection square or circle.
[Alt]-drag	Draws a selection border from the centre of the item.
[Ctrl] + any tool (except the [hand] tool and the pen tools)	Activates the [move] tool.
[Alt]-drag	To switch from the [icon] tool to the [icon] tool.
[Alt]-click	To switch from the [icon] tool to the [icon] tool.
[Alt]-drag a selection with [move] tool	Copies the selection.

Adobe Photoshop 5.5

Appendix

Any selection tool + ← or → or ↓ or ↑	Moves the selection border one pixel at a time (hold down ⇧Shift to move by 10 pixels).
⊕ tool + ← or → or ↓ or ↑	Moves the selected area one pixel at a time (hold down ⇧Shift to move by 10 pixels).
Ctrl + ← or → or ↓ or ↑	Moves the layer one pixel at a time (hold down ⇧Shift to move by 10 pixels).
The ✋ or ✋ tool + ← or →	Reduces/increases the width of the "magnetic" area.
⇧Shift -drag a guide	Aligns the guides with a ruler marker.
Alt -drag a guide	Changes the orientation of the guide.

VIEW

Double-click the ✋ tool or Ctrl 0	Displays the image so it fits the screen.
Double-click the 🔍 tool or Ctrl Alt 0	Displays the image at 100% zoom.
Ctrl +	Zooms in.
Ctrl -	Zooms out.
Ctrl space	Activates the 🔍 tool.
Alt space	Activates the 🔍 tool.
Ctrl -drag Navigator palette preview	Zooms that part of the image.

Navigation

space -drag	Activates the ✋ tool.
Home	Changes view to upper left corner
End	Changes view to bottom right corner

DRAWING TOOLS

Any drawing/retouching tool + Alt	Activates the 💧 tool.
💧 tool + ⇧Shift	Activates the 💧 tool.
💧 tool + Alt +click	Deletes a sampling point.
💧 tool + Alt + click	Selects the background colour.
Any drawing/retouching tool + a key on the numeric keypad (0 = 100%, 1 = 10%, 2 = 20% etc)	Defines the tool's opacity, pressure or exposure.

420   Adobe Photoshop 5.5

Appendix

Shortcut	Action
`Alt` `←`	Fills the selection/layer with the foreground colour in normal mode. Hold down `⇧ Shift` to keep transparent areas.
`Ctrl` `←`	Fills the selection/layer with the background colour in normal mode. Hold down `⇧ Shift` to keep transparent areas.
`Alt` `Ctrl` `←`	Fills the selection/layer from history in normal mode. Hold down `⇧ Shift` to keep transparent areas.
`!`	Activates or deactivates the **Preserve Transparency** option for the active layer.
Any drawing tool + `⇧ Shift` +click	Draws straight lines.

TYPE TOOL DIALOG BOX

`Ctrl` `⇧ Shift` `L`	Aligns text on the left.
`Ctrl` `⇧ Shift` `C`	Centres text.
`Ctrl` `⇧ Shift` `R`	Aligns text on the right.
`⇧ Shift` `←` or `→`	Selects one character to the left or right
`⇧ Shift` `↓` or `↑`	Selects one line of text below or above.
`Ctrl` `A`	Selects the whole text.
`⇧ Shift` -click	Selects all the characters between the insertion point and the place where you click.
`←` or `→`	Moves the insertion point one character to the left or the right.
`↓` or `↑`	Moves the insertion point one line down or up.
`Ctrl` `←` or `→`	Moves the insertion point one word to the left or to the right.
`Ctrl` `⇧ Shift` `:`	Increases font size by 2 points Hold down `Alt` to increase by 10 points.
`Ctrl` `⇧ Shift` `;`	Decreases font size by 2 points. Hold down `Alt` to decrease by 10 points.
`Alt` `↓` or `↑`	Reduces/increases leading by 2 points. Hold down `Ctrl` to reduce/increase by 10 points.
`⇧ Shift` `Alt` `↓` or `↑`	Reduces/increases the baseline shift by 2 points. Hold down `Ctrl` to reduce/increase by 10 points.
`Alt` `←` or `→`	Reduces/increases kerning or tracking by 20/1000 ems.
`Ctrl` `Alt` `←` or `→`	Reduces/increases kerning or tracking by 100/1000 ems.

Adobe Photoshop 5.5

Appendix

DRAWING TOOLS

[arrow] tool + [⇧ Shift] + click — Selects several anchor points

[arrow] tool + [Alt] + click — Selects the whole path.

[pen] tool + [Alt] + [Ctrl] + drag — Duplicates a path.

Any drawing tool + [Ctrl] — Activates the [arrow] tool.

[arrow] tool + [Alt] or
Any drawing tool + [Ctrl] + [Alt] — Activates the [arrow+] tool.

[Alt] — Switches from the [pen+] tool to the [pen] tool.

Any drawing tool + [Alt]
(except the [arrow] tool) — Activates the [convert] tool.

[arrow] tool + [Ctrl] + [Alt] — Activates the [convert] tool.

Any drawing tool + Enter
on the numeric keypad — Converts the path into a selection.

[Alt] + drag — Switches from the [pen−] tool to the [pen] tool.

[Alt] + click — Switches from the [pen−] tool to the [pen] tool.

WINDOWS MENU SHORTCUTS

File

Shortcut	Action
[Ctrl] N	New
[Ctrl] O	Open
[Ctrl] [Alt] O	Open As
[Ctrl] W	Close
[Ctrl] S	Save
[Ctrl] [⇧ Shift] S	Save As
[Ctrl] [Alt] S	Save a Copy
[Ctrl] [Alt] [⇧ Shift] S	Save for Web
[Ctrl] [⇧ Shift] P	Page Setup
[Ctrl] P	Print
[Ctrl] K	Preferences − General
[Ctrl] Q	Exit

Appendix

Edit

Ctrl Z	Undo
Ctrl X	Cut
Ctrl C	Copy
Ctrl ⇧Shift C	Copy Merged
Ctrl V	Paste
Ctrl ⇧Shift V	Paste Into
⇧Shift ←	Fill
Ctrl T	Free Transform
Ctrl ⇧Shift T	Repeat

Image

Settings

Ctrl L	Levels
Ctrl ⇧Shift L	Auto Levels
Ctrl M	Curves
Ctrl B	Color Balance
Ctrl U	Hue/Saturation
Ctrl ⇧Shift U	Desaturate
Ctrl I	Invert
Ctrl Alt X	Extract

Layer

Ctrl ⇧Shift N	New Layer
Ctrl J	Layer Via Copy
Ctrl ⇧Shift J	Layer Via Cut
Ctrl G	Group with Previous
Ctrl ⇧Shift G	Ungroup

Arrange

Ctrl ⇧Shift]	Bring to Front
Ctrl]	Bring Forward
Ctrl [	Send Backward
Ctrl ⇧Shift [	Send to Back

Select

Ctrl A	All
Ctrl D	Deselect
Ctrl ⇧Shift D	Reselect

Adobe Photoshop 5.5

Appendix

| Ctrl Shift | I | Inverse |
| Ctrl Alt | D | Feather |

Filter

| Ctrl | F | Last Filter |
| Ctrl Shift | F | Fade (last adjustment or last filter) |

View

Ctrl	Y	Preview CMYK
Ctrl Shift	Y	Gamut Warning
Ctrl	+	Zoom In
Ctrl	-	Zoom Out
Ctrl	0	Fit on Screen
Ctrl Alt	0	Actual Pixels
Ctrl	H	Show/Hide Edges
Ctrl Shift	H	Show/Hide Path
Ctrl	R	Show/Hide Rulers
Ctrl	;	Show/Hide Guides
Ctrl Shift	;	Snap To Guides
Ctrl Alt	;	Lock Guides
Ctrl	"	Show/Hide Grid
Ctrl Shift	"	Snap To Grid

Help

| F1 | | Help Topics |

Glossary

ACTION
An action is a type of macro a series of automated tasks that can be saved and automatically reproduced on other images.

ALPHA CHANNEL
These are used to define transparent/semi-transparent areas on certain images; these images must be saved in a format that manages alpha channels such as PNG or DCS2.0. Used within Photoshop, these channels allow you to save selections.

BITMAP
Generally speaking, this is an image that is defined with pixels, as opposed to vector drawings made in applications such as Corel-Draw or Adobe Illustrator. In Photoshop, a bitmap image is an image made up of two colours, black and white. Shades of grey are simulated by alternating black and white pixels with varied spacing.

BLENDING MODE
The chosen mode defines the way a retouch or drawing tool is applied to an image. It can also be used to apply layers with a particular effect or to combine channels.

BMP
This is the standard image format in Windows. It is recognised by most applications that work in this environment.

CHANNEL
There are three types of channel: colour, alpha and spot channels. Colour channels define the colours in an image and the mixture of these channels (which is placed on a composite channel) gives the image its colours. The number of colour channels depends on the image's colour mode (for example, on a CMYK image there are four channels). See also ALPHA CHANNEL and SPOT COLOUR.

CLIPPING
To clip an image is to isolate it from the rest of the image, by selecting it for retouching, for separation onto a layer or for transformation. See also CLIPPING GROUP.

CLIPPING GROUP
This is a special group of layers. In a clipping group, the bottom layer acts as a type of stencil on the other layers. The transparent areas on the bottom layer make the corresponding areas on the other layers equally transparent.

CMYK
This is a four-colour model that defines colours in terms of levels of Cyan, Magenta, Yellow; black is added to these colours to produce colour depth and contrast. This is the model used by colour printers. It is used in professional printing to make colour documents.

COLOUR
Colours are defined from channels of the same name. Some colours are not always correctly printed, this depends on the image mode. RGB and Lab images can use colours which are "out-of-gamut", or unprintable with CMYK inks.

Glossary

COMBINING
Combining two channels on an image can be used to produce special effects The channels are combined according to a chosen blending mode. See also BLENDING MODE.

CROPPING
Cropping an image means to make it smaller by removing part of it: imagine cropping a picture with a paper guillotine...

DCS
This image format is identical to EPS in all respects except one: in its version 2, it can save alpha and spot channels. However, it can only save CMYK and multichannel images. This is a format used for printing and is recognised by certain desktop publishing applications such as Quark XPress.

DENSITY
When referring to printed images, this represents the density of ink. The higher the density the more ink used and the darker the colour, and vice versa. For dot density, see FREQUENCY.

DUOTONE
This is an image made up of two inks, generally black and another colour, often from the Pantone book. This type of colour image is inexpensive to print and can also be used to create special effects, such as old sepia photo effects.

EPS
This is the most common format for images that are to be printed. It allows you to save a path to make a transparent mask around an image. It can save images in grayscale, duotones, RGB or CMYK images.

FILTER
Filters are used to retouch or distort images or to apply certain special effects. They can provide a vast array of effects. In addition to the default filters provided in Photoshop, it is possible to load additional filters from other sources.

FREQUENCY
This is also called screen ruling. It defines dot density in printing. The denser the dots used, the better the print quality produced. For an optimal quality, an image's resolution should be 1.5 to 2 times the size of the screen frequency. See also RESOLUTION.

GAMUT WARNING
You can use this feature before converting to CMYK mode (or before digitisation) to highlight unprintable colours in an image.

GIF
The GIF image format is often used for Internet purposes. It is limited to 256 colours but gives good results on small images or drawings. A variation of this format called GIF89a is able to save transparent areas.

GRAYSCALE
This colour model only contains one colour, black. Ink variation defines the grey: when there is less ink used, the grey is lighter, and vice versa. This is the model used for black and white photos.

HISTOGRAM
This is a graphic representation of the layout of dark/light areas in an image. It is used to analyse the distribution of luminosity or colour in an image.

Glossary

HSB This model defines colours according to their Hue, Saturation (or intensity) and Brightness. This ensures colours are defined according to visual perception. The resulting colour has a perfect equivalent in the RGB model.

INDEXED COLORS The number of colours in an image is limited to 256. These are indexed in a colour table. An image in indexed color mode can memorise a transparent colour, which partially imitates an alpha channel. Although images in indexed colors have fewer colours, they can be correctly viewed on most computer screens. This is an especially useful mode for Internet pictures.

JPEG This is a common file format on the Internet. Photos saved in this format can be highly compressed. It is not a good format for images that are to be printed, as it discards colour information in order to optimise file size.

LAB This is another colour model, which defines colours with a lightness value and two colour channels, a and b. "a" defines the colours from green to magenta and "b" the colours from blue to yellow. This model allows you to alter the amount of light in an image without affecting its colour range. It takes in the CMYK and RGB gamuts, so Photoshop uses this model when converting between RGB and CMYK.

LAYER Layers are used to separate different elements on the same image. This allows you to work on one specific area more easily. There are three types of layer: standard, type layers and adjustment layers. Standard layers can contain any image and the various items in an image can all be placed on separate layers. A type layer contains text and an adjustment layer contains retouching information that is independent of the image.

LAYER MASK A layer mask is associated with a particular layer and is used to create transparent/semi-transparent areas on that layer. It behaves in a similar way to an alpha channel, except it affects only its own layer and not the whole image.

MASK Masks are features of selections: masked areas can be removed from a selection. Photoshop also uses paths as masks to create transparent areas on images saved in EPS or DCS format.

MONOCHROME This is similar to a duotone, but uses only one ink. It works in the same way as a grayscale, but instead of black, uses a coloured ink.

PANTONE Pantone colours make up a special colour palette. They are frequently used in professional printing. In theory, using these colours guarantees colour uniformity whatever the printing medium used. They are often used for logos, in duotones and as extra spot colours in CMYK prints. Similar colour books are produced by competitors such as ANPA, DIC, Focoltone, Toyo or Trumatch.

Glossary

PATH
A vector drawing, made with Bezier curves, which you can use to select, retouch or draw on part of an image. You can also make a mask from a path to create transparent areas on images saved in EPS or DCS.

PIXEL
The pixel is the fundamental component from which images are made, images being essentially a group of dots. It is a loose abbreviation of PICTure ELement.

PIXELATION
Pixelation refers to the "staircase effect" sometimes seen when the edge pixels on an image are too noticeable. To avoid this unattractive effect you can use Photoshop's anti-alias options.

PNG
This image format can be used on the Internet, particularly for images that require a high display quality and/or that have transparent areas.

POSTERIZATION
This command is used to reduce the number of tonal levels in an image. One result of using it is the production of flat areas of colour, making a photo resemble a drawing.

PREVIEW
Previewing means viewing an effect or a retouch on an image before the changes are actually applied. See also GAMUT WARNING.

PSD
This is the standard Photoshop format. It is not recognised by many other applications, but has the advantage of saving all elements in an image such as layers, channels or paths.

RESOLUTION
This determines image quality and sharpness. At a high resolution, images are clearer with more detail. However, high resolution means large image file size, which consumes lots of memory on your disks. See also FREQUENCY.

RGB
This model defines colour with the three primary colours, Red, Green and Blue. This is the default model used by input devices such as scanners or digital cameras as well as by monitors and televisions. This is the ideal model for Internet images or video recording.

SATURATION
This refers to a colour's intensity. Nil saturation gives grey while a high saturation gives a very bright colour. Highly saturated colours are often out of the CMYK gamut (and so are unprintable). See also HSB.

SCALING
This means to change the size of a selected area or layer within an image.

SCITEX CT
This is an image format used for Scitex digital printers. This format is primarily used with imagesetters to make colour separations on films for photoengraving.

© Editions ENI - All rights reserved

Glossary

SCREENING — This technique determines how dots of colour will be overlaid in printing to achieve the required colour and density. This is a must to achieve correct colour perception on images with limited colours (such as those in indexed colors mode).

SNAPSHOT — A feature of the History palette, a snapshot is a particular stage of work on an image that you "capture" by taking a snapshot. You can use a snapshot to return to a particular version of the image (thus cancelling unsatisfactory changes) or for retouching. A snapshot is not saved with an image.

SPOT COLOUR — A spot colour is a special colour, often a Pantone colour, which can be added to an image's colour channels. On a CMYK image, this can be used to create a fifth or sixth colour. Some examples of spot colours are fluorescent and metallic colours (gold, silver etc) and varnishes but any other colour can be used.

SWATCHES — This is a special colour palette, which you can use to select particular colours more easily. You can make custom swatches (and swatch books) or use supplementary palettes such as the Pantone book.

TIFF — This is a format used for images to be printed. It is not used as often as EPS which offers some advantages in terms of print reproduction quality. TIFF format can however be used when you wish to save the alpha channels in an image.

TRAP — This is a device used to manage overlapping colours when they are printed with CMYK colour separation. A trap overlays the edges of two adjacent colours so white patches do not appear between colours. This is a device used only with professional print jobs and on drawings: it would not normally be used on photos.

TRITONE — This is a variation on a duotone; it uses three inks instead of two. See also DUOTONE.

TWAIN — This is a standard interface for communicating with image input devices such as digital cameras or scanners. The device manufacturer should provide a TWAIN data source and source manager. Photoshop will call upon the plug-in but the plug-in relies directly on the input device.

Index

A

ACROBAT

Converting an Acrobat document into a Photoshop document	402

ACTION

Actions palette	366
Creating	370
Creating an action set	369
Deleting an action/action item/set	378
Duplicating an action or a set	377
Including a path in an action	374
Inserting a menu item	375
Inserting a stop	372
Modifying options	378
Modifying playback options	384
Playing on a group of images	386
Recording a command or an action again	380
Saving a set of actions	385
Using recorded actions	367

ADJUSTMENT

Creating an adjustment layer	195
Modifying an adjustment layer	198
Softening effects	189

ALPHA CHANNEL

Converting into a Spot channel	343
Creating from a selection	325
Creating new	324
Loading a selection from an Alpha Channel	325
Modifying options	326

ANCHOR POINT

Adding/deleting	298
Moving	297
Selecting	296

ARROWS

Drawing	136

B

BACKGROUND

Converting into a layer	188

BITMAP

Converting grayscale to bitmap	231
Saving in BMP format	272
Transforming part of an image into bitmap	170

BLACK/WHITE POINT

Adjusting	157

BLENDING MODE

Associating with a layer	181
Behind	182
Clear	183
Color	187
Color burn	185
Color dodge	185
Darken	185
Difference	186
Dissolve	182
Exclusion	186
Hard light	184
How they work	181
Hue	186
Lighten	185
Luminosity	187
Multiply	183
Normal	181
Overlay	184
Saturation	186
Screen	183
Soft light	184

BLUR

Part of an image	144
Using Blur filter	145

BRIGHTNESS

Adjusting black/white point	157
Adjusting with Auto Levels	153
Adjusting with Brightness/Contrast command	150
Adjusting with the curves	154

Index

Adjusting with the histogram	151
Checking tonal range with the histogram	148
Darkening/lightening part of an image	146
Equalize	408

BRUSHES

Creating from a drawing	397
Creating standard brush	395
Deleting	399
Modifying options	399
Saving/loading a brush palette	400

C

CALIBRATION

Calibrating the monitor display	417

CHANNEL

Channels palette	322
Combining	332
Combining from two images	335
Converting an image into multichannel mode	349
Deleting	331
Duplicating	330
Merging channels into a single document	351
Mixing colour channels	339
Modifying	327
Splitting channels into several documents	351
Using Alpha channels	324
Using Spot channels	342

See also ALPHA CHANNEL, SPOT CHANNEL

CLIPPING

With a clipping path	312

CLIPPING GROUP

Creating	192
Removing a layer	193

CMYK

Converting to Lab mode	225
Converting to RGB	229
Description of colour model	53

COLOR BALANCE

See COLOUR PROPORTION

COLOR TABLE

Loading	242
Modifying	243

COLORIZE

Grayscale by modifying hue/saturation	246
Grayscale image with drawing tools/ Fill command	245
Grayscale with a duotone	247
Grayscale with Indexed Colors	248

COLOUR

Colouring a path outline	306
Configuring colour management	417
Converting colour models	225
Filling a selection	61
Selecting a range of colours	205
Selecting with the Eyedropper	57
Using a custom Color Picker	58
Using the Color Palette	54
Using the Color Picker	56
Using the Swatches palette	57

See also COLOUR CORRECTION, COLOUR MODEL, COLOUR PROPORTION, SELECTING COLOUR

COLOUR CORRECTION

Adjusting an image's colour components	163
Adjusting colour proportions in an image	159
Adjusting components with Selective Color	166
Changing colour depth	224
Creating flat areas of colour	172
Modifying saturation on part of an image	162

Adobe Photoshop 5.5 431

Index

Replacing certain colours	167	Image to duotone	234
See also COLOUR PROPORTION		Image to grayscale	230
		Text into image	108
		With Conditional Mode change	365

COLOUR MODEL

Converting CMYK/Lab into RGB	229
Converting Lab/RGB to CMYK	226
Converting RGB to Indexed Colors	238
Converting RGB/CMYK to Lab	225
Converting to grayscale	230
Description of CMYK	53
Description of grayscale	54
Description of HSB	54
Description of Lab	53
Description of RGB	52

COLOUR PROPORTION

Adjusting the colour balance	160
Adjusting the variations	159
Adjusting with the histogram/ the curves	161

COLOUR WHEEL

Description	52

CONTACT SHEET

Creating	356

CONTRAST

Adjusting black/white point	157
Adjusting with Auto Contrast	154
Adjusting with Auto Levels	153
Adjusting with Brightness/ Contrast command	150
Adjusting with the curves	154
Adjusting with the histogram	151
Equalize	408

CONVERTING

Acrobat document into a Photoshop image	402
Colour models	225
Grayscale to Bitmap	231
Image into multichannel mode	349

COPYING

Image onto another document	43
Images located on several layers	194
Layer effects	115
One selection into another	190
Onto a new layer	51
Part of an image	39
Using the clipboard	40

CREATING

Action	370
Action set	369
Adjustment layer	195
Brush	395
Clipping group	192
Contact sheet	356
Negative	169
New document	41
New layer	82
Path	287
Pattern	199
Picture package	363
Snapshot in the History palette	213
Type layer	102

CROPPING

Image	257

CURVE

Converting points (smooth to corner)	299
Description	292
Modifying	298
Moving segment	297
Selecting segment	296

CURVES

Using to adjust contrast/brightness	154

Index

D

DELETING

Action/action item/set	378
Brush	399
Channel	331
Guide	22
History state	211
Layer	85
Layer effects	115
Part of an image	117
Path	286

DISTORT

Layer/selection	95

DOCUMENT

Creating from a snapshot/state	215
Creating new	41
Defining document information	403
Opening	17
Printing	72
Revert to last saved version	38
Saving in a specific format	259

See also IMAGE

DRAWING

Curves	292
Path with the Magnetic Pen	288
Path with the Pen	290
Simple path	284
Straight lines/arrows	136
Using the Paint Bucket	138
Using the Pencil/Paintbrush/Airbrush	132
Using to create a brush	397

See also ANCHOR POINT, CURVE, PATH

DUOTONE

Creating from a grayscale	234

DUPLICATING

Action/set	377
Image zones with the Rubber Stamp	173
Layer	97
Path	309

E

EFFECT

Applying a 3D effect	405
Applying a colour fill	113
Applying a drop shadow	109
Applying a glow	111
Bevel and Emboss	112
Copying	115
Defining global angle	108
Modifying/deleting	114
Throwing light onto part of an image	409

EXPANDING/CONTRACTING

Selection by color	68
Selection outline	68
Selection with the mouse	67

EXPORTING

Paths to Illustrator	314

EXTRACT

Foreground of an image	140

F

FEATHERING

Applying to a selection	65
Description	35

FILL

Applying a fill colour to a selection	61
Filling with a pattern	201
Filling with texture	179
Path area with colour	307
Selection/layer with a gradient	121
With the Paint bucket	138

FILTER

Applying	86
Softening effects	189
Throwing light onto part of an image	409
Using Texturizer	179
Using to sharpen an image	146

Adobe Photoshop 5.5   433

Index

FORMAT

Miscellaneous formats handled by Photoshop	273
Saving GIF89A format	264
Saving in BMP format	272
Saving in GIF format	263
Saving in JPEG	261
Saving in Photoshop DCS formats	270
Saving in Photoshop EPS format	268
Saving in Photoshop PDF format	271
Saving in TIFF format	267

FREE TRANSFORM

See TRANSFORM

G

GALLERY

Creating a Web Photo Gallery	359

GAMUT WARNING

Viewing out of gamut colours before conversion	226

GIF

Using GIF format	263
Using GIF89A format	264

GRADIENT

Creating a custom gradient	123
Filling with a preset gradient	121

GRAYSCALE

Colorizing	245
Converting grayscale to bitmap	231
Converting to grayscale	230
Creating a duotone	234
Description of colour model	54

GUIDE

Adding	21
Defining appearance	22
Deleting	22
Moving	21

H

HISTOGRAM

Using for tonal range	148
Using to adjust contrast/brightness	151

HISTORY

Creating snapshot	213
Deleting states	211
Emptying palette	211
History palette	208
Modifying preferences	212
Undoing several actions	210

See also STATE, SNAPSHOT

HSB

Description of colour model	54

HUE

Modifying on a whole image	163

I

ILLUSTRATOR

Copying/pasting object in Photoshop	318
Exporting paths to	314
Opening document in Photoshop	315
Placing a document on an image	317

IMAGE

Adjusting Contrast/Brightness	150
Applying special effects to layers	108
Changing depth of colours	224
Changing size/resolution	252
Creating a contact sheet	356
Creating a negative	169
Creating a picture package	363
Cropping	257
Defining resolution automatically	407
Deleting dissimilar pixels	404
Deleting items	117
Extracting foreground	140
Importing from Illustrator	315
Modifying canvas size	249
Printing	72

Index

Scanning from Photoshop	392
Using several views on an image	401

See also DOCUMENT

INDEXED COLORS

Choosing an Indexed Color palette	239
Conversion to Indexed Colors	238
Managing a color table	242

INFO PALETTE

Using during transformation	28
Using to show colour values	28

J

JPEG

Using JPEG format	261

L

LAB

Converting to CMYK	226
Converting to RGB	229
Description of colour model	53

LAYER

Aligning the contents of linked layers	100
Applying a layer mask	126
Applying a transformation	90
Applying effects	108
Associating with a blending mode	181
Auto Select Layer	414
Changing stacking order	78
Converting background into a layer	188
Creating a clipping group	192
Creating a type layer	102
Creating an adjustment layer	195
Creating new	82
Deleting	85
Duplicating	97
Filling with a gradient	121
Layers palette	76
Linking	99
Merging	101
Modifying/deleting effects	114
Moving/copying onto a new layer	51
Removing fringe pixels	88
Removing jagged edges	89
Selecting non-transparent parts	83
Setting layer options	79
Spacing the contents of linked layers	100

See also EFFECTS

LAYER MASK

Applying	126
Applying effects	129
Deleting	129

LINES

Drawing	136

LINKING

Aligning the contents of linked layers	100
Layer	99
Spacing the contents of linked layers	100

LOADING

Brush palette	400
Saved selection	50

LUMINOSITY

See BRIGHTNESS

M

MEASURE

Using the Measure tool	412

MERGING

Layers	101

MOVING

Guides	21
One selection into another	190
Onto a new layer	51
Part of an image	37
Positioning with precision	38
Using the clipboard	40

Adobe Photoshop 5.5

Index

N

NEGATIVE
Creating a negative image	169

O

OPENING
Document	17

P

PAGE SETUP
Defining options	70

PALETTE
Actions palette	366
Brushes palette	395
History palette	208
Info palette	27
Navigator	24
Opening a palette menu	17
Using the Channels palette	322
Using the Color Palette	54
Using the Layers palette	76
Using the Paths palette	285
Using the Swatches palette	57
Working with palettes	16

PANTONE
Using a Pantone book	58

PATH
Applying colour to outline	306
Clipping an image	312
Converting a path into a selection border	303
Converting a selection border into a path	302
Creating	287
Deleting	286
Drawing curves	292
Drawing straight line with the Pen	290
Duplicating by copy/paste	309
Duplicating onto another image	310
Duplicating onto new path	309
Exporting to Illustrator	314
Extending	291
Filling path area with color	307
Including in an action	374
Modifying	296
Opening a closed path	300
Paths palette	285
Renaming	287
Saving a work path	286
Showing/hiding	301
Simple path with the Freeform pen	284

PATTERN
Applying with the Fill command	201
Applying with the Pattern Stamp	200
Creating	199
Wrapping around the edges	202

PERSPECTIVE
Effect on layer/selection	95

PHOTOSHOP 5.5
Description of the workscreen	13
Leaving	29
Setting preferences	414
Starting	12

PICTURE PACKAGE
Creating	363

POINTER
Defining presentation	19

POSTERIZE
Using to create flat areas of colour	172

PREFERENCES
Cursor presentation	19
Defining guide appearance	22
History preferences	212
Memory	416
Saving files	415
Setting general preferences	414
Work drives	416

Index

PRINTING

Defining page setup options	70
Image	72

Q

QUICK MASK

Setting preferences	337
Using to make a selection	338

R

RESIZE

Layer/selection	93

RESOLUTION

Changing image resolution	252
Defining automatically	407

RETOUCH

Blurring/sharpening part of an image	144
Creating an art reproduction of a state	220
Creating flat areas of colour	172
Darkening/lightening part of an image	146
Deleting dissimilar pixels	404
Duplicating image zones with Rubber Stamp	173
Increasing image sharpness	405
Reproducing a previous state/snapshot	217
Smudging an image	142
Transforming part of an image into bitmap	170

See also COLOUR CORRECTION

RGB

Converting to CMYK	226
Converting to Indexed Colors	238
Converting to Lab mode	225
Description of the colour model	52

ROTATE

Layer/selection	94
Text	105

RULER

Using	20

S

SATURATION

Modifying on part of an image	162

SAVING

Brush palette	400
Image for use on the Web	274
In another format	259
Saving a set of actions	385
Selection	49
Work path	286

See also FORMAT

SCANNING

Image from Photoshop	392
Selecting a digitisation source	392

SELECTING

Anchor point/segment	296
By extracting the foreground	140
Deselecting	34
Images by colour	66
In Quick Mask mode	338
Irregular items	45
Non-transparent parts of a layer	83
Range of colours	205
Regular area on an image	34
Whole image	33

See also SELECTING COLOUR, SELECTION

SELECTING COLOUR

Using a custom Color Picker	58
With the Color Palette	54
With the Color Picker	56
With the Eyedropper	57
With the Swatches palette	57

SELECTION

Adding stroke colour to border	64
Applying a fill colour	61

Adobe Photoshop 5.5

Index

Applying a transformation 90
Converting a path into
a selection border 303
Converting a selection border
into a path 302
Expanding/contracting 67
Feathering 65
Filling with a gradient 121
Inversing 69
Loading saved selection 50
Moving/copying into another selection 190
Saving 49
Smoothing 400
Transforming a selection border 251

See also SELECTING

SHARPEN

Increasing image sharpness 405
Part of an image 144
Using the Sharpen filter 146

SIZE

Changing image size 252
Cropping 257
Modifying canvas size 249

SKEW

Layer/selection 94

SNAPSHOT

Creating 213
Creating with specific state 215
Reproducing with
the Art History Brush 220
Reproducing with the Fill command 219
Reproducing with the History Brush 217
Using to create a document 215

SOFTENING

Effect of a filter, adjustment or tool 189

SPOT CHANNEL

Creating new 342
Merging with an image 347

STATE

Deleting 211
Reproducing with
the Art History Brush 220
Reproducing with the Fill command 219
Reproducing with the History Brush 217
Using to create a document 215

STROKE

Adding to a selection border 64
Colouring a path outline 306

SWATCHES

Adding colours 59
Deleting colour 59
Saving/opening a book 60
Using the Swatches palette 57

T

TEXT

Converting into image 108
Inserting into an image 102
Modifying on a type layer 107
Type tool options 104

TEXTURE

Creating 200
Using to fill parts of an image 179
Wrapping around the edges 202

TIFF

Using TIFF format 267

TOOL

Description of the toolbox 14
Softening effects 189
Using hidden tools 14
Using the Art History Brush 220
Using the Background Eraser 120
Using the Blur/Sharpen tools 144
Using the Crop tool 257
Using the Dodge/Burn tools 146
Using the Eraser tool 118
Using the Eyedropper 57
Using the Freeform Pen 284

Index

Using the History Brush	217
Using the Lasso tool	45
Using the Magic Eraser	120
Using the Magic Wand	66
Using the Magnetic Lasso	47
Using the Magnetic Pen	288
Using the Marquee tools	34
Using the Measure tool	412
Using the Paint Bucket	138
Using the Pattern Stamp	200
Using the Pen tool	290
Using the Pencil/Paintbrush/Airbrush	132
Using the Polygonal Lasso	46
Using the Rubber Stamp	173
Using the Smudge tool	142
Using the Sponge tool	162
Using the type tools	103

TRANSFORM

Applying to a selection border	251
Distorting layer/selection	95
Flipping/rotating a layer/selection	90
Perspective effect on layer/selection	95
Rescaling layer/selection	93
Rotating layer/selection	94
Skewing layer/selection	94
With precise values	91

TYPE

See TEXT

U

UNDOING

Last action(s)	38

Several actions with the History palette	210

See also HISTORY

V

VIEW

Showing a full screen image	27
Using several views on an image	401
Zooming an image	25

W

WEB

Creating a Web Photo Gallery	359
Saving images for Web use	274

Z

ZOOM

Showing a full screen image	27
Using the Navigator palette	24
Using the View menu	26
Using the Zoom tool	25

Adobe Photoshop 5.5

▲ Quick Reference Guide ▲ Practical Guide ▲ Microsoft® Approved
▲ User Manual ▲ Training CD-ROM Publication

VISIT OUR WEB SITE http://www.editions-eni.com

Please affix stamp here

Ask for our free brochure

For more information on our new titles please complete this card and return

Name: ....
....
Company: ....
Address: ....
....
Postcode: ....
Town: ....
Phone: ....
E-mail: ....

ENI Publishing LTD

500 Chiswick High Road

London W4 5RG